10582   NOV 1 3 2014

S0-ANR-128

PROPERTY OF
HOLY CROSS COLLEGE
WESTVILLE EDUCATION
INITIATIVE

Varieties of Governance in China

VARIETIES OF GOVERNANCE IN CHINA

Migration and Institutional Change in Chinese Villages

Jie Lu

OXFORD
UNIVERSITY PRESS

OXFORD
UNIVERSITY PRESS

Oxford University Press is a department of the University of Oxford.
It furthers the University's objective of excellence in research, scholarship,
and education by publishing worldwide.

Oxford   New York
Auckland   Cape Town   Dar es Salaam   Hong Kong   Karachi
Kuala Lumpur   Madrid   Melbourne   Mexico City   Nairobi
New Delhi   Shanghai   Taipei   Toronto

With offices in
Argentina   Austria   Brazil   Chile   Czech Republic   France   Greece
Guatemala   Hungary   Italy   Japan   Poland   Portugal   Singapore
South Korea   Switzerland   Thailand   Turkey   Ukraine   Vietnam

Oxford is a registered trade mark of Oxford University Press
in the UK and certain other countries.

Published in the United States of America by
Oxford University Press
198 Madison Avenue, New York, NY 10016

© Oxford University Press 2015

All rights reserved. No part of this publication may be reproduced,
stored in a retrieval system, or transmitted, in any form or by any means,
without the prior permission in writing of Oxford University Press,
or as expressly permitted by law, by license, or under terms agreed with the
appropriate reproduction rights organization. Inquiries concerning reproduction
outside the scope of the above should be sent to the Rights Department,
Oxford University Press, at the address above.

You must not circulate this work in any other form
and you must impose this same condition on any acquirer.

Library of Congress Cataloging-in-Publication Data
Lu, Jie, 1977–
   Varieties of governance in China : migration and institutional change
in Chinese villages / Jie Lu.
       p.   cm.
   Includes bibliographical references and index.
   ISBN 978–0–19–937874–6 (hardback)
1. Local government—China. 2. Village communities—China. 3. Rural-urban
migration—Political aspects—China. 4. China—Rural conditions.
5. Organizational change—China. I. Title.
   JS7353.A8L84 2014
   320.8'50951—dc23
                                                  2014009443

9 8 7 6 5 4 3 2 1

Printed in the United States of America on acid-free paper

To my parents:
Fujin Lu and Yufen Li

CONTENTS

ACKNOWLEDGMENTS

Although I was born in China, my understanding of and interest in rural China were very limited until I came to Duke in 2003. Early in my time there, I was fortunate to be involved in a project on China's grassroots democracy co-directed by Tianjian Shi and John Aldrich. As part of the research team, I visited many Chinese rural villages and urban residential communities to observe their local elections and help the Ministry of Civil Affairs (which officially supervises China's grassroots democracy) revise and standardize the electoral procedure for direct elections in these locales. During our field trips, the varying quality of electoral institutions, particularly in Chinese villages, amazed me, given the conventional wisdom of a powerful and almost omnipresent Chinese government uniformly imposing and enforcing its policies and regulations. Later, as I gradually expanded the scope of my observations in rural China from grassroots democracy to its governance in general and learned more about the evolution of numerous policies and institutions in Chinese villages, such variance became even more dramatic and perplexing. Then I decided to do some "serious research" to better understand the dynamics of governance in a significant portion of the country where I was born.

For teaching me how to do research with the rigor of modern social sciences and effectively connect my empirical work with big theoretical issues, I owe an immense intellectual debt to my advisors Tianjian Shi, John Aldrich, Karen Remmer, and Guillermo Trejo. TJ (as most people called Tianjian Shi) was an academic father-figure to me and was the best advisor any Ph.D. student could have asked for. Always encouraging and supportive, TJ was the key figure who guided me into the field of survey research, taught me survey research techniques, and offered me insightful information and opportunities to do surveys in China. My countless discussions with TJ in his office, minivan, living room, kitchen, and even hotel room gave birth to this project. Without TJ's guidance, assistance, and generosity in sharing his resources and data, this research would not have been feasible. TJ's very unfortunate and unexpected passing away in the end of 2010 greatly saddened me.

Working with John Aldrich has always been pleasant. No matter when I ask for help and suggestions, John always assists me at his earliest convenience. Discussions in John's office, conversations during our field trips to China, and our collaborations on survey projects have taught me how to do rigorous and scientific research. It is Karen Remmer who has inspired my interest in the political economy of institutions and institutional change and pushed me persistently to focus on theoretical questions. Karen's intellectual acuity and methodological sophistication have helped me avoid many mistakes that might have compromised the quality of this project. Karen's detail-oriented comments and critiques have also significantly improved the presentation of this project. Guillermo Trejo's rich knowledge of indigenous politics and governance in Latin America offered many interesting examples for placing my research in a comparative and broader perspective. My intellectual adventure at Duke has shaped my approach to political science ever since.

This project would not have been possible without those who have helped me in China with their time and experiences. I am particularly grateful to the faculty and students of the Center of Rural Governance at Huazhong University of Science and Technology. Working with them has significantly facilitated and enriched my fieldwork in rural China, due to their connections and various inputs. Special thanks are due to Xuefeng He, Leiming Dong, Xingzuo Luo, Baifeng Chen, Duanfeng Shen, Qin Liu, Dewen Lu, Shiyong Zhang, Derui Li, Liang Guo, and Hua Yang. I am also deeply grateful to Tangbiao Xiao, Yanjing Ou, and Yue Liu, who have assisted my fieldwork in Jiangxi and Shandong Province. Yun-han Chu, as the director of the Asian Barometer Survey (ABS), also merits special thanks for generously allowing me to insert my questions into the questionnaire of the second wave of the ABS survey in mainland China in order to rigorously test my hypotheses with national sampling survey data. I also would like to thank Mingming Shen, Ming Yang, Jie Yan, Jingjing Cai, Cai Zuo, He Meng, Jinrui Hua, and Xiaoli Lu, as well as many professional interviewers, at the Research Center for Contemporary China at Peking University for helping me with data collection.

At various stages of this project, conversations with Emerson Niou, Bruce Dickson, Pierre Landry, Jean Oi, Dorothy Solinger, Andrew Nathan, Edward Gu, Wenfang Tang, Ryan Kennedy, Katherine Pak, Jie Chen, Mayling Birney, Yu-tzung Chang, Anoop Sadanandan, Efren Perez, Kian Ming Ong, David McIvor, Cristina Corduneanu-Huci, Wei Shan, Tao Wang, Xuelian Chen, Jiangnan Zhu, and Jiangai Dong were very valuable.

I have benefited greatly from the generosity and insights of my colleagues at American University. Todd Eisenstadt, Eric Hershberg, Diane Singerman, Saul Newman, William LeoGrande, Adrienne LeBas, Ruth Lane, Jan Leighley, Jennifer Lawless, Candice Nelson, and David Lublin have offered comments and criticisms at various stages of this project. The Junior Teaching Release Program at American University provided me with extremely valuable resources and allowed me to work fully on the revision of the book manuscript. My thanks go especially to Todd Eisenstadt, whose encouragement, guidance, and insights on publication have made this project much easier.

I was fortunate to receive excellent and detailed comments on the entire manuscript from two anonymous referees, who have pushed me to sharpen my theoretical arguments and better connect my research to contemporary research on China's rural politics. I also would like to thank my editor at Oxford University Press, Angela Chnapko, for her interest in the project and her consideration of the professional pressures faced by a junior scholar. Sharon Bear and Amy Ruddle provided excellent editorial assistance at the last stage of this project, which significantly improved the presentation of this book.

Finally, I thank my family for their support along the way. My love, Icy Moyung, has been a source of endless love and support during the most difficult and challenging stage of the writing and revision. My little lovely niece, Ruiyan Michelle Lu, made the revision process much less boring and more entertaining. Thanks to the understanding and support from my brother, Min Lu, and sister-in-law, Hong Zhang, I could fully focus on my work, while letting them bear most of the responsibility of taking care of our parents in China. Above all, I am deeply indebted to my father, Fujin Lu, and my mother, Yufen Li. They have worked extremely hard and sacrificed a lot to give me the best education possible. It is their persistent and continuous support and encouragement that have made my academic journey from a small city in Hubei to the capital of the P.R.C. and then to the capital of the United States possible. Though neither of my parents had formal college education for historical and political reasons, their belief in the power of knowledge in changing lives and their highly respected achievements in their respective fields have been, and will always be, a source of inspiration for me. Therefore, this book is dedicated to my parents.

Varieties of Governance in China

CHAPTER 1

Introduction

It is not surprising to China scholars that the quality of governance in Chinese villages varies dramatically. As soon as I set foot on the well-maintained roads that connect the families within Qianhouzhai Village of Shandong Province, I was reminded of my experience in Su Village of Henan Province, where, on a rainy day, I trudged along a muddy road to interview villagers and found myself cursing when my brand-new sneakers were ruined by a mixture of mud and livestock excrement. In terms of local governance, the contrast cannot be any more dramatic between communities such as Su Village and Qianhouzhai Village. Although residents of both villages have a similar level of average annual per capita income (i.e., 6,500 to 7,000 RMB [around 970 to 1,044 USD]) and most villagers can afford to live in decent one- or two-story houses, the differences in their access to local public goods and projects, as well as other aspects of local governance, are too obvious to ignore.

In fact, neither Qianhouzhai Village nor Su Village has sufficient collective resources, except for some limited fiscal transfers from upper-level governments, to cover the expenses of paving their roads. Village Committee Elections (VCEs) in both villages are rigged, with township officials imposing their preferred candidates. There also are no encompassing and embedding solidarity groups (e.g., lineage or religious organizations) in either village. Nevertheless, local cadres of Qianhouzhai Village have managed to collect enough from their villagers, despite the per capita quota's far exceeding the prescribed upper limit on raising funds from peasants, to improve the condition of its within-village roads and to pave its main road with concrete. In Su Village, in contrast, neither local cadres nor average villagers have ever made any serious efforts to improve the condition of village roads, despite their dissatisfaction with them. A pair of rubber boots becomes a daily necessity for most villagers in Su Village, which is their inexpensive but private solution to the problem.

Despite the lack of collective resources and the existence of flawed formal institutions in both Qianhouzhai Village and Su Village, the residents and cadres of each village differ in their attitudes toward how their fellow villagers perceive and judge them. In Qianhouzhai Village, powerful reputation-based social sanctions have a significant impact on various aspects of people's lives. However, in Su Village, residents and cadres care only about their own material benefits, with little attention paid to how other people in the community judge them. It follows that, in Qianhouzhai Village, it is very common for villagers to help each other out during busy seasons, as well as pooling money for renting trucks to transport their agricultural products. And local cadres in Qianhouzhai Village are significantly more attentive to the demands of those under their jurisdiction.

Different from the situations of Su Village and Qianhouzhai Village, transparent and competitive VCEs are regularly held in some Chinese villages. After the Commune system, initially established and sustained by the despotic power of the Chinese Communist Party (CCP), was abolished to accommodate market-oriented reforms in the early 1980s, village committees, organized on the basis of regular, competitive, and transparent democratic elections, were proposed as an officially endorsed institution of governance in rural China (e.g., O'Brien and Li 2000; Shi 1999b). This grassroots democracy was introduced and imposed upon Chinese villages mainly, if not solely, for the purpose of improving the quality of local governance, in a decentralized and democratic way, as the authoritarian state withdrew its political control and bureaucratic influence from rural communities.

Theoretically, village committees with publicly recognized authority based on democratic elections should be able to perform effectively and decisively in sustaining local governance. Moreover, the accountability mechanism embedded in grassroots democracy also should help improve the governance in Chinese villages by making local cadres more attentive to villagers' demands and interests. This is exactly the case in villages such as Songzhuang Village of Henan Province, where grassroots democracy has become the powerhouse of local governance. For example, the village committee of Songzhuang has channeled the lion's share of its collective incomes (i.e., 300,000 RMB [around 44,800 USD]) into public projects such as paving village roads, rather than into the village cadres' personal bank accounts. Unfortunately, VCEs in a large number of rural communities, such as Su Village and Qianhouzhai Village, have not been organized in a transparent and competitive way, following the Organic Law of Village Committees, drafted in 1987, amended in 1998, and further revised in 2010. Further, serious manipulations and interventions primarily from township officials at different stages of VCEs have been widely reported (e.g., J. Lu 2012; L. Tsai 2010). It is obvious that rigged VCEs cannot work as originally designed to sustain local governance in rural China, as they are unable to provide publicly recognized authority or hold local cadres accountable.

Compared with the residents of villages like Qianhouzhai and Songzhuang, members of villages like Su are at a disadvantage: Neither powerful social sanctions nor high-quality grassroots democracy is available for sustaining their local governance. In most cases, they have to rely on themselves: They buy rubber boots for trudging along the muddy roads, solve conflicts with their fellow villagers on their own, take care of their families when financial crises strike, and use their own savings or borrow money from family and friends for small business ventures. Conversely, in villages like Qianhouzhai and Songzhuang, villagers can pool their resources to maintain irrigation projects and within-village roads; they can ask for mediation or arbitration from village cadres or some fellow villagers with publicly recognized authority to resolve conflicts; they can get assistance and secure relief from their fellow villagers or the village committee during crises; and they are also able to raise loans from their fellow villagers or apply for credit from local Rural Credit Cooperatives to finance their entrepreneurial activities. The dramatic differences between villages like Su, on the one hand, and those like Qianhouzhai and Songzhuang, on the other hand, give rise to a question with both theoretical and practical value: What are the underlying factors that drive such differences?

Most of the existing research on China's rural governance focuses on one specific institution or type of institution, like village elections (e.g., R. Luo et al. 2007; S. Wang and Yao 2010; X. Zhang et al. 2004), solidarity groups (e.g., Jie Chen and Huhe 2013; L. Tsai 2002, 2007a), rural credit associations and cooperatives (e.g., B. Hu 2004, 2007; Ong 2006, 2009, 2012), nongovernmental social organizations (e.g., Y.-t. Chang and Wu 2011; L. Tsai 2011; Xia 2011), and so forth. Together, such research strongly suggests the existence of varieties of institutional foundations of local governance in rural China; nevertheless, few scholars have tried to establish a coherent framework that can help us effectively understand rural China's varieties of governance. Instead of focusing exclusively on the performance of a specific institution or type of institution in decentralized governance in rural China,[1] this book examines the operation and effectiveness of a variety of institutions of local governance in Chinese villages. It further explores the potential dynamics among different institutions and uncovers the conditions under which some institutions can outperform others and play a dominant role in upholding the quality of governance in rural China. A series of interesting and interrelated questions are addressed in this book: When close-knit communities undergo gradual transformation into loosely coupled communities,[2] as pressured by economic modernization and the technology revolution, are indigenously cultivated relation-based institutions able to sustain governance in the transformed communities? Will rule-based institutions imposed, for whatever reasons, by national governments be enthusiastically accepted by average citizens as the new institutional foundation that upholds local governance? Under what conditions are these externally imposed rule-based institutions more likely to be well established and accepted within transformed communities and to perform effectively as the new institutional foundation of local governance?

These questions are of significance not only to China but also to other countries that aim to improve local governance through institutional innovations. Understanding how to ensure that newly imposed institutions perform as expected in sustaining local governance is a critical component for such innovations. But this is much more than just making the institutions right, as it requires systemic understanding of the social environment in which such institutions are embedded.[3] This is particularly the case for developing countries including China that face constant pressure to reform their socioeconomic and political institutions. Many of these countries (though for different reasons) are engaged in transplanting and imposing rule-based formal institutions into their societies for better governance.[4] Since many of these institutions have been crafted and practiced in societies with different socioeconomic backgrounds (e.g., developed countries) and many of the developing countries have rich histories of governance based on indigenous informal institutions (especially for local governance), the significance of understanding the interactions between the imposed and indigenous institutions, as well as their implications for governance, cannot be overemphasized for the policymakers in these countries.[5]

In addition to resonance with what is at the top of the agenda of policymakers in both developed and developing countries, changes in the institutional foundations of local governance also are of great interest to social scientists who examine the origins and consequences of institutional change (e.g., Fukuyama 2011; Greif 2006; Knight 1992; Kuran 2010; Mahoney and Thelen 2010b; North 1990; North et al. 2009; Parthasarathi 2011; Pomeranz 2000; Rosenthal and Wong 2011).

In particular, this topic is of value to the newly growing literature on informal institutions, the interactions between formal and informal institutions, and their implications for governance (e.g., Aoki and Hayami 2001; Greif 2006; Helmke and Levitsky 2004; Helmke and Levitsky 2006; MacLean 2010; Platteau 2000; Platteau and Peccoud 2011; Skarbek 2011; Tabellini 2008; K. S. Tsai 2006; L. Tsai 2007a).

Empirically, we have accumulated rich, though sometimes contradictory, findings on the performance and relative effectiveness of different institutions in sustaining local governance from a variety of regions, through both large-N statistical analyses (e.g., Manion 1996, 2006; L. Tsai 2007a, 2007b; Y. Yao and Gao 2006; Y. Yao and Shen 2006) and detailed case studies (Galvan 2004, 2007; Platteau 1994a, 1994b, 1995, 2000). Nevertheless, until now, only limited theoretical tools have been made available for resolving contemporary empirical debates, integrating different theoretical arguments, and uncovering some general and widely shared underlying mechanisms.[6] Drawing on the most recent developments in political science, political anthropology, sociology, economic history, and legal studies on institutional change and local governance, this book suggests a new and contextualized theoretical framework that, firstly, helps synthesize contrasting empirical findings on the performance and effectiveness of both indigenously developed and externally imposed institutions in upholding decentralized local governance.[7] By focusing on the influence of the surrounding environment on the performance of different types of institutions, this framework reveals the conditions under which the varying institutions can perform effectively in sustaining local governance. Secondly, this framework also allows an understanding of the potential interactions between indigenous institutions and imposed institutions that are moderated by community structural features in local communities, as well as their implications for governance in transformed communities. By bringing community structural features to the center of analysis, this framework sheds some light on critical questions like why institutions that follow the same design vary significantly across countries or even across regions within the same country in regard to their performance.

1.1 VARIETIES OF GOVERNANCE, INSTITUTIONAL FOUNDATIONS, AND INSTITUTIONAL CHANGE

Governance is conventionally understood as the exercise of power to structure, regulate, and coordinate the relationships among the populace in the management of their public affairs.[8] Good governance, if defined simply as resulting in prosperous and peaceful lives for the majority of those concerned, has been normatively prescribed and actively pursued by students of politics for centuries. This is part of the reason why Leviathan was suggested as a possible way out of the miserable situation characterized as the "nature of war" (Hobbes 1982 [1651]). This is also why "social contract" was conceived as a critical institutional innovation to channel the power of Leviathan toward the public good (Locke 1980 [1689]). Furthermore, this is why democratic and liberal reforms have been so widely promoted in today's world as a promising means of achieving prosperous and peaceful lives for most people, regardless of their skin color, language, or religious beliefs (Samuel P. Huntington 1991). "Good institutions," particularly those set down on parchment, have been widely recognized as the key to good governance (Acemoglu and Robinson 2012; Greif 2006; North 1990; North et al. 2009; M. Olson 1982; Rodrik 2007). As a consequence, institutional design and change, since the late twentieth century, have been examined with unprecedented interest and enthusiasm by both academics and policy-oriented researchers.

After decades of research, it has been widely acknowledged that institutions do matter and that "good institutions" are critical for good governance.[9] Nevertheless, when we observe the world through a comparative lens and temporarily discard the relatively parochial interest in parchment institutions, it should be easy to see the lack of a universally applicable institutional template or formula for good governance.[10] Institutions that follow the same design vary significantly across localities in regard to their performance.

Perhaps the most famous and well-analyzed example is the difference between South and North Italy in terms of institutional performance, as Putnam and his colleagues documented in their seminal work (Putnam et al. 1993).[11] Less well-known but equally thought-provoking cases can be found in many developing countries engaged in the complex project of "institution formalization and modernization" for the sake of potentially facilitating both their social transition and economic development. For example, nationally promoted land-tenure systems, widely believed by new institutional economists to be capable of securing property rights and facilitating economic growth, have generated unexpected results in African countries, some of which have been catastrophic for local communities. Specifically, in some African communities, the state-endorsed land-tenure system runs against community-shared norms of fairness and reciprocity. Resulting conflicts have led to unrest and even ruined harmonious relationships cherished by local residents (Chimhowu and

Woodhouse 2006; Daley 2005a, 2005b; Galvan 2004). Therefore, in these communities, newly imposed land-tenure systems have not been as effectively adopted as expected. Even in those communities where the state-endorsed land-tenure system has been established as designed, the resulting enormous inequality in land ownership has become a serious challenge for local governance and to economic prosperity (Platteau 1995, 2000).

In addition to numerous examples of the uneven establishment and performance of formal institutions despite the same design and settings, contemporary literature provides abundant evidence of how good governance, conventionally assumed to be closely associated with well-designed and properly performing formal institutions, has been effectively maintained in some communities without resorting to the parchment institutions that most academics and policymakers have in mind.

In the history of Europe and North America, indigenously developed informal institutions had been critical for local economic growth and prosperity as well as for the maintenance of social order (Fukuyama 2011; Greif 1989; Greif and Kandel 1995; Greif et al. 1995). Even in some rural communities of the United States in the 1990s, locally shared norms and conventions played dominant roles in resolving conflicts among residents, despite contradictions between formal legal stipulations and these local norms and conventions. In these communities, order was achieved without law (Ellickson 1991). Similar cases of good governance without formal institutions are widely available in developing countries. Blood revenge rather than criminal law has been a key deterrent against felonies in some East European and Middle Eastern underdeveloped regions (Boehm 1984; Ginat 1997). People in Indian villages still go to traditional leaders for conflict resolution (Krishna 2002). Informal money-raising organizations have played an indispensable role in facilitating local marketing in Indonesia (Hayami and Kawagoe 2001). In sum, we have varieties of governance, many of which rely not on externally imposed formal institutions but rather on indigenously cultivated informal ones.

When it comes to local governance and its associated institutional foundations, China is similar to the rest of the world. Reviewing the existing literature on China's rural governance clearly shows the salience of different and even contrasting findings on the performance of different types of institutions in Chinese villages.

Grassroots democracy in Chinese village has been evolving in a highly uneven way. VCEs have been regularly held in a transparent and competitive way in some villages but seriously and persistently manipulated in others (Kennedy 2002; Landry et al. 2010; J. Lu 2012; O'Brien 1994;

Tan 2004). Moreover, even in villages with democratic and transparent grassroots elections, VCEs' impacts on local governance are far from clear. In some communities, grassroots elections have successfully aligned villagers' and elected officials' policy preferences, increased community members' positive evaluations of local cadres' performance as well as their trust in the latter, reduced income inequality among villagers, and increased expenditures on local public projects (Manion 1996, 2006; Sato 2008; S. Wang and Yao 2010; Y. Yao and Shen 2006; X. Zhang et al. 2004).[12] However, in other villages, there is no significant relationship between the democratic nature of VCEs and the provision of local public goods.

Instead, it is solidarity groups (e.g., clan/lineage or religious organizations) that have coordinated villagers' collective activities and regulated elected officials' behaviors by creating accountability without democracy (Jie Chen and Huhe 2013; L. Tsai 2007a, 2007b; Xia 2011).[13] Institutional pluralism has also been documented in other aspects of China's rural governance, like resolving conflicts among villagers (B. Chen 2011a, 2011b; Michelson 2008; Michelson and Read 2011) and raising financial sources for entrepreneurial activities (Bislev 2012; B. Hu 2007; Nee and Opper 2012; Ong 2012; K. S. Tsai 2002).

These fascinating but puzzling findings raise the following questions: Why could the same designed and imposed rule-based institutions, working as the foundation of local governance, be effectively established in some regions but not in others? Why are indigenous relation-based institutions still the foundation of local governance in some communities, despite the availability of externally imposed rule-based institutions? Confronted with both indigenous relation-based institutions and imposed rule-based institutions, which institutional channels are community members more likely to use in dealing with various issues? Under what conditions do the coexistence of and interactions between indigenous institutions and newly imposed ones favor one over the other as the institutional foundation of local governance? Moreover, what are the implications of the answers to the aforementioned questions for contemporary literature on institutional change and local governance?

Before I present the central arguments of this book and lay out the framework for subsequent analyses, two key concepts need to be defined: indigenously developed institutions (IDIs) and externally imposed institutions (EIIs).[14] IDIs are systems of social factors, which emerge endogenously, with the potential to enable or constrain community members' behaviors. These institutions, including clan/lineage organizations, religious solidarity groups, rotating saving and credit associations, and local norms, are primarily produced out of continuous social interaction and transmitted through socialization. EIIs are exogenously designed systems of social factors with the potential to enable or constrain community members' behaviors. These institutions, including local elections, police, and judicial and banking systems, are primarily produced out of the intentional efforts of external forces and transmitted through institutionalized bureaucratic channels. Generally speaking, IDIs are primarily relation-based, more informal in the sense that they are not mandated by forces exogenous to communities such as national governments, and widely observed in traditional societies. EIIs are primarily rule-based, more formal in the sense that they are imposed through institutional bureaucratic channels and backed by forces foreign to communities, and widely practiced in modern societies.

This book makes four central arguments. Firstly, regardless of its nature, any institution can perform effectively in sustaining local governance, as long as it can effectively solve the two fundamental problems in decentralized governance: collective action and accountability. Historically, indigenously cultivated relation-based institutions have a much longer and richer tradition than do externally imposed rule-based institutions of serving the governance of local communities by addressing these two problems.

Secondly, the effectiveness of different institutions—indigenous relation-based versus imposed rule-based—in solving these two fundamental problems is, at least to some extent, contingent upon the social environment in which they are embedded. A close-knit social environment—more specifically, frequent and continuous social interaction and the existence of dense and extended social networks—favors the operation of indigenous relation-based institutions, while imposed rule-based institutions enjoy an advantage in loosely coupled communities. In contrast, in atomized communities,[15] neither can work effectively as the institutional foundation of local governance.

Thirdly, local communities' social environments are closely tied to their structural features. When communal structures are transformed to various extents due to factors such as significant outward migration, the social environments of these communities are accordingly reshaped along the spectrum that ranges from the close-knit environment at one end, through the loosely coupled one, to the atomized environment at the other end.

Finally, confronted with the coexistence of different institutions embedded in transformed social environments and serving similar functions, community members are more likely to choose the efficacious one with the lowest transaction costs, which include both switching and coordination costs in their institutional choice. Therefore, given unevenly transformed social environments in local communities, as well as community members' contextualized choices among different institutional solutions, varieties of governance can be observed under similar sets of externally imposed formal institutional arrangements. In sum, this book argues that changes in the structures of local communities, something that contemporary literature on local governance and institutional change has generally ignored or only tentatively touched upon, play a central role in explaining the existence of varieties of governance in local communities as well as transformations in the institutional foundations of decentralized governance.

1.2 CASE SELECTION, METHODOLOGY, AND DATA

China scholars generally have agreed that a "honeycomb" is an appropriate representation of the communal structures of rural China before the initiation of market-oriented reforms in the late 1970s and early 1980s (Parish 1985; Shue 1988).[16] The social environment associated with this honeycomb community structure favors the cultivation, consolidation, and operation of indigenous relation-based institutions for local governance.[17] Not surprisingly, historical studies on local governance in premodern China, particularly those on rural governance in the Song, Ming, and Qing dynasties, have provided numerous examples of indigenous institutions (including clan/lineage organizations, community granaries, and local norms) that effectively regulated and coordinated people's behaviors to sustain social order and promote local development (Kuhn 1975; A. H. Smith 1899; Wakeman and Grant 1975; Watt 1972; G. Xiao 1960; L. Yang 1961). To fulfill its ambition of modernizing governance in China, the CCP centralized its administration after its military victory in the late 1940s, oppressed the operation of various indigenous institutions in local governance, and penetrated local communities through the use of newly imposed party and mass organizations between the 1950s and 1970s. Nevertheless, the CCP's various imposed rule-based institutions, including the household registration system, the Commune system, and government-controlled urbanization and migration, actually reinforced the honeycomb structure in rural China (Bislev and Thøgersen 2012; H. Li 2009; Yep 2003).[18] Furthermore, these undisrupted, well-maintained, close-knit communal structures in rural China provided the necessary social environment for the resurrection and operation of many indigenous institutions in the early 1980s, as the CCP steadily decentralized its administration and loosened its bureaucratic control of rural communities. Later, accompanying a national program of institutional modernization to promote economic reforms and improve macro-governance, a large number of newly designed rule-based institutions, including grassroots democracy, were introduced into various aspects of rural life, beginning in the late 1980s.

Meanwhile, China's market-oriented economic reforms have significantly challenged the honeycomb structure of Chinese villages in an unprecedented way: Many villagers leave rural communities for economic opportunities and associated benefits in urban areas. According to China's most recent official statistics, more than 158 million rural laborers worked and lived in urban areas (other than their home townships) as migrant workers at the end of 2011.[19] Also, the geographic distribution of rural China's cityward migration is highly uneven.[20] As a result, the social environments of Chinese villages have been substantively transformed, *inter alia*, by rural–urban migration, and in a very uneven way. Although these villagers migrate cityward without deliberately challenging the performance of indigenous relation-based institutions within their home communities, their leaving per se has significantly reshaped the institutional and political landscapes of Chinese rural communities (Murphy 2002; Pesqué-Cela et al. 2009; Roberts 1997; Y. Xu 2000; Y. Xu and Xu 2003).

When these three things—(1) revived indigenous relation-based institutions in rural communities with a rich and deep-rooted tradition of self-governance based on such institutions, (2) the ongoing national project of modernizing and formalizing institutions for decentralized governance in rural communities, and (3) unevenly transformed rural communities due to the significant outflow of labor through rural–urban migration—come together, students of institutional change, institutional performance, and local governance are offered a rare opportunity to examine a series of interesting questions whose answers have significant implications for both policymaking and theory development. This book focuses on the particular questions of whether a variety of institutional foundations have been working in sustaining the decentralized governance in Chinese villages with transformed social environments, and why different institutional foundations have been adopted and consolidated for governance in these communities.

In addition to examining the correlations between various institutions established and adopted in Chinese villages and the quality of governance in these communities at the community level, this books goes one step further, following the methodological framework suggested by Coleman

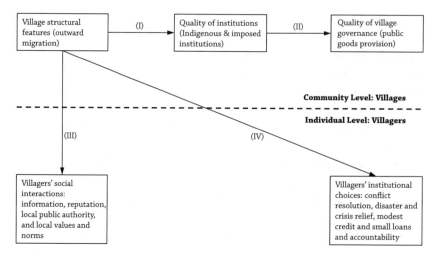

Figure 1.1:
A Multilevel System of Propositions

(1990, pp. 5–23), to examine a multilevel system of propositions, including some interesting dynamics at the individual level (Fig. 1.1).

At the community level, as illustrated in Figure 1.1, this book examines two relationships. Like most existing research on China's rural governance, this book explores the relationship between the quality of different institutions (i.e., indigenous relation-based institutions and imposed rule-based ones) and local public goods provision in Chinese villages, as indicated by Path II. However, different from contemporary pertinent research, this book traces one step back, as indicated by Path I, and examines how village communal structures (which are captured primarily by varying levels of cityward migration) shape the quality of different institutions, thus providing a contextualized understanding of institutional change and governance in rural China.

Beyond such community-level dynamics, this book further explores some micro-dynamics at the individual level that could have driven the institutional changes in rural China. More specifically, this book tries to understand how changes in communal structures shape the information environment, social sanctions based on local reputation, public authority, and cooperative norms among villagers, as indicated by Path III. All these factors are closely tied to the performance and effectiveness of indigenous relation-based institutions. Furthermore, this book also examines how the transformed social environment affects villagers' choices between different institutions (i.e., indigenous relation-based institutions vs. imposed rule-based ones) to address their variety of issues within home communities, as indicated by Path IV, like conflict resolution, disaster and crisis relief, modest credit and small loans, and accountability.

To achieve these goals, I need pertinent information on both villages, as the environments in which socioeconomic and political activities are embedded, and villagers, as the agents of contextualized decisions and consequential behaviors. Therefore, in addition to objective measures of the quality of governance in Chinese villages, their villagers' perceptions, evaluations, and normative orientations also are critical to the exploration of the micro-foundations of the operation and performance of different institutions in upholding local governance. Given such requirements, sampling surveys are the most appropriate research tool for examining the propositions of this book. The 4,205 rural respondents of the 2008 Asian Barometer Survey II Mainland China Survey (ABSMCS) and 356 administrative villages where these rural respondents lived and that were covered in the 2008 National Village Survey (NVS) are the key subjects of this book's empirical examination.[21]

To be able to design appropriate survey instruments, I spent three months in the summer of 2006 immersed in the villages of Hubei, Henan, Shandong, and Shanxi provinces to (1) familiarize myself with the substantive issues that could offer the most analytic leverage when examining the performance of different institutions and (2) identify valid but not region-specific proxies that could be used to measure such performance. Partnered with students and faculty from the Center of Rural Governance (CRG) at Huazhong University of Science and Technology, I worked as part of a team comprising three or four groups living in three or four adjacent villages.[22] Following an outline that I prepared, with cues and potential questions on various aspects of local governance and villagers' perceptions and evaluations of different institutions, each group worked independently in a preselected village, interviewing village cadres and villagers and closely observing relevant activities. Every other night, all groups met for a two-hour discussion on what each group had found, what should be further explored, and what should be paid extra attention to in subsequent fieldwork. Through this effective collaboration, I not only became knowledgeable about more cases but also built a deeper understanding of each individual case through comparison. This collaboration based on group efforts helped to maximize the validity of proposed survey instruments when later applied to villages that I did not visit in person.

A pilot survey was conducted in the summer of 2007 in the villages of Hunan, Anhui, and Jiangxi provinces. Partnered again with the CRG, I tested two sets of questionnaires designed for both villagers and their villages.[23] After further revising the survey instruments based on pilot survey results and securing permission from the principal investigators of the Asian Barometer Surveys (ABS),[24] I included some key survey instruments in the mass questionnaire of the 2008 ABSMCS. I also worked with the ABS II to incorporate the village questionnaire that I tested into its community questionnaire for the 2008 NVS as a means to collect socioeconomic, political, and structural features of the sampled Chinese villages. Moreover, to ensure that this survey could cover as many temporal and seasonal migrants in rural areas as possible, it was scheduled between December 2007 and March 2008, with the Chinese Spring Festival (*chunjie*) in between, when most temporal and seasonal migrants go home for family reunions. Nevertheless, an unexpected and unprecedented snowstorm attacked more than twenty provinces in central, south, and northwest China in early January 2008 and significantly delayed the implementation of this survey, which was not completed until late May 2008.

To offset the widely recognized deficiency of quantitative analyses in uncovering underlying causal mechanisms and fleshing out theoretical arguments, I also compiled qualitative evidence, based on rounds of fieldwork in rural China between 2006 and 2008, through semistructured interviews, participant observation, and documentary studies.[25] The value of these qualitative data in this book is twofold. First, snapshot survey data can only offer cross-sectional information on the correlations among key variables of interest, with exclusive emphasis on the variance along the spatial dimension. However, the temporal dimension also plays a significant role in the process of institutional change and performance, particularly if we are interested in the impacts of evolving outward migration on communal structures and local social environments. For this research, despite my lack of access to longitudinal survey data, process tracing within a rural community, based on villagers' recall and memories, could offer some extra analytic leverage in understanding the impacts of transformed communal structures on local social environments from a longitudinal perspective as well as how the performance of different institutions changes as evolving national socioeconomic and political policies drive the outflow of villagers.

Secondly, following most-similar and most-different research strategies (King et al. 1994; Przeworski and Teune 1970; Ragin 1989), comparative case studies also offer a further advantage in addition to isolating the influence of the variables of interest. Average villagers' and local cadres' reflections on social sanctions, village politics, local governance, and the performance of different institutions, as well as their answers to how they prefer some institutions over others, provide vivid examples of the "contextualized rationality" that is critical for understanding the logic of decentralized governance and institutional change in rural communities. All such rich information cannot be recovered simply through statistically analyzing survey data.

It is important to remind readers that although this book's quantitative and qualitative evidence comes primarily from rural China, its theoretical framework and arguments are not just valid for and relevant to decentralized governance in Chinese villages. Instead, this book offers a contextualized understanding of changes in the institutional foundations of local governance in any community that faces the coexistence of indigenous relation-based institutions and imposed rule-based ones and simultaneously witnesses the transformation of community structures driven by external socioeconomic and political forces. As local communities move away from the close-knit type to the loosely coupled type or even the atomized one, the institutional foundations of governance in such communities change accordingly. Thus, identifying the social environments in which different institutions operate and perform, and bringing the transformation of social environments back into our theorization of institutional change and local governance, can significantly deepen our knowledge of how institutions change, perform, and affect local governance. Moreover, it can enrich our understanding of the conditions under which institutional modernization or engineering may succeed or fail.

1.3 OVERVIEW OF THE BOOK

Chapter 2 establishes the theoretical foundation and offers a coherent framework to guide subsequent empirical analyses. After reviewing contemporary literature on the origins of and changes in institutions and local governance, I raise the key research questions of this book. Subsequently, both macro- and micro-views of the origins of indigenously developed relation-based institutions and externally imposed rule-based institutions in local communities are presented as critical background information. Building upon stylized game-theory models, I show the effectiveness of reputation-based multilateral social sanctions, which I argue are the linchpin of most indigenous institutions, in solving the problems of collective action and accountability in close-knit communities. Juxtaposing externally imposed rule-based institutions and indigenous relation-based ones, I also demonstrate the advantage of the former in sustaining governance in loosely coupled communities. I then lay out the framework for a contextualized understanding of institutional choices in local communities confronted with the coexistence of different institutions and unevenly transformed social environments. In the end, major hypotheses regarding how the institutional foundations of local governance may undergo transition because of the changes in communal structures (primarily driven by outward migration) are derived for subsequent empirical examination.

Chapter 3 offers a broad historical review of the evolution of local governance in China, as well as its institutional foundations, and the evolution of rural–urban migration since the late 1970s. One focus of this chapter is how structural features of Chinese villages have moderated the performance of various institutions imposed by central governments in Chinese history. A brief review of institutions adopted by the Ming and Qing dynasties and the Kuomintang regime for governing rural China offers some examples of how indigenous relation-based institutions were intentionally and effectively incorporated by the central governments into their respective institutional designs to uphold the governance in Chinese villages. An introduction to the totalitarian and later authoritarian institutions imposed upon Chinese rural communities by the CCP before the late 1970s, as well as the grassroots democracy introduced into rural China after the 1980s, provides the necessary background for understanding villagers' institutional choices and the existence of varieties of governance in contemporary rural China. The other focus of this chapter is the evolution of the outflow of villagers through rural–urban migration in contemporary China. With the help of national statistics collected from different sources, I present the uneven distribution of rural–urban migration in Chinese villages. These statistics attest to the plausibility of uneven transformation in the social environments of the rural communities examined in subsequent chapters.

Chapter 4 focuses on the decentralized provision of local public goods (i.e., Paths I and II in Fig. 1.1), a critical aspect of local governance in rural China, using empirical evidence collected at the village level from the 2008 NVS. After establishing the validity of the proxies used for indigenous relation-based and imposed rule-based institutions, this chapter presents an examination of the data on local public goods provision in 356 administrative villages, with the help of structural equation modeling. I first show that, regardless of its nature, any institution that can solve the problems of collective action and accountability is capable of sustaining the provision of local public goods in a decentralized way, wherein required resources come primarily from the collective incomes of villages and/or voluntary contributions from villagers. I then demonstrate that changes in communal structures, caused primarily by outward migration, have a significant impact on whether and how public goods in Chinese villages can be provided in a decentralized way. As confirmed by statistical results, this structural feature exerts its influence primarily and indirectly via shaping the performance of different institutions, thus providing empirical support for theoretical Paths I and II. Three case studies, with anecdotal and qualitative stories, are presented to show the validity of the causal stories uncovered by statistical modeling.

Chapters 5 and 6 provide some micro-level evidence for the macro-picture presented in Chapter 3. Chapter 5 shows how outward migration at the village level has transformed the close-knit social environment and eroded the social foundations for the operation and performance of indigenous relation-based institutions in some Chinese rural communities (i.e., Path III in Fig. 1.1). Outward migration, albeit unintentionally, induces changes in villagers' information environment, their responses to possible social sanctions, and perceptions of public authority as well as normative orientations toward collective interests, long-term relationships, and conflict avoidance. Such changes are systematically examined by the use of discrete choice models that combine both individual characteristics collected from the 2008 ABSMCS and community features collected from the 2008 NVS. In addition to cross-sectional evidence, a case study on changes in the social environment of a village since the People's Commune era is presented. This case study offers some qualitative and longitudinal evidence of how the social foundations for the effective performance of indigenous relation-based institutions in the village have gradually eroded due to the transformation in the village's community structure driven by increasing outward migration, which in turn supports theoretical Path III.

Chapter 6 moves beyond the induced changes in social environments and focuses on villagers' choices among different institutional solutions for handling a variety of issues as well as on their assessment of different institutions for monitoring village cadres and holding them accountable (i.e., Path IV in Fig. 1.1). As such, imposed rule-based institutions are the focus of this chapter. Villagers' evaluations of imposed rule-based institutions for conflict resolution, disaster/crisis relief, modest credit and small loans, and regulating village cadres' behaviors are systematically examined using discrete choice models that combine individual characteristics collected from the 2008 ABSMCS and community features collected from the 2008 NVS. As expected, in loosely coupled villages, characterized by a medium level of outward migration, imposed rule-based institutions, *ceteris paribus*, are more likely to attract villagers' attention and become their choice for addressing local governance issues. Imposed rule-based institutions are also more likely to be used for supervising village cadres and holding them accountable. This not only supports theoretical Path IV but also emphasizes the influence of structural features on the villagers' choice to use imposed rule-based institutions, an important point for policymakers.

Chapter 7 provides a conclusion and comprises summarized findings. In addition, I address a serious challenge that faces most students of institutions: Are institutions epiphenomenal? I argue that rural China' experiences under the CCP regime confirm the significant influence of institutions on its governance, which cannot be fully attributed to the institutions' simply transmitting the impact of structural conditions. I also provide suggestions on how to adequately contextualize our understanding of institutional change and its consequences. Particularly, I emphasize the necessity of establishing a comprehensive framework to examine the possible dynamics among different types of institutions and moving beyond the institutional environment by bringing in the pertinent social environment. I further discuss the broader implications of this research for the literature on formal and informal institutions, institutional change, local governance, and social capital.

The epilogue (Chapter 8) contains some reflections on whether the increasing number of migrant workers returning to rural China due to the 2008 financial crisis and China's efforts to upgrade its economic structure might offer some opportunities to revive China's rural governance, particularly that in those villages atomized or paralyzed due to a high level of cityward migration. I argue that whether returned migrant workers can contribute to reviving these communities' governance depends on whether they can be attracted to resettle in their home villages and whether their attachment to these villages can be regenerated and strengthened. Furthermore, I also discuss how to effectively use China's increasing budget for *Sannong* (agriculture, villages, and peasants) to revive its rural communities for better institutional performance and improved governance. I particularly emphasize the salience of channeling critical resources into rural communities and intentionally cultivating the cooperation and coordination capacity among Chinese villagers for Chinese leaders.

CHAPTER 2
Local Governance in Transformed Communities

It has been widely acknowledged that the problems of collective action and accountability have prevented many communities from enjoying the benefits of good governance (e.g., Gibson et al. 2000; G. Hardin 1968; Ostrom 1990; L. Tsai 2007a). To solve these problems, facilitate cooperation among community members, and channel efforts and resources toward public interest, a variety of institutional solutions have been proposed and practiced. Some of the institutional solutions are indigenously cultivated and refined through a trial-and-error process embedded in long-term, within-community social interaction, while others are externally imposed and established on the basis of sophisticated institutional engineering. The effectiveness of different institutions is contingent upon the surrounding social environment as well as on community members' contextualized responses. Further, when communal structures are transformed to various extents due to socioeconomic and political forces foreign to local communities, the institutional foundations of local governance, as well as their associated quality, vary accordingly.

This chapter draws upon the most recent developments in sociology, cognitive science, anthropology, economic history, legal studies, and political science to (1) establish a coherent theoretical framework and (2) derive major hypotheses to guide subsequent empirical chapters. In particular, this chapter theoretically engages the following questions: (1) How do different types of institutions perform effectively to sustain local governance? (2) Under what conditions, particularly the features of social environments and communal structures, do different types of institutions have an advantage in working as the foundation of local governance? (3) When different types of institutions that serve similar functions are simultaneously available in local communities, how does the interplay among them shape the institutional foundations of local governance? Finally, (4) as communal structures are transformed by various socioeconomic and political forces foreign to local communities, how do the dynamics among different types of institutions for local governance evolve?

2.1 GOVERNANCE WITHOUT PARCHMENT INSTITUTIONS IN CLOSE-KNIT COMMUNITIES

Although parchment institutions generally have been recognized as the foundation of good governance, the existence of a peaceful and stable social life, which is critical to governance, has been widely documented by social scientists in numerous communities without anything even remotely resembling rule-based institutions in the modern sense.[1] In these communities, social control has been well maintained and enforced not through parchment institutions but rather via endogenous relation-based institutions that are primarily supported by effective social sanctions and that emerge out of long and stable within-community social interaction.[2]

For example, in some tribal communities in Sub-Saharan Africa, people are expected to share what they have and are normatively prescribed not to hoard extra food or economic benefits. Such egalitarian norms provide a critical hedge against uncertainties in food production and economic activities and ensure the survival of the community in the long run. Anyone found hoarding extra food or other material resources is likely to be cursed by other community members, with the help of witches, or to have his property destroyed. Given the deterrence of community sanctions and punishment, egalitarian norms thus are widely obeyed in these tribal communities (Platteau 1994a, 1994b, 2000). Similar stories were reported for some Japanese villages in the early 1900s, wherein villagers who were caught or even suspected of stealing could be ostracized from their village and even be subject to having marks tattooed on their faces (Nakane 1967; R. J. Smith 1967). These stigmatized villagers were unlikely to be accepted by other villages, which implied a miserable end to their lives.

In addition to such implicit but community-recognized norms, indigenously developed but clearly stipulated rules also are enforced in some communities to regulate their members' behaviors. An example is the village compacts in rural China. Fieldwork and archival studies in different regions of rural China have repeatedly confirmed that well-stipulated village compacts played an important role in ensuring governance in Chinese villages, at least before the Chinese Communist Party (CCP)'s victory in 1949 (Duan 2007; Duara 1988; Freedman 1958; P. C. Huang 1985, 1996; H. Li 2005; Niou 2005; Unger 2002; G. Xiao 1960). In many villages, compacts comprised specific rules about what was appropriate or inappropriate in particular aspects of villagers' lives—for example, attitudes toward people with different social status, daily dealings with neighbors and relatives, and rituals for weddings and funerals. Some even provided procedures on how civil and criminal cases, such as adultery and theft, should be addressed. Villagers who violated such rules could be scolded or whipped in public, have their names removed from their genealogy, or even be drowned or burned to death, depending on the nature of their transgressions.[3]

This kind of governance without parchment institutions is not limited to rural communities in less-developed countries, as some conventional wisdom may suggest. In Shasta County of Northern California, in the early 1990s, gossip and stigmatization still played a dominant role in regulating people's daily interaction and resolving conflicts. The norm of neighborliness trumped legal entitlements in social interaction, and the philosophy of "live and let live" guided people's behavior and successfully maintained local governance in this American community (Ellickson 1991). Further, the concept of community should not be narrowly construed as a geographic concept. Mutually shared norms, widely cherished reputation, and internally enforced arbitration systems also have effectively dominated the regulation of the activities of businessmen in the contemporary diamond industry, despite the availability of a modern legal system (L. Bernstein 1992). These businessmen may not live in the same area or region, but they still prefer extralegal contractual relations to legal ones.[4] In this industry, a binding agreement could be made by a handshake with the words *mazel u'broche* (luck and blessing). An envelope folded and sealed in a specific way, with the stone inside, signature over the seal, and specialized terms and conditions included, can work as the formal contract of transaction with binding power.

Given the documentation of governance without parchment institutions in these communities with different historical and cultural traditions, varying socioeconomic characters, and distinct geographic distribution features, a question naturally arises: What are the shared features of these communities that make their governance without parchment institutions possible? A succinct answer is that they all are close-knit communities with two prominent structural characteristics: (1) frequent and continuous within-community interaction and (2) extended and dense social networks that connect community members.[5] In reality, these two community structural features are related to some extent; however, they do have distinct theoretical and empirical implications for the performance of indigenous relation-based institutions supported by effective social sanctions. Thus, they are addressed respectively.

Frequent and Continuous Interaction

In close-knit communities, due to either geographic or other structural constraints,[6] interaction among members is frequent and continuous. In some Chinese villages, for example, people not only work in lands bordering each other but also deal with each other in other activities: They buy daily groceries from one or two shops for years or decades; they go to each other's parties, weddings, and funerals; and they may even spend most of their time in the village with those who have been their friends since childhood. "You always see each other when raising your head, though you may not realize their existence when lowering your head" (*ditou bujian taitou jian*) is the most frequently used phrase by Chinese villagers to describe their relationships with their fellow villagers. This is why Chinese villages have been characterized as "communities of acquaintances" (Fei 1939, 1992). And this frequent and continuous interaction among community members has serious implications for how they behave when dealing with local governance issues.

Because most local governance problems are related to community members' and local leaders' transgressing in order to obtain personal gains at the cost of community benefits, the Prisoners' Dilemma (PD) game is generally used in this context to demonstrate the effects of frequent and continuous interaction on the possible outcomes of local governance.[7] In a one-shot PD game, both players move strategically and simultaneously to attain the best outcome given their opponent's possible moves. Regardless of the opponent's moves, "Defection" is always a winning strategy for both players. Because no player has an incentive to change his strategy, "Defection, Defection" becomes a Nash-equilibrium.[8] Nevertheless, this individual strategic calculation prevents the two players from achieving the collectively optimal outcome, "Cooperation, Cooperation."

To overcome this dilemma, one solution is iteration. Basically, if the PD game can be played over and over again, transforming the one-shot PD game into an iterated PD game, "Cooperation" might be the preferred strategy for both players and become a Nash-equilibrium out of many other equally possible ones (Axelrod 1984, 1997; Camerer 2003; Nachbar 1989).[9] In plain language, in close-knit communities, frequent and continuous interaction can transform the nature of social interaction by enabling social sanctions that reward cooperation and penalize deviant and opportunistic behavior (La Ferrara 2011). Thus, with this heavy shadow of the future, pessimistic predictions for the lack of cooperation among self-interested individuals (G. Hardin 1968; Mancur Olson 1971) may not necessarily come true in close-knit communities, even though community members are still rational in pursuing their own interests rather than being tricked into some altruistic mental state.

After continuous and repeated interactions, due to human beings' cognitive features, beneficial strategies in social interaction might gradually become autonomously and subconsciously retrieved responses in dealing with similar situations (Mantzavinos 2001; North 2005). Moreover, through community socialization, such effective responses might be disseminated among community members and across generations, become gradually internalized by most community members, and finally develop into norms or cultural values that prescribe and regulate future social interaction (Coleman 1986; Cook and Hardin 2001; Ellickson 2001; Hechter and Opp 2001; Horne 2001; Ullmann-Margalit 1977). These norms and values not only provide internal sanctions (e.g., guilt) that lead community members to self-regulate their behavior, they also further ease and empower external social sanctions (e.g., shame) within the community (Coleman 1990, Chapter 3; de Hooge et al. 2007; Gilbert 2003; Hechter 1987; Scheff 1988).

In summary, thanks to the beneficial communal structure of close-knittedness, the expectation of future interactions plays a significant role in people's rational calculations in close-knit communities. Further, given how embedded these members are within the community's socialization, they are likely to hold stable expectations of each other's behavior. Thus, norms and cultural values that prescribe behaviors such as reciprocity and self-discipline in social interactions are likely to be cultivated and internalized by community members.[10] All this contributes to the effective performance of indigenous relation-based institutions supported by social sanctions that may ease cooperation, facilitate the emergence of order, and sustain quality local governance in the absence of parchment institutions.

Dense and Extended Social Networks

In addition to frequent and continuous interaction among members, dense and extended social networks are another critical structural feature of close-knit communities that contributes to effective governance without parchment institutions. Two key functions are served by dense and extended social networks for local governance issues: generating cross-issue linkages and easing information transmission.

In rural China, for example, it is common to find villages with a majority of residents sharing the same surname, worshiping the same ancestors, and participating in the same rituals and ceremonies. In some villages, it is easy to identify systematic connections among the villagers if provided with detailed information on villagers' names and statuses in the genealogical record (Freedman 1958, 1966; L. Liu and Murphy 2006; Qian 1994; L. Zhao 1999). Dense and extended social networks also span across villagers' socioeconomic, political, and cultural lives in rural China: Besides socializing at birthday parties, weddings, and funerals, they may pool money for small businesses, call upon each other's support to address their grievances against local officials, or offer each other their respective expertise and skills when asked. It is not uncommon for villagers who are good at cooking to help their fellow villagers prepare banquets for weddings, funerals, and parties without charging for their work in rural China. In turn, they expect to be repaid by their fellow villagers when they need help or some other villager's expertise is requested (Fei 1939, 1992; X. He 2003a).

Iteration, as previously discussed, is one solution to the PD game, which creates the shadow of the future via repeated interaction. This solution is particularly effective when applied to continuous social interaction within specific issue domains over the long run. Meanwhile, embedded in dense and extended social networks, members of close-knit communities are simultaneously engaged in interactions across multiple issue domains in their daily lives. In other words, the dense and extended social networks of close-knit communities make within-community interaction multiplex rather than simplex. Therefore, the "games" played in these communities are not isolated games but, rather, are interlocked, which creates the shadow of cross-issue linkages and further contributes to the endogenous emergence of cooperation and order.[11] Given their interlocked nature, deviation from cooperation in one game is likely to be punished by exclusion from many or even all other games. In other words, spontaneous cooperation and order can be achieved in a meta-game that consists of numerous simultaneously played games, even if transgression might be the dominant strategy for players in any individual game. An extreme example is the ostracism used by some communities to punish transgressors: Deviation in social interaction leads to the cancellation of community membership, which could be detrimental for those whose lives depend on their community (Nakane 1967; R. J. Smith 1967).[12]

In addition to generating cross-issue linkages that empower social sanctions with higher costs for transgressors (Lacy and Niou 2004; Martin 1993) and facilitate the realization of collectively optimal results, dense and extended social networks in close-knit communities ease the transmission of information that is indispensable for ensuring order and governance in the absence of parchment institutions. The role of information in sustaining indigenous relation-based institutions supported by effective social sanctions has been repeatedly emphasized in contemporary research (Clay 1997; Coleman 1986, 1990; Geertz 1973, 1980; Greif 1989, 1993, 2006).[13] Further, it is apparent that information can be more quickly disseminated through dense social networks—that is, social networks with a high degree of dyadic connection among a covered population.[14]

Embedded within such social networks, people can easily get information about other community members through various sources. Any member's good or bad behavior, including his or her words, is very likely to be in the public domain and accessible to the whole community. In rural China, gossip plays an important role in village social interaction (Fei 1939, 1992; X. He 2003b; H. Li 2009; L. Su 2000) and used to be the major entertainment medium for most villagers before TV became widely accessible in Chinese villages in the early 1990s.[15] Therefore, given their embeddedness in dense and extended social networks, it is much more difficult for people to cover up their words and deeds, and their transgressions, if any, are very likely to be identified and sanctioned. Moreover, once their transgressions are uncovered, the transgressors are expected to be stigmatized with a bad reputation transmitted via word of mouth, which, in turn, makes them no longer acceptable to other community members.[16] As a consequence, spontaneous order and governance are more likely to be sustained.

In summary, governance without parchment institutions in close-knit communities is not only consistent with theory but is also widely practiced. Two critical structural features of these communities, (1) frequent and continuous within-community interaction and (2) dense and extended social networks that connect community members, have enabled governance via indigenously developed relation-based institutions supported by effective social sanctions. Embedded within this social environment that is characterized by a heavy shadow of the future, overarching cross-issue linkages, and quick transmission of information, community members are likely to establish stable expectations of their fellow members' behavior. Endogenously evolved norms and values that prescribe behaviors such as reciprocity and self-discipline in social interactions are more likely to be diffused and internalized. Transgressions and opportunistic behavior can largely be successfully deterred or effectively punished once they occur. Therefore, efficacious social sanctions, together with self-regulation driven by internalized norms, not only facilitate cooperation among community members (the collective action problem) but also regulate the behavior of local leaders who are embedded within the same social environment (the accountability problem). In sum, indigenous institutions supported by powerful social sanctions can effectively solve the problems of collective action and accountability and, thus, work as the foundation of local governance in close-knit communities.[17]

Nevertheless, such close-knit communities are not isolated from but rather embedded within the outside world. This embeddedness indicates that all the aforementioned community structural features that are favorable for the cultivation, establishment, and performance of indigenous institutions are thus subject to the impact of transformations in the outside world. Such transformations can erode the favorable communal structures and reshape the performance of indigenous institutions. Once the forces of economic modernization and technological innovation are unleashed, this embeddedness becomes increasingly salient and consequential for local governance.

2.2 MODERNIZATION AND IMPOSED PARCHMENT INSTITUTIONS

As a key theme of the nineteenth and twentieth centuries, modernization generally has been acknowledged as a process of transformation that goes far beyond individuals and involves essential changes in social, economic, and political institutions.[18] Accompanying modernization, nation-states have gradually taken over tribal communities, city-states, and principalities as the dominant political entities in the world. Market economies based on secure property rights and other institutions buttressed by national governments, or centrally planned economies that cover extended geographic areas, have shadowed barter economies or locally circumscribed commercial activities. Legal systems monopolized by nation-states with predominant jurisdiction over their respective territories have successfully established their status against possible rivals.

Generally, parchment institutions primarily sanctioned and imposed by nation-states have played indispensable roles in modern politics, economies, and various social issues.[19] The role of indigenous institutions and their corresponding influence have been significantly reduced and weakened, if not completely eliminated, in modern societies. To fully understand the impact of modernization on institutional innovation and change, it is valuable to understand these effects from two analytically different but interrelated perspectives: bottom-up momentum versus top-down incentives.

Bottom-up Momentum due to Increased Mobility

Empowered with increased physical mobility and augmented material resources, people have been largely freed from geographic constraints as well as associated socioeconomic restrictions. With the availability of cross-regional and even cross-national commercial activities, people are more likely to get out of their home communities to capitalize on novel economic opportunities in other places. Therefore, interaction with strangers becomes increasingly likely. Even those who choose to stay in their home communities have to face new realities and deal with strangers either doing business or residing in their neighborhood. Consequently, the effectiveness of indigenously developed institutions supported by effective social sanctions that coordinate or regulate social interaction has been significantly challenged, primarily for two reasons.

First, when strangers, whom people may come across only a limited number of times or even just once, take up a significant portion of social interaction, the essence of social relation moves away from iterated interaction and toward a one-shot game. As previous discussions on the difference between one-shot and iterated PD games show, this change dramatically lessens the weight of the shadow of the future on people's utility calculations. Thus, as induced by short-term and immediate interest, deviant and opportunistic behavior is more likely to emerge.

Second, given their exclusive reliance on personal ties and connections, locally circumscribed social networks cannot effectively encompass social interaction across geographically dispersed communities. As the geographic scope of social interaction expands, critical information can no longer be efficiently disseminated through locally circumscribed social networks in a timely manner due to the limited number or even lack of links among dispersed localities. Thus, without access to necessary information such as reputation validation or behavior confirmation, the performance of social sanctions in deterring and punishing deviant and opportunistic behavior is seriously undermined. Moreover, given the alternatives available in other localities and the low cost of moving around, the effectiveness of indigenous institutions based on effective social sanctions is severely weakened.

Confronted with the impaired capacity of indigenous institutions to coordinate and regulate transformed and expanded social interaction, people naturally look for new institutional solutions to resume order and governance.[20] This was why commercial guilds in towns and cities during medieval times in European countries, which used to be dominant players in regional business, gradually dwindled when the integration of national markets developed (Greif 2006; Greif et al. 1995). This also was why Italian city-states began to participate on behalf of resident merchants in commercial activities, as the latter expanded their business into foreign cities (Greif 2006). This not only is the case in the history of European countries but is also well documented in developing societies that embarked on their journeys of modernization in the nineteenth or twentieth century, including China. For example, as contemporary literature on the evolution of China's financial and capitalist institutions shows, the development of China's modern banking system (L. Cheng 2003) and commodification of land and labor (Pomeranz 2000; Reed 2004) were spearheaded in more-developed regions with a relatively higher level of social mobility, mostly urban areas. Comparatively speaking, the influence of such bottom-up momentum rarely penetrated into rural China before the Republican era (1911–1949), except for some villages located on the border of developed urban areas (P.C. Huang 1990).[21]

Top-Down Incentives due to Expanded Scale of Governance

The building of nation-states, as a critical political process, has accompanied modernization since the nineteenth century. As a consequence, nation-states have gradually taken over tribal communities, city-states, and principalities as the dominant political entities in the world. In his seminal examination of social engineering in nation-states for effective governance, Scott (1998) cogently argues that a key issue for modern nation-states is "the legibility of a society," which can be improved with the help of simplification and abstraction via rule-based institutions. Similarly, as she examines China's state building and governance, with a particular emphasis on rural China, Shue (2012, pp. 224–225) also argues:

What historians and political scientists refer to as the modern state, in particular, relies on its capacity to devise and deploy sound, rational organizations through which to order all activities aimed at governing its people and at governing itself. . . . Modern states, furthermore, work to inscribe and project suitably modern, legible systems of organizations around, over, and into the human communities under their rule. These, typically precise and hierarchical, state-made arrangements for ordering supervision over space, for demarcating time into schedule and programs, and for specifying the requisites of accepted knowledge, training, and labor all serve to erect a framework within which individuals, groups and communities are meant to place themselves, their activities, and the conduct of their lives. . . . To be organized—rationally and visibly so—is one of the defining qualities of being modern. Exhibiting internal organization and projecting external organizational schemes onto forms and routines of social life that are regarded otherwise as being inscrutable and non-modern, is one of the signature techniques of rule deployed by modern states.[22]

Thus, in addition to the previously discussed dramatic bottom-up momentum for new institutional solutions (e.g., parchment institutions) to replace impaired indigenous institutions for governance, political leaders of nation-states are confronted with the unprecedented challenge of ensuring effective governance over substantially expanded territories that include residents with different backgrounds, experiences, and even cultural traditions.[23] This fundamentally transformed nature of governance (with a much broader geographic scale compared to the governance in local communities) has made indigenous relation-based institutions no longer effective for nation-states and has pushed political leaders to identify new institutions that can significantly reduce the transaction costs of national governance to a manageable level. In this case, rule-based parchment institutions have an advantage.

As shown in previous sections, the efficacy of indigenous institutions relies on frequent and continuous within-community interaction as well as the dense and extended social networks that connect community members. Essentially, indigenous institutions, which emerged in close-knit communities, are primarily relation-based.[24] For these relation-based institutions, there are few fixed costs—for instance, there are few formally stipulated codes, no specialized agents to enforce these codes, and limited use of contracts. Nevertheless, due to the lack of clearly articulated rules and procedures for evaluation, the marginal cost for each individual case is relatively high (compared to the low fixed costs) because each case has to be addressed by taking its specificities into consideration.

As Li (2003, p. 657) argues, under the governance of relation-based institutions, "one needs to screen, test and monitor each and every transaction partner. The acquired relational information is implicit and person-specific, and hence non-(publicly) verifiable and nontransferable." Fortunately, the rich information efficiently disseminated through dense and extended social networks in close-knit communities, by making pertinent information easily accessible, publicly verifiable, and transferable, significantly eases the performance of such relation-based institutions. As a consequence, to ensure good governance, the total transaction costs associated with indigenous institutions in close-knit communities can be maintained at an acceptably low level. However, given the scale of governance for nation-states, the total transaction costs can be prohibitively high and even unbearable if indigenous relation-based institutions are used as the foundation of national governance over geographically dispersed and experientially varied residents. In other words, to achieve the goal of making their societies legible (Scott 1998) and organized (Shue 2012), political leaders of nation-states have to identify new institutional solutions.

Different from indigenous relation-based institutions, parchment institutions are rule-based and involve high fixed costs. Codes and regulations have to be drafted, implemented, and enforced; specialized agents have to be trained and provided; and a comprehensive information infrastructure has to be established and maintained. Nevertheless, the marginal cost for each additional case to be addressed by rule-based institutions is significantly lower or even negligible (compared to the high fixed costs), given the explicit, impersonal, and standardized relationships involved. Basically, with the help of rule-based institutions, national leaders no longer need to deal with their constituencies in a case-by-case style but, rather, more effectively in a mass-production style.[25] Therefore, taking advantage of the economy of scale by adopting standardized rule-based institutions, national leaders can effectively reduce the total transaction costs to a manageable level when dealing with geographically dispersed and diverse residents. In other words, to ensure effective governance over substantially expanded territories that include residents with different backgrounds, experiences, and cultural traditions, political leaders of modern nation-states have strong incentives to establish and impose appropriate rule-based socioeconomic and political institutions via systematic institutional engineering. Meanwhile, the abundant resources generated from economic modernization or the enhanced state capacity of resource extraction also make it possible for political leaders to financially support their institutional engineering and afford the huge fixed investment for establishing rule-based institutions.

In summary, modernization, particularly as promoted by technological innovations and economic growth, has fundamentally transformed the social interaction in local communities and brought about new challenges for local governance. Increased physical mobility enables people to explore various opportunities beyond their home communities and in broad geographic areas. This broadened scope of social interaction significantly weakens the capacity of indigenous relation-based institutions supported by social sanctions to regulate and coordinate people's behavior and, thus, generates bottom-up demand for new institutional solutions. In addition, dramatically expanded geographic scales of territories, including widely dispersed residents with varying backgrounds, experiences, and cultural traditions, also pressure political leaders of modern nation-states to identify new institutional solutions that can make their societies legible and organized, and in turn, keep the transactions costs of effective national governance at a manageable level. The resources generated from economic modernization or the enhanced capacity of resource extraction make it possible for nation-state leaders to make significant investments in building information infrastructure and strengthening state capacity, thereby establishing and imposing rule-based institutions as the foundation of national governance.

As societies witness increased mobility and a significantly expanded scale of social interaction, the bottom-up momentum and top-down incentives for the transition from indigenous relation-based institutions supported by social sanctions to imposed rule-based institutions backed up by nation-states' coercive power may feed upon each other and generate a virtuous cycle that pushes for further institutional innovation and social development (e.g., Greif 2006; Kuran 2010; Mokyr 2002, 2008). However, there also might be a significant disparity between institutional innovation and social development, especially in today's developing countries in which political leaders can easily adapt or import rule-based institutions that have been long practiced in developed countries and impose such institutions onto their respective societies (Berkowitz et al. 2003a, 2003b; Boettke et al. 2008; Scott 1998). Fukuyama (2004, p. 35) succinctly summarizes the noteworthy implications of the dynamic between the bottom-up momentum and top-down incentives for institutional change for the performance of imposed parchment institutions and the quality of governance:

The majority cases of successful state-building and institutional reform have occurred when a society has generated strong domestic demand for institutions and then created them out of whole cloth, imported them from the outside, or adapted foreign models to local conditions. . . . Insufficient domestic demand for institutions or institutional reform is the single most important obstacle to institutional development in poor countries.

2.3 INSTITUTIONAL SYNCRETISM AND INSTITUTIONAL CHOICE

When bottom-up momentum and top-down incentives for institutional change interact, which side takes the lead and to what extent the supply of rule-based institutions matches the demand for parchment institutions can lead to very different scenarios in regard to the performance of imposed parchment institutions and associated governance. The demand-driven scenario has been widely reported in contemporary literature on institutional change in both developed and developing countries (Boix 1999; Cuscak et al. 2007; Greif 2006; Greif et al. 1995; Knight 1992; Thelen 2003, 2004; K. S. Tsai 2005, 2006).[26] Conversely, the supply-leading scenario is more likely to occur in contemporary developing countries and has been noticeably observed in such contexts (Berkowitz et al. 2003a, 2003b; Boettke et al. 2008; Galvan 2004; Scott 1998; Sil and Galvan 2007).

Developing countries are not among the first groups to undergo modernization, and thus they usually are learners or importers of rule-based institutions that have been practiced and established in developed countries. Different from the scenario of demand-driven institutional change, in many developing countries, it is their political leaders who have taken the initiative and imposed parchment institutions to make their societies legible and organized.[27] Nevertheless, due to the relatively low level of economic growth and limited experience with transition in many developing countries, particularly those that won their independence in the twentieth century, social transformation is still at an embryonic stage. In these countries, the economic situation has improved but still hovers at a relatively low level; communication and transportation facilities have been established but still suffer from poor conditions; and the scope of social interaction has been expanded but is still significantly constrained. Further, in most developing countries, there is a large unevenness across localities with respect to the impact of modernization. In metropolitan areas such as Beijing, Mexico City, New Delhi, Dakar, and Cape Town, people can enjoy the numerous benefits of modernization in the same way as their counterparts in developed countries. Meanwhile, in most rural areas of developing countries, physical mobility is still limited and many people are still engaged in traditional ways of production and living. Under these conditions, an "over-supply" or "mismatched supply" of rule-based institutions, or the so-called transplant effect (Berkowitz et al. 2003a, 2003b), is very likely to happen.[28]

In this supply-leading scenario, as rule-based institutions imposed by political leaders are promoted and established in a predetermined and standardized way, the imposed rule-based institutions, especially those of local governance, may fail to operate as effectively as expected (T. L. Anderson and Hill 2004; Boehm 1984; Ellickson 1991; Ginat 1997; Krishna 2002; Platteau 2008; Scott 1998). In rural China, for example, village elections have been officially sanctioned and imposed as the key rule-based institution for organizing self-governance in Chinese villages (Kelliher 1997; O'Brien and Li 2000; Shi 1999a, 2000c).[29] The Organic Law of Village Committees (OLVC) (trial version in 1987 and revised in 1998 and 2010), as the constitution for self-governance in rural China, clearly stipulates the institutional procedures on how such elections should be organized and how decisions on local governance issues should be made. Nevertheless, in practice, the implementation of village elections is far from even in rural China: Some village elections have been implemented closely in accordance with the OLVC, ensuring competition among multiple candidates and the quality of the whole electoral institution, while other village elections have been manipulated to varying extents. As many scholars have already documented, *inter alia*, different levels of economic development in the villages (R. Hu 2005; Oi 1996; Shi 1999a, 2000c), village clan and lineage cleavages (J. Lu 2012; T. Xiao 2010), and manipulation by upper-level governments (particularly township governments) over political and policy concerns (Kennedy 2002, 2009; Landry et al. 2010; Shi 1999b) have contributed to the varying quality of grassroots democracy in rural China.

Contemporary scholarship on institutional transplant further attests that this kind of "over-supply" or "mismatched supply" of rule-based institutions without taking local socioeconomic structures into account could lead to inefficiency and even negative impacts on local governance, particularly in developing countries (Aoki 2001b; Aoki and Hayami 2001; Berkowitz et al. 2003a, 2003b; Boettke et al. 2008; Galvan 2004; Lesorogol 2008; North et al. 2009; Platteau 1995, 2000; Roland 2004). For example, among all regimes in Chinese history, the CCP may have done the best job of establishing formalized judicial institutions in rural communities (Liebman 2012; Peerenboom 2007). Since the mid-1980s, the CCP has launched waves of campaigns of "sending law to rural China" (*songfa xiax-iang*) to reshape and formalize the judicial practice in Chinese villages (Qiang 2003; L. Su 2000, 2002). Nevertheless, in many areas, the linger-ing influence of a culture of anti-litigation (*yansong*) significantly impedes the CCP's efforts (Z. Liang 2002; Michelson 2007, 2008; X. Zhao 2003). Moreover, in some cases, such imposed formal judicial practice contra-dicts locally shared norms and cherished conventions regarding related issues; thus, the enforced formal judicial practice generated uneasiness among villagers, ruined local social relationships, exacerbated local con-flicts, or has even mobilized negative sentiment toward imposed judicial institutions (L. Dong 2008; X. Guo and Xing 2010; X. He 2013; Qiang 2003; L. Su 2000, 2002).

A critical factor identified by contemporary research on the perfor-mance and consequences of imposed parchment institutions in local com-munities is the deep-rooted indigenous relation-based institutions in these communities.[30] Therefore, it is critical to understand the interplay between imposed rule-based institutions and indigenous relation-based institutions in local governance as well as how members of such commu-nities, embedded in this mixed institutional environment, may respond and behave.

Institutional Syncretism and its Critics

A majority of contemporary research on institutional change formulates or tests its frameworks with examples in the history of developed coun-tries and then applies such frameworks with assumed universal applica-bility (Greif 2006; Greif and Laitin 2004; Knight 1992; Kuran 2010; Ma-honey and Thelen 2010b; North 1990). However, as previously discussed, such examples overwhelmingly represent demand-driven institutional change, with little room left for the supply-leading institutional change that is equally significant and widely observed in today's world. As criti-cal reflections over this "biased" situation of contemporary literature on institutional change increase, a new scholarship of institutional syncre-tism has been developed to capture the differences in the dynamics of institutional change in the demand-driven vis-à-vis the supply-leading scenarios (S. Anderson and Francois 2008; Bickford 2007; Galvan 2004; Galvan and Sil 2007; Kearney 2007; Scott 1998; Sil 2007; L. Su 2000, 2002). This line of research shows particular interest in institutional changes witnessed by developing countries that are currently engaged in the project of institutional import/transplant and criticizes the implicit analytic universalism in contemporary mainstream studies on institutional change.[31] Galvan and Sil (2007, p. 6) summarize the goal of this newly developed literature:

> It tries to understand the dilemmas of deploying rules, practices, and designs of institutions that have been imported or imposed from external environments in locales where actors are enmeshed in historically embedded complexes of interests, norms, collective memories, social relations, and knowledge structures.

In his analysis of land market and other reforms in Senegal, Galvan (2004, pp. 15–20) suggests a generic framework for examining the establishment, adoption, and performance of rule-based institutions in developing countries, which are usually imposed by national policymakers onto local communities.[32] In this layered model of institutional organization and performance, Galvan identifies some habituated patterns of action, values, attitudes, and beliefs as the "institutional infrastructure" for institutional organization and performance,[33] while formal rules and administrative structures are conceptualized as the "institutional superstructure." To achieve effective performance and good local governance, the institutional infrastructure and superstructure should be compatible with each other. Moreover, because the change in institutional superstructure, compared to that in institutional infrastructure, is much easier, and the institutional infrastructure cannot be easily and successfully transplanted,[34] the adoption and performance of imposed institutions usually are contingent upon the interplay between the superstructure of imposed institutions and the infrastructure of indigenous institutions.

In view of this, Galvan (2004, pp. 216–223) argues that four scenarios are theoretically plausible: (1) Institutional syncretism: The legitimacy of imposed rule-based institutions is established upon existing indigenous institutions, thanks to permeation between the two and the new elements created in both the institutional superstructure and infrastructure; (2) Pseudo-syncretic grafting: The superstructure of imposed institutions and the infrastructure of indigenous institutions stick together but with little or no transformation in either institutional element; (3) Institutional disarticulation: Imposed institutions exist only as hierarchical administrative rules, are incapable of ever establishing or developing corresponding institutional infrastructure, and work like a "state floating above society"; and (4) Modernizing transformation: Imposed rule-based institutions successfully transform the infrastructure of indigenous institutions to uphold the imposed institutions' performance. This institutional syncretism framework is further refined by Galvan and Sil (2007, p. 7) as "a set of interpretative processes through which actors in local settings selectively transform newly imposed or transplanted institutional features, while adopting portable elements of preexisting social institutions to produce innovative institutional configurations."[35] This emerging literature on institutional syncretism contributes to contemporary research on institutional change by systematically incorporating the experiences of developing countries engaged in institutional transplant and formalization. It also makes a valuable effort to provide an integrated framework for analyzing the dynamics involved in institutional transplant or supply-leading institutional change.

Although existing research on local public goods provision (Y.-t. Chang and Wu 2011; R. Luo et al. 2007; L. Tsai 2007b, 2011; X. Zhang et al. 2004), conflict resolution (L. Dong 2008; X. Guo and Xing 2010; X. He 2013; Qiang 2003; L. Su 2000, 2002), and local financing (A. He and Hu 2000; B. Hu 2004, 2007; Ong 2006, 2012) in Chinese villages does not explicitly follow the framework of institutional syncretism for theorization and empirical analysis, their findings actually attest to the significance of the interplay between imposed rule-based institutions and indigenous relation-based institutions for understanding contemporary rural China's governance.

Unfortunately, this literature pays overwhelming attention to successful cases of institutional syncretism, so as to promote its preferred agenda of institutional change in developing countries.[36] Methodologically, this overemphasis on successful institutional syncretism may hinder our comprehensive and systematic understanding of institutional change in the supply-leading scenario. Institutional syncretism, as the literature recognizes, is just one of four plausible results when rule-based institutions are externally imposed into local communities. Pseudo-syncretic grafting, disarticulation, and modernizing transformation are not only theoretically plausible, they also have been empirically observed. Thus, a more intriguing and compelling question is: Under what conditions is the interplay between indigenous institutions and imposed ones more likely to result in institutional syncretism, pseudo-syncretic grafting, disarticulation, or modernizing transformation? Specifically, how can we effectively explain the varying performance of grassroots democracy, formal judicial institutions, or rural financial institutions in rural China's governance? Unfortunately, students of institutional syncretism fail to determine why institutional syncretism succeeds in some situations but fails in others.

Moreover, their exclusive emphasis on the interaction between the superstructure of imposed institutions and the infrastructure of indigenous institutions, while ignoring the possible impact of the surrounding social environment shaped by national socioeconomic and political policies, prevents them from offering a comprehensive understanding of institutional change embedded in the unprecedented socioeconomic transformation in developing societies or of its implications for transformed governance in these societies.

If we temporarily put aside the hidden (and in many cases unfounded) assumption of the advantage of imposed rule-based institutions over indigenous relation-based institutions in improving local governance and focus on the effects of different possible institutional configurations on local governance, more interesting questions arise: What are the implications of institutional syncretism, pseudo-syncretic grafting, disarticulation, and modernizing transformation for local governance? Are pseudo-syncretic grafting and disarticulation always bad for local governance? Is institutional syncretism the most-preferred method for improving local governance in transition societies, regardless of community structural features? In other words, by treating imposed rule-based institutions and indigenous relation-based institution as equally competent (functionally speaking) in supporting local governance and including both successful and failed cases of institutional syncretism, we can more effectively understand (1) why the interplay between indigenous institutions and imposed ones could result in institutional syncretism, pseudo-syncretic grafting, disarticulation, or modernizing transformation, as well as (2) how such different institutional configurations affect local governance. Then we will be more likely to appreciate the complexity and contingency of institutional change and be better equipped to understand the dynamics of institutional engineering and local governance in developing societies.

Moreover, once we consider the performance of both imposed institutions and indigenous institutions, as well as the interplay between them, as variables that are at least partially shaped by surrounding social environments, instead of simply assuming invariance in one or the other,[37] a more contextualized understanding of institutional change and local governance can be achieved.

Contextualized Institutional Choice

Different from the aforementioned research on institutional change in developing countries, wherein institutional transplant prevails, I do not privilege institutional syncretism for either ideological or normative reasons but, rather, propose a contextualized and agent-based understanding of how externally imposed rule-based institutions are established in local communities and how they perform in supporting local governance. As Fafchamps (2011) and Onoma (2010) suggest, people's adoption and use of institutions are critical for the institutions' diffusion and performance. Nee and Opper (2012, p. 25) specifically argue that students of institutional change should "bring individual utility expectations to the center of analysis" if we want to effectively understand the different aggregate outcomes resulting from competing formal and informal institutions. Following this line of research, I focus on the conditions under which community members, given their access to both imposed rule-based institutions and indigenous relation-based institutions, choose one over the other for local governance issues.

In particular, I argue that, logically, institutional choice "precedes and determines" whether institutional syncretism, pseudo-syncretic grafting, disarticulation, or modernizing transformation may emerge. Only after imposed rule-based institutions are adopted by community members, for whatever reasons, can we then talk about the interaction between the superstructure of imposed institutions and the infrastructure of indigenous institutions, and in this case, either institutional syncretism or modernizing transformation may develop. However, if the community members show no interest in imposed institutions and still prefer indigenous ones for their socioeconomic and political lives, then pseudo-syncretic grafting or disarticulation is more likely to be observed.

As previously discussed, both indigenously developed relation-based institutions and externally imposed rule-based institutions can help sustain local governance by solving the problems of collective action and accountability. Indigenous relation-based institutions have lower fixed costs but higher marginal costs for operation. In close-knit communities, however, the high marginal costs can be effectively offset by the convenient access to sufficient information disseminated through extended and dense social networks. As the scope of social interaction is significantly expanded and close-knit communities are transformed into loosely coupled ones due to increased mobility, the marginal costs of using indigenous institutions grow dramatically and may even become prohibitively high.

The situation is essentially different for imposed rule-based institutions. Their operation is characterized by higher fixed costs but lower marginal costs. Although the high fixed costs of using rule-based institutions might be too much for most local communities, they are usually affordable for nation-states with the resources accumulated through economic growth and state extraction. Moreover, rule-based institutions, compared with relation-based institutions, are much better equipped to address the critical issue of scale that confronts all political leaders of nation-states (i.e., more serious problems of collective action and accountability, involving geographically dispersed individuals with distinct backgrounds, experiences, and cultural traditions). This is a key reason that contemporary nation-states rely more on rule-based institutions to make their societies legible and organized and reduce the transaction costs of effective governance to a manageable level.

However, as contemporary research and previous discussions also have shown, this does not necessarily mean that once rule-based institutions are imposed, they are embraced by local communities without resistance. I further argue that, confronted with the choice between institutional alternatives, members of local communities usually take three factors into consideration: (1) the respective effectiveness of distinct institutions in dealing with specific issues; (2) the switching costs incurred for adopting unfamiliar institutions; and (3) the coordination costs incurred due to their fellow members' choices.[38]

Theoretically, people can pursue varying institutional solutions for distinct issues, based on their contextualized evaluations, and this is exactly what some scholars have observed. For example, in rural China, villagers use local courts more often to collect their unpaid salaries from local enterprises but rely primarily on within-village mediation for collecting debts from their fellow villagers (Read and Michelson 2008). Thus, for those issues that have been substantively transformed by socioeconomic and political changes and demand regulation and coordination far beyond the scope of local communities, imposed rule-based institutions seem to be the natural choice. Nevertheless, if local communities still define the scope of required regulation and coordination for specific issues, the choice between imposed institutions and indigenous institutions is unlikely to be clear-cut. Further, such issues are usually the gist of local governance in developing countries as well as the focus of subsequent examination.

As long as indigenous institutions supported by social sanctions perform well in local communities, as information misers, community members are less likely to switch to imposed institutions because they are already familiar with the procedures involved and persons to whom they should go when dealing with local governance issues using indigenous institutions. In this case, imposed institutions are too expensive due to the lack of pertinent experiences as well as the costs associated with acquiring necessary information (Ellickson 1991; Nye 2008). Moreover, when most other community members still prefer indigenous institutions for coordination and regulation, one's opting for imposed institutions might be interpreted as violating community-shared norms and may even be sanctioned as deviation from a cherished goal of local harmony (Dixit 2004). In these cases, any switching or coordination costs can deter the use of imposed institutions. Hence, in close-knit communities, thanks to the powerful social sanctions that ensure the effectiveness of indigenous institutions, imposed institutions are less likely to be embraced.

However, this does not necessarily imply that imposed rule-based institutions are more likely to be embraced by members of atomized communities that are characterized by collapsed social networks and a dearth of vibrant within-community social interaction. Theoretically, the operation of any institution requires some minimum level of coordination among the individuals involved (Eggertsson 2005). Thus, in loosely coupled communities, wherein within-community social interaction and social networks may not enable powerful social sanctions that ensure the effective performance of indigenous relation-based institutions, there are strong incentives among community members to seek alternative and more effective institutional solutions. Imposed institutions are a viable alternative, despite the unavoidable switching costs; meanwhile, the impaired but somewhat functional social networks in loosely coupled communities can help overcome the incurred coordination costs. Consequently, community members can still manage to coordinate their choices of imposed institutions as the publicly recognized and accepted institutional solutions for locally circumscribed governance issues. Therefore, given the weakened efficacy of indigenous institutions and the impaired but somewhat functional social networks, imposed institutions are more likely to be embraced in loosely coupled communities.

Not surprisingly, in extreme cases of atomized communities characterized by a dearth of vibrant within-community interaction and collapsed social networks, neither indigenous relation-based institutions nor imposed rule-based ones can survive. This situation, to some extent, resembles a locally circumscribed "state of nature" in the Hobbesian sense. Although there are strong incentives among the community members to seek alternative and effective institutional solutions to replace vitiated indigenous institutions and even bear the necessary switching costs, they suffer from the lack of the minimum level of indispensable coordination for the establishment and effective performance of imposed institutions. In these cases, the incurred coordination costs are too high to overcome. Then, private solutions based on personal connections or even violence may emerge as alternatives.[39] In some atomized

Table 2.1. CONTEXTUALIZED INSTITUTIONAL CHOICES

		Institutional Choice
Community Structural Features	Close-knit	Indigenous Institutions
	Loosely coupled	Imposed Institutions
	Atomized	Private Solutions

Chinese villages, for example, due to a lack of publicly recognized authority for effective mediation or the prohibitively high costs of using formal judicial institutions, villagers rely on themselves for conflict resolution. In these villages, it is not uncommon for violence or death to be the only tool available to the strong or the weak to address the wrongs that have been done to them (B. Chen 2011a, 2011b; L. Dong 2008; X. Xu 2005). Community members' contextualized choices between indigenously developed relation-based institutions and externally imposed rule-based institutions in communities with distinct structural features are summarized in Table 2.1.

In reality, there are a variety of factors that contribute to the structural transformation of local communities, which, as displayed in Table 2.1, have implications for the establishment and performance of different types of institutions in these communities. One salient factor is closely related to a major phenomenon in developing countries that are witnessing the transition from agrarian to industrial societies: rural–urban migration.[40]

2.4 RURAL–URBAN MIGRATION AND TRANSFORMED LOCAL GOVERNANCE

During the transition from agrarian to industrial societies, urbanization, *inter alia*, has been one of the most salient features, particularly in the twentieth century. According to the United Nations World Urbanization Prospects report, a rapid urbanization of the world's population was observed in the twentieth century. The global proportion of urban population rose dramatically from 13% (220 million) in 1900 to 29% (732 million) in 1950 and further to 49% (3.2 billion) in 2005. This statistic is projected to be around 60% (4.9 billion) in 2030 (United Nations et al. 2005). What has been dramatically contributing to this growing urbanization is significant rural–urban migration, with people leaving rural communities and settling in urban areas temporarily or permanently for economic opportunities and associated benefits.[41] For example, according to the most recent official statistics in China, which is the largest transition society in today's world, over 158 million rural laborers worked and lived in urban areas (other than their home townships) as migrant workers at the end of 2011. For the first time in its history, in early 2012, there were more urban residents (51.27%) than rural residents in mainland China.[42] With such a significant number of rural residents moving cityward, what are the implications, although unintended in many cases, for their communities of origin, particularly for the performance of indigenous and imposed institutions in upholding these rural communities' governance?

As previous discussions show, community structural features have significant influence over the efficacy of indigenous relation-based institutions as well as on how community members respond to imposed rule-based institutions. When local communities are close-knit, due to either political or socioeconomic constraints (e.g., the household registration [hukou] system[43] or underdeveloped transportation infrastructure), the frequent and continuous interaction among community members and the within-community dense and extended social networks ensure the efficacy of indigenous institutions supported by social sanctions. Once such close-knit communities are forced to open up, either by internal or external pressures, with some community members' leaving, within-community social interaction and connections are challenged. For those who make their living in urban areas, rural communities may no longer be the primary concern in their daily lives, and the communication and interaction with other members of their home communities become more expensive and less relevant. For those who stay in rural communities, their interest and attention also shift more toward the outside world (e.g., due to the significance of the remittances sent back by the migrants) or their domestic issues (e.g., due to the increased burden for taking care of their families given the absence of the migrants). Moreover, when some community members are absent most of the time, the opportunities for social interaction on multiple and interrelated occasions dwindle. Thus, because of outward migration, the frequent and continuous interaction among community members is disrupted and the dense and extended social networks are loosened.

Disrupted social interaction significantly relieves the shadow of the future on community members' utility calculation and makes the surrounding social environment less fertile for the cultivation and preservation of cooperative norms (Coleman 1986, 1990; Cronin 1999; Geertz 1980;

Gintis 2005; Opp 1986). Reduced opportunities for social interaction on multiple and interrelated occasions weaken overarching issue linkages across various aspects of community lives. Loosened and shrunk social networks also hinder the in-time transmission of and easy access to necessary information for effective social sanctions (Greif 1989, 1993; Platteau 1994a, 1994b, 2000). Thus, deviant and opportunistic behavior may be left unpunished and less effectively deterred in subsequent social interaction. In addition, rural–urban migration provides a convenient channel of exit for community members who may benefit from circumventing possible social sanctions.[44] When community members can easily move out of the community and make their own living in urban areas, punishing them for deviant and opportunistic behavior through social sanctions becomes much less credible and meaningful. Even depriving transgressors of their community memberships is no longer as threatening as it once was. Thus, the performance of indigenous relation-based institutions is seriously challenged and impaired by outward migration.[45] Consequently, because of outward migration, the original close-knit community may be transformed into a loosely coupled one. Moreover, once this outward migration approaches exodus, this structural challenge may even lead to an atomized community.[46]

Nevertheless, rural–urban migration is not a prevailing phenomenon that affects all rural communities to the same extent. In many cases, it develops in a very uneven way across rural areas for geographic, physical, and economic reasons. Taking China as an example, there is clearly a difference between sending and receiving regions when it comes to rural–urban migration.[47] Sichuan, Hubei, Hunan, Jiangxi, and Shaanxi are provinces with a large number of rural residents who leave for jobs in metropolitan cities or provinces such as Beijing, Shanghai, Tianjin, Zhejiang, Guangdong, and Fujian. Rural communities in these receiving regions, due to booming private businesses or collectively owned enterprises, do not necessarily witness significant outward migration. In other words, the close-knit communal structures are relatively well maintained in these rural communities. Even in sending regions, due to different natural endowments, some rural communities can still keep their members residing in villages rather than moving into urban areas. For these communities, indigenous institutions supported by social sanctions may still perform effectively and play an important role in providing institutional solutions to local governance issues. Thus, thanks to the uneven distribution of rural–urban migration among rural communities of a society, we are likely to see significant variance in the efficacy of indigenous institutions in upholding the respective governance in these communities. Moreover, in most cases, the sources of this variance also can be primarily and legitimately attributed to the dynamics exogenous to and beyond local communities (e.g., natural endowments and national economic policies).[48]

I argue that when political leaders launch the programs of establishing rule-based institutions for more effective national governance and impose such institutions following unified procedures and codes into local communities with unevenly transformed communal structures, we are likely to see diverse responses from community members to the imposed institutions.[49] Basically, as previously discussed, with the level of outward migration in local communities moving along the spectrum from the very low to the very high, local communities witness a structural transformation from close-knit, through loosely coupled, to atomized. Accordingly, as shown in Table 2.1, community members' contextualized institutional choices also may shift away from indigenous relation-based institutions toward imposed rule-based institutions. However, in an atomized community, no institutions can perform effectively, and private solutions might be community members' only choices. Moreover, as has been emphasized, good governance can be achieved in local communities as long as effective institutional solutions are available to address the problems of collective action and accountability, regardless of their institutional nature. Indigenously developed relation-based institutions and externally imposed rule-based institutions both can be relied on to provide solid foundations for quality local governance. Based on this information, Table 2.2 presents a summary of the impacts of rural–urban migration on rural communities' structural features, their members' contextualized institutional choices, and the possible quality of community governance.

In communities with well-maintained, close-knit structures and a low level of outward migration, indigenous relation-based institutions can still play a dominant role in sustaining quality local governance. In loosely

Table 2.2. OUTWARD MIGRATION, INSTITUTIONAL CHOICE, AND GOVERNANCE QUALITY

		Community Type	Institutional Choice	Governance Quality
Outward Migration	Low	Close-knit	Indigenous Institutions	High
	Medium	Loosely coupled	Imposed Institutions	High
	High	Atomized	Private Solutions	Low

coupled rural communities, with some members' leaving for economic opportunities and associated benefits in urban areas, externally imposed rule-based institutions may be adopted as the new institutional foundation to uphold local governance. Therefore, in both close-knit and loosely coupled communities, we may expect good governance despite their reliance on different institutions to address the problems of collective action and accountability. However, the governance in atomized communities with a dramatic outflow of community members through rural–urban migration is expected to be significantly worse. Because the social environments in these communities are atomized, even a minimum level of coordination is difficult to sustain; thus, neither indigenous nor imposed institutions can perform effectively. In such cases, the community members left behind usually have to rely on private solutions, such as personal connections or even violence. Without effective institutional assistance in solving the problems of collective action and creating accountability, quality governance usually eludes atomized communities.

2.5 CONCLUSION

To ensure quality governance, efficacious institutions are indispensable. However, the task of searching for and establishing the right institutions for governance, particularly those for local governance in developing countries, is not straightforward. Good local governance does not necessarily follow institutional transplant or grafting, even though the institutions transplanted or grafted may have shown their efficacy in upholding quality local governance in other regions or countries. We, thus, have a variety of governance outcomes with similar institutional settings, rather than one type of institution that can be universally applied to improve local governance.

Indigenously developed relation-based institutions have been widely adopted in close-knit communities to uphold governance, without resorting to laws or other parchment institutions. Abundant examples of well-maintained local governance based on indigenous institutions have been found in both developing and developed countries, from medieval times to the twenty-first century. Cooperative norms cultivated through frequent and continuous social interaction and transmitted through socialization are conducive to cooperation and collective efforts among community members. The within-community dense and extended social networks facilitate both the timely transmission of information and the creation of cross-issue linkages in social interaction. Embedded within such a favorable social environment, indigenous institutions supported by social sanctions can effectively regulate and coordinate social interaction within the communities, punish and deter deviant and opportunistic behavior, and hold local leaders accountable.

When dramatic socioeconomic transformation unleashed by the process of modernization increases people's physical mobility and expands their scope of social interaction, indigenous institutions become less competent in regulating and coordinating people's interactions. The increased mobility and expanded social interaction are particularly challenging for political leaders of modern nation-states, who want to make their societies legible and organized and aspire for effective macro-governance with affordable transaction costs. The scale of their governance is no longer constrained to a specific local community but, instead, covers geographically expanded territories and widely dispersed residents with different backgrounds, experiences, and even cultural traditions. Despite the rule-based institutions' demand for significant investments in providing detailed codes and procedures, specialized agents, and a solid information infrastructure, from the perspective of national leaders, these rule-based institutions are much more effective than are indigenous relation-based institutions in sustaining governance in modern states. Therefore, rule-based institutions, most of which have arisen and been practiced in developed countries, are borrowed or imported into developing countries. Nevertheless, when imposed upon local communities for governance, community members' responses to these rule-based institutions may not be as enthusiastic as expected by their national leaders. How community members respond to imposed institutions is contingent upon their access to other institutional alternatives, such as indigenous institutions that have been relied on for local governance long before the imposed rule-based institutions.

Generally, in close-knit communities, imposed rule-based institutions are less likely to be adopted for local governance issues due to community members' access to and familiarity with the still-functioning indigenous relation-based institutions. The switching costs for using imposed institutions are too high. In loosely coupled communities, the imposed institutions are more likely to be accepted and to perform as the new institutional foundation for community governance. In these communities, weakened indigenous institutions generate sufficient incentives for community members to incur the switching costs for adopting the imposed institutions, while the still-somewhat-functioning within-community social networks also enable them to successfully coordinate their institutional choices for community governance.

Furthermore, in atomized communities where indigenous institutions are ineffective, despite the strong incentives to seek alternative institutional solutions, community members suffer from the lack of a minimum level of coordination to effectively embrace imposed institutions. The coordination costs for using imposed institutions are too high. In many cases, members of these communities have to count on private solutions based on personal connections or even violence.

In almost all developing countries, rural–urban migration, *inter alia*, plays a significant role in reshaping the structures of their rural communities and, thus, generates diverse social and institutional environments for the imposed rule-based institutions as a part of their national programs of institutional formalization. Some communities simply collapse, with most members' leaving for economic opportunities and associated benefits in more developed regions. Some communities, while enjoying the fruits of economic growth and industrialization, succeed in maintaining their close-knit communal structures. Others fall in between, witnessing the transformation of the original close-knit environment into a loosely coupled but not an atomized one, with a certain number of members' leaving for better lives in urban areas. Therefore, in rural communities with different levels of outward migration, community members' contextualized choices between indigenous institutions and imposed institutions, as well as corresponding institutional change and syncretism in local governance, are likely to unfold in distinct ways, given their respective and unevenly transformed communal structures.

In general, indigenous institutions are more likely to be preferred over imposed institutions if a low level of outward migration has done limited damage to the frequent and continuous interaction among community members or the within-community dense and extended social networks. Thus, given the indigenous institutions' dominant role in sustaining local governance, institutional disarticulation or grafting is likely to occur. As a medium level of outward migration transforms close-knit communities into loosely coupled ones, externally imposed institutions are more likely to be favored over indigenous institutions and to serve as the foundation for community governance. Therefore, institutional syncretism or even modernizing transformation is likely to be observed. In both cases (i.e., communities with a low or medium level of outward migration), quality local governance can be much more effectively sustained, despite their distinct institutional foundations. However, a very high level of outward migration can paralyze and atomize local communities; thus, neither indigenous institutions nor imposed institutions can function effectively, due to the lack of a minimum level of coordination among community members. In these cases, private solutions based on personal connections or even violence are likely to prevail, leading to a radical degeneration of local governance.

The following chapters use evidence collected through sampling surveys and semistructured interviews in rural China to show how indigenously developed relation-based institutions and externally imposed rule-based institutions have succeeded or failed in upholding quality governance in Chinese villages. The evidence also will be used to show the role of rural–urban migration in the dynamics of institutional change and transformed governance in rural China.

CHAPTER 3

Evolution of China's Rural Governance and Rural–Urban Migration

Regardless of the features of their regimes (e.g., feudal dynasties until the early twentieth century, the pseudo presidential democracy of the Kuomintang [KMT] before 1949, and the totalitarian and later authoritarian system of the Chinese Communist Party [CCP] since 1949), Chinese national leaders have been confronted with an unrelenting challenge to its rural governance: How can they ensure order and sustain quality governance in rural China while efficiently extracting resources, given the nation's geographic vastness, the large number of residents, and the significance of agriculture to China's economy? Most of the time, this challenge has been exacerbated by each regime's lack of sufficient resources to effectively establish and sustain official administration exclusively based on parchment institutions, particularly in rural China. Thus, institutional engineering and related trials, aimed at ensuring effective local governance, have been regularly seen in Chinese history, resulting in both continuity and dramatic change. Before we delve further into the investigation of contemporary local governance in rural China, it is valuable to understand the evolution of governance in Chinese history, the rationale for various institutional projects, and corresponding transformations in rural China's socioeconomic environments and communal features.

More specifically, this chapter documents the history of indigenous relation-based institutions serving rural China's governance, how such indigenous institutions were incorporated or repressed by different regimes in their respective related institutional engineering, and how indigenous institutions' performance has been affected by the changing socioeconomic and political environments of rural China. This review demonstrates the rich legacy of indigenous relation-based institutions in rural China's governance, their significance to the institutional environment and for examining villagers' institutional choices, and their indispensability for understanding the performance of imposed rule-based institutions. After this historical synopsis, the chapter further discusses the evolution of rural–urban migration in China as a response to the economic reforms that have been unfolding since the late 1970s as well as the characteristics of migration's uneven geographic distribution. These discussions show how the unevenly distributed cityward migration in Chinese villages has reshaped their communal structures and, thus, may have generated diverse social and institutional environments for the imposed rule-based institutions. Overall, this chapter provides critical background information about the primary challenge facing China's present-day rural governance: the outflow of surplus labor through cityward migration, which became a phenomenal issue in the early 1990s and reached an unprecedented scale in the early 2000s.

3.1 RURAL CHINA THROUGHOUT HISTORY

China has been an agrarian society for most of its history; thus, rural communities have played a critical role in Chinese society.[1] This is clearly reflected in two key aspects of the society: (1) the large number of residents who live in rural areas and (2) the significance of agricultural production in China's national economy.

Even after decades of aggressive industrialization initiated by the CCP regime in the early 1950s, the majority of Chinese citizens still lived in rural areas, and the majority of its population was involved in agriculture. As displayed in Figure 3.1, the percentage of the Chinese population who lives in rural areas has remained over 50%, and only as recently as 2012 has this not been the case.[2] In 1954, just five years after the establishment of the People's Republic of China, over 86% of Chinese lived in rural areas. Although this percentage has been decreasing steadily, at the end of 2009, over 53% of the Chinese population remained in rural communities.[3] A related indicator of the importance of rural China is the total number of its agricultural population, the definition of which is closely associated with the household registration system (*hukou*) in China.[4]

According to China's national statistics, the percentage of its agricultural population also has been declining since 1954, when it was

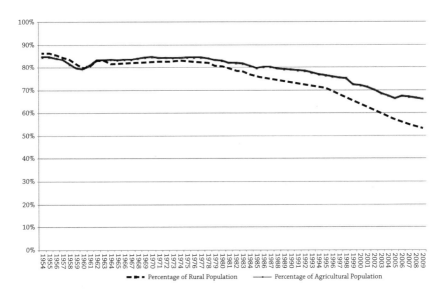

Figure 3.1:
Rural Population in China
Source: China Labor Statistical Yearbook, 2007–2010.

approximately 85%. Nevertheless, at the end of 2009, over 66% of Chinese citizens were still registered as part of the agricultural population. That a large majority of Chinese citizens live in rural areas or are primarily engaged in agricultural production also captures the reality of the Republican era under the KMT government as well as that of even earlier feudal dynasties such as the Ming (1368–1644 A.D.) and Qing (1644–1911 A.D.), when the level of industrialization was even much lower.[5]

In addition to the concentration of its population in rural settlements, before the 1940s, China's economy was supported primarily by its agricultural production (Feuerwerker 1976, pp. 77–94). The earliest systematic industrialization program launched by the Chinese government can be traced only to the late Qing dynasty, after a series of military defeats against foreign powers. Such limited industrialization was implemented only in some metropolitan cities such as Shanghai, Tianjin, and Wuhan (Cohen 2005; Feuerwerker 1958; Pomeranz 2000) and had highly constrained influence over China's rural areas (P. C. Huang 1990).[6] Even after some efforts from the KMT regime in the Republican era, the role of secondary industry in China's national economy was still dwarfed by that of agriculture.[7]

At the beginning of the aggressive industrialization launched by the CCP, as illustrated in Figure 3.2, China's primary economy (i.e., agriculture)

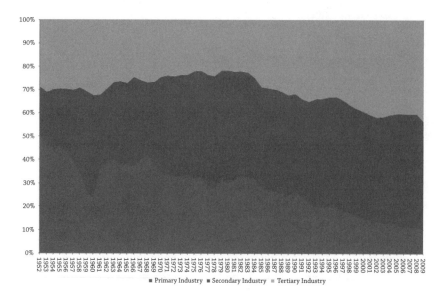

Figure 3.2:
Structure of China's Economy
Source: China Labor Statistical Yearbook, 2007–2010.

still contributed to over 50% of its GDP. This number significantly dropped to around 23% in 1960 with the dramatically improved production in China's secondary industry, which accounted for more than 44% of its GDP.[8]

After the economic reforms that began in the late 1970s, China's secondary industry's damaged production capacity, due to the Cultural Revolution (1966–1976), has recovered and even improved. As a consequence, although absolute production from agriculture also has been substantially expanded, its relative role in China's national economy has shrunk. At the end of 2009, only around 10% of China's GDP came from its agricultural production, with more than 46% from its secondary industry and the rest (around 44%) from its tertiary industry. Clearly, it was only after industrialization, forcefully pushed forward by the CCP, that China's economy has gradually shifted away from the dominance of agriculture. However, the approximately 65 years of CCP governance is only a very small fraction of China's 5,000-year history, during which it was primarily an agrarian society.

In light of the dominant role played by agriculture in China's economy, as well as the large number of residents concentrated in its rural areas, ensuring the quality of governance in rural communities has been a major concern for all national leaders of different regimes throughout Chinese history. As Wong (1999, pp. 214–227) argues in his comparative analysis of the political economy of governance in China and Europe:

> Europe's state-making dynamics unfolded amidst territorial states expanding their powers in competition with each other, while Chinese state formation and reproduction focused upon creating and managing an agrarian empire seeking to expand its territory and increase its population, confident that it was at the center of the world, or at least that part of it that truly mattered. . . . Chinese political economy [of an agrarian empire] tied production and distribution together through its commitment to reducing or ameliorating relative inequalities and guaranteeing some absolute minimal standards for survival to Chinese families. . . . The state's virtue was manifested by peasant security and well-being.

For the legitimacy and survival of their reign, China's leaders must ensure a minimal level of satisfaction among their rural residents as well as cultivate and sustain their political loyalty. Therefore, they have to find an effective means of addressing socioeconomic issues in rural communities—for example, resolving the conflicts among villagers, improving public security, sustaining or even boosting local economies, and instilling favorable ideological and cultural doctrines. Given the predominant role of agricultural production and agricultural population, these national leaders also need to efficiently extract economic and labor resources from rural communities. Specifically, they have to establish a cost-effective means to levy taxes, collect fees, and conscribe labor for both military and civil projects. As discussed in Chapter 2, what constitutes a cost-effective means for serving these political and socioeconomic purposes is contingent upon the communal structures of rural China and the resources available to the leaders during different historical periods.

The Chinese villages that Smith (1899) visited in the late nineteenth century, despite their socioeconomic and political modernization since the late Ming dynasty, were representative of rural China throughout history.[9] Historically, in most of China, people lived in concentrated settlements, hamlets, villages, towns, and cities. The connections and interactions among different settlements were infrequent and were primarily constrained to proximate villages. Although local settlements were loosely integrated into a hierarchical system under the administration of the national government through larger towns and cities, the significance of local communities far outweighed that of higher-level administrative units in rural residents' daily lives. The self-sufficient economy of ancient China did not offer many opportunities for most rural residents to engage in commercial activities.[10] The majority of their necessities or demands for consumption could be well covered by their villages or with the help of itinerant merchants or doctors who traveled among proximate villages and towns.[11] With respect to social and political interaction, local communities were even more critical for rural residents. Given the lack of convenient and inexpensive transportation facilities, rural residents' social interaction was primarily limited to their neighbors and fellow villagers. Visiting relatives in other villages was an occasional activity, mainly reserved for weddings, funerals, or important holidays such as the Spring Festival (*chunjie*).

This village-anchored life in rural China was further reinforced by limited opportunities to make a living outside of villages. Relatively underdeveloped commercial economies and industrialization in towns and cities could not provide enough jobs for the surplus labor in villages. Further, to be eligible to serve as a government official, beginning with the Sui dynasty (580–618 A.D.), the Chinese people had to pass a series of imperial examinations (*keju kaoshi*).[12] The enrollment rate for these examinations, however, was extremely low. For instance, the enrollment for the lowest level of imperial examination at the end of the Ming dynasty was around 3.3% (P. Guo 2006). Moreover, taking the imperial examinations was a significant investment, as it included both educational expenses and a loss of income due to reduced labor for agricultural production; this investment was generally beyond the means of most Chinese peasants, who usually lived at a subsistence level.

This community-anchored life in Chinese villages, however, offered a favorable environment for the cultivation, diffusion, consolidation, and preservation of communal relationships based on geographic identities and kinships. The reason that "place of origin was one of the major ascribed statuses in Chinese society" (Cohen 2005, p. 47) can be partially attributed to these historically cultivated features of social interaction embedded in China's agrarian society. As a consequence, China scholars have characterized Chinese rural communities as "societies of acquaintances," where almost everyone knows about others in the same community due to long-term interaction within a geographically demarcated and relatively stable social environment (Fei 1939, 1992). It is common to find Chinese villages with a majority of residents' sharing the same surname, worshiping the same ancestors, and participating in the same rituals and ceremonies. In such communities, it is also easy to identify systematic connections among the villagers if provided with detailed information on villagers' names and statuses in the genealogical record (Freedman 1958, 1966; L. Liu and Murphy 2006; Potter 1970; Qian 1994; L. Zhao 1999).[13]

In summary, Chinese villages throughout history closely resemble close-knit communities, defined in Chapter 2 as characterized by frequent and continuous within-community interaction and the existence of dense and extended social networks that connect community members. Their close-knittedness was primarily shaped and driven by the nature of China's agrarian economy and community-anchored life in rural China, which did not change essentially until the great social transformation launched by the CCP after its victory.[14] This close-knit communal structure of rural China also served as the social foundation for local governance throughout Chinese history and was intentionally exploited by some national leaders for institutional engineering and related trials.

3.2 EVOLUTION OF RURAL GOVERNANCE IN CHINESE HISTORY

Self-governance has been a central feature of Chinese villages throughout Chinese history, regardless of whether decentralization was a *de facto* or *de jure* institutional feature of its official administration system.[15] Two key factors contributed to this decentralized self-governance in rural China. First, before the CCP took power in the late 1940s and due to a scarcity of administrative resources, official bureaucracies (the dominant means of local governance) had rarely been extended into rural communities.[16] Thus, although villages were incorporated into the centralized political and administrative system before the CCP regime, their loose integration was mainly established indirectly and with the help of some indigenous relation-based institutions or local social forces. Second, the close-knit social environments of Chinese villages provided the foundation for the development and operation of various indigenous institutions in enforcing social control and sustaining local governance, without the need for substantial interference from official bureaucrats, who usually were "strangers" to local communities.

Decentralized Governance with Incorporated Indigenous Institutions

According to Shue (1988, 2012), since the beginning of China's history as a centralized state, rural China has rarely been under complete and systematic control of national bureaucracies. The incompetency of Chinese bureaucracies in rural governance should be partially attributed to insufficient administrative resources for dealing with a large number of residents in geographically dispersed rural communities, as noted above.

In Late Imperial China, more specifically the Ming and Qing dynasties, counties (*xian*) were the smallest administrative unit in most of China, where the administrative office (*yamen*) of a magistrate was established. In general, large numbers of people were under the jurisdiction of a magistrate, with an average of 100,000 people in 1749 and 250,000 in 1819 (G. Xiao 1960, p. 5).

Given the restricted economic and personnel resources available to magistrates (Qu 1962; Wakeman and Grant 1975; Watt 1972; G. Xiao 1960), it was almost impossible for them to take full responsibility for local governance. Hence, magistrates, as the only government officials responsible for the daily administration of all governance issues, had to rely on assistance from intermediate agents such as clerks, runners, and gentries who were local residents and who had the necessary information for local governance. In most cases, Chinese villages in the Ming and Qing dynasties were indirectly "governed" by local magistrates via securing the intermediate agents' access to indigenous resources and institutions.[17] Thus, it is no wonder that the national leaders of the Ming and Qing dynasties intentionally incorporated these local resources and indigenous institutions into their institutional engineering for rural governance as well as for extracting resources.[18] Among the institutions established by the Ming and Qing dynasties for rural governance, the neighborhood administrative system (*lijia*), watch-group system (*baojia*), and rural district pledge system (*xiangyue*) were the most important ones.[19]

The *lijia* system was designed and introduced by the first emperor of the Ming dynasty, Ming Taizu. The immediate aims of the *lijia* system were to reduce the transaction costs of extracting economic resources and administration by having the citizenry collect taxes and implement other government policies by themselves. Under the *lijia* system, all households in the empire were organized into groups of 110, with each group's representing an administrative neighborhood (*li*). Within an administrative neighborhood, the ten wealthiest families were appointed to serve annually, in turn, as neighborhood leaders. The remaining one hundred families were further divided into ten units (*jia*) of ten families. Because the dense and extended social networks within close-knit communities ease the spread of and access to local information, members of the same *jia* and *li* were very familiar with each other's various information, including their fiscal situation. Moreover, thanks to the powerful social sanctions within these communities and all members' having to provide similar services in turn, it was difficult for anyone to dodge his obligations. Later, the *lijia* system was further empowered and expanded for rural jurisdiction. Each administrative neighborhood nominated elders for selection by their magistrates. These nominated elders had to be more than fifty years old, upright, well respected, and robust enough to undertake the position. Once confirmed by their magistrates, the elders assumed legal and social services for their neighborhoods. Without consulting the magistrates except in extreme situations, the elders' jurisdiction was binding and covered matrimonial and property suits and even physical assault cases.

The *baojia* system also was designed during the Ming dynasty, primarily for self-defense and public security in local communities, and was revised and expanded in the Qing dynasty. Under the *baojia* system, groups of ten households were established in all urban and rural districts. Leaders were selected for each group of ten, one hundred, and one thousand households. Within each group, members guaranteed and were collectively responsible for each other's security and behavior. As required, suspicious activities were reported to local officials at the time that they occurred. At the end of each month, group leaders were ordered to submit signed statements to the official concerned for inspection, regarding whether there had been any unlawful activities. The group leaders were also required to bring all fugitives from justice to light as best they could. Moreover, if any illegal activities were concealed, all households in the same *baojia* would be held responsible and punished. Similar to the *lijia* system, the *baojia* system took advantage of the wealth of information disseminated through the dense and extended social networks of communities to check on the whereabouts of people, ensure the provision of mutual aid in case of attack, and identify criminal activities. The collective responsibility mechanism of the *baojia* system further deterred potential deviant behavior in local communities.

The *lijia* and *baojia* systems were complemented by the *xiangyue* system. While the former two addressed community governance issues through formal rules and organizations backed up by coercive forces and social sanctions, the latter provided "soft" power for local governance, mainly as "a vertically integrated system that specialized in moral indoctrination" (R. B. Wong 1997b, p. 318). In the Ming dynasty, the *xiangyue* system was designed to cover a wide variety of activities, ranging from moral inculcation to mutual aid and social entertainment. Each *xiangyue* had a staff of sixteen to twenty officers, including three registrars who kept records of the names and businesses of all community members as well as their good and bad behaviors. Under the *xiangyue* system, community members were required to follow certain principles in their social interaction, such as honoring tax obligations and acting humanely when conducting private and public businesses. Any violations of such principles would be registered and publicly revealed at monthly community meetings. In essence, the linchpin of the *xiangyue* system was within-community cooperation and controls through indigenous relation-based institutions supported by powerful social sanctions.

Later in the Qing dynasty, this *xiangyue* system was developed into the widely adopted village lecture (*jiangyue*) system, which aimed to incite the virtues of public-mindedness and loyalty rather than to register personal behaviors and reputations. For instance, the six maxims issued by the Shunzhi emperor and the sixteen maxims issued by the Kangxi emperor, as well as the ten-thousand-word official amplification issued by the Yongzheng emperor, were ordered to be expounded and clarified, as needed, on a regular basis, to members of local communities via the *jiangyue* system. These maxims urged people to live in harmony with their relatives and neighbors, to maintain a viable income, and to fulfill the requirements of the government, with an emphasis on the bonds of filial duty and loyalty. Essentially, the *xiangyue* system and the later *jiangyue* system were used mainly by the national governments in Late Imperial China to provide moral indoctrination and pressure for local governance, assisted and enforced primarily by social sanctions.[20]

The national leaders of the Ming and Qing dynasties took advantage of the close-knit communal structures of Chinese villages and systematically incorporated their indigenous resources and institutions to facilitate their governance in rural China. Compared with a specialized official agency outside rural communities in charge of levying taxes and implementing government policies, the *lijia* system was expected to be much more cost effective, given its easy access to the necessary information. The publicly recognized authority of the older and experienced villagers also was an invaluable resource for resolving conflicts and sustaining community order. Through the "collective responsibility" institution stipulated by the *baojia* system, cooperation for collective defense and public security were secured. Similarly, the *xiangyue* system capitalized on the value of personal reputations in close-knit villages to regulate their members' behaviors; gossip, avoidance, and even ostracism could be used to detrimentally affect the lives of those villagers who misbehaved. With its education and indoctrination of norms that emphasize harmonious relationships, conflict avoidance, filial duty, and loyalty, the *jiangyue* system also contributed to local governance by further empowering moral pressures exerted through both external and internal sanctions.

Moreover, the rulers of the Ming and Qing dynasties also selected publicly recognized local authoritative figures such as gentries and headmen of clan/lineage organizations, given the respect they commanded from villagers by virtue of their special qualifications like age, wealth, learning, kin status, or personal capacity (C.-l. Chang 1955; Miller 2009; G. Xiao 1960), to serve as their intermediate agents for local governance.[21] These authoritative figures assumed various functions in governing Chinese villages: They settled disputes; conducted fund-raising campaigns; commanded local defense; organized moral education, rituals, and ceremonies; and provided other kinds of leadership. They also were expected to protect villagers against injustice; give them relief in times of calamity; and participate actively in promoting local welfare, including education.[22] These local authoritative figures were "indispensable to the realization of certain of the government's aims" (Qu 1962, p. 168).

Nevertheless, the performance of such institutions was not as satisfying or effective as the rulers of the Ming and Qing dynasties had expected, particularly in regard to extracting resources from rural China.[23] The deficiency of such institutions in extracting resources to finance the national governments in the Ming and Qing dynasties can be found in the dual identities of local authoritative figures who were recruited as intermediate agents for effective rural governance in Late Imperial China. On the one hand, for the *lijia*, *baojia*, and *xiangyue* systems to work, recruited intermediate agents needed to have sufficient community standing for effective action, which was closely tied to their local identity and their willingness and ability to promote local interests (Kuhn 1975; Wakeman and Grant 1975). On the other hand, the rulers also expected the intermediate agents to align their interests with those of the national government, particularly when levying taxes or conscripting labor—activities that frequently ran against the interests of their fellow villagers. In practice, the two identities collided quite often.

As Duara (1988) demonstrates, the authority and legitimacy of these intermediate agents were mainly established, maintained, and consolidated through their embeddedness in indigenous ceremonies, clan/lineage and religious organizations, or locally shared norms, all of which Duara defined as a "cultural nexus." This cultural nexus, while effectively regulating and coordinating villagers' behavior and upholding effective rural governance, also significantly restricted these local authoritative figures' pursuit of personal gains at the cost of their fellow villagers and held them accountable via effective social sanctions. Had these intermediate agents gone all out to help the national government with unpopular policies and extracting resources, their authority and legitimacy could have been challenged, weakened, or even rejected by their fellow villagers. Given their embeddedness in the cultural nexus, these intermediate agents behaved more like "protective brokers," whose interests were primarily aligned with those of the locals. Therefore, the Ming and Qing governments' extraction of resources from rural China, via the assistance of the recruited intermediate agents, was not as effective as expected.

This conflict between the dual identities of these intermediate agents became even more salient during the late Qing dynasty, when the national government's military expenses significantly increased due to the wars against foreign powers. To increase its revenue and cover military expenses, the national government demanded more substantial extraction from rural China. Thus, the local authoritative figures had to either bear the cost of social sanctions—including alienation from their fellow villagers as the local leaders succumbed to the national government—or refuse to carry out their officially assigned responsibilities. Gradually, "entrepreneurial brokers," who cared only about personal gains and were not concerned with social sanctions,[24] replaced "protective brokers" as the intermediate agents of official bureaucracies for the governance in rural China. Not surprisingly, brute force then prevailed in Chinese villages and significantly worsened the quality of governance.

When the Qing dynasty was overthrown by the Xinhai Revolution (1911) and succeeded by the Republic of China, due to continuous military mobilization and conflicts, the governance in rural communities was further worsened. Landed gentries, who previously served as the intermediate agents of official bureaucracies in local governance, gradually left for residence in more urbanized areas.[25] The KMT's state-making process incited a local culture of violence against regional warlords, communists, and some of its former military commanders or allies. Thus, to consolidate its power, the KMT focused primarily on the suppression of local opposition rather than on ensuring public order and welfare (H. Li 2005; Myers 1980; Thornton 2007). During this period, Chinese peasants were held to "increasingly brutal and disadvantageous relationships with few sound institutions to turn to for relief or recourse" (Jackson 2011, p. 79).[26] As Duara (1988, pp. 159, 223) documents, in the Republican era, the governance in rural communities suffered from the intrusiveness of the state and of battling armies:

> The patron type of leader increasingly abandoned village offices, which were then filled by men of another sort. Although from diverse social backgrounds, these men shared a basic perception of the rewards of politics and village office. Office was no longer pursued as a way of expressing leadership aspirations or gaining prestige because these goals could no longer be realized through these means. . . . The new type of village official who began to emerge in the late Republic had to base his power on the sources outside of the cultural nexus.

In sum, to overcome the lack of sufficient administrative and economic resources, the national governments in Late Imperial China took advantage of the close-knit communal structures of Chinese villages, intentionally incorporated their indigenous resources and institutions, and recruited local authoritative figures as intermediate agents in crafting their institutions for China's rural governance. Nevertheless, due to some internal tensions, this institutional engineering was not as effective as expected. Further, when national leaders became primarily concerned with resource extraction for political and military campaigns in the Late Qing and Republican era, entrepreneurial brokers replaced protective brokers as the intermediate agents in China's rural governance. These brokers were no longer constrained by indigenous institutions when pursuing personal interests; rather, they were rewarded for their attempts to squeeze every penny out of Chinese villagers.[27] This deterioration in China's rural governance became too serious to be overhauled with anything less than a revolution, both political and institutional.

Centralized Governance with Imposed Totalitarian Institutions

According to Li (2009, p. 5), the inefficiency of integrating rural communities into a centralized administrative system in China was not effectively addressed until the establishment of the CCP regime in the late 1940s:

> Unlike an insulated community in the imperial times, where impersonal relations were subject primarily to the regulation of endogenous social hierarchies and shared values, state making in twentieth-century China exerted a profound impact on power relations in the villages through the vigorous expansion of the formal government system into the countryside and the diffusion of new, national-level values among the rural dwellers.

By consolidating its party organizations in villages as well as systematically extending its administrative bureaucracies below the level of counties and into townships and even villages, the CCP regime thoroughly penetrated rural China. New village governments, which were controlled by locally recruited communist party members, were also created to formally address numerous local governance issues. To align these local leaders' interests with those of the national government, the CCP intentionally recruited those whose fortunes were tied primarily to the CCP's revolution and continued rule. These local leaders were expected to be highly loyal to the party and to prioritize the government's interests, even at the cost of their fellow villagers. In practice, local leaders were more likely to come from rural households with relatively low economic status, and they were held accountable to their superiors in the upper levels of government through a cadre evaluation and appointment system.

There was a key difference between the institutions established by the CCP and those adopted by the Ming and Qing dynasties and inherited by the KMT regime. Leadership roles in local governance were no longer assigned to those with privileges, as related to seniority, learning, wealth, or kin status, but to those who were ideologically and politically attached to the CCP. With the help of ideological and political affiliations, the CCP regime could, to some extent, ensure that their agents in rural communities would take the government's side and be faithful should the government's interests run against those of rural residents.

In addition to identifying more faithful local agents, the CCP also made enormous efforts, primarily through socioeconomic and political campaigns, to ensure that local leaders' ideological and political affiliations with the CCP generated sufficient authority and legitimacy for rural governance. With the help of land reform and social class designation, the CCP significantly challenged the socioeconomic basis of traditional authority, power, and social relations.[28] For instance, Chinese communists confiscated clan/lineage organizations' corporate lands and distributed them among poor peasants. They also organized poor peasants to humiliate, attack, and expropriate the property of rich peasants and landlords, who might be their kinsmen (Madsen 1984). Thus, through varying means, the CCP made rural residents' loyalty and responsibility to their class their most salient concern.

Moreover, the CCP also intentionally cultivated and indoctrinated its people with communist norms and values (such as collectivism that prioritized national interests over local ones) through newspaper reading in study groups and radio programs broadcast through high-volume speakers in local communities.[29] This propaganda and value indoctrination, together with the socioeconomic and political campaigns, substantively transformed the nature of the local cultural nexus that contributed to the authority and legitimacy of local leaders. Embedded in this transformed cultural nexus, village cadres' ideological and political affiliations with the CCP gave them the necessary authority and justified their legitimacy in village governance. Further, the moral pressures within Chinese villages, thanks to the transformed cultural nexus, were less likely to drive a wedge between village cadres' interests and those of the CCP regime and more likely to reinforce the alignment between the two. Therefore, as Parish and Whyte (1978) suggest, with the help of radio broadcasts, films, and study groups that exposed villagers to messages from the outside, the CCP regime penetrated rural communities to an unprecedented extent and dramatically increased the vertical integration between the villagers at the periphery and the national government in Beijing.

This significantly increased the integration of and tightened control over rural communities, and their residents were further strengthened by the establishment of the People's Commune (*renmin gongshe*) following the agricultural collectivization of the mid-1950s. At the bottom of the commune system was the production team (*shengchan xiaodui*), which consisted of one or two hundred people from the same community. The members of a production team shared the work and output on collectively owned lands. The next higher unit was the brigade (*shengchan dadui*), which had anywhere from two to two dozen teams. A brigade also ran most rural industries, when there were any. At the top of the commune system was the commune (*gongshe*) itself, which had around ten to twenty brigades under its administration.[30]

A key job of communes was to ensure that brigades and production teams fulfilled their respective production quotas allocated by the county government (Kelliher 1992). In addition to overseeing agricultural production and other rural economic activities, communes also assisted the CCP regime in various other aspects of local governance, such as conflict resolution, education, social welfare provision, and disaster relief.[31] In sum, under the commune system, village cadres, who were loyal agents of the CCP regime and who were given a monopoly over socioeconomic and political resources in rural China, had effective control over almost every aspect of their villagers' lives (Oi 1985, 1989). This imposed totalitarian institution contributed to the effective integration of rural China into a national administrative system for centralized governance.[32] The successful establishment and performance of the imposed institution should be attributed to the CCP's continuous socioeconomic, political, and ideological campaigns as well as to its willingness to use coercive power—in some cases even terror and systematic violence—to enforce the imposed institution and to stifle potential competition from some indigenous institutions by attacking their social and cultural bases.[33]

Nevertheless, despite the CCP's extensive political, economic, and social engineering, the close-knit communal structures of rural China were maintained and even strengthened as an unintended byproduct of the commune system (i.e., a form of apartheid system for Chinese rural households). Although their national horizons had been expanded through continuous propaganda and indoctrination, as well as their systematic integration into the centralized administrative system, Chinese rural residents were still geographically restricted and intentionally circumscribed to their home villages. For instance, under the commune system, villages not only defined the boundary of residence but also marked the boundaries of production, consumption, and social interaction. Villagers' leaving the commune for alternative ways of life was extremely difficult, if not impossible; and even shifting between brigades was rare. Additionally, rural residents' limited physical mobility was further constrained by the household registration (*hukou*) system that was adopted by the CCP to ensure effective resource extraction for financing and subsidizing its ambitious project of industrialization.[34]

The *hukou* system was originally developed to subsidize the industrialization program by providing underpriced and rationed daily necessities to urban workers as well as guaranteed access to education, housing, and other social welfare (K. W. Chan and Zhang 1999; T. Cheng and Selden 1994; F.-l. Wang 2004, 2005; X. Wu and Treiman 2004; X. Yang 1993). Generally, under the *hukou* system, Chinese citizens were categorized as either an agricultural or non-agricultural population. Only those who were registered as part of the non-agricultural population qualified for benefits such as grain rations, employer-provided housing, and health care. Although there were still opportunities for changing the household registration type from agriculture to non-agriculture, the quotas were strictly controlled.[35] Thus, due to the *hukou* system, Chinese rural residents, who, as noted, were mostly registered as an agricultural population, were effectively tied to the land, with limited possibilities of moving out. They also were prevented from cityward migration and even punished for trying to reside in cities.

As Shue (1988) observes, the planned economy, together with the household registration system, reinforced the "honeycomb" structure in rural China.[36] The well-maintained, close-knit communal structures of Chinese villages allowed the preservation of some indispensable resources for the operation of indigenous relation-based institutions. That is part of the reason why clan/lineage organizations, as well as traditionally cultivated norms, still shaped the socioeconomic and political arenas to some extent in many villages in the 1960s and 1970s, even after the CCP intensively campaigned against them (e.g., A. Chan et al. 1984; Madsen 1984; Ruf 1998). When the CCP later relaxed its control and gradually retreated from rural China beginning in the late 1970s, the close-knit communal structures of Chinese villages effectively facilitated the revival of indigenous institutions and provided the necessary social foundation for their effective performance.[37]

Decentralized Governance with Imposed Grassroots Democracy

It is clearly the case that the commune system made a critical contribution to China's industrialization in the 1950s and 1960s. As previously illustrated in Figure 3.2, the percentage of China's GDP from its secondary industry increased considerably during the first two decades after the CCP's victory. Nevertheless, the commune system also suffocated the development of local economies, due to the lack of effective mechanisms for resource allocation, as well as glorified self-sufficiency and sacrifice in Chinese villages for China's national defense and urban industrialization.[38] After the chaotic ten years of the Cultural Revolution (1966–1976), the economic situation in rural China in particular showed a striking deterioration. The depressing economic performance of Chinese villages triggered economic and, later, administrative and political reforms in rural China, respectively, in the form of the household responsibility system (*jiating lianchan chengbao zerenzhi*) and self-governance based on grassroots democracy (*jiceng minzhu zizhi*).

In response to the legacy of totalitarianism in China, particularly its control over almost every aspect of the Chinese society, the reform coalition of national leaders, headed by Deng Xiaoping, gradually loosened the government's domination of commerce and industrial enterprises, reduced the role of central planning, and encouraged a vast array of entrepreneurial ventures. In rural China, in particular, they introduced the household responsibility system in 1979 and dismantled the commune system in the early 1980s. China scholars believe that these reform measures have considerably relieved the constraints imposed on Chinese villages, resulted in significant enthusiasm and incentives for agricultural production among Chinese peasants, and made an invaluable contribution to China's continuous economic growth (A. Chan et al. 1992; Kelliher 1992; Parish 1985; Walder and Zhao 2006; K. X. Zhou 1996).

Economic prosperity, however, is only one (albeit a critical) dimension of governance in rural China. When the CCP decentralized its economic system to provide incentives for agricultural production and later dismantled the commune system, other socioeconomic and political functions previously assumed by the communes (e.g., public goods provision) were left unattended in many Chinese villages. Moreover, the village cadres' authority and legitimacy, based primarily on their political and ideological affiliations with the CCP, were also, at least partly, rejected by villagers after their witnessing some of the catastrophic consequences of the totalitarian system. The gradual erosion of village cadres' monopoly over socioeconomic resources after the economic reforms further expedited the rejection of their claimed legitimacy in Chinese villages. This "public authority vacuum" in a large number of Chinese villages had negative consequences for China's rural governance in the 1980s and 1990s.

Despite their no longer having control and publicly recognized authority and legitimacy in rural communities in the 1980s and 1990s, village cadres were still compelled to extract resources from rural residents and to implement unpopular policies such as family planning. Given the pressure from upper-level governments that pushed for fulfilling quotas and implementing policies, as well as the upper-level governments' control over their material benefits and political careers, many village cadres resorted to brute force in rural governance (T. Bernstein and Lu 2008; X. He 2007a; X. Lu 1997; D. Shen 2006). Moreover, to compensate for the reputational and social assets they lost within villages as they subverted their fellow villagers' interests to their own and those of the government, it is not surprising that many village cadres engaged in a variety of rent-seeking activities and behaved like the "entrepreneurial brokers" in the Ming, Qing, and Republican eras (Duara 1988). This resulted in a rural governance crisis in the 1980s and 1990s, characterized by deteriorating and increasingly confrontational cadre–villager relationships (X. He 2007a, 2009; L. Li and Xiong 1998). This governance crisis eventually pushed the CCP to try an essentially different institutional solution for its decentralized governance in rural China: self-governance based on grassroots democracy.

As established by the scholarship on Chinese rural politics, in the early 1980s village committee elections were initiated by some Chinese peasants to fill the public authority vacuum and to tackle the declining social order in their villages (O'Brien and Li 2000; Shi 1999a, 2000c). After intense internal debates on whether such bottom-up initiatives should be officially endorsed and promoted in all Chinese villages, and owing to some national leaders' individual efforts and insistence (Kelliher 1997; Shi 1999a), a trial version of the Organic Law of Village Committees (OLVC) was approved by the National People's Congress (NPC) in November 1987, despite lingering opposition.[39] Proponents of this new institution for rural governance claimed that democratic village elections could (1) help the government revive its governance in Chinese villages, given the ongoing reforms of decentralization and withdrawal of the state's presence in rural China; (2) ease the increasingly confrontational cadre–villager relationships, which might evolve into a significant political crisis, by making village cadres accountable to their constituencies; and (3) facilitate the implementation of government policies and secure villagers' compliance (Kelliher 1997). After another decade of practice and debate, the OLVC was further revised by the NPC and promulgated in November 1998 (further revised in October 2010) as the "constitution" for self-governance in rural China. Although internal debates continued on whether villagers should be granted such autonomy and whether village leaders should be directly elected,[40] the promulgation of the OLVC in 1998 meant that the Chinese central government acknowledged the benefits of granting villagers more autonomy in its decentralized rural governance and was determined to formalize its institutional foundation, mainly in the form of grassroots democracy, for even greater gains.[41]

In addition to promoting and establishing grassroots democracy as the officially sanctioned institutional foundation for its rural governance, the Chinese government has also pushed forward rural fiscal and administrative reforms since the early 1990s to address its rural governance crisis. The basic idea of such reforms is to relieve villagers of the tax and fee burden that had been eroding their incomes (J. Y. Lin and Liu 2007; Oi and Zhao 2007; Yep 2004). In the early 1990s, the Chinese government tried experiments of tax-for-fee reforms (TFR) in Anhui, which was officially designated as the provincial TFR test point in 2000. In 2002, the TFR was broadly introduced to twenty other provinces.[42] To further reduce villagers' burden, the central government completely abolished the agricultural tax in 2006. Meanwhile, to balance the loss of local revenues in rural China due to fiscal reforms, the central government also pushed for downsizing its local administrative agencies and cutting administrative expenditures.[43] Fiscal transfers from the central government have also been increased to compensate for local revenue shortfalls (B. Huang and Chen 2012; C. Shen et al. 2012).

Despite their undisputable effectiveness in reducing villagers' burden (Kennedy 2007b; Tao and Qin 2007), the TFR and abolition of the agricultural tax's negative impact on China's rural governance has been well documented (Kennedy 2007a; R. Luo et al. 2007; Oi and Zhao 2007; Sato et al. 2007; Yep 2004). More specifically, due to the loss of local revenues, insufficient fiscal transfers from upper-level governments, and administrative downsizing, fiscal and personnel resources at the disposal of township and village cadres are extremely limited; thus, many townships have become administrative shells and are not even able to provide basic services. Particularly, as Yep (2004) argues, village-level administration is the major victim of the financial squeeze.[44] In most cases, raising funds from villagers via the "one task, one meeting" (*yishi yiyi*) system has become indispensable for financing local public goods and welfare provision.[45] As numerous empirical studies have shown, the exacerbated fiscal situation of rural China, primarily driven by its TFR and abolition of agricultural taxes, has further increased the salience of grassroots democracy in contemporary rural China's decentralized governance (R. Luo et al. 2007; X. Meng and Zhang 2011; Pesqué-Cela et al. 2009; Tao and Qin 2007; S. Wang and Yao 2010) as the only officially sanctioned formal institution for generating public authority, mobilizing resources, creating accountability, coordinating people's behavior and expectations, and sustaining quality governance.

As shown in previous sections, before the CCP regime, the close-knit communal structures of Chinese villages occupied a central role, either explicit or implicit, in different institutional solutions proposed by national leaders. Due to insufficient administrative and fiscal resources, national bureaucracies were rarely extended into Chinese villages in the Ming and Qing dynasties. Thus, rural community leaders, with their recognized authority and legitimacy embedded in the local cultural nexus, were systematically recruited as intermediate agents of district magistrates for administrative purposes; and indigenous relation-based institutions, supported by powerful social sanctions, also were intentionally incorporated into official institutions such as the *lijia*, *baojia*, and *xiangyue* systems for effective rural governance. Although the KMT regime relied primarily on "entrepreneurial brokers" in extracting resources to support its continuous military mobilization and power consolidation while leaving other aspects of rural governance unattended, it also took advantage of the close-knit social environments of Chinese villages for necessary information, mobilization, and social control.

Different from its predecessors, the CCP regime, for the first time in Chinese history, successfully penetrated almost every aspect of rural Chinese life. With the help of widely established party organizations, newly organized village governments, and, later, the commune system, the CCP effectively integrated Chinese villages into the centralized and totalitarian administrative system. The necessary authority and legitimacy of newly recruited village cadres for effective rural governance also were successfully established, thanks to the CCP's continuous socioeconomic and political campaigns as well as value/norm cultivation and indoctrination. Thus, the CCP ensured the establishment and performance of the imposed totalitarian institution in China's rural governance, through the essentially transformed local cultural nexus and, if necessary, coercive power and violence.

Despite its success in channeling administrative bureaucracies and imposing the totalitarian institution onto Chinese villages, the commune system, together with the household registration system, actually reinforced the close-knit communal structures of Chinese villages. Thus, the influence of indigenous relation-based institutions on rural residents' behavior and on village socioeconomic and political dynamics was not completely eliminated, as the CCP had originally hoped. Further, in some villages, indigenous institutions were quickly revived in the 1980s and 1990s to fill the public authority vacuum in local governance (e.g., Hansen 2008; Svensson 2012; T. Xiao 2010), which was caused by various socioeconomic and political reforms launched by the CCP beginning in the late 1970s as well as by the CCP's gradual withdrawal of its presence in Chinese villages.

Therefore, when grassroots democracy, as the only officially sanctioned institution for decentralized self-governance, was tentatively introduced in the late 1980s and officially imposed upon rural China in the late 1990s, in many cases it was actually imposed upon rural communities with a rich tradition and memories of local governance mainly supported by indigenous relation-based institutions. Confronted with possible competition from the indigenous institutions, the place of grassroots democracy as the dominant and effective institutional foundation for decentralized governance in rural China is not certain. Empirically, the quality of Chinese village elections, as well as their impact on local governance, has been subject to debate among China scholars (J. Chen and Zhong 2002; J. Lu 2012; Manion 1996, 2006; Sato 2008; Shi 1999c; L. Tsai 2007b, 2010; Y. Yao and Shen 2006).

Before we systematically and thoroughly examine the respective roles of indigenous relation-based institutions and imposed rule-based institutions in contemporary rural China's decentralized governance, we need to establish a deeper understanding of the substantial but uneven transformation of Chinese villages' communal structures and social environments beginning in the 1990s. This significant communal structural change, *inter alia*, is driven primarily by the large-scale outflow of rural surplus labor through cityward migration, as a consequence of the ongoing market-oriented economic reforms in China. This rural–urban migration poses an unprecedented challenge for Chinese political leaders in their rural governance, as it seriously complicates the institutional engineering used to ensure quality decentralized governance in Chinese villages.

3.3 RURAL–URBAN MIGRATION IN CONTEMPORARY CHINA

When agricultural output constitutes the majority of the national economy and the level of industrialization is relatively low, the transfer of rural labor across sectors and regions through migration is unlikely to be significant. Partly because of the scarcity of alternatives for surplus rural labor, "involution in agricultural production" (P. C. Huang 1985), in which the marginal input of labor generally outweighs the marginal output of agricultural production, had been a prevalent phenomenon in nineteenth- and early twentieth-century rural China. As discussed in previous sections, before the economic reforms in the late 1970s, outward migration of rural labor, particularly for economic opportunities and associated benefits in urban areas, was rarely a large-scale phenomenon in China for both socioeconomic and political reasons. Further, the low physical mobility of rural residents helped maintain the close-knit communal structures of most Chinese villages.[46]

Evolving Rural–Urban Migration

Accompanying its market-oriented economic reforms in urban China beginning in the early 1980s, the Chinese government increased its resource allocation for industrialization, particularly for light industries. As a consequence, China's increasingly expanding industrial production demanded much more inexpensive labor. Meanwhile, the widely implemented household responsibility system in rural China helped further release surplus labor from agriculture and facilitated the transfer of the surplus labor to non-agricultural sectors. According to the China Agricultural Development Report (2007), the percentage of rural labor employed in non-agricultural production increased steadily from 9% in 1983 to 41% in 2005.[47]

However, this significant transfer of rural surplus labor from agriculture to non-agricultural sectors did not necessarily mean that Chinese villagers had to leave their residential communities and make a living as migrant workers. Doing so was their second choice and was not observed on a large scale until the 1990s. Locally available employment opportunities in non-agricultural sectors can be very attractive, particularly given the lower economic, emotional, and psychological costs involved (Guang and Zheng 2005; Y. Zhao 1999, 2002). During the early 1980s, at the initial stage of this dramatic labor transfer in rural China, township and village enterprises (TVEs) absorbed most of the surplus labor released from agriculture (Xin Meng 2000; Nee and Opper 2012).[48]

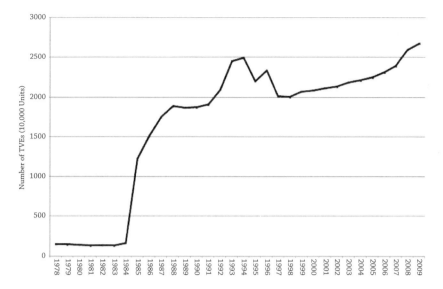

Figure 3.3:
The Number (in Thousands) of Township and Village Enterprises
Source: China Township and Village Enterprises Statistics (1978–2002) and China Labor Statistical Yearbook 2010.

As illustrated in Figure 3.3, the number of TVEs in China increased exponentially, from 1.65 million in 1984 to 12.22 million in 1985, a growth of more than sevenfold. This momentum of growth was sustained until 1993, when the number of TVEs peaked at 24.52 million. Moreover, in the early 1980s, other institutional controls that blocked labor mobility, such as the household registration system, had not yet been relaxed. Therefore, most rural surplus labor used the strategy of leaving the land without leaving the villages (*litu bu lixiang*) and seized newly available economic opportunities in rural industries.

These rural residents no longer worked exclusively as peasants but, rather, lived on salaries, worked in enterprises outside of their villages, and helped their families with agricultural production when needed. Nevertheless, they still stayed in rural communities and continued to work together with their families, neighbors, and fellow villagers. Compared with the situation under the commune system, these rural residents had more freedom in choosing their occupations and ways of life, but they were still closely attached to rural communities, with most social interaction geographically constrained to where they lived. In other words, although rural surplus labor was successfully transferred to non-agricultural sectors in the 1980s, this change was realized mainly through the expansion of the TVEs in rural China rather than via cityward migration. Thus, the close-knit communal structures of most Chinese villages were not seriously challenged during that time. Even today, in some rural regions of coastal and eastern provinces where TVEs continue to prosper, "leaving the land without leaving the villages" is still the dominant pattern of rural surplus labor transfer.

Encountering severe competition from state-owned enterprises (SOEs) and joint ventures as well as unfavorable government policies in the late 1980s and early 1990s, a large number of TVEs closed down (Nee and Opper 2012). As illustrated in Figure 3.3, the number of TVEs in China dropped to 22.02 million in 1995 and further down to 20 million in 1998. The surplus labor in rural China responded accordingly and sought economic opportunities in urban areas farther away from their home villages. To further demonstrate this transformation in the nature of rural labor transfer since the early 1990s, the percentages of the household population who worked in TVEs and as migrant workers between 1986 and 1999 are displayed in Figure 3.4. Before 1993, the percentage of household labor who worked in TVEs had been consistently higher than those who worked as migrant workers. However, the latter climbed from its relatively lower level in 1992, surpassed the former, and has maintained this momentum of steady growth through the rest of the twentieth century. Clearly, when non-agricultural sectors in rural China could no longer accommodate the

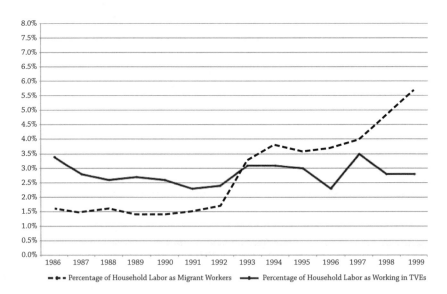

Figure 3.4:
Percentages of Household Labor Working in TVEs and as Migrant Workers
Source: China Agricultural Development Report 2001.

surplus labor released from agriculture, the latter continued their search for economic opportunities by moving to urban areas.

Similar to what classical economic theories on migration posit (Harris and Todaro 1970; Lewis 1954) and what has been observed in the histories of developed countries (Hagood and Sharp 1951; Hochstadt 1999; J. Patten 1973) and in contemporary developing countries (Bhuyan et al. 2001; Joshi and Verma 2004; Kutsche 1994; Mortuza 1992; Oberai et al. 1989; Yadava 1989), the rural–urban disparity, in regard to economic opportunities and benefits, significantly contributes to this cityward outflow of rural labor in contemporary China (Bakken 1998; Cai and Bai 2006; Day and Ma 1994; Hare 1999; Hussain and Wang 2010; Lall and Selod 2006; C. Luo and Yue 2012; X. Yang 1996; Linxiu Zhang et al. 2010; M. Zhang 2003; Y. Zhao 1999). Given China's rigid household registration system and discriminatory policies that favor urban residents in various ways, rural–urban inequality in terms of living standards has been substantial; unfortunately, this inequality has been enlarged in the reform era.

As illustrated in Figure 3.5, the ratio between the per capita disposable income of urban China and that of rural areas has been persistently larger than 2 since the beginning of the 1990s, when it rose from 1.86 in the mid-1980s. Despite a temporary decline between 1994 and 1997 (probably due to the reforms in the SOEs that resulted in large-scale layoffs

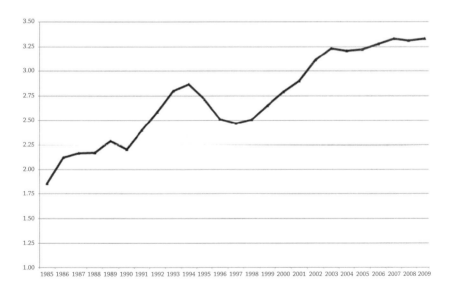

Figure 3.5:
Ratio of Per Capita Disposable Income Between Urban and Rural China
Source: China Agricultural Development Report 2007–2010.

in urban China),[49] this ratio increased continuously as the economic reforms unfolded in China and reached 3.33 at the end of 2009.

Moreover, China's substantially expanded urban industries, most of which are at the lower end of the value chain in the world market and specialize in labor-intensive production, also generate a huge demand for inexpensive labor with a moderate level of education (i.e., junior or senior high school graduates). In many cases, this demand for inexpensive labor with basic skills cannot be fully accommodated by the limited labor pool in urban China alone. Fortunately, owing to the compulsory nine-year education program widely promoted in China, there is a large pool of surplus labor in rural villages that meets the needs of Chinese urban industries.[50] Further, when high-quality urban laborers move upward into jobs with higher requirements in terms of education, skills, and human capital, there are significant opportunities left for rural laborers to take dirtier, more exhausting, and more labor-intensive jobs in Chinese cities.[51] Naturally, rural surplus laborers take advantage of these opportunities, move into urban areas, and explore a new way of life as migrant workers.

As expected, rural migrant workers bring enormous economic benefits for both receiving and sending regions in terms of boosting local economies.[52] Because performance-related indicators such as GDP play a significant and even dominant role in China's cadre evaluation system and in shaping government officials' career trajectory (Bo 2002; Landry 2003, 2008), Chinese local governments, in the late 1990s and in competition against each other, gradually adopted a variety of policies that facilitated the cityward migration, as well as migrant workers' settlement in urban regions. Despite the lingering impacts of the half-century-old household registration system, this bottom-up momentum in promoting rural–urban migration finally led to policy changes at the central government level. In the early 2000s, a series of national regulations in regard to migrant workers were promulgated.[53] With much more favorable official policies, cityward migration has rapidly grown into a major means of rural surplus labor transfer in contemporary China (Weston 2012).

As displayed in Figure 3.6, the percentage of total rural labor who worked as migrant workers, regardless of their destination, increased from 6.8% in 1983 to 28.4% in 2009, a growth of almost fourfold in sixteen years. Also shown in Figure 3.6 are two time periods with much more significant growth (i.e., steeper slopes) in the number of migrant workers— the early 1990s and the early 2000s. This pattern is compatible with the aforementioned arguments on the declining capacity of the TVEs to absorb rural surplus labor in the early 1990s as well as the positive impacts of a

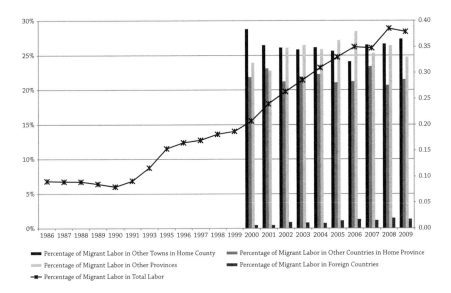

Figure 3.6:
Percentage of Total Rural Labor as Migrant Workers
Source: China Agricultural Development Report 2001–2010 and National Rural Social-Economy Survey
Data Collection (1986–1999).

series of favorable government policies on cityward migration in the early
2000s.

With more rural residents' joining the significant cityward migration,
the destinations of migrant workers also change significantly: An increasing number of villagers find their temporary or permanent jobs in urban
areas that are farther away from their home communities. Although there
is little detailed information on the destinations for migrant workers in
the 1980s and 1990s, we can still see the patterns with the information
available for the early 2000s. As shown in the right-hand portion of
Figure 3.6, the percentage of migrant workers who worked in other towns
in their home counties decreased from 38.4% in 2000 to 32.3% in 2006.
Partly due to the global economic recession in the late 2000s, this percentage witnessed some increase and reached 36.5% at the end of 2009 but
was still lower than that of 2000. The percentage of migrant workers who
worked in other counties or cities in their home provinces was relatively
stable between 2000 and 2009, hovering around 29%. In contrast, the
percentage of migrant workers with jobs in other provinces or even foreign countries increased over this nine-year span, with the former's increasing from 31.9% to 33.0% (with a peak of 38.0% in 2006) and the latter's from 0.6% to 1.8%.[54] Considering the costs involved in migration, it
is understandable that rural surplus laborers are more likely to take jobs

in proximate towns and counties and gradually move to other cities and provinces when proximate opportunities run out.

Currently, Chinese villagers no longer simply leave the land without leaving the villages but are forced to or voluntarily choose to leave both the land and their home villages as migrant workers and move to urban areas, where they face a new way of life and new challenges (Fong and Murphy 2006; Jacka 2005; W. Tang and Yang 2008; Thireau and Linshan 2007; C. Zhao 2004). This transformed pattern of rural–urban migration also is expected to have considerable impacts on the communal structures and social environments of Chinese villages, in which different institutions for local governance are embedded.[55]

Uneven Distribution of Rural-Urban Migration

Despite the increasing transfer of surplus labor through rural–urban migration and the growing number of rural migrants who work in urban areas far away from their home communities, the distribution of rural migrant workers in China is far from geographically balanced, particularly in terms of long-distance migration (e.g., interprovincial migration).

Figure 3.7 presents the percentages of rural migrants working in other towns of their home counties, other counties of their home provinces,

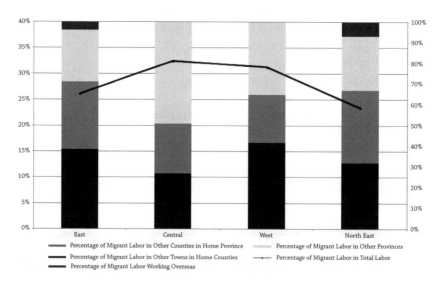

Figure 3.7:
Composition of Rural Migrant Workers in Different Regions
Source: China Agricultural Development Report 2009.

other provinces, and overseas, respectively, for East, Central, West, and Northeast China in 2008.[56] As indicated by the left y-axis, the percentage of rural laborers working as migrants in urban areas was the highest in Central China, more than 32.4% in 2008. The percentages for West and East China were 31.3% and 26.1%, respectively, while Northeast China had the lowest percentage of rural migrant workers, at 23.5%. After dividing such figures according to the destinations of rural migrants, as indicated by the right y-axis, we see that the vast majority of rural migrant workers from Central China, 49.1%, found jobs outside of their home provinces in 2008. For West China, 35.0% of its rural migrants worked temporarily or permanently in other provinces. This figure was substantively lower for East and Northeast China. Only 25.2% of rural migrant workers from East China chose to work in other provinces; the corresponding number for Northeast China was 26.3% in 2008.

This uneven spatial distribution of rural laborers' long-distance cityward migration becomes even clearer when we examine the information from each provincial-level administrative unit. Table 3.1 presents statistics on temporary residents working in industries in all provinces and metropolitan cities of China in 2005.[57] The first column contains the total number of temporary residents working in industries in each provincial unit. The second column includes the percentages of the temporary residents from the counties of other provinces, which can be interpreted as a rough proxy of rural migrant labor from other provinces through long-distance cityward migration.

Clearly, there is huge variation in regard to the percentage of rural migrant workers from other provinces in a provincial unit, ranging from 14.6% to 83.7% in 2005. In Shanghai, Zhejiang, Beijing, and Tianjin, more than 70% of temporary residents who worked in industries were supplied through rural labor's interprovincial migration from other provinces. For Hunan, Sichuan, Chongqing, Gansu, Anhui, Hubei, Henan, Shandong, and Jilin, fewer than 25% of their temporary residents who worked in industries were recruited from the rural migrant workers from other provinces. It is not a coincidence that the second group of provinces also are the sending regions of the majority of rural migrant workers in China today.

This uneven spatial distribution of cityward migration also is reflected in the varying sources of Chinese rural residents' income. Table 3.2 shows the percentages of rural households' net income from wages, working as migrants, and working in local townships, based on the 2008 China Rural Household Survey. Again, there are huge variances across regions. In 2008, salary-based net income accounted for more than 50% of rural

Table 3.1. TEMPORARY RESIDENTS WORKING IN INDUSTRIES
IN DIFFERENT REGIONS

	Total Number of Temporary Residents Working in Industries	Temporary Residents (from the Counties of Other Provinces) Working in Industries
Shanghai	4,491,424	83.68% (3,758,297)
Zhejiang	10,398,032	75.70% (7,871,081)
Tianjin	1,204,762	71.94% (866,745)
Beijing	2,584,907	71.88% (1,857,968)
Tibet	101,167	63.91% (64,660)
Xinjiang	526,460	61.12% (321,789)
Shanxi	522,553	50.49% (263,851)
Guangdong	20,002,931	49.67% (9,934,499)
Jiangsu	6,816,938	47.74% (3,254,311)
Ningxia	57,284	47.44% (27,174)
Fujian	2,637,683	44.81% (1,181,975)
Hebei	811,444	40.37% (327,564)
Hainan	125,278	38.91% (48,741)
Yunnan	1,074,382	38.47% (413,315)
Liaoning	729,194	37.60% (274,166)
Inner Mongolia	731,334	28.27% (206,779)
Qinghai	246,393	26.47% (65,228)
Guizhou	506,225	26.10% (132,113)
Jiangxi	201,864	25.70% (51,875)
Heilongjiang	434,425	25.55% (111,010)
Guangxi	483,510	25.43% (122,963)
Shaanxi	640,765	25.25% (161,804)
Jilin	222,053	24.74% (54,945)
Shandong	2,156,984	23.82% (513,755)
Henan	781,818	22.80% (178,233)
Hubei	691,777	21.43% (148,280)
Anhui	313,704	20.34% (63,823)
Gansu	166,798	20.19% (33,673)
Chongqing	341,356	18.14% (61,910)
Sichuan	1,029,017	14.82% (152,475)
Hunan	625,242	14.58% (91,189)

Source: National Compiled Statistics on Temporary Residents 2006.

Table 3.2. PERCENTAGES OF DIFFERENT SOURCES OF RURAL
HOUSEHOLD NET INCOME

Net Income from Wage	Net Income from Working as Migrants	Net Income from Working in Local Townships
Shanghai (70.90%)	Guangdong (32.54%)	Shanghai (45.38%)
Beijing (59.90%)	Hunan (27.96%)	Tianjin (40.55%)
Guangdong (57.60%)	Chongqing (27.91%)	Zhejiang (39.78%)
Jiangsu (53.00%)	Anhui (25.63%)	Beijing (38.94%)
Tianjin (51.40%)	Sichuan (25.39%)	Shanxi (32.69%)
Zhejiang (49.60%)	Jiangxi (24.46%)	Jiangsu (29.36%)
Hunan (44.10%)	Ningxia (24.01%)	Hebei (23.50%)
Chongqing (42.80%)	Hubei (23.60%)	Shandong (23.30%)
Shanxi (41.80%)	Qinghai (21.99%)	Fujian (22.80%)
Anhui (41.40%)	Shaanxi (19.68%)	Guangdong (19.87%)
Hebei (41.30%)	Guangxi (18.72%)	Liaoning (17.52%)
Shandong (40.10%)	Gansu (17.67%)	Shaanxi (17.15%)
Shaanxi (39.60%)	Jiangsu (17.49%)	Guizhou (15.82%)
Sichuan (39.30%)	Henan (17.15%)	Hunan (14.38%)
Jiangxi (39.20%)	Guizhou (14.50%)	Yunnan (13.17%)
Fujian (39.10%)	Hebei (14.37%)	Guangxi (12.77%)
Hubei (37.40%)	Shanghai (14.18%)	Henan (12.74%)
Liaoning (36.50%)	Shandong (12.27%)	Chongqing (12.28%)
Guizhou (35.80%)	Tibet (12.17%)	Hubei (11.78%)
Guangxi (34.80%)	Beijing (11.98%)	Anhui (11.43%)
Ningxia (34.20%)	Liaoning (10.88%)	Jiangxi (10.98%)
Henan (33.70%)	Fujian (10.87%)	Sichuan (10.77%)
Qinghai (32.10%)	Hainan (7.91%)	Heilongjiang (8.73%)
Gansu (31.90%)	Inner Mongolia (6.57%)	Ningxia (8.65%)
Tibet (23.90%)	Heilongjiang (6.37%)	Gansu (8.64%)
Yunnan (19.90%)	Jilin (6.30%)	Tibet (8.41%)
Heilongjiang (18.90%)	Zhejiang (6.15%)	Jilin (7.69%)
Hainan (18.40%)	Shanxi (5.14%)	Hainan (7.45%)
Inner Mongolia (17.30%)	Xinjiang (4.16%)	Inner Mongolia (7.35%)
Jilin (16.40%)	Yunnan (3.90%)	Qinghai (6.16%)
Xinjiang (12.10%)	Tianjin (0.53%)	Xinjiang (5.01%)

Source: China Rural Household Survey Report 2009.

households' net income in Shanghai, Beijing, Guangdong, Jiangsu, and Tianjin, while this percentage was below 20% in Xinjiang, Jilin, Inner Mongolia, Hainan, Heilongjiang, and Yunnan.

The salary-based income also is earned in a variety of ways. In some provinces, non-agricultural rural laborers primarily work as migrant workers in cities far away from their home communities. For instance, migrant workers' contribution to rural households' net income accounted for more than 20% in Guangdong, Hunan, Chongqing, Anhui, Sichuan, Jiangxi, Ningxia, Hubei, and Qinghai in 2008. In some other provincial units, their non-agricultural laborers do not move far away from their home villages but primarily work in local townships. For example, in 2008, at least 30% of rural households' net income in Shanghai, Tianjin, Zhejiang, Beijing, Shanxi, and Jiangsu came from villagers' working in local townships.

In summary, after the economic reforms beginning in the late 1970s, particularly the household responsibility system in rural China and expanded industrialization in urban China, rural surplus labor released from agricultural production has been seeking alternative economic opportunities outside the villages. In the 1980s, widely established TVEs in rural China absorbed a significant portion of rural surplus labor. This localized labor transfer made it possible for a large number of Chinese villagers to leave the land without leaving their villages. As a consequence, the close-knit communal structures of Chinese villages were not seriously challenged at the initial stage of the transfer of rural surplus labor. When the economic performance of TVEs deteriorated in the early 1990s, *inter alia*, due to the increasing competition from reformed SOEs and joint ventures, as well as the government's unfavorable policies, rural surplus laborers were increasingly forced to seek new alternative economic opportunities and were attracted by the much higher living standard in urban China. The expanded Chinese urban industries also generated increasing demand for inexpensive rural labor with appropriate education and skills. All these factors came together and triggered an unprecedented large-scale cityward migration, which is a dominant way of transferring rural surplus labor in China today. Further encouraged and facilitated by favorable government policies, the rural–urban migration in contemporary China continues to grow substantially and is characterized by two salient features: (1) An increasing number of peasants not only leave the land and the villages but also move outside of their home counties or provinces for jobs and (2) The geographic distribution of cityward migration is uneven, with more rural migrant workers' leaving Central and West China and making their living in East China.[58]

Although rarely systematically addressed and sometimes even ignored in contemporary research on Chinese rural politics and governance, this significant but uneven outflow of rural labor has serious implications for the communal structures and social environments of Chinese villages.[59] And these substantially but unevenly transformed rural communities, in which both indigenous relation-based institutions and imposed rule-based institutions are embedded, experience varieties of decentralized governance, despite having the same officially sanctioned and imposed formal institutional settings.

3.4 CONCLUSION

For most of Chinese history, agriculture played a dominant role in its national economy and the overwhelming majority of its citizens lived in concentrated rural settlements. Thus, ensuring the stability and security in Chinese villages, as well as efficiently extracting resources from rural China, has always been a key concern for China's national leaders. Unfortunately, due to insufficient administrative resources, before the CCP's victory, rural China had rarely been effectively integrated into the centralized administrative system. To overcome this administrative insufficiency, Chinese national leaders proposed various institutional solutions that took advantage of the close-knit communal structures of Chinese villages, intentionally incorporated indigenous relation-based institutions, and systematically recruited local authoritative figures as their intermediate agents for rural governance.

During the Ming and Qing dynasties, the recruited intermediate agents, whose publicly recognized authority and legitimacy were based on their senior status in the genealogical hierarchy, better education, or other personal qualities such as moral character, played a critical role in China's rural governance. They helped collect taxes and uphold justice through the *lijia* system, ensured local public security and defense through the *baojia* system, and cultivated and indoctrinated officially canonized norms/values through the *xiangyue* and later *jiangyue* system. Nevertheless, their embeddedness in the local cultural nexus prevented the interests of such "protective brokers" from being successfully aligned with those of the national government, particularly when the government's policies seriously contravened the interests of rural residents. As the late Qing government gradually shifted to "entrepreneurial brokers" for more effective resource extraction to cover its military and other expenses, brute force prevailed in the governance of Chinese villages.

In the Republican era, the chaos and constant military mobilization under the KMT regime also prevented the national government from implementing effective new institutional solutions to address this persistent problem in China's rural governance. Moreover, the constant military conflicts and mobilization also significantly shortened Chinese villagers' time horizon and impaired the performance of indigenous institutions, despite the maintained close-knit communal structures of Chinese villages.

It was only after the establishment of the CCP regime that China's national government successfully penetrated its villages with the help of widely established party organizations, newly organized village governments, and, later, the imposed commune system. In addition to recruiting loyalists as local agents for rural governance, the CCP regime also transformed the nature of the local cultural nexus in Chinese villages, through political and ideological campaigns, to effectively align the interests of its local agents with its own and to minimize potential disagreements due to local moral pressures. However, the new institutional solutions offered by the CCP for China's rural governance, together with its industrialization program and other complementary institutions such as the household registration system, actually reinforced the close-knit communal structures of Chinese villages. This maintained the "honeycomb" structure of rural China and preserved some critical resources for the revival of indigenous relation-based institutions for local governance when the CCP gradually withdrew its presence in and control over Chinese villages.

To revive China's economy, which was shattered by the Cultural Revolution and substantiated the problems of its centralized totalitarian system, the CCP introduced the household responsibility system into Chinese villages, decentralized its rural governance, gradually retreated from its rural regions, abolished the commune system, and returned the self-governance status of rural China. Although Chinese villages did witness soaring economies after the economic reforms beginning in the late 1970s, a large number of them also suffered from the collapse of public authority in local governance, which previously was based on village cadres' political and ideological affiliation with the CCP. As a consequence, rural governance crises, as well as deteriorating cadre–villager relationships, distressed many Chinese villages. To address these issues, fill in the public authority vacuum, and revive its rural governance, grassroots democracy was tentatively introduced into Chinese villages in the late 1980s and then officially sanctioned as the legitimate parchment institution for China's rural governance in the late 1990s. However, quite different from the situation of previously imposed totalitarian institutions, grassroots democracy was imposed upon a rural China that witnessed a significant but uneven transformation in its communal structure, *inter alia*, primarily driven by the dramatic outflow of rural surplus labor through cityward migration that began in the 1990s.

When previously inaccessible alternatives became available, rural surplus laborers were eager to leave agricultural production and even rural communities for better economic opportunities. When TVEs were prosperous in the 1980s, most rural surplus laborers left the land without leaving the villages and worked in local TVEs. Even then, they still lived in villages and were closely attached to rural communities in various ways. Nevertheless, when TVEs could no longer effectively accommodate the rural surplus labor, beginning in the 1990s, Chinese peasants had to seek employment opportunities in urban areas farther away from their home communities. Gradually, as proximate opportunities ran out, long-distance cityward migration, such as between provinces, was increasingly embraced by rural surplus laborers. Moreover, this large-scale cityward migration's geographic distribution is far from even, with substantial surplus rural labor from Central and West China's leaving for jobs in East China.

As previously discussed, this significant but unevenly distributed cityward migration has challenged the original close-knit communal structures of Chinese villages to various degrees and resulted in serious implications for their decentralized rural governance. Some villages, with their surplus laborers' working primarily in local industries, may have maintained their close-knit communal structures. Some villages may have been transformed into loosely coupled communities, with a medium level of outward migration. Still other villages may have been seriously challenged and even paralyzed due to an exodus-level outflow of labor and, thus, have become atomized communities. When rule-based institutions such as grassroots democracy are imposed upon such unevenly transformed rural communities for their decentralized governance, their performance, as well as the quality of these villages' respective governance, is highly likely to be significantly varied, despite the standardized and unified settings and procedures specified by parchment institutions.

CHAPTER 4

Local Public Goods Provision, Institutional Performance, and Rural–Urban Migration in Chinese Villages

As previously discussed, since the economic reforms of the late 1970s, rural China has witnessed significant changes in its socioeconomic and political institutions: the establishment of the household responsibility system, collapse of the commune system, introduction of grassroots democracy, tax-for-fee reforms, and, most recently, the abolition of agricultural taxes. Some of these important institutional changes were launched at the same time many Chinese villages experienced an unprecedented large-scale outflow of labor through cityward migration. This substantial but geographically unevenly distributed rural–urban migration presents a challenge to the historically close-knit communal structures of Chinese villages to various extents and has reshaped the social environments in which different institutions are embedded and expected to perform. Without taking this significant community structural transformation into consideration, it is difficult to provide a contextualized understanding of the varying performance of imposed rule-based institutions in supporting China's decentralized rural governance, in particular, and the institutional change in rural China, in general.

Governance is a multidimensional and fuzzy concept, which makes it difficult to operationalize in social scientific inquiry, particularly quantitative research.[1] Thus, many students of local governance focus primarily on the provision of public goods as the key indicator (Banerjee and Iyer 2005; Banerjee et al. 2005; Habyarimana et al. 2007; R. Luo et al. 2007;

Miguel and Gugerty 2005; Sato 2008; L. Tsai 2002, 2007a, 2007b, 2011; X. Zhang et al. 2004).[2] Theoretically, the provision of public goods speaks directly to the two fundamental problems of local governance: collective action and accountability. Therefore, in this chapter I follow this conventional approach and study the provision of local public goods in Chinese villages as a key indicator of the quality of local governance in rural China.[3]

Moreover, this chapter focuses on the dynamics of public goods provision at the village level through an assessment of the capability of both indigenous and imposed institutions to support local public goods provision in Chinese villages with varying levels of cityward migration—that is, Paths I and II shown in Figure 1.1. More specifically, I use the information from the 2008 National Village Survey (NVS) to (1) describe the state of local public goods provision in contemporary rural China, (2) examine the performance of both indigenous relation-based and imposed rule-based institutions in supporting local public goods provision in Chinese villages, and (3) study how unevenly distributed cityward migration may have affected the performance of both indigenous and imposed institutions, thus contributing to the varieties of governance in rural China.

4.1 DECENTRALIZED PROVISION OF LOCAL PUBLIC GOODS IN CONTEMPORARY RURAL CHINA

Decentralization is a prominent feature of China's contemporary rural governance, in general, and the provision of local public goods in Chinese villages, in particular (e.g., Kung et al. 2009; R. Luo et al. 2007; Sato 2008; L. Tsai 2007a, 2011; X. Zhang et al. 2004).[4] This decentralized nature of China's rural governance has gradually increased after a series of changes in its socioeconomic institutions, starting with the introduction of the household responsibility system, via subsequent tax-for-fee reforms, and reaching its zenith in 2006 with the abolition of the 2,600-year-old agricultural taxes.[5]

Especially before the economic reforms of the late 1970s, communes (equivalent to today's townships) were fully responsible for the provision of local public goods in Chinese villages, given their comprehensive control over various resources under the commune system. Moreover, due to a lack of capital and the then-national policy of subsidizing industrialization through agricultural surplus, most local public goods in rural China, such as irrigation projects and roads, were provided through compulsory participation of rural residents and their contribution of in-kind labor.

Despite its inefficiency in generating incentives for agricultural production and economic activities, this "totalitarian model" was quite effective in accumulating sufficient resources for building reservoirs, paving roads, and establishing village-wide medical networks (W. Lin 2003; S. Wang 2011; S. Wu 2002; Ye 1997; B. Zhang and Chu 2006).[6]

Once the commune system was abolished, townships no longer bore the full responsibility for local public goods provision in Chinese villages. Village cadres had to come up with ways to at least partially fund various activities related to local public welfare, such as maintaining irrigation projects, paving roads, providing running water, and improving local education facilities. Before the late 1990s, village cadres could obtain financial resources from the village retention (tiliu) and various subsidies from the township comprehensive fee (tongchou), both of which were levied upon villagers.[7] However, since these fees were levied to some extent at village cadres' discretion, this generated serious problems in rural China— for example, widespread corruption among village cadres, an increased financial burden on villagers, and increasingly confrontational villager– cadre relationships. As previously discussed, because these problems posed significant challenges to the legitimacy of the Chinese Communist Party (CCP) regime and weakened the stability of its governance in rural areas, the Chinese government, after several local experiments and evaluations, launched the tax-for-fee reforms in the early 2000s and finally abolished agricultural taxes in 2006 (Kennedy 2007a; L. C. Li 2006; Sato 2008; L. Tsai 2011; Yep 2004).

Due to the loss of both economic and political leverage to secure financial resources or in-kind labor from villagers and insufficient fiscal transfers from upper-level governments, as well as administrative downsizing, fiscal and personnel resources at the disposal of township and village cadres are extremely limited. And, as Yep (2004) argues, village-level administration is the major victim of the financial squeeze; thus, many Chinese villages are left with limited capacity to provide local public goods. For instance, at the end of 2010, according to the most recent statistics from the Ministry of Water Resources (2011), only 54.7% of Chinese rural residents had access to tap water, and 50.4% of the arable lands in rural China did not have adequate and functional irrigation systems. This deficiency in local public goods provision in today's rural China goes beyond a large number of villagers' lack of access to running water and insufficient irrigation systems for agricultural production. To comprehensively evaluate the state of local public goods provision in Chinese villages, the 2008 National Village Survey (NVS) collected relevant information from 356 administrative villages, as shown in Table 4.1.

Table 4.1. LOCAL PUBLIC GOODS PROVISION IN RURAL CHINA

Local public goods	
Tap water	59.83% (213)
Paved roads within villages	71.63% (255)
Maintenance of irrigation projects	54.78% (195)
Maintenance of other public facilities	41.01% (146)
Provision of other public welfare	64.33% (229)

Source: 2008 National Village Survey (*N* = 356).
Note: Raw frequencies in parentheses.

Among all of the 356 sampled villages in 2008, 59.8% had access to tap water;[8] 71.6% of the sampled villages had paved roads. With regard to the maintenance of irrigation projects and other public facilities, the situation is much less favorable. At the time of the survey, only 54.8% of the sampled villages had maintained their irrigation projects in the past three years, and 41.0% of these villages had maintained other public facilities in the past three years. With respect to the residual category, "provision of other public welfare in the past three years," 64.3% of the village cadres responded with positive answers.[9] Given the size of rural China (with around 700,000 administrative villages) and the survey results, it is reasonable to argue that a huge number of Chinese villages suffer from the underprovision of local public goods.

Practically, there are three potential ways to fund the decentralized provision of local public goods in Chinese villages: fiscal transfers from upper-level governments, resources from village-owned collective economies, and contributions from villagers.[10] Although the Chinese government has steadily increased its fiscal transfers to agriculture and rural areas, there are still not enough resources to fund the provision of local public goods. According to a national sampling survey administered in late 2003, which covered 6 provinces, 36 counties, 216 townships, and 2,459 villages in China, only 36% of public projects in sampled villages were fully funded by fiscal transfers from upper-level governments, nearly half (46%) were funded by matching funds from both villages and their respective upper-level governments, and the rest (18%) were funded by villagers themselves (R. Luo et al. 2007). Similar results have been found by other scholars, using various local surveys (Kung et al. 2009; Sato 2008; X. Zhang et al. 2004). It seems that funding the provision of local public goods in contemporary rural China relies heavily on villages and the villagers themselves. Unfortunately, previous studies do not provide detailed information on the specific ways in which Chinese villages mobilize resources for their local public goods provision. To systematically evaluate the ways in which some Chinese villages raise the money for their local public goods, in the 2008 NVS, village cadres and treasurers were asked to provide detailed information on how they had managed to fund the provision of some local public goods in their villages by asking, "What was the key channel through which your village raised the money for that?" Their answers are coded and shown in Table 4.2.

Among the 195 villages that had maintained their irrigation projects over the past three years at the time of the survey, 35.9% primarily relied on fiscal transfers from upper-level governments and 39.5% of the sampled villages funded the maintenance of irrigation projects mainly out of village collective incomes, such as rents paid for collectively owned lands or profits from village-owned enterprises. Except for a small percentage of villages (3.1%) that borrowed money from banks and credit unions, the remaining villages relied primarily on money collected from all villagers (27.3%) or on donations from villagers (2.1%). The situation does not

Table 4.2. FUNDING SOURCES FOR LOCAL PUBLIC GOODS

Maintenance of irrigation projects (195)

Fiscal transfers from upper-level governments	35.90% (70)
Village collective income	39.49% (77)
Money collected from villagers	27.28% (53)
Donation from some villagers	2.05% (4)
Bank and credit union loans	3.08% (6)

Maintenance of other public facilities (146)

Fiscal transfers from upper-level governments	34.25% (50)
Village collective income	46.58% (68)
Money collected from villagers	20.55% (30)
Donation from some villagers	4.79% (7)
Bank and credit union loans	5.48% (8)

Providing other public welfare (229)

Fiscal transfers from upper-level governments	57.21% (131)
Village collective income	12.23% (28)
Money collected from villagers	24.89% (53)
Donation from some villagers	3.06% (7)
Bank and credit union loans	0.87% (2)

Source: 2008 National Village Survey (*N* = 356).
Note: Percentages do not add up to 100%. Answers mentioning different funding sources are coded for all appropriate categories.
Raw frequencies in parentheses.

change much in terms of the maintenance of other public facilities over the past three years: Among the 146 villages that had maintained other public facilities, 34.3% paid for this maintenance mainly using fiscal transfers from upper-level governments, 46.6% relied on village collective incomes for such projects, and the rest funded their maintenance primarily with the money collected from all villagers (20.6%) or from donations from villagers (4.8%). A small percentage of villages (5.5%) borrowed the money from banks or credit unions to pay for their public facility maintenance.

Although upper-level governments played a relatively active role in providing other public welfare—57.2% of the 229 villages that had provided other public welfare in the past three years relied primarily on their fiscal transfers—40.1% of the villages still had to fund the provision of public welfare mainly through their collective incomes (2.2%), money collected from villagers (24.9%), or donations from villagers (3.1%). Thus, in reality, a majority of Chinese villages depend on internal funding to provide local public goods, through collective incomes, contribution from villagers, or donations from some wealthy villagers.

Several interesting questions then arise: Confronted with the same decentralized provision of local public goods and lack of adequate fiscal transfers from upper-level governments, how do some villages manage to raise enough resources to pay for local public goods, while the others fail to do so? How do those villages solve the problem of collective action when asking for contributions from their villagers? Moreover, how can villagers hold village cadres accountable once economic resources are collected and at the disposal of their local leaders?

4.2 VARIOUS INSTITUTIONS FOR THE DECENTRALIZED PROVISION OF LOCAL PUBLIC GOODS

As discussed in Chapter 2, the two key problems of local governance, in general, and decentralized local public goods provision, in particular, are collective action and accountability. These two problems can be solved provided that appropriate institutions are available, regardless of the nature of these institutions. The literature on collective action contains abundant examples of different institutional solutions, ranging from relation-based institutions embedded in stable and reiterated interaction (Axelrod 1984; Nachbar 1989; Ostrom 1990) and community/social networks (Grould 1993; Lichbach 1995) to rule-based institutions with an intentional incorporation of selective incentives (Mancur Olson 1971), internal hierarchical structure, and contract systems (Lichbach 1995). The literature on accountability also contains various institutionalized means of holding bureaucrats or leaders accountable, again ranging from rule-based institutions that enforce the supervision of bureaucrats through meritocratic selection and evaluation (Evans 1995; Moe 1984) and transparent and competitive democratic elections (Przeworski et al. 1999; Strom et al. 2003) to relation-based institutions that are supported by encompassing and embedding solidarity groups (L. Tsai 2007a, b). More specifically, in local governance, both indigenous relation-based institutions (supported by powerful social sanctions) and imposed rule-based institutions (supported by effective enforcement) can deter and punish deviant and opportunistic behavior among community members and local leaders, although in distinct ways. Chinese villages also have varying experiences with both types of institutions in their decentralized provision of local public goods.

Indigenous Social Sanctions

As shown in Chapter 3, villages in rural China have had long and rich experiences of indigenous relation-based institutions in their local governance. Powerful social sanctions, gossip, moral pressure, and the enforcement of indigenous organizations such as religious or clan/lineage groups all have contributed to the regulation and coordination of within-village social interaction (e.g., Cohen 2005; Fei 1939, 1992; Kuhn 1975; L. Tsai 2007a, b; Wakeman and Grant 1975; G. Xiao 1960). As discussed in Chapter 2, social sanctions in villages are critical to the performance of indigenous relation-based institutions. Nevertheless, although there is extensive anecdotal evidence of the powerful social sanctions in many rural communities of contemporary China (e.g., B. Chen 2011a, 2011b; L. Dong 2008; X. He 2000, 2003a, 2007b, 2009; X. Zhao 2003), there is little systematic evidence. A major challenge to such research is the convergence of many of the consequences of both indigenous relation-based institutions and imposed rule-based institutions in Chinese villages. They impose similar constraints on villagers and local leaders in many domains and shape their behavior and attitudes in the same direction. Thus, it is difficult to establish a clear indicator of the strength of social sanctions in Chinese villages.

Taking advantage of the features of China's land-tenure system, I developed an objective indicator to gauge the strength of social sanctions in Chinese villages: the difficulty of adjusting land allocation to accommodate demographic changes in a village. I argue that despite its deficiencies, this indicator can objectively and effectively measure how powerful social sanctions are in a Chinese village, which reflects the effectiveness of indigenous relation-based institutions supported by the social sanctions.

In China, land is either state owned or collectively owned, and its dual land-tenure system separates land ownership from land-use rights. According to its Land Administration Law (drafted in 1986 and amended in 1998 and 2004), the state owns all urban land, while farmer collectives own all rural land. During the commune era, all villagers worked on collectively owned land and were compensated following a work-credit system. Since the reforms in 1978 and to generate more incentives for agricultural production, collectively owned land has been contracted out to be run by villagers independently for crop farming, forestry, animal husbandry, and fishery production. This practice was first officially endorsed in 1982 by the Chinese government and has been repeatedly upheld in subsequent official documents and policies. Further, to encourage peasants to invest more in agricultural production by increasing the stability in their land contracts, the central government officially stipulated that the term of land contracts should be at least fifteen years, which was extended to thirty years, and is now part of the Land Administration Law.[11] These long-term land contracts, however, also have generated some problems in rural China by depriving villages of flexibility and capacity in adjusting land allocation to accommodate demographic changes (Unger 2005, 2012; Hui Wang et al. 2011).

The allocation of land in the mid-1990s was based on the then-size of each family. After a number of years, allocated land may not be enough to support some families that now include daughters- and sons-in-law and newborns. Thus, there is a very strong demand in almost every village for reallocating land after some years to accommodate demographic changes. Nevertheless, since reallocating land indicates that some people are required to give up some of their land and others acquire more, it is understandable that villagers may have distinct views on this issue. Using survey data collected from rural China in 2008, Wang and his colleagues (2011, p. 811) find that:

> Compared to an interviewee whose family had no population change or experienced a net decrease in population from 1998, an interviewee whose family had added new members since 1998 was more likely to have negative view on land tenure policy. In other words, these villagers wanted more frequent farmland reallocation or readjustment. On the contrary, the significant and negative

coefficients for Landpc [land per capita] in these models indicate that families with higher landholding tend to be more reluctant to give up their land and be more supportive for land tenure policy. Likewise, the coefficients for Fampop [family size] are all negative and statistically significant, meaning that larger families are more likely to support long-term farmland tenure security. This is consistent with their interest of preserving the status quo and preventing their existing holdings from being redistributed.[12]

Because most land contracts were renegotiated in the mid-1990s, which was considered a second round of land contracting, they are still under the protection of the thirty-year contract term. Given the still-valid land contracts, no one can force villagers to give up any piece of their land, unless they voluntarily consent. In other words, thanks to the law and government policies—rule-based institutions imposed by the Chinese government—discontented villagers can effectively obstruct the reallocation process. And it is not rare to hear stories of land reallocation's being sabotaged by a single or a few villagers (L. Guo 2010).

Therefore, for successful land reallocation, it is critical to get the consent of those who will lose land in order to secure village-level consensus,[13] which is very challenging thanks to the land-tenure system endorsed by the Chinese government. Powerful social sanctions that enforce the indigenous norm of "live and let live," however, can help achieve village-level consensus for land reallocation. In a village of Shandong Province that I visited in the summer of 2006, villagers often cited a local saying—"Snakes shed every five years (*changchong tuibi, wunian yici*)"—to express their recognition of the need to adjust land allocation to accommodate demographic changes.[14] As long as everyone follows the locally shared norm (either due to one's internalization of the norm or because one is deterred by the possible sanction of being denounced and loathed by one's fellow villagers for rejecting land allocation) and recognizes the legitimacy of regular land reallocation, it should not be very difficult to secure the necessary village-level consensus for land reallocation.

In this case, imposed rule-based and indigenous relation-based institutions orient villagers' attitudes and behavior in opposite directions. The former legitimizes some villagers' self-interest in keeping their allocated land and exacerbates the challenge for adjusting land allocation; the latter enforces the indigenous norm of "live and let live" and helps secure the consent even from those who might be required to give up some of their land. Thus, if adjusting land allocation to accommodate demographic changes can be easily implemented within a village, it is reasonable to conclude that social sanctions are still powerful and that indigenous relation-based institutions supported by the social sanctions can still effectively perform in the village.

This measure, however, may underestimate the strength of social sanctions and the effectiveness of indigenous relation-based institutions. On many occasions, this kind of village-level consensus is not necessary for indigenous institutions to exert their influence, for instance, on conflict resolution or the maintenance of local order. Further, in many cases, indigenous institutions do not need to compete against the counteracting influence of rule-based institutions in order to shape villagers' attitudes and behavior, for instance, in regard to irrigation project maintenance. Given the difficulty of establishing a refined and continuous measure of the strength of social sanctions, I adopted this measure as the second-best choice. Moreover, this measure, due to the aforementioned deficiency, is likely to bias the empirical analyses toward null findings, thus rejecting my arguments.[15] Therefore, if I can still find strong evidence for the positive role of indigenous institutions in the decentralized provision of local public goods in Chinese villages, I should have more confidence in my theoretical arguments. In the 2008 NVS, village cadres were asked how difficult it was to adjust land allocation to accommodate demographic changes in their respective villages; their answers are displayed in Table 4.3.

As seen in the Table 4.3, 41% of the sampled villages found it impossible to adjust land allocation to accommodate demographic changes. Nearly the same percentage of these villages (39.6%) faced serious difficulty in reallocating land. This widely reported resistance in adjusting land allocation to accommodate demographic changes in rural China is compatible with other scholars' findings on the infrequency of land reallocations in Chinese villages since the 1990s (Brandt et al. 2002; Kung 2000; Hui Wang et al. 2011). It also speaks to the effectiveness of the thirty-year-long land contracts and related national policies in securing the stability of Chinese peasants' land-use rights.

Table 4.3. DIFFICULTY IN ADJUSTING LAND ALLOCATION

Is it possible to adjust land allocation among villagers to accommodate demographic changes within the village?	
Impossible	41.01% (146)
Very difficult	39.61% (141)
Easy to implement	14.04% (50)

Source: 2008 National Village Survey (*N* = 356).
Note: Nineteen villages without pertinent information.
Raw frequencies in parentheses.

As previously discussed, villagers who are not happy with land reallocation can legitimately reject and obstruct the whole process, thanks to the
Rural Land Contract Law and the Land Administration Law. However,
adjusting land allocation to accommodate demographic changes still can
be done in certain villages, despite the hurdles.[16] As seen in Table 4.3, 14%
of the sampled villages found it easy to reallocate land among their
villagers. In these villages, social sanctions are still very powerful
in enforcing indigenously cultivated norms, reorienting villagers' attitudes and behavior, and perhaps even counteracting the influence of rule-
based institutions imposed by the government. This also suggests the
potentially effective role of indigenous relation-based institutions, as
supported by powerful social sanctions, in these villages' local public
goods provision.

Given the recent research on the role of solidarity groups in the provision of local public goods in rural China (L. Tsai 2002, 2007a, 2007b;
T. Xiao 2002, 2010), it is reasonable to question whether the aforementioned measure of the strength of social sanctions is simply an intervening variable that connects solidarity groups to village local public goods.
Although the existence of solidarity groups might address the problems of
collective action and accountability through the provision of social identities or cleavages for mobilization, these groups are neither sufficient nor
necessary for effective social sanctions against deviant and opportunistic
behavior in local communities. In some villages in North China without a
history of active solidarity groups, scholars still observe powerful social
sanctions in regulating and coordinating villagers' behavior and social
interaction (e.g., X. He 2003a; Pomeranz 1993; X. Zhao 2003). Once the
authority and resources of clan/lineage organizations, a critical type of
solidarity group in rural China, are weakened or deprived, however, their
existence does not necessarily guarantee effective social sanctions (T. Xiao
2010). In this book, I argue that powerful social sanctions are a critical
foundation for any indigenous relation-based institution, in the form of
solidarity groups or other facades. Thus, to effectively study the role of
indigenous institutions in the provision of local public goods, in particular, and decentralized governance, in general, in rural China, scholars
should pay more attention to the foundations and underlying mechanisms, rather than specific facades, of indigenous institutions.

Given the salience of clan/lineage organizations in rural China,
I specifically check the possible relationships between various conventionally used measures of clan/lineage organizations and my measure of
the strength of social sanctions in Chinese villages. Table 4.4 presents
information on clan/lineage organizations in all sampled villages, using

Table 4.4. CLAN/LINEAGE ORGANIZATIONS IN RURAL CHINA

Power of clans before 1949	
No clans	66.85% (238)
Some but not powerful	28.65% (102)
Very powerful	3.65% (13)

Number of ancestor halls with spirit tablets	
None	80.61% (287)
One	10.39% (37)
Two	2.81% (10)
Three	0.84% (3)
Four +	5.34% (19)

Clan structure	
One clan	3.93% (14)
One dominant clan with several other small ones	6.46% (23)
Two clans with equivalent power	2.53% (9)
Three clans with equivalent power	1.97% (7)
Two major clans with several other small ones	4.21% (15)
Three major clans with several other small ones	3.37% (12)
Multiple surnames	66.29% (236)

Source: 2008 National Village Survey (*N* = 356).
Note: Raw frequencies in parentheses.

different measures: (1) respondents' perceptions of the power of clans before 1949, (2) the number of ancestor halls with spirit tablets, and (3) village cadres' description of the clan structure within their respective villages.

Depending on the measures used, from 66.3% to 80.6% of the sampled villages did not witness active clan/lineage organizations at the time of the survey, and 66.9% of the villages reported a lack of powerful clan/lineage activities even before the CCP penetrated rural China, imposed its totalitarian institutions, and actively campaigned against clan/lineage organizations. In regard to the encompassing and embedding clan/lineage organizations that contemporary literature on China's rural governance emphasizes, the situation is even more discouraging: Only 10% of the sampled villages had encompassing and embedding clan/lineage organizations (i.e., a dominant clan for the whole village).[17]

Moreover, there is insufficient empirical evidence that encompassing and embedding clan/lineage organizations generate powerful social sanctions that facilitate land reallocation for accommodating demographic changes in Chinese villages. Table 4.5 displays the results of the cross-tabulation of the difficulty of land reallocation with the existence of encompassing and embedding clan/lineage organizations.

As shown in Table 4.5, Chinese villages with encompassing and embedding clan/lineage organizations reported less difficulty in reallocating land. For instance, using the number of ancestor halls with one spirit tablet as the proxy, villages with encompassing and embedding clan/lineage organizations were 9.7% more likely to report ease in land reallocation to accommodate demographic changes. This relationship, however, is statistically insignificant even at the 0.1 level. When a different measure (reported clan structure) is used, the advantage of villages with encompassing and embedding clan/lineage organizations vanishes. Moreover, a number of villages without encompassing and embedding clan/lineage organizations did report ease in land reallocation.

Based on the above information, it appears that social sanctions in some Chinese villages are still powerful enough to effectively regulate villagers' behavior, and that these social sanctions are not necessarily related to encompassing and embedding clan/lineage organizations. In these villages, social sanctions even counteract the externally imposed land-tenure system as well as secure consensus among villagers for land reallocation to accommodate demographic changes. As discussed in Chapter 2, such powerful social sanctions are critical to indigenous relation-based institutions and, thus, strongly suggest the effective role of such indigenous institutions in rural China's decentralized provision of

Table 4.5. LAND REALLOCATION AND ENCOMPASSING/EMBEDDING CLAN ORGANIZATIONS

	Adjusting Land Allocation	
Ancestor halls with spirit tablets	Impossible or very difficult	Easy
Other	86.14% (261)	13.86% (42)
One dominant clan	76.47% (26)	23.53% (8)
(Chi-square, DF)	(2.261, 1) with p-value = 0.133	
Clan structure		
Other	85.66% (227)	14.34% (38)
One dominant clan	85.71% (30)	14.29% (5)
(Chi-square, DF)	(0.0001, 1) with p-value = 0.993	

Source: 2008 National Village Survey (N = 356).
Note: Raw frequencies in parentheses.

local public goods. Moreover, this new measure of the strength of social sanctions is not simply an intervening variable that connects encompassing and embedding solidarity groups to local public goods. It speaks more broadly to the foundation and underlying mechanisms of indigenous relation-based institutions that could have varying facades. In the following analyses, this measure of the strength of social sanctions is used as the proxy for the effectiveness of indigenous relation-based institutions.

Imposed Grassroots Democracy

As discussed in Chapter 3, grassroots elections in rural China were originally developed by some villages to fill the vacuum of public authority caused by the collapse of the commune system in the early 1980s (O'Brien and Li 2000). Later, this institutional innovation, after some debate, was recognized and endorsed by the Chinese government as the official institution for self-governance in rural China. After some discussion of its institutional form and associated settings, in 1998, village committees, selected and organized on the basis of direct elections, were officially imposed upon Chinese villages as the officially sanctioned rule-based institution for their governance. According to the 2008 NVS, all sampled villages had regularly organized grassroots elections to choose local leaders at the time of the survey and 96.4% had organized more than three rounds of village elections.

Village committees' officially sanctioned role in rural China's governance, particularly in providing local public goods and improving local public welfare, is clearly stipulated in the eleventh article of China's Constitution and the second article of the Organic Law of Village Committees (OLVC):

> Article 2: The village committee is the primary mass organization of self-government, in which the villagers manage their own affairs, educate themselves, and serve their own needs and in which elections are conducted, decisions are adopted, administration is maintained, and supervision is exercised by democratic means. The village committee shall manage the public affairs and public welfare undertakings of the village, mediate disputes among the villagers, help maintain public order, and convey the villagers' opinions and demands and make suggestions to the people's government.

In addition to overseeing the socioeconomic and political lives of rural communities, village committees are required to assist cooperation among villagers and coordinate their behavior, as stipulated in the fifth article of the OLVC:

> Article 5: The village committee shall support the villagers and assist them in their efforts to set up various forms of cooperative and other economic undertakings in accordance with law, provide services and coordination for production in the village, and promote the development of rural production and construction and the socialist market economy.

To ensure that village committees have the recognized authority for effective governance and to establish built-in mechanisms to constrain village cadres' behavior, particularly their abuse of power, the Chinese government identified democratic elections as the only legitimate means of selecting and organizing these village committees. This is clearly stipulated in the eleventh article of the OLVC:

> Article 11: The chairman, vice-chairman (vice-chairmen) and members of a village committee shall be elected directly by the villagers. No organization or individual may designate, appoint or replace any member of a village committee.

Theoretically, village committees organized through democratic elections can take advantage of their publicly endorsed authority to govern locally. More specifically, endowed with the popular mandate via democratic elections, village cadres are expected to effectively promote cooperation among villagers and secure necessary resources from villagers and other sources to fund local public goods provision. Further, facing regular and competitive democratic elections, village cadres are expected to be held accountable to their constituents, the villagers. Therefore, villagers' evaluations and ballots, as well as the real possibility of being voted out of office, are expected to channel village cadres' efforts and performance toward the public interest and, thus, effectively deter them from various rent-seeking activities. As a consequence, well-established grassroots democracy is expected to improve China's rural governance (Manion 1996, 2006; L. Tsai 2008), in general, and its local public goods provision, in particular (Y.-t. Chang and Wu 2011; R. Luo et al. 2007; Sato 2008; X. Zhang et al. 2004).[18]

All of these expected positive impacts of grassroots democracy on rural China's governance are contingent upon its transparent and competitive nature. Only transparent and competitive elections can generate the publicly endorsed authority for village cadres and simultaneously hold village cadres accountable to their constituencies, which addresses the problems of collective action and accountability in Chinese villages' decentralized provision of local public goods. Unfortunately, the implementation of village elections is far from even in rural China, as many scholars have already documented, for reasons such as manipulation by upper-level governments (particularly township governments) for political and policy motives (Kennedy 2002, 2009; Landry et al. 2010; Shi 1999b) and different levels of economic development in the villages (R. Hu 2005; Oi 1996; Shi 1999a, 2000c).[19] In practice, some village elections have been implemented closely in accordance with the OLVC, ensuring competition among multiple candidates and the quality of the whole electoral institution, while other village elections have been manipulated to varying extents, which significantly weakens the embedded mechanism of accountability and elected village cadres' public authority (J. Lu 2012; L. Tsai 2010).

In addition to promulgating that administrative leaders of any village should be directly elected by its residents and such elections should be held every three years, the OLVC also provides detailed stipulations on how to implement village elections:

Article 13: Members of Village Election Committee should be recommended by Villager Assembly (*cunmin huiyi*) or Villager Small Groups (*cunmin xiaozu*).

Article 14: Nominations should be directly made by eligible villagers. And the number of candidates should be more than the number of positions.

To what extent are the elections in Chinese villages implemented according to such stipulations? In the 2008 NVS, village cadres were asked for detailed information on various electoral procedures adopted in their most recent village elections by the time of the survey; the results are summarized in Table 4.6.[20]

In their most recent elections, by the time of the survey, 29.9% of the sampled villages followed recommendations from their villager assemblies and 9.3% took recommendations from villager small groups, both of which are compatible with the OLVC. Nevertheless, 53.7% used villager representative assemblies, 3.7% followed the instructions of party branches, and a small percentage of villages took orders from township governments (0.8%) or outgoing village committees (1.7%).

Similar variances emerge when the measures used for nominating candidates are examined. Compatible with the OLVC, primary election (*haixuan*) (51.1%), joint nomination by eligible villagers (30.6%), and self-nomination (10.1%) were adopted by a fair number of the sampled villages. Nevertheless, in some villages, party branches (5.9%), higher-level officials (1.7%), villager small groups/villager representative assemblies

Table 4.6. MEASURES ADOPTED FOR VILLAGE COMMITTEE ELECTIONS

Organization of village election committee	
Recommended by the villager assembly	28.93% (103)
Recommended by villager small groups	9.27% (33)
Recommended by the villager representative assembly	53.65% (191)
Recommended by the party branch	3.65% (13)
Recommended by the outgoing village committee	1.69% (6)
Recommended by the township government	0.84% (3)
Nomination of candidates	
Primary election (*haixuan*)	51.12% (182)
Joint nomination by eligible villagers	30.62% (109)
Self-nomination	10.11% (36)
Nomination by the party branch and other organizations	5.90% (21)
Nomination by higher-level officials	1.69% (6)
Nomination by villager small groups or villager representative assembly	27.81% (99)
Nomination by village election committee	5.90% (21)
Finalization of formal candidates	
Pre-election (*yuxuan*)	42.98% (153)
Finalized by villager representative assembly	48.60% (173)
Finalized through internal negotiations (*xieshang yunniang*)	12.64% (45)
Finalized by village election committee	9.55% (34)
Finalized by the party branch	1.97% (7)
Finalized by higher-level officials	3.65% (13)
Multiple candidates	
Committee chairman	90.45% (322)
Committee members	90.45% (322)

Source: 2008 National Village Survey (*N* = 356).
Note: Percentages do not add up to 100% due to the adoption of multiple measures at some stages. Raw frequencies in parentheses.

(27.8%), or village election committees (5.9%) also played significant roles, which is expressly barred by the OLVC.

When there are too many candidates, the candidate pool has to be narrowed. Accordingly, 43.0% of the sampled villages used pre-election (*yuxuan*). Other sampled villages chose different strategies: Villager representative assemblies (48.6%), internal negotiations (*xieshang yunniang*) (12.6%), village election committees (9.6%), party branches (2.0%), or higher-level officials (3.7%) influenced the selection of finalists.

With regard to adopting multiple-candidate elections (*cha'e xuanju*), the results presented in Table 4.6 suggest much less variance. Of the sampled villages, 90.5% used multiple-candidate elections to select the chairmen of their village committees, and the same percentage of the villages adopted the multiple-candidate elections for choosing other members of their village committees.

Because more than one measure could be used at various stages of village elections, to rigorously evaluate the quality of these villages' electoral institutions, I strictly assess each procedure against the OLVC. Any measure not officially sanctioned by the OLVC is coded as a violation. Table 4.7 shows the percentages of the sampled villages that strictly followed the OLVC in implementing their most recent elections by the time of the survey. For the longitudinal comparison, I also include comparable information collected from another two national village surveys implemented in 2002 and 2005, respectively.[21]

Among the Chinese villages surveyed in 2008, 38.2% organized village election committees strictly following the OLVC, and 65.2% nominated their candidates through various legitimate means. With regard to finalist identification, only 31.7% did not violate the OLVC. Furthermore, 86.5% had multiple candidates for both chairman and member elections. The situation is quite worrisome when the overall quality of village elections is examined. In this case, to be an overall high-quality village election, all stages of the election must be implemented by strictly following the OLVC. When this criterion is strictly applied, as shown at the bottom of Table 4.7, only 10.4% of the sampled villages had executed high-quality electoral institutions, ensured by noncompromised democratic and transparent electoral procedures, in their most recent village elections by the time of the survey. When compared to the situation revealed in comparable surveys in 2002 and 2005, we can conclude that (1) the overall quality of grassroots democracy in rural China does vary dramatically across vil-

Table 4.7. QUALITY OF ELECTORAL INSTITUTIONS IN RURAL CHINA

	2002	2005	2008
Organization of village election committee	42.32% (102)	48.48% (183)	38.20% (136)
Nomination of candidates	51.87% (125)	75.73% (287)	65.17% (232)
Finalization of formal candidates	29.46% (71)	36.94% (140)	31.74% (113)
Multiple candidates	79.67% (192)	91.03% (345)	86.52% (308)
Electoral institution as a whole	11.20% (27)	16.62% (63)	10.39% (37)

Sources: 2002 (*N* = 241), 2005 (*N* = 379), and 2008 (*N* = 356) National Village Surveys.
Note: Raw frequencies in parentheses.

lages and (2) almost ten years after grassroots democracy was officially sanctioned and imposed on Chinese villages as the institutional foundation for local governance, this rule-based institution has not yet been widely established as stipulated by the OLVC.

With rigged elections, villagers cannot effectively punish village cadres with their ballots or hold them accountable for their unsatisfying performance or rent-seeking activities. Moreover, once such breaches in village elections are observed by average villagers, the public authority associated with village committees is likely to be impaired, and villagers may no longer regard elected village cadres as local leaders with a popular mandate. Consequently, village cadres, due to rigged elections, may not be able to effectively promote cooperation among villagers, secure necessary resources from villagers and other sources to fund local public goods provision, or improve local governance. In the following analyses, I use the overall quality of electoral institutions in village elections as the proxy for the quality of imposed rule-based institutions in Chinese villages.

Empirically, there are two ways to operationalize the quality of electoral institutions: a summary index or a binary indicator. The first strategy assigns equal weight to different procedures, while the second strategy assigns "veto power" to each procedure in determining the democratic nature of village elections. Because (1) the violation in any electoral procedure may make villagers perceive their elections as rigged and challenge the public authority of elected village cadres and (2) there is no information to evaluate the relative importance of different electoral procedures in shaping villagers' assessment of the integrity of village elections, I take the second approach and assign "veto power" to each procedure in assessing the overall quality of electoral institutions in Chinese villages. Similar to the measure of the strength of social sanctions in rural China, this more rigorous measure of the quality of electoral institutions is likely to bias my subsequent empirical analyses toward null findings. Again, significant findings on the positive role of transparent and competitive village elections in contributing to local public goods provision, once confirmed, should lead to much more confidence in my arguments.

Indigenous and Imposed Institutions and Local Public Goods Provision

As discussed in Chapter 2, institutions, whether relation-based or rule-based, can help sustain local governance, providing they can effectively address the problems of collective action and accountability. For the decentralized provision of local public goods in rural China, this argument is expected to be valid as well. Thus, any villages that have either indigenous relation-based institutions supported by powerful social sanctions or high-quality, imposed rule-based institutions as embodied in transparent and competitive village elections should witness better provision of public goods, *ceteris paribus*. For villages with neither type of institution, their provision of public goods is likely to suffer from the curse of the collective action problem or the lack of any mechanism to hold local leaders accountable. Table 4.8 displays the institutional environments of the sampled villages, based on previously discussed proxies of indigenous relation-based (strength of social sanctions) and imposed rule-based institutions (quality of electoral institutions).

As shown in Table 4.8, in 12.4% of the sampled villages, there were still powerful social sanctions that could effectively ensure that indigenous relation-based institutions enforce community-shared norms, facilitate cooperation, and deter deviant and opportunistic behavior among villagers and village cadres. In these villages, however, grassroots democracy did not follow the OLVC in practice. In 7.9% of the sampled villages, grassroots elections did follow the OLVC in practice; therefore, these transparent and competitive elections could have generated widely recognized public authority associated with village cadres, eased resource mobilization for local public welfare and public goods provision, and held cadres accountable. In these villages, however, social sanctions were not powerful enough to secure village-level consensus on issues such as land reallocation. In 1.7% of the sampled villages, both powerful social sanctions and transparent and competitive village elections were observed. Unfortunately, in 72.8% of the sampled villages, neither indigenous relation-based nor imposed rule-based institutions seemed to work, and, thus, the vast majority of villages may witness some inadequate provision of public goods. In sum, 21.9% of the sampled villages had functional institutions, either indigenous relation-based or imposed rule-based, and are expected to enjoy a higher level of provision of local public goods.[22]

Table 4.8. INSTITUTIONAL ENVIRONMENTS IN RURAL CHINA

Rural institutional environment	
Quality indigenous relation-based institutions only	12.36% (44)
Quality imposed rule-based institutions only	7.87% (28)
Both quality indigenous and imposed institutions	1.69% (6)
None	72.75% (259)

Source: 2008 National Village Survey (N = 356).
Note: Raw frequencies in parentheses.

The cross-tabulation results presented in Table 4.9 provide some preliminary evidence on the impact of relation-based and rule-based institutions on the decentralized provision of local public goods in Chinese villages. As shown in Table 4.9, the level of public goods provision in the sampled villages with functional institutions, either indigenous relation-based or imposed rule-based, is higher across the board. Specifically, when villagers' access to tap water (9.8%), within-village paved roads (12.9%), and provision of other public welfare (8.8%) are examined, the differences are statistically significant.

To more rigorously examine the effects of indigenous and imposed institutions on rural China's local public goods provision, I use a more appropriate and sophisticated statistical modeling technique, while controlling for various socioeconomic, demographic, ecological, and political features of the sampled villages.[23]

Economic Features

As discussed in previous sections, the provision of local public goods in rural China has been highly decentralized. Due to limited fiscal transfers from upper-level governments, villages have to fund their public projects, facilities, and welfare programs primarily through their collective incomes or contributions from villagers. Therefore, economic resources available to villages and villagers should be of great significance in this decentralized local public goods provision. To measure the economic resources that villagers have for the provision of local public goods through their collective efforts, I use the annual per capita income in a village in 2007.[24] The

---

Table 4.9. PUBLIC GOODS PROVISION IN DIFFERENT INSTITUTIONAL ENVIRONMENTS

	Tap Water	Paved Roads	Irrigation Project Maintenance	Other Public Facility Maintenance	Other Public Welfare
Institutional solutions					
Relation-based or rule-based	70.00%	83.95%	56.37%	47.44%	74.36%
None	60.16%	71.06%	55.56%	41.57%	65.59%
(T, *p*-value)	(1.581, 0.115)⁺	(2.152, 0.032)**	(0.129, 0.898)	(0.915, 0.361)	(1.444, 0.149)⁺

Source: 2008 National Village Survey (N = 356).
Note: ⁺One-tailed test significant at the 0.1 level.
**Two-tail test significant at the 0.05 level.

collective income of a village in 2007 is used to measure the financial capacity of a village in providing local public goods.[25]

Demographic and Ecological Features

The size of the population who stays in villages, excluding those working as migrants in other cities or provinces, is used as a control for the impact of group size (Mancur Olson 1971) and the potential demand for public goods on the provision of local public goods.[26] The existence of encompassing and embedding clan/lineage organizations also is included as a critical control (L. Tsai 2007a, b).[27] The pattern of housing is an important control for the ecological features of Chinese villages. In some villages, houses cluster together within a very small space, while in other villages, the houses are scattered across a large area; thus, different ecological features may have varying impacts on villagers' social interactions, which can have significant consequences for their collective action (D. Zhao 1998) and local public goods provision.[28] Lastly, the dominance of rice in local agricultural production is used to control for possible varying demand for irrigation facilities and projects.[29]

Political Features

The distance to township seats is used as a proxy for possible influence from upper-level governments.[30] If village committees have signed "political contracts" with upper-level governments in regard to local public goods provision, they are under pressure to fulfill these obligations.[31] Being designated as a model village of self-governance also is expected to be associated with the provision of local public goods in a village, due to either more fiscal transfers from upper-level governments or upper-level governments' intentional selection of villages with more satisfying performance in providing local public goods.[32]

In the previous cross-tabulation analysis, as shown in Table 4.9, specific public goods are treated as independent from each other; nevertheless, in reality, the provision of the specific public goods is likely to be under the same budget and other socioeconomic constraints. To effectively account for these socioeconomic constraints in subsequent empirical analysis, and given the dichotomous nature of the dependent variables, I follow the strategy of multivariate probit regression (MPR) (Cappelari and Jenkins 2003) and implement statistical analysis in the framework of structural equation modeling (SEM).[33] It is worth noting that the corresponding null-hypotheses for this empirical exercise are:

H4.1: *The impact of a transparent and competitive village election is not statistically different from zero across all five equations simultaneously.*

H4.2: *The impact of powerful social sanctions is not statistically different from zero across all five equations simultaneously.*

Table 4.10 provides detailed results of MPR with nonstandardized regression coefficients and robust standard errors corrected for clustering. Due to the classic problem in analyzing survey data (i.e., missing items), the MPR results are based on the averaged information from five imputed complete datasets, following Rubin's Rule (King et al. 2001; Rubin 1987).[34]

The focus of this analysis is Path II displayed in Figure 1.1—that is, the impacts of indigenous relation-based institutions and imposed rule-based institutions on local public goods provision in Chinese villages. The pertinent information is highlighted in Table 4.10. It is important to point out that, given the correlated error terms in the MPR model, the appropriate statistical test for the impacts of indigenous and imposed institutions is not the conventional Z-test for the individual coefficient associated with each specific public good but, rather, the joint Chi-square test shown in the last column of Table 4.10. As indicated by the significant F-statistics, there is sufficient statistical evidence for the significant and positive contribution of both indigenous relation-based institutions (measured by the strength of social sanctions) and imposed rule-based institutions (measured by the quality of electoral institutions) to the decentralized provision of public goods in rural China, even after controlling for possible confounding factors.[35] This also confirms some recent research's findings on the positive impacts of both formal and informal institutions on public goods provision in rural China (Kung et al. 2009).[36]

Some control variables perform as expected. First, economic resources matter a lot. Both annual per capita income and village collective income play significant positive roles in local public goods provision. The more economic resources available to Chinese villages and their residents, *ceteris paribus*, the better the provision of local public goods. Second, model village status also is strongly associated with better local public goods provision in Chinese villages. Third, communal ecological features also matter in the decentralized provision of local public goods. Villages in which residents live close to each other, *ceteris paribus*, perform better

Table 4.10. MULTIVARIATE PROBIT REGRESSIONS FOR LOCAL PUBLIC GOODS PROVISION IN RURAL CHINA

Structural model	Tap Water	Paved Roads	Irrigation Projects	Other Public Facilities	Other public welfare	Averaged Joint Chi-square Test
Size of population staying in village	0.065 (0.125)	0.403 (0.152)***	-0.031 (0.118)	0.151 (0.117)	0.046 (0.119)	
Distance to the township seat	-0.375 (0.128)***	-0.140 (0.147)	-0.008 (0.101)	0.126 (0.115)	-0.125 (0.124)	
Annual income per capita	0.259 (0.140)*	0.358 (0.155)**	0.174 (0.122)	0.201 (0.112)*	0.333 (0.119)***	
Village collective income	0.011 (0.018)	0.055 (0.021)***	0.082 (0.019)***	0.081 (0.021)***	0.033 (0.020)*	
Transparent and competitive village election	0.159 (0.290)	1.343 (0.453)***	-0.335 (0.230)	0.125 (0.255)	0.391 (0.231)*	$F_{(5, 618.7)} = 2.555$**
Easiness of reallocating land	0.438 (0.247)*	0.264 (0.252)	0.209 (0.212)	0.133 (0.240)	0.486 (0.272)*	$F_{(5, 2009.9)} = 1.890$*
A dominant clan	-0.301 (0.230)	-0.153 (0.250)	-0.230 (0.223)	0.085 (0.233)	0.633 (0.306)**	
Model village of self-governance	0.394 (0.157)**	0.421 (0.188)**	-0.076 (0.161)	0.174 (0.159)	0.033 (0.164)	
Official obligation to public goods provision	-0.074 (0.206)	-0.095 (0.247)	0.122 (0.222)	0.286 (0.217)	0.131 (0.219)	
Clustered housing	0.167 (0.133)	0.441 (0.143)***	0.196 (0.105)*	0.227 (0.114)**	0.079 (0.142)	
Rice as the primary agricultural product			0.245 (0.147)*			
Intercept	2.134 (1.364)	6.372 (1.622)***	2.288 (1.282)*	4.606 (1.275)***	2.876 (1.165)**	

Covariance between variance components

	Tap Water	Paved Roads	Irrigation Projects	Other Public Facilities
Paved roads	0.297 (0.104)***			
Irrigation projects	0.014 (0.095)	0.013 (0.113)		
Other public facilities	0.240 (0.098)**	0.244 (0.028)**	0.373 (0.088)***	
Other public welfare	0.141 (0.083)*	0.234 (0.103)**	0.145 (0.097)	0.169 (0.089)*

(continued)

[107]

Table 4.10. (CONTINUED)

Structural model	Tap Water	Paved Roads	Irrigation Projects	Other Public Facilities	Other public welfare	Averaged Joint Chi-square Test
Model fit indexes						
Chi-square	Mean = 2.501, Standard Deviation = 1.199, MI = 5					$F_{(4, 49.01)} = 0.225$
CFI	Mean = 0.999, Standard Deviation = 0.001, MI = 5					
TLI	Mean = 0.997, Standard Deviation = 0.003, MI = 5					
RMSEA	Mean = 0.003, Standard Deviation = 0.006, MI = 5					

Source: 2008 China Village Survey (N = 356).
Note: WLSMV estimation in Mplus 6.11.
Averaged coefficients in cells (five imputed datasets with the MI procedure in STATA 11).
Averaged robust standard errors in parentheses, corrected for clustering around counties.
* $p < 0.1$ ** $p < 0.05$ *** $p < 0.01$.

[108]

than those in which houses are scattered, with significant distance in between. Further, in terms of the regular maintenance of irrigation projects, villages in which rice is the key crop outperform others in which wheat and corn are the key crops.

In summary, empirical data from the 2008 NVS show that, *inter alia*, both indigenous relation-based and imposed rule-based institutions significantly improved the decentralized provision of local public goods in the sampled villages. More specifically, as previously discussed, powerful social sanctions support the performance of indigenous relation-based institutions in Chinese villages, which in turn enforce community-shared norms, facilitate cooperation among villagers, and deter deviant and opportunistic behavior among average villagers and village cadres. Transparent and competitive grassroots elections also can generate publicly recognized authority associated with elected village cadres, facilitate the mobilization of resources for local public goods and other public welfare, and hold cadres accountable to the public interest.

4.3 A HYBRID VERSION OF LOCAL PUBLIC GOODS PROVISION AND RURAL–URBAN MIGRATION

An important finding from the aforementioned empirical analyses, as shown in Table 4.8, is that neither indigenous relation-based institutions nor imposed rule-based institutions perform equally effectively across Chinese villages. Significant variance is observed in rural China in regard to the quality of indigenous and imposed institutions. In some villages, only indigenous relation-based institutions work; in other villages, only imposed rule-based institutions function; and, in still other villages, neither indigenous institutions nor imposed institutions perform well. What, then, can account for this variance in the institutional foundations of the decentralized local public goods provision in Chinese villages? I argue that, as discussed in detail in Chapter 2 and summarized in Table 2.2, Chinese villages' communal structural features significantly shape the performance of indigenous relation-based and imposed rule-based institutions in supporting their local public goods provision; moreover, such communal structure features are transformed by the numerous socioeconomic changes brought about by the modernization process, including more contact with the outside world, exposure to different information and values, and opportunities to leave villages for different, if not better, lives in urban areas. Among these changes, cityward migration poses the most serious challenge.

Thanks to their well-maintained close-knit community structure, in Chinese villages with a low level of cityward migration, cooperative norms cultivated through frequent and continuous social interaction and transmitted through socialization are conducive to cooperation and collective efforts among villagers. Their within-community dense and extended social networks facilitate both the timely transmission of information and the creation of cross-issue linkages in social interaction. Embedded within such a favorable social environment, indigenous institutions supported by social sanctions can effectively regulate and coordinate social interaction within the villages, punish and deter deviant and opportunistic behavior, and hold village cadres accountable. Nevertheless, cityward migration can disrupt the frequent and continuous interaction among villagers and loosen the dense and extended social networks, which in turn challenges and impairs the performance of indigenous relation-based institutions.

H4.3: *The effectiveness of indigenous relation-based institutions declines as more villagers leave their home communities and work in cities far away as migrant workers.*

As demonstrated in Chapter 3, when newly designed rule-based institutions are imposed onto Chinese villages, they are not transplanted into an institutional vacuum but, rather, into a social environment with a long and rich history of various indigenous institutions. When both institutional settings are available in Chinese villages for similar purposes, their change and performance are determined by villagers' contextualized choices, which are again constrained and shaped by their respective communal structural features. In loosely coupled villages, within-community social interaction and social networks may not enable powerful social sanctions that ensure the effective performance of indigenous relation-based institutions. Thus, there are strong incentives among villagers to seek alternative and more effective institutional solutions. Meanwhile, the impaired but somewhat functional social networks in loosely coupled villages can help overcome the incurred coordination costs; thus, villagers can still manage to coordinate their choices of imposed institutions as the publicly recognized and accepted institutional solutions for local governance issues. Therefore, given the weakened efficacy of indigenous institutions and the impaired but somewhat functional social networks, imposed institutions are more likely to be embraced in loosely coupled villages.

In extreme cases of atomized villages characterized by a dearth of vibrant within-community interaction and collapsed social networks, neither indigenous relation-based institutions nor imposed rule-based ones can survive. Although there are strong incentives among villagers to seek alternative and effective institutional solutions to replace vitiated indigenous institutions and even bear the necessary switching costs, they suffer from the lack of the minimum level of coordination necessary for the establishment and effective performance of imposed institutions. In these cases, the incurred coordination costs are too high to overcome. As previously discussed, with increasing cityward migration, original close-knit villages may be transformed into loosely coupled ones. In some places, when this cityward migration approaches exodus, the structural challenge may even lead to atomized villages.

> H4.4: *Imposed rule-based institutions are more likely to be established and practiced with high quality in villages with a medium level of cityward migration.*

> H4.5: *In villages with a very high level of cityward migration, neither indigenous institutions nor imposed institutions can function effectively.*

Again, I use the 2008 NVS data to test the three hypotheses. In the 2008 NVS, the number of villagers who worked as migrants in places far away from their home communities in 2007 was reported from each sampled village.[37] I divide this number by the total population of each village to get a percentage and use this as the proxy of the impact of cityward migration on the communal structures of Chinese villages. Then I determine how the cityward migration in rural China affects its institutional environments.

For illustrative purposes, I divide all villages into ten groups, with each representing an evenly divided interval of the distribution of the percentage of migrant workers.[38] Then the respective percentages of villages within each group that (1) have organized transparent and competitive elections (i.e., imposed institutions, represented by black columns) and (2) reported ease in adjusting land allocation to accommodate demographic changes (i.e., indigenous institutions, represented by gray columns) are illustrated in Figure 4.1.

As displayed in Figure 4.1, in the ninth and tenth groups of the sampled villages with a high level of outward migration, none found it easy to reallocate land to accommodate demographic changes. On the contrary, in villages with a lower level of outward migration, for instance, the first group, over 20% of these villages found it easy to reallocate land. Despite some irregularities, the general trend is that, as outward migration increases, social sanctions are less effective in securing village-level consensus on critical issues such as land reallocation. This indicates that the effectiveness of indigenous relation-based institutions may decrease as more villagers leave via cityward migration.

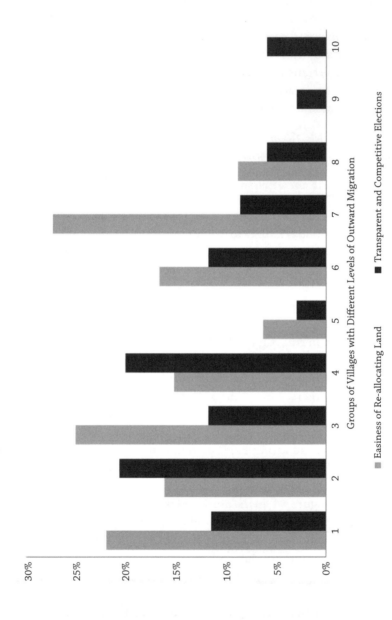

Figure 4.1:
Cityward Migration and Different Institutional Environments
Source: 2008 China Village Survey (*N* = 356).

The situation for organizing transparent and competitive elections is different in Chinese villages with different levels of outward migration. Among the sampled villages with a high level of outward migration, for instance, in the ninth and tenth groups, the percentages of villages with transparent and competitive elections were low, hovering around 5%. In contrast, in the second and fourth groups, those with medium levels of outward migration, much higher percentages of villages used transparent and competitive elections, around 20%. In villages with a low level of outward migration, for example, the first group, the percentage of villages with high-quality electoral institutions was close to the national level, at 11.4%. This indicates a possible curvilinear relationship between the effectiveness of grassroots democracy in Chinese villages and their levels of outward migration.

The preliminary empirical evidence in Figure 4.1 seems to support H4.3 through H4.5: Indigenously developed relation-based institutions work better in close-knit villages and become less effective when outward migration increases and, as a result, challenges the close-knit social environment. Externally imposed rule-based institutions are more likely to be established and practiced with high quality in loosely coupled villages with a medium level of outward migration, wherein the transformed social environment can no longer ensure the effectiveness of the indigenous relation-based institutions but can still enable some coordination among villagers for adopting and using the imposed rule-based institutions. In atomized villages with a very high level of outward migration, however, neither indigenous institutions nor imposed institutions can work effectively, due to these villages' paralyzed social networks and the absence of minimally required coordination among villagers.

To comprehensively and rigorously scrutinize the complex relationships among decentralized local public goods provision, different institutional environments, and transformed communal structures in Chinese villages, I need to examine Paths I and II displayed in Figure 1.1 simultaneously in an integrated statistical model. In other words, in addition to the model estimated in Table 4.10 (which corresponds to Path II), I need to include another model that captures the influence of Chinese villages' transformed communal structures on the effectiveness of indigenous and imposed institutions (which corresponds to Path I). Statistically, this suggests a path analysis that examines how unevenly transformed communal structures of Chinese villages affect their decentralized local public goods provision, via shaping their institutional environments. Therefore, I use an integrated SEM, the most effective and appropriate modeling strategy, for this empirical exercise.

More specifically, in this integrated SEM there are two components. The first component basically replicates the MPR analysis shown in Table 4.10. For this component, indigenous and imposed institutions are used as key independent variables (together with other village-level socio-economic, demographic, ecological, and political factors) to explain the variation in Chinese villages' local public goods provision. The second component tries to explain the variation in Chinese villages' institutional environments shown in Table 4.8. For this component, indigenous and imposed institutions are instead examined as dependent variables; the percentage of villagers who worked as migrant workers in cities far away from their home villages[39] and its quadratic item (as indicators of the transformed communal structures of Chinese villages due to cityward migration) are used as key independent variables (together with other village-level socioeconomic, demographic, ecological, and political factors) to explain the varying performance of indigenous and imposed institutions in rural China. Figure 4.2 summarizes the integrated SEM model using a path diagram.

As illustrated in Figure 4.2, the dependent variables are again five specific local public goods. The two key intervening variables are indigenous relation-based institutions (measured by the strength of social sanctions) and imposed rule-based institutions (measured by the quality of electoral institutions). In addition to their direct impact on local public goods provision, the aforementioned socioeconomic, demographic, ecological, and political features of the sampled villages are also specified to indirectly affect local public goods provision via shaping the effectiveness of indigenous or imposed institutions.[40] Cityward migration is the key explanatory

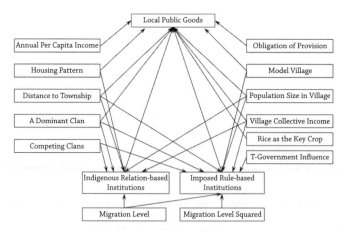

Figure 4.2:
Path Diagram for the SEM on Local Public Goods Provision

variable for the quality of indigenous and imposed institutions. To capture the possible linear negative impact of outward migration on indigenous relation-based institutions (H4.3), I specify the percentage of migrant workers to have a direct impact on the strength of social sanctions. To capture the possible curvilinear impact of outward migration on imposed rule-based institutions (H4.4), this percentage and its quadratic item are both specified to have direct impacts on the quality of electoral institutions.[41] Following contemporary research on Chinese village elections, I include two more variables as controls when analyzing the quality of electoral institutions. A binary variable is created for the existence of competing clan/lineage organizations (B. He 2003; J. Lu 2012; T. Xiao 2002, 2010),[42] and an ordinal variable is used to measure the nature of the working relationships between village committees and their respective township governments (B. He 2007; Landry et al. 2010).[43]

Following the MPR model reported in Table 4.10, I specify all error terms of the five specific local public goods to be correlated with each other. The error terms of indigenous and imposed institutions are also specified to be correlated with each other to model the possible aggregated effect of villagers' contextualized institutional choices.[44] Taken together, the specified SEM is a system of seven equations, all of which are probit models and simultaneously estimated. Table 4.11 provides detailed results of the SEM.[45]

The first five columns present the direct impacts of different variables on local public goods provision in Chinese villages, and they further confirm the MPR results shown in Table 4.10. Significant averaged joint Chi-square tests again show that both effective indigenous relation-based institutions (supported by powerful social sanctions) and imposed rule-based institutions (embodied in transparent and competitive grassroots elections) significantly contribute to the decentralized provision of local public goods in Chinese villages. Similarly, various socioeconomic and ecological features of Chinese villages also matter in their local public goods provision, as previously discussed.

The sixth and seventh columns present the direct impacts of different variables on the institutional environments in Chinese villages. As expected, outward migration has a significant and negative impact on how easily a village can reallocate its land to accommodate demographic changes. Controlling for other factors, as an increasing number of villagers leave via cityward migration, the strength of social sanctions is weakened, and, consequently, indigenous relation-based institutions become less effective in regulating villagers' and village cadres' behaviors and enforcing community-shared norms. The size of the population who stay in Chinese villages also has a significant but negative impact on the

Table 4.11. SEM FOR OUTWARD MIGRATION, INSTITUTIONAL ENVIRONMENT, AND LOCAL PUBLIC GOODS PROVISION IN CHINESE VILLAGES

Structural Model	Tap Water	Paved Roads	Irrigation Projects	Other Public Facilities	Other Public Welfare	Transparent and Competitive Election	Easiness of Reallocating Lands	Averaged Joint Chi-square Test
Size of population staying in village	0.072 (0.136)	0.482 (0.158)***	−0.008 (0.131)	0.164 (0.117)	0.135 (0.128)	−0.197 (0.161)	−0.374 (0.164)**	
Distance to the township seat	−0.356 (0.134)***	−0.062 (0.168)	−0.006 (0.104)	0.134 (0.119)	−0.152 (0.120)	−0.049 (0.178)	0.124 (0.162)	
Annual income per capita	0.219 (0.125)*	0.342 (0.142)**	0.198 (0.127)	0.188 (0.117)*	0.359 (0.114)***			
Village collective income	0.014 (0.017)	0.044 (0.024)*	0.081 (0.019)***	0.077 (0.022)***	0.030 (0.021)	0.007 (0.024)	−0.009 (0.027)	
Transparent and competitive village election	0.075 (0.118)	0.544 (0.158)***	−0.133 (0.102)	0.018 (0.114)	0.192 (0.098)**			F (5, 7259.52) = 4.363***
Easiness of reallocating land	0.139 (0.082)*	0.032 (0.140)	−0.097 (0.099)	0.047 (0.121)	0.210 (0.115)*			F (5, 13353.79) = 2.019*
A dominant clan	−0.408 (0.262)	0.094 (0.324)	−0.237 (0.255)	0.162 (0.235)	0.628 (0.282)**	−0.294 (0.476)	0.202 (0.316)	
Competing clans						0.195 (0.253)	−0.189 (0.379)	
Model village of self-governance	0.391 (0.161)**	0.486 (0.199)**	−0.049 (0.160)	0.222 (0.161)	0.035 (0.168)	−0.053 (0.184)		

(continued)

Table 4.11. (CONTINUED)

Structural Model	Tap Water	Paved Roads	Irrigation Projects	Other Public Facilities	Other Public Welfare	Transparent and Competitive Election	Easiness of Reallocating Lands	Averaged Joint Chi-square Test
Official obligation to public goods provision	-0.173 (0.210)	-0.125 (0.255)	0.115 (0.235)	0.226 (0.225)	0.104 (0.235)			
Clustered housing	0.148 (0.129)	0.345 (0.142)**	0.174 (0.103)*	0.200 (0.122)*	-0.014 (0.144)		0.157 (0.162)	
Rice as the primary agricultural product			0.257 (0.151)*					
Township government influence						-0.071 (0.100)		
Village-level migration						-0.618 (0.245)**	-0.581 (0.284)**	
Village-level migration squared						-0.062 (0.028)**		
Intercept	2.428 (1.385)*	6.447 (1.527)***	2.688 (1.343)**	4.375 (1.287)***	2.453 (1.213)**	-0.763 (1.664)	1.887 (2.025)	
Covariance between variance components								
Paved roads	0.244 (0.110)**							
Irrigation projects	0.044 (0.098)	0.079 (0.123)						
Other public facilities	0.216 (0.113)*	0.211 (0.112)*	0.383 (0.087)***					
Other public welfare	0.157 (0.101)	0.177 (0.116)	0.144 (0.098)	0.170 (0.099)*				
Easiness of reallocating lands						0.067 (0.127)		

(continued)

Table 4.11. (CONTINUED)

Structural Model	Tap Water	Paved Roads	Irrigation Projects	Other Public Facilities	Other Public Welfare	Transparent and Competitive Election	Easiness of Reallocating Lands	Averaged Joint Chi-square Test
				Model fit indexes				
Chi-square	Mean = 33.844, Standard Deviation = 0.576, MI = 5							$F_{(34, 35854.04)}$ = 0.986
CFI	Mean = 0.998, Standard Deviation = 0.002, MI = 5							
TLI	Mean = 0.999, Standard Deviation = 0.016, MI = 5							
RMSEA	Mean = 0.003, Standard Deviation = 0.003, MI = 5							

Source: 2008 China Village Survey (N = 356).
Note: WLSMV estimation in Mplus 6.11.
Averaged coefficients in cells (five imputed datasets with the MI procedure in STATA 11).
Averaged robust standard errors in parentheses, corrected by clustering around counties.
$*p < 0.1 **p < 0.05 ***p < 0.01$.

strength of social sanctions. With a large number of people who stay in villages, it is more difficult to reallocate land to accommodate demographic changes. This is compatible with the conventional wisdom on the influence of group size on collective action (Mancur Olson 1971) as well as the influence of a larger number of veto players on policy stability and change (Tsebelis 2002).

In regard to the quality of grassroots elections, both outward migration and its quadratic item are negative and statistically significant, which indicates a curvilinear and upward convex relationship. Essentially, *ceteris paribus*, it is in villages with a medium level of outward migration that elections are more likely to be organized in accordance with the OLVC, which ensures their transparency and competitiveness. In other words, it is in loosely coupled villages, rather than close-knit or atomized ones, that grassroots democracy is more likely to be established and practiced following stipulated rules and standardized procedures. This well-established rule-based institution can generate publicly recognized authority associated with elected village cadres, ease their resource mobilization for local public goods provision, and hold them accountable to the public interest.

In sum, both indigenous relation-based and imposed ruled institutions can help rural China enjoy better local public goods provision. Nevertheless, which institutions can be well established and perform effectively in Chinese villages is closely tied to their respective communal structural features. In Chinese villages where the close-knit communal environment has been well maintained, indigenous relation-based institutions can still effectively address the problems of collective action and accountability, with the help of powerful social sanctions. Then indigenous institutions can improve local public goods provision and ensure the quality of governance in these close-knit communities in rural China.

Cityward migration induced by the growing disparity between rural and urban China in terms of economic opportunities and benefits substantially challenges the close-knit communal structures of Chinese villages. With some villagers leaving, within-community social interaction is disrupted, social networks are loosened, and the strength of social sanctions is weakened. As a consequence, indigenous institutions can no longer effectively support village governance. In such cases, externally imposed rule-based institutions such as grassroots democracy are more likely to be embraced by villagers and established with high quality. Transparent and competitive grassroots democracy can effectively address the problems of collective action and accountability and, thus, contributes to the decentralized provision of local public goods in these loosely coupled villages. However, as the exodus-level outward migration paralyzes

Chinese villages and atomizes the relationships among villagers, even the imposed institutions cannot work effectively, due to a lack of minimally required coordination among villagers. As a consequence, in atomized villages, the quality of local governance is likely to deteriorate and local public goods provision is likely to be insufficient.

The 2008 NVS data clearly show that, as the unprecedented large-scale but unevenly distributed rural–urban migration transforms the communal structures of Chinese villages to different extents, we indeed see a hybrid array of institutional environments in rural China. Notably, these villages' varying institutional environments have consequential implications for the quality of their local public goods provision, in particular, and local governance, in general.

4.4 SOME QUALITATIVE EVIDENCE

Systematic quantitative exercises with survey data can help generate a broad picture of the decentralized provision of local public goods in Chinese villages, given their different socioeconomic situations, ecological features, communal structures, and associated institutional environments. Despite large-N quantitative modeling's efficiency in reducing possible biases driven by selective and limited cases, such modeling has considerable limitations in uncovering underlying causal mechanisms, particularly when applied to observational data such as the 2008 NVS. To substantiate the broad picture generated by the regression coefficients and associated p-values, I select three comparable cases out of the villages that I visited for fieldwork between 2005 and 2008. In the following case studies, I primarily focus on what I have learned from average villagers and village cadres in regard to the performance of indigenous relation-based and imposed rule-based institutions, as well as local public goods provision in their respective communities.

Qianhouzhai Village

Qianhouzhai Village is under the administration of Qingzhou City, Shandong Province, which I visited in the summer of 2006. This is a village with two major surnames (i.e., Zhang and Cui) among its approximately 700 residents. Most villagers are engaged in agricultural production, primarily vegetables grown in vinyl tunnels. Instead of selling vegetables in the market, villagers of Qianhouzhai wholesale their products to intermediate agents who drive to the village for business. The average annual per capita income was around 6,500 RMB (around 970 USD) in 2005. Qianhouzhai does not have a very profitable collective economy. Rents from collectively owned land and limited fiscal transfers from upper-level governments are the major collective incomes, together around 50,000 RMB (about 7,500 USD) per year. Except for a few young villagers' commuting daily to work in Qingzhou city, which is just 10 miles away, Qianhouzhai had a very low level of outward migration (less than 2%) when I visited. Like most other villages in Shandong, family houses in Qianhouzhai are built very close to each other; for instance, many families share side walls. Clustered housing with a very low level of outward migration effectively maintains the close-knit communal structure of Qianhouzhai and makes it a typical "community of acquaintances" (*shuren shehui*).

In Qianhouzhai, within-village social interaction is not only continuous and frequent but also spans across multiple issue domains: Weddings, funerals, and building new houses are major village events, during which villagers voluntarily help each other out. This is clearly demonstrated in the conventional practice of building a new house in Qianhouzhai, as informed by Ming Zhang, the host of the family with which I stayed during my fieldwork:

> We only hire professional workers for technically challenging and difficult jobs (*dagong*). And we help each other out with those minor jobs (*xiaogong*). Except for providing food and drink, we do not pay each other for the minor jobs. Eventually, everyone needs to build a house, either for themselves or for their children. And it is very important to follow the village's customs when building new houses: your house should not be taller than that of your backyard neighbor; there should be no windows in your back wall.[46]

During my visit, conversational groups in the street were regularly observed, particularly in the late evening, after dinner. Different from other villages in which the elderly dominate such street conversations, in Qianhouzhai I saw a mixture of people of different ages. These casual conversations not only efficiently spread information but also exerted significant influence on people's behavior. The experience of a college student, Min Cui, who came back for summer vacation when I stayed in the village, indicates the power of social sanctions in Qianhouzhai:

> According to our custom, people cannot use umbrellas except for rainy days, no matter how strong the sunshine is. Otherwise, people sitting on both sides of the street may reprimand you. I have to be very cautious about my behavior

when I come back, which makes me feel really uneasy. In our village, a young female walking with a young male can easily generate suspicion. Even the trivial issues of each family can be quickly spread and become public knowledge. Reputation is very important in our village. It is very difficult for a family with a tarnished reputation to find a wife or husband for their child, despite that the family might be rich.[47]

Thus, in Qianhouzhai, villagers' behavior can be effectively regulated and coordinated with the help of community-shared norms that are enforced by powerful social sanctions. Thanks to this, the land in Qianhouzhai has been under regular adjustment every five years to ensure that every household has enough land for agricultural production. When asked for the reasoning behind regular land adjustment, several villagers stated, "It would be terrible to imagine that your children will not have land. Everyone has to live, right?"

Such powerful social sanctions not only effectively regulate the average villager's behavior but also significantly affect how the village cadres behave. In Qianhouzhai's elections, the township government dominates the nomination of candidates; therefore, the elected village cadres are not effectively held accountable to villagers through this rule-based institution.[48] Moreover, the salaries for village cadres in Qianhouzhai are relatively low. The annual salary for the chairman of the village committee is 1,600 RMB (around 240 USD) and even lower for other committee members. Occasionally, village cadres cannot even get paid on time. Nevertheless, rent-seeking activities are rare among village cadres. Honor and reputation are the key incentives for many village cadres to serve. As the committee chairman, Maode Cui, told me:

> I do this not for money. My salary cannot even cover my phone bills. However, if you have worked as the chairman, people may still remember you as the ex-chairman after your retirement. They will greet you and call you ex-chairman (*lao zhuren*) in public.[49]

Thanks to this close-knit environment, villagers in Qianhouzhai also enjoy significant power in supervising village cadres' performance. The ex-chairman of the village committee in Qianhouzhai, who had a very close relationship with township officials, was actually thrown out of the office by villagers when they were informed that he had embezzled some collective income. According to a witness:

> Upon knowing the chairman was engaged in embezzlement, many villagers went to his house. Some even took away his belongings. I thought 80% of them

were there just for fun, without any idea or opinion. If everyone went there and you did not, you might be picked up later. If everyone else thought he was corrupt and not good, my impression of him could not be good either.[50]

In regard to local public goods provision, such relation-based institutions supported by powerful social sanctions also play a critical role. Due to a lack of sufficient collective income, most public projects in Qianhouzhai rely on voluntary contributions from villagers. For instance, as the villagers' wholesale vegetable business grew, more intermediate agents drove their trucks to Qianhouzhai for business; their trucks were frequently stuck in Qianhouzhai's muddy roads in bad weather like rain or snow. Given villagers' complaints, in early 2006, Qianhouzhai organized its villagers to improve the condition of its within-village roads and to pave its main road with concrete. Although Qianhouzhai's collective income covered 70% of the expense, each household still paid 170 RMB toward this project.[51] According to the chairman, after village cadres paid their dues, it was easy to collect money from all villagers, with no complaints.

As expected, Qianhouzhai's close-knittedness provides a favorable environment for the performance of indigenous relation-based institutions supported by powerful social sanctions in regulating and coordinating villagers' behavior, enforcing community-shared norms, and deterring deviant and opportunistic behavior among villagers and local leaders. Despite its lack of sufficient collective income, Qianhouzhai still manages to mobilize enough economic resources from its villagers to provide local public goods.

Songzhuang Village

Songzhuang Village, with approximately 1,300 villagers and multiple surnames, is located in the middle of Henan Province. Its closeness to both township and county seats provides abundant opportunities for local businesses as well as convenient access to transportation facilities for cityward migration. Instead of cultivating crops such as rice and wheat, most villagers in Songzhuang grow vegetables. The farmer's markets located in township and county seats offer a stable place for their daily business. Despite locally available employment opportunities, there are still some villagers, particularly the youth, who work as migrants in coastal cities such as Shenzhen and Haikou after their graduation from junior or senior high school. The migrant workers make up about 10% to 15% of the village population.

Average annual per capita income in Songzhuang varies across the years due to weather conditions and ranges from 3,000 to 4,000 RMB (around 450 to 600 USD). Different from Qianhouzhai Village, Songzhuang has a village-owned enterprise, Yellow River Boiler Accessory Factory (*huanghe guolu fujian chang*). Since its establishment in 1966, this collectively owned enterprise has been the major source of income for Songzhuang. In the 1980s and 1990s, taxes and fees levied upon Songzhuang villagers were partly covered by the profit from this enterprise. Starting in the late 1990s, each year, the village committee can claim around 300,000 RMB (around 44,800 USD) from this enterprise as part of its collective income.

Family houses in Songzhuang also are built close to each other, and all villagers live in a clustered area. However, one is much less likely to find villagers sitting in groups or chatting in the street. Even when such street conversations happen, they are more likely to be among the elderly, who get together for mahjong, with few young villagers involved. When I stayed in one villager's home during my fieldwork, the husband drove his tractor to the farmer's market every morning to sell freshly harvested vegetables and did not come back until early evening. The wife went to their land twice, in the morning and afternoon, and then spent the rest of the day at home watching television or doing housework. Their only son worked in Zhenzhou, the capital city of Henan, as a salesman. When I asked the husband about the situation of other families in Songzhuang, he told me:

> This is very typical here. Vegetables cannot stay too long in the land. We are close to the farmer's market, so we can make more money by commuting every day, rather than selling vegetables to those merchants who come over to purchase. Vegetables are different from crops such as rice, and you have to take care of them all the time. After the children leave for work in cities, adults in every family are fully occupied by agricultural production. Basically, you just feel exhausted after a whole day's work, and you no longer have the energy and interest to chat with your fellow villagers.[52]

More attention shifted to personal and family business and infrequent social interaction among villagers have made villagers in Songzhuang less enthusiastic about gossiping and worrying about other villagers' issues. For most residents of Songzhuang, making money is their priority. Paying professionals or fellow villagers with special expertise to help with major family events like weddings, funerals, and building houses has become widely accepted in Songzhuang. As the communal structure of this village deviates from the ideal type of close-knit communities and moves closer to loosely coupled ones, the effectiveness of indigenous relation-based institutions supported by social sanctions is weakened. Until the early 1990s, Songzhuang still had the custom of land reallocation every five years, but this has not been repeated since the second round of land contracting in 1999. As village cadres reported,

> There are always some villagers who are not happy with giving away a piece of their land. And there is nothing I can do to force them to give up their land. We have no way to enforce this, given the government's laws and regulations (*guo youfa, wo wufa*). As long as one or two fishwives (*pofu*) stand against this, land reallocation is impossible.[53]

Generally, elected village cadres play dominant roles in Songzhuang's governance: 90% of the conflicts among villagers are resolved by village cadres, and they are the first choice for conflict resolution within the village.[54] Village cadres also control a significant amount of collective income, which further contributes to the competitiveness in Songzhuang's village elections, which have been regularly organized since the mid-1990s. Since the 2002 election, voluntary election campaigns have been regularly organized, and village elections have become increasingly attractive to middle-aged villagers. The turnout rate in Songzhuang is very high: According to my interview, the turnout rate in the 2005 village election was very close to 100%. Even those who worked in nearby cities were called back for voting. The primary election (*haixuan*) was the only way of nominating and finalizing candidates, and each family received multiple visits from the candidates for their votes. During the campaigns in 2005, what kind of public projects would be built and how public welfare would be sustained were the key issues for all candidates. When I asked one villager whether he believed all those campaign promises could be realized after the election, he laughed at my question:

> They are not doing this for one term, right? I am not that stupid to vote for him again if he just lies and does nothing. Every three years, they have to show what they have done. This is not something that you can cheat on. With broken irrigation tunnels, muddy roads, and village money spent for nothing, they cannot easily get away (*bu haohun*).[55]

One anecdote clearly reveals the nature of those campaign activities: When two candidates invited some villagers over for dinner and talked about what they would like to do for the villagers once elected (e.g., compensation for the elderly and beneficial policies for school-age children), one villager approached them and raised his concern:

Do not give me cheap talk. I just want to know where the compensation for our villager small group's eight *mu* lands that were confiscated one year ago is. You two were in charge of this then. You should tell us what happened to the money.[56]

As expected, this villager's question ruined the campaign dinner. Nevertheless, that the residents of Songzhuang do care about elected village cadres' performance and can hold them accountable through grassroots democracy is a reality that has been confirmed by both villagers and village cadres. Despite some material benefits that the village committee provided for villagers, such as a barrel of cooking oil for every family during the Spring Festival and compensation for the elderly, what villagers seriously care about is how village cadres spend the collective income and what village cadres have done for the whole of Songzhuang and its residents. Thanks to the election-based mechanism of accountability, as well as abundant collective income, local public goods in Songzhuang are effectively provided: Within-village roads are paved, irrigation projects and tunnels are regularly maintained, and even garbage is collected and disposed of by a specialized agency recruited by the village committee.

Su Village

Su Village also is located in Henan Province, but in the northeast part. This is a village of approximately 1,500 people and multiple surnames. Very different from the situations in Qianhouzhai Village and Songzhuang Village, a majority of Su Village's residents, around 60%, work as migrant workers in other provinces and coastal cities. Ever since the mid-1990s, salaries earned by migrant workers have been the major source of income for the residents of Su Village. According to my interview in 2007, on average, remittances from migrant workers contributed 60% to 75% of a household's annual income. In 2006, the average annual per capita income in Su Village was around 7,000 RMB (around 1,050 USD). Contrary to the collective economic resources enjoyed by villagers in Qianhouzhai and Songzhuang, Su's collective income is limited, except for an annual fiscal transfer from upper-level government of 28,000 RMB (around 4,200 USD).

The most salient feature of Su Village is the coexistence of two- and three-story houses built in clustered areas and the muddy roads in between. The local custom of Su Village puts heavy emphasis on each family's capacity to build houses, and the majority of each family's income is spent on house building and decoration.[57] Most families own motorcycles, and some rich families even own private cars. Since the beginning of 2000, dozens of migrant workers drive all the way back from where they work, even faraway cities such as Guangzhou, during the Spring Festival, and park their cars along the muddy roads. Nevertheless, when the village committee asked for contributions for paving the main road in the village in 2005, few villagers responded. The only donation, about 5,000 RMB (about 750 USD), that the village committee received was from a business-man who moved out years ago.

Almost all young people leave and work as migrants after graduating from junior high school. Even middle-aged villagers work primarily as migrant workers in nearby cities rather than staying at home for agricul-tural production. When walking in the village, one is more likely to come across elderly villagers and children; it is a challenge to find a young or middle-aged villager to interview. Street conversations or group chatting is not something that is regularly observed in Su Village. Even when vil-lagers get together, they are more interested in discussing various oppor-tunities outside, as well as their experiences as migrant workers, rather than anything related to the village itself. Given the atomized communal structure and fragmented social networks, indigenous relation-based institutions in Su Village are impotent in regulating villagers' behavior and coordinating their efforts. For instance, in the late 1980s and early 1990s, land in Su Village was under regular reallocation, with a minor adjustment every three years and a major one every five years, following demographic changes. However, there was no more land reallocation after the second round of land contracting in 1998.

Village cadres in Su Village do not possess highly recognized public authority and cannot even resolve the conflicts among villagers: about 80% of such conflicts are either left unaddressed or reported to the judi-cial organizations at the township seat. Although the compensation for village cadres in Su Village is similar to that in Qianhouzhai Village, around 2,000 RMB (about 300 USD) each year, few villagers are interested in these positions. The chairman told me:

> What can you do with so little money? If you want to do something, you just do not have money. Asking for money from villagers is like pulling out feathers from iron roosters (tiegongji bamao). To get money from upper-level govern-ments, I have to spend my own money for banquets and gifts. Why should I do that? Do you know that if I work in the nearby city for one day, I can easily get 50 RMB? If I had not needed to take care of my sick wife at home, I would have been in Shenzhen with a much higher and more stable salary. I will definitely leave and go out after this term when my wife gets better.[58]

Villagers in Su Village are also apathetic about local elections, given their insignificance in their lives. Candidates are usually appointed by the township government, and the final result is not based purely on the number of ballots but determined primarily by the township government, which may not even take the villagers' votes into consideration. In the 2005 election, including proxy votes, fewer than 50% of Su's registered voters cast their ballots. According to the OLVC, this election should have been invalid. Nevertheless, after mysterious extra ballots were delivered by the heads of villager small groups, the predetermined candidate won the election and passed the double-majority threshold. When I approached a few senior villagers for questions about village elections, they usually just laughed and told me:

> That was just a show (*zuoxiu*). Everyone knew what the township government wanted. Only those like us who cannot go out to make money stay here. If they had not promised to give each people 5 RMB for attending the election, I would not have been there. Who the chairman is has nothing to do with me. No matter who is elected, he will not give me extra money or benefits. I really do not care. It is just a joke.[59]

Given the lack of any effective institutional foundations for the governance in Su Village, it is easy to understand why those villagers who walked onto the muddy roads out of their beautifully decorated two-story buildings did nothing about the roads except wear their rubber boots and occasionally curse at the roads. It is also not surprising to witness increasing conflicts among the villagers during the season when the demand for water exceeds the capacity of existing irrigation projects, but few villagers are willing to pay for their maintenance and expansion.

The relevant information about Qianhouzhai Village, Songzhuang Village, and Su Village is summarized in Table 4.12 for comparison purposes. Neither Qianhouzhai nor Su has sufficient collective income to fund local public goods provision. However, despite their rigged elections, the village cadres in Qianhouzhai still managed to collect money from villagers to pave the main roads within the village, while their counterparts in Su failed in a similar attempt. It is Qianhouzhai's indigenous relation-based institutions, supported by powerful social sanctions, that have enforced community-shared norms, facilitated the cooperation among villagers, held village cadres accountable, and contributed to its local public goods provision.

Songzhuang relies primarily on its collective income to fund local public goods provision. Its transparent and competitive elections have

Table 4.12. CASE STUDIES ON LOCAL PUBLIC GOODS PROVISION

Village information	Qianhouzhai	Songzhuang	Su
Province	Shandong	Henan	Henan
Population size	700	1340	1500
Collective village income (RMB)	50,000	300,000	28,000
Annual per capita income (RMB)	6,500	3,500	7,000
Distance to township seat (KM)	5	2	5
Outward migration	Low	Medium	High
Clustered housing	Yes	Yes	Yes
A dominant clan	No	No	No
Land reallocation	Easy	Difficult	Difficult
Village election	Manipulated	Democratic	Manipulated
Public goods provision	Good	Good	Poor

Source: Fieldwork in Rural China between 2005 and 2008.

held elected village cadres accountable and deterred them from embezzling collective resources for personal gains. Although indigenous relation-based institutions are not as effective in Songzhuang as in Qianhouzhai, due to Songzhuang's relatively higher level of outward migration, which has loosened and fragmented its communal structure and social environment, Songzhuang's village committee, organized through transparent and competitive elections, has, instead, performed as the key institutional foundation for its local public goods provision.

While their counterparts in Qianhouzhai and Songzhuang work industriously for their villages, the village cadres of Su are neither willing to do nor capable of doing anything, given the lack of necessary resources. Because their fellow villagers also do not care that much about village affairs and are even less likely to reward the village cadres for doing anything for the village, the village cadres of Su choose to govern by doing nothing. Thus, the poor quality of local public goods in Su, an atomized Chinese village paralyzed by its very high level of outward migration, should not be surprising.

4.5 CONCLUSION

The provision of local public goods in contemporary rural China has been significantly decentralized, particularly after the collapse of the commune system, subsequent tax-for-fee reforms, and the final abolition of agricultural taxes. With limited fiscal transfers from upper-level governments,

Chinese villages must mobilize and secure economic resources by themselves to fund local public projects and public welfare. Therefore, they must either rely on collective incomes from various sources or collect money from their residents. To effectively fund local public projects and welfare and to address the problems of collective action and accountability in this decentralized provision of local public goods, Chinese villages need effective institutional solutions. Accordingly, the quality of local public goods provision in Chinese villages varies significantly and is closely tied to villagers' access to such effective institutional solutions.

Various institutional solutions can be used to address the problems of collective action and accountability. Indigenously developed relation-based institutions, as supported by powerful social sanctions, can regulate and coordinate villagers' behavior and relieve the problem of collective action. Village cadres, as local leaders, also can be held accountable to the public interest, provided such indigenous institutions can effectively deter their rent-seeking through social sanctions. Externally imposed rule-based institutions also can be of great help in improving local public goods provision. Transparent and competitive elections can not only make elected village cadres accountable to their electorates and channel their efforts toward the public interest but also generate highly recognized public authority that is indispensable for coordinating villagers' behavior and mobilizing necessary resources for local public goods provision. The national village survey data show consistent and significant evidence of the effectiveness of different institutional solutions in improving the decentralized provision of local public goods in Chinese villages.

Nevertheless, the performance of these institutions also varies significantly in rural China, and their effectiveness is contingent upon some communal structural features that are significantly but unevenly transformed by the large-scale cityward migration. In Chinese villages with a very low level of outward migration, indigenous relation-based institutions embedded in the well-maintained, close-knit environment and supported by powerful social sanctions can still perform effectively to address the problems of collective action and accountability. When the level of outward migration increases, the effectiveness of these indigenous institutions is weakened. Then, in the somewhat transformed and loosely coupled villages, imposed rule-based institutions are more likely to be established with high quality and perform effectively in addressing the two problems. As outward migration approaches the exodus level, the communal structures of Chinese villages are fundamentally transformed and their social networks are seriously fragmented. In this atomized environment, neither indigenous institutions nor imposed institutions can perform effectively to alleviate the problem of collective action and hold village cadres accountable. Both quantitative and qualitative evidence have confirmed the indirect impacts of outward migration on the decentralized provision of local public goods in Chinese villages, via shaping the performance of indigenous and imposed institutions.

In summary, in rural China, the quality of local public goods provision varies; we have a hybrid version of local public goods provision based on distinct institutional foundations. Chinese villages' respective institutional environments are further tied to their communal structures, which have been transformed to varying extents, *inter alia*, by the unprecedented large-scale but unevenly distributed outflow of rural labor through cityward migration.

CHAPTER 5

Transformed Social Foundations of Governance in Rural China: Rural–Urban Migration and Social Environments in Chinese Villages

Chapter 4 presents village-level information on the decentralized provision of local public goods, a key aspect of local governance, and associated institutional foundations in contemporary Chinese villages. Both quantitative and qualitative evidence confirm that, by solving the problems of collective action and accountability, indigenously developed relation-based institutions and externally imposed rule-based institutions play significant and positive roles in improving local public goods provision in rural China. Moreover, the effectiveness of these institutions is contingent upon some communal structural features that are significantly but unevenly transformed by, *inter alia*, the large-scale cityward migration in rural China.

More specifically, in Chinese villages with a very low level of outward migration, indigenous relation-based institutions embedded in the well-maintained close-knit environment and supported by powerful social sanctions can still perform effectively to address the problems of collective action and accountability. When the level of outward migration increases, the effectiveness of these indigenous institutions is weakened. Then, in the somewhat transformed and loosely coupled villages, imposed rule-based institutions are more likely to be established with high quality and perform effectively in addressing the two problems. As outward migration approaches the exodus level, the communal structures of Chinese villages are fundamentally transformed and their social networks are seriously fragmented. In this atomized environment, neither indigenous institutions nor imposed institutions can perform effectively to alleviate the problem of collective action and hold village cadres accountable. Therefore, these distinct communal structures result in a hybrid version of various institutions being used for the decentralized provision of local public goods in rural China, and with the communal structures influencing how effective the institutions are in this endeavor.

These findings at the village level offer some understanding of the institutional foundations of local governance as well as institutional performance and change in rural China, which corresponds to Paths I and II in Figure 1.1. Nevertheless, the underlying micro-dynamics, which correspond to Paths III and IV in Figure 1.1, are simply described rather than systematically examined and tested. This chapter and the next one examine the micro-dynamics of the change and performance of indigenous relation-based institutions and imposed rule-based ones in Chinese villages. This chapter, in particular, focuses on the transformed social foundations of governance in rural China (Path III in Figure 1.1). More specifically, this chapter uses both village-level and individual-level survey data to examine the impacts of cityward migration on the social environments in Chinese villages as well as its implications for critical local social norms.

5.1 INFORMATION ENVIRONMENT, SOCIAL SANCTIONS, AND PUBLIC AUTHORITY IN TRANSFORMED COMMUNITIES

As discussed in Chapter 2, frequent and continuous interaction among community members and dense and extended social networks are the defining features of close-knit communities. These structural features make local governance based on indigenous relation-based institutions not only possible but also effective. Importantly, when information about community members' behavior can be spread quickly, accessed easily, and shared widely and when local reputation and community membership play a significant role in members' daily lives, indigenous relation-based institutions, supported by powerful social sanctions, can work effectively in regulating and coordinating community members' behavior and holding local leaders accountable (L. Bernstein 1992; Clay 1997; Greif 1989, 2006; Platteau 2000; L. Tsai 2007a). These close-knit communities, with their wealth of easily accessible local information and powerful, community-wide social sanctions, can be characterized as "societies of acquaintances" (Fei 1939, 1992; X. He 2003a, b; A. H. Smith 1899). As reviewed and discussed in Chapter 3, this was particularly the case for most Chinese villages before the economic reforms of the late 1970s, when the "honeycomb" structure covered most of rural China (Shue 1988).

Before the emergence of plentiful outside opportunities, most Chinese rural residents' economic and social activities were limited primarily to their home communities or some adjacent villages. Therefore, information about villagers' behavior and even private concerns could be spread quickly within the villages through word of mouth, and such information also contributed to villagers' daily gossiping (*jiang shifei*), a form of entertainment. Thus, in this close-knit environment, it was difficult, if not impossible, for villagers to hide information from their fellow villagers. Moreover, in this close-knit social environment, villagers cared a great deal about their local reputations. "Reputation is as important to a person as the bark to a tree" (*renhuo yikouqi; shuhuo yizhangpi*), a local saying that many villagers cited during my fieldwork, attests to the significance of within-community reputation even in some of today's Chinese villages after decades of economic reforms. In this way, powerful community-wide social sanctions could effectively regulate villagers' behavior and deter deviant and opportunistic activities. Under the pressure of social sanctions, some villagers even resorted to extreme measures such as suicide.[1]

Publicly recognized local authority is also critical for maintaining local governance (Arendt 1958; Easton 1955, 1958; Friedrich 1958, 1972). In close-knit social environments, such authority is usually conferred on someone with those attributes most respected in local communities and is cultivated and sustained through local socialization and social sanctions. The foundations of such publicly recognized local authority may vary according to cultural traditions and historical inheritances. For example, in some close-knit Chinese villages with a long history of clan/lineage organizations, genealogical seniority could be a decisive factor in the selection of authoritative figures to address local socioeconomic and political issues (Cohen 2005; Freedman 1958, 1966; Potter 1970; Qian 1994; J. Tang 2001; L. Zhao 1999). In other close-knit villages where there are no such rich traditions of clan/lineage activities, locally respected personal attributes, primarily moral character (usually combined with access to resources), may play a major role in the determination of local public authority (Duara 1988; H. Li 2005; Pomeranz 1993; G. Xiao 1960).[2]

However, when outside alternatives become available and more attractive, and some villagers opt for better economic opportunities in other cities or provinces and leave their home communities, the close-knit environment becomes seriously challenged. As argued in Chapter 2, when outward migration in Chinese villages grows, the transformed social environment may impede the convenient information access that is indispensable to timely and effective social sanctions against deviant behavior, weaken the strength of social sanctions that support the performance of indigenous relation-based institutions, and reshape the foundations of publicly recognized local authority.

To empirically examine the changes in some key features of the social environments of Chinese villages, the 2008 ABS Mainland China Survey (ABSMCS) asked rural respondents about their familiarity with their fellow villagers, the significance attached to their local reputations, and their perceptions of local public authority in their respective villages: (1) "How much do you know about your fellow villagers?"[3] (2) "Do you care about how people in the village evaluate you?"[4] and (3) "In your opinion, who has the highest publicly recognized authority (*weiwang*) in your village?"[5] The weighted frequencies of their answers are presented in Table 5.1.[6]

In close-knit villages, the residents are assumed to be familiar with and have extensive information about their fellow villagers. Were the close-knit environment still well maintained in rural China, when approached about their familiarity with fellow villagers, "Almost everything" would be widely selected. However, the close-knittedness in many villages is disappearing, as one villager expressed during an interview:

> As more and more people leave, and the rest focus on their own business, we no longer care that much about other people's business. Thus, there is nothing worth talking or gossiping about (*shenbian de shiqing mei shenme liaotou*).[7]

Due to the unprecedented magnitude of migration in China, one would expect a growing number of Chinese villagers to no longer be interested in the lives of their fellow villagers. Thus, it is not surprising to find that, as shown in Table 5.1, only 9.3% of Chinese rural residents report extensive familiarity with their fellow villagers, while 28.1% report a lack of any familiarity with their fellow villagers. Further, a majority of Chinese rural residents (59.3%) know only something or just something superficial about those who live in the same village. Because most Chinese villagers no longer have access to sufficient information about their fellow villagers, it is much more challenging for them to evaluate and hold stable expectations of those who live in the same village. This not only generates more leeway for possible opportunistic and deviant behavior but also

Table 5.1. INFORMATION ENVIRONMENT, LOCAL REPUTATION,
AND PUBLIC AUTHORITIES IN RURAL CHINA

How much do you know about your fellow villagers?

Almost nothing	28.06% (1,188)
Something superficial	45.77% (1,903)
Something	13.55% (560)
Almost everything	9.31% (411)
Don't know	3.31% (143)

Do you care about how people in the village evaluate you?

Not at all	43.80% (1,897)
Care	47.34% (1,903)
Care a lot	2.74% (113)
Don't know	6.12% (292)

In your opinion, who has the highest publicly recognized authority in your village?

Senior people in the clan hierarchy	7.92% (308)
Villagers with the best moral character	45.11% (1,866)
Village cadres	26.89% (1,157)
Villagers making the most money	7.31% (312)
Ruthless villagers with physical power	0.66% (40)
Don't know	12.11% (522)

Source: 2008 ABSMCS Rural Subpopulation (*N* = 4,205).
Note: Weighted percentages.
Raw frequencies in parentheses.

weakens the timely and effective enforcement of social sanctions, which impedes the performance of indigenous relation-based institutions.

In regard to the significance that Chinese villagers attach to how their fellow villagers evaluate them, nearly half (49.1%) either care or care a lot about such evaluations; however, 43.8% of Chinese rural residents show a lack of concern over how their fellow villagers assess them. This roughly equal division between those who care and those who do not care about their local reputations further suggests the transformation of social environments in Chinese villages. In other words, many Chinese villagers no longer live in a close-knit community, in which a good reputation is critical to social interaction. Again, once villagers no longer care about their local reputations, the power of social sanctions is impaired.

In addition, Chinese villagers' perceptions of who has the highest publicly recognized authority in their respective villages demonstrate that rural life may no longer be consistent with the picture painted by the scholars who characterized Chinese villages as "societies of acquaintances" (e.g., Duara 1988; Fei 1939, 1992; A. H. Smith 1899; G. Xiao 1960). As shown in Table 5.1, a majority of Chinese rural residents (53%) still choose those with genealogical seniority (7.9%) or best moral character (45.1%) as having the highest publicly recognized authority in their respective villages. Both genealogical seniority and moral character are widely reported as critical components of local public authority supported by a village's "cultural nexus" (Duara 1988). These local authoritative figures usually assumed leadership for China's rural governance that heavily relied on indigenous relation-based institutions (Fei 1939; Qu 1962; G. Xiao 1960). However, as Zhao (2003) reports, based on his more recent qualitative research in North China, the foundations of local public authority in Chinese villages have been significantly diversified. The data in Table 5.1 confirm this, as 26.9% of Chinese villagers believe that village cadres have the highest publicly recognized authority in their villages, and villagers who make the most money (7.3%) or those who are ruthless with physical power (0.7%) are also regarded as the most authoritative figures in their communities.[8]

In summary, the characteristics of the social environments in many Chinese villages have significantly deviated from those of close-knit communities: Villagers know little about or have superficial information about their fellow villagers, and local reputation plays a less important role in villagers' daily lives. Moreover, the foundations of publicly recognized local authority in many villages also are significantly diversified; current authoritative figures may not be able to effectively assume the leadership for village governance based on indigenous institutions. Notably, increasingly limited information and the decreasing significance attached to local reputation characterize the environment of social interaction for many rural residents in contemporary China. This has serious implications for the performance of indigenous relation-based institutions that rely on easy access to sufficient local information and powerful social sanctions within local communities. Is this, as theoretically specified, at least partly a consequence of outward migration in rural China?

Integrating the information on villages (collected through the 2008 National Village Survey [NVS]) and their respective residents (collected through the 2008 ABSMCS), I examine the role of cityward migration in shaping (1) villagers' knowledge about their fellow villagers, (2) the significance that villagers attach to their local reputations, and (3) villagers' perceptions of public authorities in their respective communities.[9] All communal structural features, including cityward migration, the size of the population that stays in their home communities, villages' economic situation (both average per capita income and collective income), and ecological characteristics, are operationalized as described in Chapter 4. For individual rural residents, key demographic features and socioeconomic and political status are used as controls, including age,[10] educational attainment,[11] gender,[12] media exposure,[13] migration experience,[14] Chinese Communist Party (CCP) affiliation,[15] and family economic situation.[16]

To facilitate comparisons across all three dependent variables and focus on the features of the social environment closely associated with close-knit communities, I dichotomize all three dependent variables. For villagers' responses about their knowledge of fellow villagers, knowing basically everything about their fellow villagers is coded as 1. For the significance that villagers attach to their local reputations, caring or caring a lot is coded as 1. For villagers' perceptions of public authority, selecting genealogical seniority or moral character as the key factor determining the highest publicly recognized authority in their villages is coded as 1. Following the empirical strategy of analyzing dichotomous variables in Chapter 4, I use probit models for multiple regression analysis.

According to the regression results of all three probit models, the only communal structural feature with persistent and significant impacts on all three dependent variables is the level of outward migration in Chinese villages.[17] More specifically, *ceteris paribus,* with a larger percentage of fellow villagers who leave for economic opportunities and associated benefits in other cities and provinces, Chinese rural residents are less likely to be well informed about their fellow villagers, pay less attention to how other villagers evaluate them, and are less inclined to associate the highest publicly recognized local authority with those who either have genealogical seniority or possess the best moral character.[18]

To help visualize the impacts of cityward migration, I have run simulations for the predicted probabilities, as well as associated 95% confidence intervals, for all three dependent variables, as the level of cityward migration in a typical village grows from 0.5% to 50%.[19] The simulation results are displayed in Figure 5.1.

A steady, declining trend is seen in all three parts of this figure. As outward migration in a Chinese village increases from 0.5% to 50%, (1) the probability that an average villager has extensive information about his fellow villagers declines from 11.8% to 8.1%, with a difference of 3.7%;[20] (2) this villager is 7.9% less likely to care about his or her local reputation, with the probability's dropping from around 52.8% to 44.9%; and (3) this villager is 18.6% less likely, with the probability decreasing from 55.4% to 36.8%, to recognize those who have either genealogical seniority or the

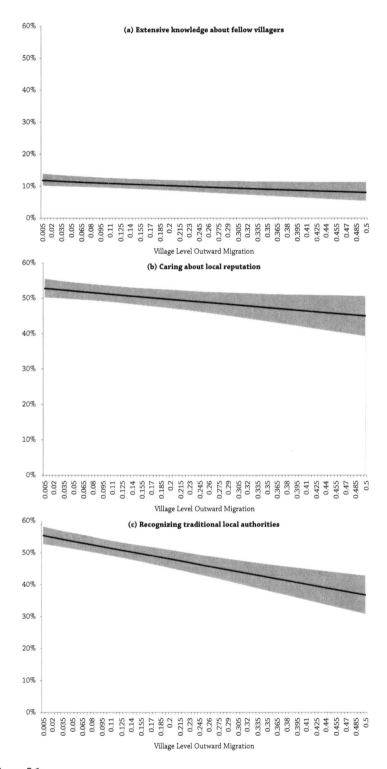

Figure 5.1:
Predicted Probabilities on Information Environment, Local Reputation, and Public Authorities in Rural China

best moral character as the figures with the highest publicly recognized authority in the village. All of the predicted changes are statistically significant and the relative changes are substantively salient. The predicted changes correspond to (1) a 31.4% drop in Chinese rural residents' extensive knowledge of their fellow villagers, (2) a 14.9% drop in the significance they attach to their local reputations, and (3) a 33.6% drop in the recognition of traditional authorities in their villages.

In sum, due to growing cityward migration, as Chinese villages deviate farther from the ideal type of close-knit communities, their local information environment, the effectiveness of local social sanctions that center on the significance of villagers' local reputations, and the recognition of local public authorities also witness dramatic transformation. Such changes are unfavorable for the performance of indigenous relation-based institutions supported by villagers' convenient access to local information and powerful social sanctions. Such changes also tamper with the recognition of traditional authorities, whose leadership has been closely associated with China's rural governance based on indigenous institutions.

5.2 TRANSFORMED SOCIAL NORMS INDUCED BY RURAL–URBAN MIGRATION

The influence of cityward migration in reshaping the social foundations of local governance in rural China moves far beyond the environment of social interaction. It also leaves a significant imprint on the local social norms that prescribe how some critical local issues should be addressed and how villagers should appropriately behave in their villages.

As discussed in Chapter 2, the close-knit environment has made possible the equilibrium switch from "default, default" to "cooperation, cooperation" in the Prisoners' Dilemma game and contributed to the generation of cross-issue linkages that empower social sanctions with higher costs for transgressors and facilitate the realization of collectively optimal results. However, this rational-choice explanation of how indigenous relation-based institutions work in close-knit communities does not necessarily mean that indigenous institutions only exert their influence via transforming incentive structure and utility calculation. According to Opp (1986), community cohesion, the extent and frequency of interaction, and the density of the structure of communication and interaction are critical for realizing possible cooperation. The effects of these features on the fate of cooperation work through (1) cooperation as a first move, (2) the formation of coalitions, (3) possible sanctions, and (4) cooperative norms. The first two intervening variables are related to incentive structure and utility calculation, while the remaining two intervening variables directly or indirectly tap social norms.[21]

As discussed in Chapter 2, for reiterated games, the existence of multiple equilibria is normal. Therefore, the coordinated choices of community members among the multiple equilibria are of significance for institutional change. In many cases, such institutional choices are prescribed by social norms that are cultivated, transmitted, and reinforced through social interaction as well as through long-term and persistent intra- and inter-generational socialization (Greif and Tabellini 2010; Greif and Tadelis 2010; Platteau 2000; Platteau and Peccoud 2011; Tabellini 2008). Thus, the norms of cooperativeness, reciprocity, and fairness, as well as others, speak directly to the cooperation and coordination among community members and are critical for the emergence, consolidation, and performance of the indigenous relation-based institutions that help sustain local governance (Coleman 1986; Cook and Hardin 2001; Dixit 2004; Ellickson 2008). Moreover, in addition to promoting cooperation directly, such social norms contribute to the performance of indigenous relation-based institutions indirectly, through easing social sanctions against possible deviant and opportunistic behavior. According to Coleman (1990, pp. 278–282), both heroic and incremental social sanctions also are likely to be undermined by the problem of collective action. One effective way of solving this second-order collective action problem is in the internalization of appropriate norms, which can lower the obstacles to timely and effective social sanctions and, thus, improve the performance of indigenous institutions.[22]

Horne (2001, p. 9) particularly notes: "Norms thus emerge when behavior produces externalities, when people recognize a right to sanction such externality-producing behavior, and when the group has the ability to enforce this decision." Although this functional argument may no longer be appealing to political scientists, recent developments in cognitive science show that, when dealing with uncertainties and unexpected changes, people do count on habitual responses. Such habitual responses are learned through trial-and-error processes, reinforced through their effectiveness in similar experiences, transmitted among community members, and eventually transformed into norms that guide subsequent social interaction and behavior (Aoki 2001a; DiMaggio 1997; Hechter and Opp 2001; Ullmann-Margalit 1977).[23] In close-knit communities, prevailing multiplex interaction among members makes the emergence of externalities unavoidable, and the existence of extended and dense social networks makes sanctions against externality-producing and deviant behavior possible. Therefore, norms that facilitate cooperation and/or justify sanctions against possible deviant behavior are likely to be cultivated, diffused, and internalized within close-knit communities. In the case of China, to ensure the quality of local governance in rural communities, whether through intermediate agents recruited from local elites or gentries in the Ming and Qing dynasties (Duara 1988; Qu 1962; G. Xiao 1960) or widely established party branches embedded in the commune system under the governance of the CCP before the 1980s (Parish 1985; K. X. Zhou 1996), the Chinese government has promoted and even indoctrinated specific norms that sustain local order.[24] The norms that are of critical significance for the performance of indigenous relation-based institutions are (1) prioritizing collective interest over individual interest, (2) emphasizing long-term relationships over short-term benefits, and (3) avoiding conflict in social interaction.[25]

The norm that prioritizes collective interest over individual interest resembles the principle of "the general will" that Rousseau recommended for good governance in any polity (Rousseau 1968 [1762]). If all players assign higher priority to collective interest, the essence of the Prisoners' Dilemma game can then be changed from a noncooperative game into a cooperative one, and, thus, the socially optimal and efficient outcome can be much more easily achieved. Owing to its prioritizing collective interest, this norm, once internalized, also provides an effective individualized mechanism for holding village cadres accountable through internal sanctions and channeling their efforts toward the public interest in rural China.

The norm that emphasizes long-term relationships over immediate benefits also is of critical value in inducing more cooperation among villagers and reducing opportunistic behavior in Chinese rural communities. The effective internalization of this norm further adds value to those benefits that can only be harvested through cultivating and maintaining long-term relationships. Through this norm, opportunistic behavior that is driven primarily by the temptation of snatching short-term or immediate interests is likely to be minimized by "the shadow of the norm," in addition to "the shadow of the future" cast upon social interaction.

The norm of conflict avoidance also assists the performance of indigenous relation-based institutions in Chinese villages. Due to villagers' frequent and continuous social interaction in close-knit rural communities, conflicts are very likely to occur. And because the villagers are involved in long-term and multiplex social relationships, once conflicts cannot be effectively resolved in a timely manner and grow out of control, future cooperation and coordination become endangered. Thus, how to effectively deal with such conflicts becomes critical to maintaining order and ensuring quality governance in these communities. If there is a lack of sufficient administrative and legal resources for conflict resolution,[26] the norm that prescribes that people should compromise and constrain their demands during conflicts is of significant value for local governance, particularly governance that relies on indigenous relation-based institutions.

To measure these social norms, three questions are used. Respondents were asked whether they completely disagreed, disagreed, agreed, or completely agreed with the following statements: (1) "In contemporary society, people should no longer sacrifice personal interest for collective interest"; (2) "When dealing with others, ensuring immediate self-interest should be more important than cultivating a long-term relationship"; and (3) "Once there is conflict, it should be critical to make it crystal clear who is right and who is wrong." The answers "Completely disagree" or "Disagree" indicate possible internalization of the social norms that prioritize collective interest, long-term relationships, and conflict avoidance in social interaction. The weighted frequencies of Chinese rural respondents' answers in the 2008 ABSMCS are displayed in Table 5.2.

After decades of market-oriented reforms and significant socioeconomic transformations (key components of the unfolding modernization process in contemporary China), many residents in rural China are still attached to the social norms that prioritize collective interest, long-term relationships, and conflict avoidance. As shown in Table 5.2, 56.8% of Chinese villagers still believe in the necessity of sacrificing personal interest for collective interest; 47.2% still assign priority to long-term relationships over immediate interests when dealing with others; and 33.1% believe in the need to avoid conflict. Nevertheless, a change in Chinese villagers' normative orientations is also clear, particularly in regard to appropriate responses to conflicts: 53.8% of Chinese villagers insist on being crystal clear as to who is right and who is wrong during conflicts rather than following the traditional way of mediating disputes at the cost of principle (*huoxini*) or blaming both sides equally (*geda wushi daban*) when conflicts arise. For the tradeoff between collective interest and personal gains, as well as that between short-term benefits and long-term relationships, 25.4% and 36.7% of Chinese villagers, respectively, assign priority to personal gains over collective interest and prefer securing immediate benefits at the cost of long-term relationships. It is expected that, once Chinese villagers' normative orientations shift away from the priority assigned to collective interest, long-term relationships, and conflict avoidance, the normative foundation, as a critical part of the

Table 5.2. SOCIAL NORMS IN RURAL CHINA

In contemporary society, people should no longer sacrifice personal interest for collective interest.

Completely disagree	4.68% (184)
Disagree	52.14% (2,131)
Agree	23.44% (981)
Completely agree	2.03% (72)
Don't know	17.71% (837)

When dealing with others, ensuring immediate self-interest should be more important than cultivating a long-term relationship.

Completely disagree	4.13% (149)
Disagree	43.08% (1,713)
Agree	34.50% (1,501)
Completely agree	2.17% (85)
Don't know	16.12% (757)

Once there is conflict, it should be critical to make it crystal clear who is right and who is wrong.

Completely disagree	2.02% (81)
Disagree	31.09% (1,246)
Agree	50.30% (2,124)
Completely agree	3.48% (134)
Don't know	13.11% (620)

Source: 2008 ABSMCS Rural Subpopulation (N = 4,205).
Note: Weighted percentages.
Raw frequencies in parentheses.

social foundations, of the performance of indigenous relation-based institutions will be notably weakened.

To systematically examine whether cityward migration plays a major role in the erosion of the social norms that facilitate the performance of indigenous institutions in Chinese villages, multiple regressions are used to control for possible confounding variables. Rather than differentiating between "Completely disagree" and "Disagree" or between "Completely agree" and "Agree," I collapse this 4-point Likert scale into a binary variable indicative of Chinese villagers' possible indoctrination of the aforementioned three norms.[27] All individual-level features and village-level variables follow the same operationalization used for previous analysis. Following the same empirical strategy adopted in Chapter 4, I use MPR for appropriate and efficient statistical modeling.[28]

According to the results of the MPR model, after accounting for the influence of demographic features, media exposure, and other individual characteristics, community structural features were still found to play significant roles in shaping the normative orientations internalized by Chinese villagers.[29] More specifically, cityward migration significantly erodes the social norms that prioritize collective interest, long-term relationships, and conflict avoidance. In other words, with more villagers' leaving for economic opportunities and associated benefits in other cities or provinces, Chinese rural residents are more likely to deviate from the normative orientations that generally facilitate the performance of indigenous relation-based institutions.[30] Following the same simulation strategy used for Figure 5.1, Figure 5.2 illustrates the substantive erosive effects of outward migration on different normative orientations internalized by Chinese villagers.

Similar to the patterns observed in Figure 5.1 in regard to the impacts of cityward migration on the information environment, local reputation, and public authorities in Chinese villages, a stable declining trend is shown in Figure 5.2. More specifically, as cityward migration in a Chinese village increases from 0.5% to 50%, (1) the probability that an average villager normatively prioritizes collective interest over individual interest experiences an 8.4% drop, from 66.3% to 57.9%; (2) the propensity that the same villager emphasizes long-term relationships over immediate benefits falls by 9.3%, from 50.2% to 40.9%; and (3) this villager also is 15.3% less likely to avoid conflict by making compromises and, instead, insist on an arbitration clearly indicating who is right and who is wrong, with the probability's dropping from 40.1% to 24.8%. All predicted changes are statistically significant and the relative changes are substantively salient. The predicted changes correspond to (1) a 12.7% drop in Chinese villagers' internalization of the norm prioritizing collective interest; (2) an 18.5% drop in their normative emphasis on long-term relationships; and (3) a 38.2% drop in their accepting the normatively prescribed avoidance of conflict in social interaction.

In other words, in Chinese villages that witness the outflow of their residents through cityward migration, due to the transformed social environment, local social norms that facilitate the performance of indigenous institutions also are eroded. With more emphasis shifted toward individual interest, lower priority assigned to long-term relationships, and the depreciated value attached to the harmonious relationships with fellow villagers, the propensity of cooperation among villagers is diminished and social sanctions are impaired.[31] Thus, deviant and opportunistic behavior among villagers and local leaders is less likely to be deterred

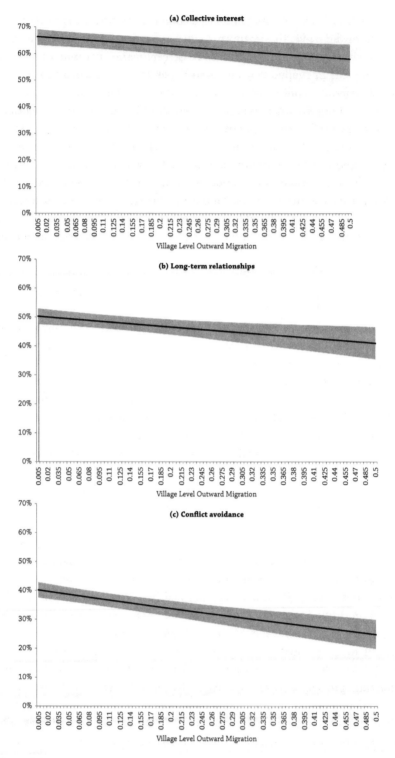

Figure 5.2:
Predicted Probabilities on Social Norms in Rural China

effectively. Essentially, the erosive effects of cityward migration in Chinese villages significantly transform the social norms internalized by Chinese villagers, and such transformed social norms pose serious challenges to the performance of indigenous relation-based institutions and have serious implications for institutional change and local governance in rural China.

5.3 A CASE STUDY OF THREE-SPRING VILLAGE

With the help of cross-sectional survey data, I find some empirical evidence that, as more and more villagers leave for better economic opportunities and benefits in urban areas, Chinese villages gradually move away from the ideal type of close-knit communities. The social environment in these transformed local communities no longer favors the performance of indigenously developed relation-based institutions: The information environment becomes characterized by less exchange; local reputation becomes increasingly irrelevant for villagers' social interaction; the foundations of local public authority are increasingly diversified; and local social norms shift away from prioritizing collective interest, long-term relationships, and conflict avoidance. In this substantially transformed social environment, indigenous relation-based institutions cannot effectively regulate and coordinate villagers' social interaction, deter deviant and opportunistic behavior, or hold local leaders accountable; thus, they cannot sustain quality local governance in Chinese villages.

Nevertheless, the statistical results can reveal only that, in villages with a higher level of cityward migration, the social environment is less favorable for the performance of indigenous institutions. The results cannot show whether cityward migration effectively drives these changes in the social environment, as I previously argue, via dramatically decreasing the stakes that villagers attach to their home communities and significantly reshaping the social interaction among villagers. To address this, I select a typical Chinese village, wherein cityward migration has been a salient phenomenon since the mid-1990s, for detailed examination. In the summer of 2006, I spent approximately three weeks in Three-Spring Village, where I interviewed its residents, of varying backgrounds, to ascertain their memories and impressions of the changes in their surrounding social environment as well as observe their social interaction on various occasions. With the help of semistructured interviews and participant observations in this village, following the strategy of process tracing (Brady and Collier 2004; Collier 2011; Mahoney 2010), I can better examine the underlying mechanisms that drive the observed empirical associations. In this way, I also hope to uncover some temporal dynamics of the relationship between cityward migration and social environment in Chinese villages, beyond the spatial dynamics revealed in previous statistical analyses.

Three-Spring Village is located in the mountainous northern part of the Dongbao District of Jingmen City in Hubei Province. This is a typical Chinese rural community without any local industries. Most of its residents are engaged primarily in agricultural production. It takes about one-and-a-half hours by bus to commute between the township and the county seats to which Three-Spring Village belongs. From the village to the township seat, villagers have to walk or bike (some rich villagers can afford motorcycles) on a muddy road for about twenty to forty minutes. With its 1,680 residents dispersed among eight villager small groups, Three-Spring Village has around 1,202 *mu* of farmland for agricultural production.[32] The residents of Three-Spring Village have multiple surnames, with more than ten surnames for each villager small group. Even the most widely shared surname, Liao, only accounts for less than 10% of the total village population.

Because of limited local access to economic opportunities other than agricultural production, and the relatively convenient access to public transportation, most young and middle-aged villagers of Three-Spring work as migrants in other cities or provinces. According to its village cadres, villagers working as migrant workers in other cities or provinces accounted for over 40% of the total population in 2005. Notably, remittances from migrant workers have been playing an important role in the lives of Three-Spring residents since the mid-1990s.

Currently, the standard of living in Three-Spring Village is slightly below the average of all villages in the Dongbao District.[33] However, before the initiation of economic reforms and the collapse of the commune system, the standard of living in Three-Spring was actually higher than that of many other villages in the same district. Two medium-scale reservoirs were constructed in the late 1960s, which provided abundant water for agricultural production, with rice as the dominant crop. In addition, villagers also profited from the fruits, herbs, and wild animals that could be harvested in the nearby mountains. In the mid-1970s, the work points (*gongfen*) villagers earned each day in Three-Spring were worth more than two times that of most other villages in the same district. Chengsha Liao, the host of the family with which I stayed during my fieldwork, recalled:

Our village was a model village in the commune era. Even during the Three Years of Natural Disasters [*sannian ziran zaihai*, 1959–1961], no one died of hunger. The two reservoirs built in the late 1960s significantly improved the conditions for agricultural production in our village. Members of other villages in the same township envied us, and our male villagers had no problem finding wives.[34]

Nevertheless, this kind of self-sufficient agricultural economy was no longer that attractive when other economic opportunities were available. By the early 1980s, township and village enterprises (TVEs), which offered much more attractive economic opportunities as compared to agricultural production, were widely established in rural China. However, because of Three-Spring Village's location in a mountainous area with geographic constraints and a lack of resources, local industries could not be easily established. In the mid-1980s, some villagers of Three-Spring started to commute to work in TVEs that specialized in the production of phosphate fertilizers in adjacent townships. Xiaosha Liao, the oldest son of my host and the owner of a small-scale chemical plant that produces phosphate fertilizers in an adjacent township, previously worked for a TVE in the mid-1980s. He stated:

> You had to compete for the jobs in those TVEs and bribe village cadres for a position. Working in a TVE was much better than digging dirt at home (*zaijia wa niba*). Basically, you biked to work in the day and came back in the evening. Although my salary was nothing compared to what the managers could get, it was much better than what my parents could get out of the land. After that, I had the idea to have my own enterprise and make more money. Agriculture simply cannot make you rich.[35]

In the mid-1990s, many of these TVEs were shut down due to low product quality as well as competition from a more effective, large-scale chemical plant established in a town seat about an hour's drive from Three-Spring Village. Around the same time, more economic opportunities were opening up in coastal areas, and official constraints on the mobility across regions were lessened. The much higher income from working as migrants in coastal areas attracted most young villagers, who usually left Three-Spring after junior or senior high school. Gradually, even middle-aged villagers began to find better economic opportunities in nearly big cities, such as Wuhan (the capital city of Hubei) and Xiangfan.[36] Currently, the pattern of cityward migration in Three-Spring Village is relatively stable: (1) Most villagers between 16 and 25 are working in coastal areas; (2) Most of them eventually come back for marriage and to have children; (3) After that, one member of most couples leaves for a job in an adjacent big city and the other stays at home to take care of the family and farmland; and (4) Except for a few villagers who can move their entire family to urban areas, most come back to the village when they are too old for laborious work in big cities.

With a significant portion of its villagers working in other cities or provinces most of the time,[37] as well as the much lower stakes and less intimacy they associate with their home community and fellow villagers, the social environment of Three-Spring Village has undergone some significant changes. A major difference is seen in with whom to socialize. Under the commune system, the village was the most important space for socialization. In addition to collective work assigned by brigade cadres, dropping in (chuanmen) had been the primary or perhaps the only available social activity for most villagers. Thus, interactions among villagers were frequent and continuous, and the village was a "community of acquaintances," in which nearly everyone knew a great deal about everyone else.

This situation changed somewhat after the initiation of the economic reforms in the late 1970s, which centered on the household responsibility system. Such reforms shifted villagers' attention to their own farmland and agricultural production, with less time left for socialization. The interaction among extended family members and neighbors took the lion's share of the villagers' socialization, with even less time left for fellow villagers, particularly those who lived farther away. Nevertheless, at that time, villagers' social interaction was still dominated by their fellow villagers.

The situation changed dramatically after the mid-1990s, when many people began to work in other cities or provinces as migrants. Exploring economic opportunities outside of the village became a key concern for most villagers. Even those who stayed in Three-Spring tried to find some odd jobs (linggong) in adjacent townships, counties, or cities. Friends, particularly those in other places who might provide business and economic opportunities, gradually replaced their fellow villagers as the more important subjects of most Three-Spring residents' social relations and connections. When I asked Xiaosha Liao what he usually did during the Spring Festival, the most important time for relation/connection building and social activities in China, he told me:

> Except for paying visits to my parents, brothers, and in-laws, I usually take the bus to adjacent townships and counties to visit my friends. Networking is critical for making money. Only my friends can provide valuable information and opportunities. Staying in the village can just starve you.[38]

The same feeling is shared by a man in his twenties, Xiaolin Chen, who came back to Three-Spring Village and monopolized the sale of a local beer in the village, using the money he had accumulated when working in Shenzhen. He even looked down on his fellow villagers for being out of date and undereducated:

> What could you get out of dealing with them? They knew nothing but playing mahjong. I mostly socialize with the friends I met in Shenzhen and those in Jingmen [the mother-city].[39]

Such decreasing social interaction among fellow villagers is further confirmed by the much less frequent dropping in among the residents of Three-Spring. During my approximately three-week stay in the village, only two people visited the house where I was staying. One was the brother-in-law of the host, and the other was the village clerk who was collecting some fees that the host had not paid on time.

As expected, this gradual shift in the locus of social interaction from within-village to out-of-village has noteworthy consequences for potential cooperation among villagers, their attitudes toward each other, their behavior, and the power of social sanctions.

Before the mid-1990s, mutual help was common among villagers, particularly for wedding or funeral ceremonies. Generally, the villagers who knew a lot about ceremonial details and procedures would be invited over as an emcee (*zhike*) to preside over the entire ceremony, which might continue for four or five days. These villagers would not be paid in cash for this service but, rather, would be rewarded through other means (e.g., receipt of help when needed or gifts during festivals). According to my interviews, the situation changed significantly after 1995, when many qualified villagers were no longer in the village or were not willing to sacrifice their time for such free work. Then, paying eligible villagers to preside over ceremonies gradually became an accepted practice and cost around 50 to 80 RMB, depending on how many days the ceremony lasted. Mingying Deng, whose son got married right before I came to the village, complained about the difficulty in finding eligible villagers who could help with her son's marriage ceremony:

> My son wanted to do this his way, like those people in the cities. But here, you still have to follow the old tradition, as many friends and relatives would come over. It was very difficult to find a qualified emcee, especially one who could help with everything and know the whole procedure. Those who are qualified for this do not want to waste four days for so little money. Finally, I had to ask

for help from an old friend whose uncle knew everything about the ceremony and paid him 100 RMB and a large box of cigarettes.[40]

Moreover, according to my interviews with villagers from different age cohorts, the power of social sanctions within Three-Spring also decreased significantly after the mid-1990s, when many villagers began to leave and find jobs through cityward migration. This decrease in the power of social sanctions is illustrated in the first suicide due to senior abuse in the history of Three-Spring Village, which occurred in 1996: An old villager hung himself because of his son and daughter-in-law's maltreatment. Although the abuse had been going on for some time, unfortunately, no villager stood up and denounced the couple's behavior in public. Many villagers believed that the couple had behaved badly in abusing their father and gossiped a lot in private about this; however, this "private opinion" did not have any effect on constraining or sanctioning the couple's deviant behavior. After that, several similar suicide cases were reported. When I asked Ms. Deng why those senior villagers killed themselves, she stated:

> These old people (lao jiahuo) just could not think straight (xiang bukai). It is not like the old days when children have to support their parents. Nowadays, parents still have the obligation to pay for their kids' education, build houses for their marriage, and even support them when they cannot make a living by themselves. But you have to count on yourselves, rather than relying on your children, when you get old. . . . It is other people's family business and has nothing to do with me. I have my own problems to worry about.[41]

In addition, premarital pregnancy also became a big problem for village cadres after 1995. According to the Chinese government's policy, village cadres would be held responsible for violations of birth-control policies and even incur penalties when young females under their administration became pregnant without official certificates and documents.[42] Most such cases occurred among young women who worked as migrant workers. One retired brigade cadre complained to me about the transformed local attitudes toward intimate relationships:

> It would have been unimaginable for young people to have sex (shui zai yiqi) before marriage, even if they were engaged, in the 1980s, not to mention the 1970s. A woman committed suicide by drinking pesticide in 1975 out of shame and guilt when accused of adultery with another villager, when I was the brigade cadre. Now young people are working outside and beyond the reach of

parents. They can behave recklessly (*hulai*) without incurring too much trouble. Some are even shamelessly proud of this. Morals are degenerating day by day (*shifeng rixia*).[43]

More seriously, due to the lack of powerful sanctions against deviant and opportunistic behavior, as well as the limited capacity of collective action among villagers, since the mid-1990s, gangsters have gradually penetrated Three-Spring Village. Hooligans from adjacent townships and counties colluded with a number of ruthless villagers in taking over public assets at a very low price, monopolizing the operation of the farmer's market by renting out booths, and controlling the local illegal lottery industry. While doing my fieldwork, I was surprised to find that the price of pork in Three-Spring is 8 RMB (about 1.2 USD) higher per kilogram than in adjacent townships. It was the gangsters' monopolization of the sale of pork that had driven the price up.[44] Instead of standing up for the public interest, village cadres of Three-Spring tried every means to avoid dealing with these local bullies.

Clearly, the communal structure of Three-Spring Village is no longer close-knit but, rather, is characterized by infrequent social interaction among the villagers and fragmented social networks. With a large number of villagers' working in other cities or provinces, and most villagers' attention shifted toward the outside world, the significance that villagers attach to their home community, local reputations, and relationships with fellow villagers has declined. Consequently, the power of social sanctions within the village also has been significantly impaired. This, in turn, has exacerbated the gradual collapse of traditional social norms and further deprived Three-Spring residents of the capacity for collective action and coordination. Within this transformed social environment, the performance of indigenous relation-based institutions is unlikely to be satisfying, which leaves more opportunity for negative social forces that may drive further degeneration of the governance of Three-Spring.

5.4 CONCLUSION

Communal structural features of close-knit communities (e.g., frequent and continuous interaction among community members and the existence of dense and extended social networks) induce a favorable social environment for the emergence, consolidation, and performance of indigenously developed relation-based institutions in facilitating cooperation, deterring deviant and opportunistic behavior, holding local leaders accountable, and, thus, improving local governance. In close-knit Chinese villages, convenient access to local information that is quickly and widely spread through local social networks ensures timely and effective social sanctions. High stakes associated with local communities increase the significance attached to local reputation, which further strengthens the power of social sanctions against possible deviant and opportunistic behavior and to hold local leaders accountable. As previously discussed, powerful and timely social sanctions are critical to indigenous relation-based institutions and determine its effectiveness in regulating and coordinating community members' behavior, as well as channeling local leaders' efforts toward the public interest.

In addition, this close-knit social environment of rural China eases the cultivation, diffusion, and internalization of social norms that prioritize cooperation, reciprocity, collective interest, long-term relationships, and conflict avoidance in social interaction. Such social norms not only directly enhance the cooperation and coordination in Chinese villages but also contribute to the performance of indigenous institutions in rural China by solving the second-order collective action problem through norm-based internal sanctions.

However, once the close-knit communal structures of Chinese villages are transformed to various extents due to the large-scale cityward migration, their social environments and foundations for local governance are reshaped accordingly. With a large number of rural residents' leaving for better economic opportunities in cities, villagers' personal stakes in their home communities are likely to be reduced, and their social interactions with fellow villagers are likely to be disrupted and become less frequent. As expected, the local information environment becomes characterized by fewer exchanges, which results in many villagers' knowing little about their fellow villagers. The significance that villagers attach to their local reputations also decreases, as their attention has shifted to the outside world. All of these transformations impair the power of social sanctions and weaken the performance of indigenous institutions. The increasingly diversified foundations of local public authority exacerbate the situation, given the dominant role of traditional authorities in upholding and enforcing these indigenous institutions.

Cityward migration also erodes certain social norms in Chinese villages that are a critical component of the social foundations for China's rural governance. When deviant and opportunistic behavior cannot be punished in a timely and effective manner, a cascade of similar deviant behavior may be triggered (Bikhchandani et al. 1992; Kuran 1998; Watts and Dodds 2007) and may even result in the transformation or collapse of social norms that favor the performance of indigenous relation-based institutions. As expected, in Chinese villages with a higher level of outward migration, residents are less likely to internalize the norms that prioritize collective interest, long-term relationships, and harmonious relationships within the villages. In these transformed rural communities, villagers are more likely to be self-centered in social interaction—for example, care more about their own interest and short-term benefits and insist on being crystal clear about who is wrong and who is right once conflicts arise. All such transformation challenges the performance of indigenous relation-based institutions.

Quantitative and qualitative analyses result in converging evidence: As the close-knit communal structure of Chinese villages is transformed, *inter alia*, by the large-scale cityward migration, the social foundations of China's rural governance are changed as well. The transformed social environment in many Chinese villages, particularly those that witness a relatively higher level of outward migration, becomes no longer favorable for the performance of indigenous relation-based institutions supported by powerful social sanctions. Thus, alternative institutional solutions are needed to address such problems and reconfigure the institutional foundations of the governance in Chinese villages.

CHAPTER 6

Rural–Urban Migration and Contextualized Institutional Choices in Rural China

Both survey data and a detailed case study have confirmed the significant impact of cityward migration on the social foundations of China's rural governance. As more Chinese villagers leave for economic opportunities and associated benefits in urban areas, the transformed environment of social interaction in rural China can no longer ensure the effective performance of indigenously developed relation-based institutions in upholding village governance. Given the depleted information environment, weakened social sanctions, diversified foundations of public authority, as well as reshaped normative orientations, Chinese villagers in these transformed rural communities are expected to seek more effective institutional alternatives for local governance. This chapter focuses on Path IV in Figure 1.1 and presents some empirical evidence on Chinese villagers' contextualized institutional choices for local governance.

Different from the discussions of Chapter 4 (i.e., decentralized local public goods provision), this chapter looks at other, at least equally important, aspects of local governance in Chinese villages—conflict resolution, disaster and crisis relief, modest credit and small loans—and different ways of regulating and supervising local political leaders. Due to the lack of valid and objective measures of these issues at the village level,[1] such important issues in China's rural governance have not been systematically examined in contemporary literature in the same manner as local public goods provision.[2] Nevertheless, they are closely related to the daily lives of Chinese villagers and constitute a critical component of China's rural governance. In the 2008 ABS Mainland China Survey (ABSMCS), rural respondents were interviewed about their choices among institutional alternatives in various issue domains. Using such self-reported measures, this chapter identifies individual-level dynamics of the impacts of cityward migration on institutional change and performance in Chinese villages.

6.1 LOCAL GOVERNANCE BEYOND PUBLIC GOODS PROVISION

To ensure quality local governance, institutional solutions should be available to sustain order, facilitate cooperation, uphold accountability, and improve the welfare of community members, despite possible interest conflict and divergent goals among them. Thus, effective local governance is a scheme not for establishing "harmonious communities" through social optimization but for an improved situation compared to the "state of nature," in which anarchy dominates and everyone has to rely on himself or herself to respond to certain problems.[3] Although the provision of local public goods has been a key topic for the literature on local governance, few people would argue that it is the only or even the most important issue for local governance.

To ensure and sustain the quality of their governance, local communities must find effective ways to serve various functions, not just the provision of local public goods. For instance, they need some means to resolve conflict among community members and control its potential spillover into other social relationships. When disasters or crises occur, local communities need resources to help them survive; providing such resources, in turn, can reinforce the cohesion within communities and thwart possible erosion in community identification. To increase the material benefits available to their members and improve the local standard of living, communities also should identify some means to facilitate cooperation in production and help their members raise the capital that is necessary for more diverse economic activities. In contemporary rural China, similar to the situation of decentralized local public goods provision, there are various institutions that address these issues. Some institutions are indigenously developed and relation-based and have existed in Chinese villages for many years. Others are externally imposed and rule-based and are part of the Chinese government's ambitious program of modernizing and formalizing its political, administrative, judicial, and socioeconomic institutions for more effective macro-governance.

Conflict Resolution in Rural China

Conflict is not uncommon in Chinese villages. It happens within families—for example, disputes over the division of family assets, quarrels between husbands and wives, and dissension between mothers-in-law and daughters-in-law. It also occurs between families or groups of families (e.g., disputes over farmland, land for housing, or irrigation). Such conflict, if not resolved appropriately and in a timely manner, could lead to personal injuries, battle royal, or even suicide.[4] Moreover, unresolved conflict, even if temporarily cooled down, might still sour relationships among villagers, contaminate the social interactions within the village, trigger significant (even disastrous) events, and disrupt local social order. Thus, to resolve the conflict among villagers effectively and minimize its possible negative impacts on local social order, Chinese villages must offer institutional solutions.

As scholars of sociology, cultural anthropology, legal studies, and political science note, social order has long been sustained in some communities with the help of indigenous relation-based institutions (Abel 1974; Ellickson 1991; Felstiner 1974; Ginat 1997; Noland 1981). A similar situation is found in Chinese villages as well, particularly before the 1980s (L. Dong 2008; Fei 1992; P.C. Huang 1996, 2001; A. H. Smith 1899; G. Xiao 1960; X. Zhao 2003). With the help of local authoritative figures such as senior villagers or the gentry, indigenously cultivated and shared norms, and villagers' observance of local customs, most conflict can be effectively resolved within Chinese villages without being reported to administrative or judicial agencies. Further, according to various legal scholars, a so-called culture of anti-litigation (*yansong*) was widely observed in ancient China, particularly in rural areas (P. C. Huang 1996, 2001; L. Liang 2008; Z. Liang 1996). The lingering influence of this anti-litigation culture is still perceivable in today's rural China (Z. Liang 2002; Michelson 2007, 2008; X. Zhao 2003).

In a village of Jiangxi Province I visited in the summer of 2004, most family asset divisions are negotiated with the presence of local authoritative figures, who usually are villagers with genealogical seniority but from different families. Sons and their parents can present their own proposals on how family assets should be divided and how the support of parents should be arranged, which usually differ significantly and can result in intrafamilial tension.[5] If they are left to develop a settlement by themselves, not only could the relationship between siblings be soured but also support for their parents might be avoided by all the siblings due to the estrangement resulting from conflict over the family asset division.

Usually, with mediation from the local authoritative figures, a compromise can be achieved, and an informal contract can be drafted on the spot and signed by all parties in the family and the local authoritative figures.[6] Although this is not a legal document with binding power, few villagers would breach such informal contracts. In other rural communities, it may not be the villagers with genealogical seniority who play the role of chairing negotiation, mediating disputes, and resolving conflict; rather, it may be those who have been publicly recognized as upright and fair in dealing with fellow villagers (L. Dong 2008; X. Guo and Wang 2004; X. He 2003a; X. Zhao 2003).

As a result of modernization and state building in China, in addition to access to such indigenous relation-based institutions for conflict resolution, Chinese villagers also have access to externally imposed rule-based institutions. Among all regimes in Chinese history, the Chinese Communist Party (CCP) may have done the best job of providing formalized judicial and administrative institutions in rural communities.[7] Since the 1930s, when the CCP was still in competition against the Kuomintang for the control of China, it has been building a system of conflict resolution, the community mediation system, in both rural and urban communities. Rather than relying on senior villagers and locally recognized authoritative figures, the CCP formalized the community mediation system by providing mediation services initially in communes (the rural part) and street councils (the urban part), with specialized agents chairing mediation committees.[8] After the administrative reforms and the promulgation of the Organic Law of the Urban Residents Committees (drafted in 1989) and the Organic Law of Village Committees (drafted in 1987 and amended in 1998 and 2010), the service of mediation has been reassigned to village committees in rural China and resident committees in urban areas. Currently, village cadres are heavily involved in resolving conflict among Chinese villagers (L. Dong 2006a, b, 2008; X. Guo and Wang 2004; Zweig 2010). A critical source of village cadres' authority in effectively adjudicating conflict within their communities is their officially endorsed and publicly elected office. In addition, village cadres work closely with the courts and police stations, usually located at township seats, to formally address conflict with serious consequences through judicial procedures (Qiang 2003; L. Su 2000, 2002).

Despite universally established village committees in rural China, as well as a rich history of indigenous relation-based institutions for conflict resolution in many Chinese villages, it is not necessarily the case that most conflict can be effectively resolved before having a significant negative impact on the local social order. In some villages, neither village committees and local judicial agencies nor indigenous institutions can effectively resolve conflict and ensure the social order for local governance due to a lack of required authority or the prohibitively high transaction costs. In these instances, villagers must rely on their own solutions. Occasionally, violence or death might be the only tool available to the strong or the weak to address the wrongs that have been done to them (B. Chen 2008a, 2011a; L. Dong 2008). Consequently, the social order in such villages is disrupted, and peaceful village life, to say nothing of quality governance, is jeopardized.

Disaster and Crisis Relief in Rural China

The multifaceted welfare system in China is a form of social security (*shehui baozhang*) that has three broad components: (1) social insurance (*shehui baoxian*) that includes arrangements for pensions and medical treatment; (2) social services (*shehui fuwu*) that provide specialized support for the elderly, disabled, and abandoned; and (3) social relief (*shehui jiuzhu*) that involves assistance in cash and kind to the elderly and disabled or those who need help due to disasters, crises, or emergencies. Unfortunately, as some China scholars incisively point out, the social welfare system has been quite restricted in rural China, particularly compared to the subsidized services and insurance programs offered to its urban counterpart. Except for some state subsidies for certain special categories of villagers, poor and remote villages, and villagers who need help due to disasters and crises, there are limited systematically established schemes for social insurance and social services in rural China (Croll 1999; Hebel 2003; G. Wang 2004; S. Wang 2011; Lirong Zhang and Li 2000). [9] Given the theme of this chapter, contextualized institutional choices in Chinese villages, I focus on social relief in rural China, which is perhaps the most meaningful issue for most Chinese rural residents.

Similar to the situation in many local communities in other countries (e.g., Platteau 1994b; Platteau and Seki 2001), some indigenous relation-based institutions in rural China offered critical social relief to their community members when the administrative capacity of the government could not effectively do so. Granary systems were established in the Qing dynasty to alleviate the hardships of peasants in response to natural disasters (G. Xiao 1960, Chapter 5). [10] Solidarity groups, particularly clan/lineage organizations and religious organizations, used their collective resources to also contribute to disaster and crisis relief (Cohen 2005; Freedman 1958, 1966; J. Liang 2004, Chapter 5; Potter 1970; Qian 1994;

G. Xiao 1960, Chapter 8). Another equally important indigenous means of disaster and crisis relief is voluntary contributions from fellow villagers on an ad hoc basis, through either cash/materials or in-kind labor. This custom of mutual help is indicative of the norms that are repeatedly and explicitly emphasized in various village compacts (Niou 2005) and cultivated through local socialization: "Give mutual help and protection; and offer mutual assistance in case of sickness and crisis" (*shouwang xiangzhu, jibing xiang fuchi*).

A typical case of social relief based on this indigenous mutual help system occurred while I visited a village in Shandong Province in the summer of 2006. Mr. Yao tried to earn extra money for his son's college tuition through a temporary job in a nearby brickyard, where he worked 12 hours a day. Unfortunately, one evening he was struck by a truck that was backing up to load bricks. As a result, Mr. Yao incurred a 4,000 RMB debt due to medical expenses. After learning of this accident and without any intentional mobilization, most of his fellow villagers came to his house with eggs, pork, and even cash. Altogether, Mr. Yao received a total of 5,275 RMB from about 250 households within the village. The amount of money could not cover everything but did significantly alleviate his burden for paying both his medical expenses and his son's tuition. Although Mr. Yao made a record of each monetary donation and insisted that he would pay back the money after he recovered, this in-time voluntary financial assistance (essentially an interest-free loan) from his fellow villagers offered a great deal of relief.[11]

Before the economic reforms of the late 1970s, the Chinese government's contribution to the social relief in rural communities, except for some provisional relief work, was made primarily and indirectly via the commune system. Stable membership in the communes guaranteed each villager's share in local resources, even beyond active labor participation. However, the situation has changed since the 1980s after the collapse of the commune system and the institutionalization of independent economic activities based on the household responsibility system. Thereafter, village committees, together with local agencies of civil affairs funded primarily by township governments and usually located at township seats, have assumed the key responsibility of providing social relief to Chinese villagers. In addition to ensuring the on-time delivery of allowances and compensation for specific groups of villagers[12] and helping select eligible candidates to receive money and resources from upper-level governments,[13] village committees may use some of their collective incomes for such purposes when necessary. For instance, after Mr. Yao's accident, the village committee gave him 500 RMB as a donation and helped his son file an application for a possible reduction in tuition, as well as educational loans, from the college.

In addition to the aforementioned communal voluntary mutual help and government-sponsored social relief programs, support from families, relatives, and close friends plays a major role in times of disasters and crises in Chinese villages.[14] And this means of social relief is based primarily on private connections or consanguineous obligations.[15] However, given the limited number of people involved in such intimate relationships, the capacity to pool sufficient resources for disaster and crisis relief is usually constrained. Moreover, after the enforcement and implementation of the "one-child policy" in rural China, the capacity of such private solutions for disaster and crisis relief has been further constrained due to reduced family size.[16]

Modest Credit and Small Loans in Rural China

Whether involved in agricultural or non-agricultural production, Chinese villagers usually need some capital for investments, either for buying necessities such as fertilizers or seeds or for starting a small business. Most of the time, they use personal savings, but often, they need some credit and loans when their savings are insufficient. Thus, modest credit and small loans are of great significance for local economies in Chinese villages. Notably, if villagers cannot raise enough money for investments, local economic activities are likely to be restricted. As a consequence, the local standard of living could decrease and there may not be sufficient economic resources for decentralized local public goods provision, particularly when villagers' contributions make up the lion's share in funding local public facilities and welfare programs, as shown in Chapter 4.

According to the most recent estimates, only about 25% of the credit and loans in rural China are raised from banks and Rural Credit Cooperatives (RCCs); over 70% is raised through other informal channels (W. He et al. 2005). This finding is compatible with many scholars' observations of the role of indigenous relation-based institutions in raising capital to sustain local economic activities, not only in rural China (B. Hu 2007; K. S. Tsai 2002) but also in many local communities in other regions (Besley et al. 1993, 1994; Besley and Levenson 1996; Hayami and Kawagoe 2001). Among many indigenous institutions for raising capital, such as usury, pawn-broking, and private money houses, rotating savings and credit associations (ROSCAs) are a typical indigenous relation-based institution that provides credit and loans in rural China (B. Hu 2004; Ong 2012; A. H. Smith 1899, Chapter 14; K. S. Tsai 2002, Chapter 2; Z. Wang 1935; L. Yang 1961, Chapter 8).[17] Villagers organize a ROSCA to pool their limited economic resources and grant loans to their association members according to their predetermined rules. The loans that villagers can obtain from ROSCAs range from several hundred dollars to even hundreds of thousands of dollars, and, according to detailed case studies in rural China, few ROSCA members default and bad debts rarely occur (W. He et al. 2005, Chapter 21; B. Hu 2007, pp. 104–117).

The Chinese government also has made extensive efforts to provide formal financial services in rural China, primarily through the Agricultural Development Bank of China, the Agricultural Bank of China, and RCCs. Nevertheless, there are widely recognized deficiencies in extending credit and loans to Chinese rural residents through these financial institutions (A. He and Hu 2000; W. He et al. 2005; G. Li 2005; Yongfu Yan 2004; J. Zhang 2003). The Agricultural Development Bank of China is a policy-related bank and is engaged in loans primarily for the procurement of agricultural products and infrastructure construction in rural areas, with little involvement in providing credit and loans for Chinese villagers. The Agricultural Bank of China has a few branches in townships, and even fewer in villages, and is engaged in loans primarily for poverty relief rather than for the promotion of production. Further, many of the Agricultural Bank of China's rural branches were withdrawn in the 1990s due to concerns over operating costs. Thus, RCCs are the major formal financial service provider in rural China, particularly in extending modest credit and small loans to Chinese villagers. By the end of 2002, approximately 90% of RCCs had extended modest credit and small loans to Chinese villagers.[18] In practice, due to the lack of a credit system in China, RCCs must bear the risk of default when extending credit and loans to villagers. To save the cost of information collection/confirmation and minimize the risk of default, RCCs usually work together with village committees to evaluate the villagers' applications for credit and loans, given the latter's rich knowledge about each case.[19] Moreover, a village committee's endorsement can save the provision of guaranty from villagers when applying for credit and loans from RCCs, which is a big relief for many villagers. Once credit and loans are granted, village cadres are often entrusted with the obligation of dunning villagers to pay their loans on time.[20]

Nevertheless, given the potential risk of raising capital through indigenous institutions such as ROSCAs and the costs of applying for loans through RCCs, many Chinese villagers still prefer to borrow money for economic activities from families, relatives, and friends. Such private capital raising constitutes a majority of credit and loans in rural China (W. He et al. 2005; Ong 2006, 2009, 2012). However, similar to the situation of providing disaster and crisis relief through private solutions, these channels of capital raising based on personal connections also have limited capacity to pool sufficient resources for economic activities.

6.2 CONTEXTUALIZED INSTITUTIONAL CHOICES IN TRANSFORMED RURAL COMMUNITIES

The previous section shows that Chinese villagers can resort to indigenously developed relation-based institutions, externally imposed rule-based institutions, or private solutions when dealing with local governance issues such as conflict resolution, disaster and crisis relief, and modest credit and small loans. Thus, identifying the conditions under which villagers are more attracted to a specific type of institution to solve their problems in these domains is critical to our understanding of the performance of such institutions in sustaining China's rural governance. Further, Chinese villagers' contextualized choices of various institutions in their daily lives also shed some light on the micro-dynamics of institutional change and transformed governance in rural China.

As presented in Chapter 2, I argue that Chinese villagers' contextualized institutional choices for local governance issues are shaped primarily by three factors: (1) the respective effectiveness of distinct institutions in dealing with specific issues, (2) the switching costs incurred for using unfamiliar institutions, and (3) the coordination costs incurred due to their fellow villagers' choices. These three factors are closely associated with the communal structural features of Chinese villages. More specifically, in close-knit villages, imposed rule-based institutions are less likely to be adopted for locally circumscribed governance issues, given villagers' access to and familiarity with the still-functioning indigenous relation-based institutions. Essentially, the switching costs are too high for using imposed institutions. In loosely coupled villages, the imposed institutions are more likely to be accepted and perform as the new institutional foundation for local governance. In these villages, weakened indigenous institutions generate sufficient incentives for villagers to incur the switching costs for using the imposed institutions, while the still-somewhat-functioning within-village social networks also enable villagers to successfully coordinate their institutional choices. In atomized villages, despite strong incentives to seek alternative institutional solutions, due to the paralyzed within-village social networks, villagers do not have the minimum level of coordination capability to effectively embrace imposed institutions. In many cases, they must rely on private solutions based on personal connections or even brute force.

In practice, powerful social sanctions and favorable locally cultivated norms and values in close-knit Chinese villages ensure the effectiveness of indigenous institutions in resolving conflict, providing disaster and crisis relief, and raising capital for villagers' economic activities. For example, the binding power of village seniors' adjudication and arbitration is based on their publicly recognized authority, derived from locally cultivated norms and customs rather than from official endorsement or violence-based enforcement. Community-based mechanisms of social relief are buttressed by local reciprocal norms and the priority that villagers assign to long-term relationships in social interaction. The effectiveness of ROSCAs in raising capital for local economic activities also relies on powerful social sanctions that deter potential default. Embedded in this close-knit social environment and due to powerful social sanctions, the behavior of local leaders and authoritative figures is also effectively supervised and well regulated.

As shown in Chapter 5, with a large number of villagers' leaving for economic opportunities and associated benefits in urban areas via cityward migration, the transformed social environment in these villages no longer favors the performance of indigenous relation-based institutions. As a consequence, imposed rule-based institutions, as an alternative solution for locally circumscribed governance issues and embodied primarily through the performance of village committees, become more attractive to villagers. In these loosely coupled rural communities, for instance, village cadres are heavily involved in conflict resolution and dispute mediation to sustain social order, which is one of their officially prescribed services. They also are frequently included in the work of local judicial and law enforcement agencies on cases with serious consequences or high stakes. Moreover, without the assistance of village committees, local agencies of civil affairs and RCCs would incur extremely high costs in identifying eligible candidates for delivering social relief and extending modest credit and small loans. As a complement to these imposed rule-based institutions, transparent village elections provide effective checks on village cadres and can hold them accountable to the public interest.

To take advantage of these imposed rule-based institutions, villagers need to collect enough information on how these imposed institutions operate and acquire the skills and knowledge required to use them. To ensure the effectiveness of the imposed institutions in improving local govern-ance and increasing public welfare, villagers must have a minimum level of coordination of their institutional choices and the ability to hold local leaders accountable. Otherwise, for instance, village cadres' significant in-fluence on the decisions of local judicial agencies, agencies of civil affairs, and RCCs might be abused for their personal gains.[21] Villagers' distrust of village cadres is also unlikely to endow the latter with the authority needed for conflict resolution and dispute mediation. Therefore, in atom-ized Chinese villages in which the within-village coordination capacity is paralyzed due to a high level of outward migration, villagers are more likely to be forced to use private solutions to address their problems. Be-cause neither indigenous nor imposed institutions can work effectively in atomized villages, personal connections or brute force may prevail in local governance.

To comprehensively evaluate Chinese villagers' contextualized institu-tional choices in the domains that are critical for quality local governance, I use three questions from the 2008 ABSMCS: (1) "When the conflict be-tween you and your fellow villager(s) cannot be resolved among yourselves through negotiation, who will you contact first for resolution?"[22] (2) "If your family experiences an economic crisis due to some unexpected issues, such as sickness or disaster, who will you contact first for help?" and (3) "When you need some capital to buy production necessities or to start a small business, who will you contact first for credit and loans?" Chinese villagers' choices among the preselected answer categories are presented in Table 6.1.[23]

As shown in Table 6.1, imposed rule-based institutions such as village committees (65.0%), villager councils (4.5%), and local judicial agencies (7.6%) dominate Chinese villagers' institutional choices for conflict reso-lution. Taken together, 77.1% of the interviewed villagers selected rule-based institutions as their first choice for conflict resolution. Neverthe-less, 7.9% of the respondents preferred some indigenous relation-based institutions, such as clan/lineage councils or upright and fair fellow vil-lagers with recognized authority as mediators. It is interesting to note that 5.7% of the villagers prefer private solutions, including fighting, either on their own or by asking for help from local bullies (*hunhun*).

The picture changes dramatically when Chinese villagers look for disas-ter and crisis relief or try to secure modest credit and small loans: Private solutions dominate their institutional choices in these two domains. When villagers need help to survive disasters and crises, families, rela-tives, and friends are still the unchallenged first choice (62.5%). Imposed rule-based institutions attract 27.3% of the villagers, who may contact

Table 6.1. INSTITUTIONAL CHOICES FOR CONFLICT RESOLUTION, DISASTER AND CRISIS RELIEF, AND MODEST CREDIT AND SMALL LOANS IN RURAL CHINA

Conflict resolution	
Clan/lineage council	0.94% (43)
Other upright and fair villagers with recognized authority	6.92% (276)
Villager council	4.46% (168)
Village committee	65.00% (2,747)
Judicial agencies at township seat	7.63% (344)
Local bullies (*hunhun*)	0.13% (4)
On my own	5.58% (248)
Don't know	9.34% (375)
Disaster and crisis relief	
Clan/lineage council	0.56% (21)
Neighbors	2.56% (104)
Villager council	1.64% (66)
Village committee	19.53% (824)
Agencies of civil affairs at township seat	6.10% (258)
Families, relatives, and friends	62.46% (2,663)
Don't know	7.14% (269)
Modest credit and small loans	
Organizations like ROSCAs within the village	0.41% (16)
Neighbors	2.79% (134)
RCCs	16.34% (709)
Families, relatives, and friends	72.34% (3,025)
Don't know	8.12% (320)

Source: 2008 ABSMCS Rural Subpopulation (*N* = 4,205).
Note: Weighted percentages.
Raw frequencies in parentheses.

village committees (19.5%), villager councils (1.6%), or local agencies of civil affairs at the township seat (6.1%) for help. Only a small percentage of the villagers might ask neighbors (2.6%) or clan/lineage councils (0.6%) for assistance, once affected by disasters or crises.[24] Private solutions also dominate Chinese villagers' institutional choices when they try to raise capital for economic activities: 72.3% of the respondents said they would first ask families, relatives, and friends for modest credit and small loans when necessary. Additionally, 16.3% of the interviewed villagers identified RCCs as their first choice when trying to get modest credit and small loans. Only 3.2% would try to raise capital through community-based means: borrowing from neighbors (2.8%) or participating in organizations such as ROSCAs (0.4%).[25]

Table 6.1 shows that Chinese villagers choose a variety of institutional solutions to address their problems with various locally circumscribed governance issues. From this, a question naturally arises: Are their institutional choices shaped by Chinese villages' communal structures, as theoretically expected? To systematically examine Chinese villagers' contextualized institutional choices for resolving conflict, alleviating unexpected and negative impacts of disasters and crises, and raising modest credit and small loans for economic activities, information on the villagers themselves (e.g., demographic features, economic status, media exposure, and village community structural features such as cityward migration and clan structures) should be included for analysis. Adopting the same strategy for empirical analysis as in Chapter 5, I combine villager-level information (collected through the 2008 ABSMCS) and village-level information (collected through the 2008 National Village Survey [NVS]) for multiple regression analysis. The operationalization of variables that capture village-level features is the same as that in Chapter 4, while the operationalization of variables capturing villager-level features is the same as that in Chapter 5.

Theoretically, for Chinese villagers, as the level of cityward migration increases, imposed rule-based institutions are expected to become more attractive in addressing various problems in local governance. However, as cityward migration grows to an even higher level, even imposed rule-based institutions may no longer work, due to the lack of a required minimum level of cooperation among villagers. Thus, a curvilinear (more specifically, an inverted-U) relationship is expected between the propensity of villagers' preferring imposed institutions and the level of cityward migration in their village.[26] To effectively capture this expected curvilinear relationship, both the level of cityward migration and its quadratic term are included in the probit regression models on Chinese villagers' choice of imposed rule-based institutions in three issue domains: conflict resolution, disaster and crisis relief, and modest credit and small loans. [27]

According to the regression results of all three probit models, there are some village-level features that show persistent impacts on Chinese villagers' choice of imposed institutions.[28] Notably, the level of cityward migration and its quadratic term are both statistically significant, and the negative sign of the quadratic term confirms an inverted-U relationship between the level of cityward migration in Chinese villages and their residents' propensity to choose imposed rule-based institutions for resolving conflict, alleviating disasters and crises, and securing modest credit and small loans. In other words, villagers of a rural community with a medium level of outward migration, *ceteris paribus*, are more likely to adopt imposed institutions for local governance issues.[29]

To visualize the impacts of cityward migration on Chinese villagers' contextualized institutional choices, I run simulations to demonstrate the change in an average villager's propensity to choose imposed rule-based institutions for conflict resolution, disaster and crisis relief, and modest credit and small loans, as the village level outward migration increases from 0.5% to 50%.[30] Other variables are set at their respective means and medians. The predicted probabilities and their associated 95% confidence intervals are shown in Figure 6.1.

Externally imposed rule-based institutions, as Figure 6.1a shows, have been widely accepted by Chinese villagers for resolving conflict in their daily lives. Even in a village with a relatively lower level of migration (i.e., 0.5%), the average villager is very likely to contact the village committee, villager council, or local judicial agencies for conflict resolution, with a probability of 81.6%. As outward migration increases, this propensity grows and achieves its highest value, at 90.5%, when the village-level outward migration is around 20%. However, further increases in outward migration reverse the trend of growth and reduce the average villager's propensity to choose imposed institutions. When the village-level outward migration grows to 50%, the propensity of the villager's contacting the village committee, villager council, or local judicial agencies for helping resolve conflict is still high but drops to 74.1%.

Although Chinese villagers are more likely to use private solutions when asking for assistance in face of disasters and crises, as shown in Table 6.1, some also contact village committees or local agencies of civil affairs (i.e., imposed rule-based institutions) for assistance. As seen in Figure 6.1b, in a village with a low level of outward migration (0.5%), the propensity for an average villager to contact the village committee or local agencies of civil affairs for help to respond to disasters and crises is 30.1%. As the level of outward migration increases to around 23%, this propensity also grows and achieves its highest value at 42.3%. Afterward, as outward migration further increases, the average villager's preference for imposed institutions drops. When almost half of the villagers leave to work in cities and provinces far away (50%), the propensity that the average villager will contact the village committee or local agencies of civil affairs for assistance in case of disasters and crises drops to 26.5%.

As illustrated in Figure 6.1c, RCCs are not the first choice for most Chinese villagers when they try to obtain modest credit and small loans for

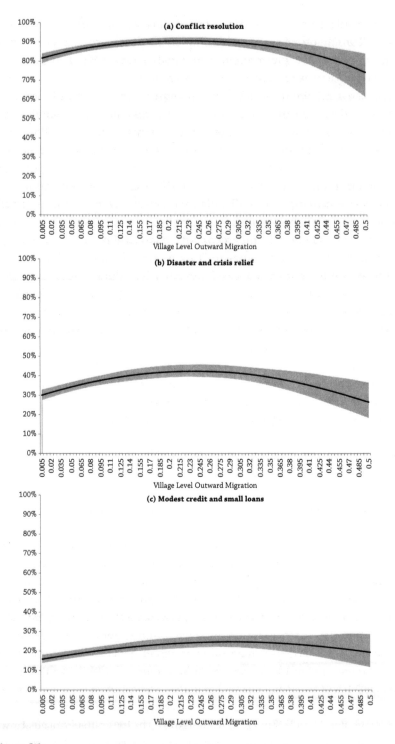

Figure 6.1:
Predicted Probabilities on Chinese Villagers' Contextualized Choice of Imposed Rule-Based Institutions in Different Issue Domains

economic activities. In a close-knit village, where the level of outward migration is as low as 0.5%, the propensity of an average villager's applying for modest credit and small loans from an RCC is 15.9%. As outward migration increases, RCCs become relatively more attractive: When the level of outward migration reaches 28.5%, the average villager's propensity of going to a local RCC for modest credit and small loans increases to its maximum value of 24.8%. Further growth in outward migration makes it more challenging for the average villager to secure modest credit and small loans from the local RCC. When the level of outward migration reaches 50%, the average villager's propensity to contact the local RCC for modest credit and small loans drops back to 19.4%.

In summary, no matter whether externally imposed rule-based institutions play a dominant role (e.g., in conflict resolution) or a minor role (e.g., in disaster/crisis relief and modest credit/small loans) in specific local governance issues, *ceteris paribus*, Chinese villagers of a loosely coupled village featuring a medium level of outward migration are more attracted to the imposed institutions.[31] In other words, as outward migration increases from a low to a medium level, imposed rule-based institutions become more attractive. However, when further increasing outward migration significantly erodes the coordination capacity among Chinese villagers and atomizes China's rural communities, such imposed institutions become less competent in effectively upholding village governance. In these atomized villages, private solutions based on personal connections or even brute force, most of the time, are used to address various governance issues.

6.3 ACCOUNTABILITY AGAIN

In addition to collective action, a key issue for the governance in Chinese villages is how to hold local leaders accountable to the public interest. For indigenous relation-based institutions, the leaders' embeddedness in local social interaction and networks generates necessary accountability through powerful social sanctions. For imposed rule-based institutions, ensuring the accountability is more challenging.

As previous sections show, in Chinese villages, village cadres' evaluations and endorsements have a significant impact on whether villagers can obtain disaster and crisis relief or secure modest credit and small loans through imposed rule-based institutions. If village cadres are interested only in their personal gains and can abuse their power, they can easily channel these resources and loans to their families, relatives, and friends or to those who offer bribes. Once villagers observe or learn of such insider transactions, their confidence in the effectiveness of imposed rule-based institutions is expected to drop accordingly. Therefore, to ensure the effective performance of imposed rule-based institutions in Chinese villages, a complementary rule-based accountability mechanism is required.

As discussed in previous chapters, grassroots democracy was introduced into rural China over two decades ago as the fundamental institutional setting for its decentralized governance. A key function of rural China's grassroots democracy is to provide a rule-based accountability mechanism for elected village cadres. Contemporary research on how effective village elections and other associated institutions are in holding village cadres accountable provides mixed findings. There is evidence of the effectiveness of village elections in increasing local expenditures on public goods (R. Luo et al. 2007; Sato 2008; S. Wang and Yao 2007; X. Zhang et al. 2004), reducing income inequality among villagers and benefiting the poor (Y. Yao and Gao 2006; Y. Yao and Shen 2006), increasing the convergence between villagers and village cadres in terms of policy preferences and even the former's trust in the latter (Kennedy et al. 2004; Manion 1996, 2006), and reducing village cadres' propensity to falsify village income statistics (L. Tsai 2008). However, there also is evidence of the insignificant role of China's rural grassroots democracy in improving local public goods provision (L. Tsai 2007a, b).

One problem with existing studies is that they rely primarily on indirect evidence of whether grassroots democracy in rural China can hold village cadres accountable: If there is a positive and significant association between competitive and transparent village elections and other dependent variables such as public goods provision, local expenditure on public projects, and reduced income inequality among villagers, researchers then infer that accountability is created and well maintained via grassroots democracy in Chinese villages. Otherwise, grassroots democracy is believed to have failed in holding village cadres accountable to the public interest. Unfortunately, few have presented direct evidence on how villagers evaluate the effectiveness of village elections and of different institutions in holding village cadres accountable.

Instead of examining villagers' participation in village elections or campaigning activities, as other scholars of Chinese rural politics (e.g., J. Chen and Zhong 2002; J. Lu and Shi 2009; Shi 1999c; F. Su et al. 2011) have done,[32] I draw on survey questions that tap villagers' evaluations of the effectiveness of village elections and other means of regulating and supervising village cadres' behavior. In the 2008 ABSMCS, rural respondents were asked to answer two questions: (1) "Do you think village elections can select the right leader for better governance in your village?" and (2) "From your perspective, which of the following means/institutions is most effective in regulating and supervising village cadres' behavior?" The weighted percentages of villagers' answers are presented in Table 6.2.

As shown in Table 6.2, when probed for their evaluations of the effectiveness of village elections in selecting the right leader for better governance in their respective villages, 59.7% of the interviewed villagers chose "Yes, for sure" or "Most of the time." Even if the "Don't know" category is treated as a non-positive answer, more than a simple majority of the interviewed villagers endorsed the effectiveness of village elections for choosing quality village cadres who can improve local governance. The villagers' answers to the second question further confirm the widely perceived effectiveness of China's rural grassroots democracy. When confronted with different means and institutions, 48.4% of the rural respondents indicated that they believe that either villager councils (21.6%) or village elections (26.9%), both of which are critical components of China's rural grassroots democracy, are most effective in regulating and supervising

Table 6.2. EFFECTIVENESS OF VILLAGE ELECTIONS AND DIFFERENT VILLAGE CADRE SUPERVISION MECHANISMS

Can village elections select the right leader for better governance in your village?	
Yes, for sure	27.26% (1,162)
Most of the time	32.41% (1,324)
Occasionally	15.95% (654)
Impossible	8.16% (387)
Don't know	16.22% (678)

Most effective means of supervising village cadres	
Clan/lineage council	0.47% (23)
Local public opinion and gossip	2.95% (136)
Villager council	21.55% (827)
Village election	26.86% (1,156)
Appealing to higher-level governments	11.94% (472)
Brute force (*dajia*)	0.08% (5)
Other villagers with connections	0.47% (15)
Don't know	35.69% (1,571)

Source: 2008 ABSMCS Rural Subpopulation (*N* = 4,205).
Note: Weighted percentages.
Raw frequencies in parentheses.

village cadres' behavior. In contrast, indigenous relation-based means, such as clan/lineage councils or gossip/public opinion, received endorsement from only 3.4% of the villagers as the most effective way to regulate and supervise village cadres' behavior. The rest chose to rely on violence (0.1%), personal connections (0.5%), or petitioning to county or even higher-level governments (11.9%).[33]

Before moving on to more sophisticated statistical analyses, it is critical to understand the "Don't know" category, which accounts for 35.7% of all answers, in Chinese villagers' responses to the second question regarding the most effective means of regulating and supervising village cadres. If "Don't know" is primarily the result of the respondents' difficulty in retrieving relevant information in forming an answer, similar to the situation in many other survey item non-responses (Luskin and Bullock 2011; Tourangeau et al. 2000), I can address the "Don't know" category as ordinary item non-responses in subsequent analysis using appropriate statistical tools (Rubin 1987). Nevertheless, "Don't know" also can be interpreted as villagers' apathy toward China's rural grassroots democracy; they might think that there is no way to effectively regulate and supervise village cadres' behavior, which is not unimaginable in rural China. If this is the case, then "Don't know" is a meaningful answer and should be categorized as a special type of private solution, characterized by inaction due to villagers' cynical attitudes toward China's grassroots democracy. To adjudicate between these two possibilities, I calculate the mean value of trust in village committees for respondents' choosing distinct institutions as most effective in regulating and supervising village cadres, with "Don't know" coded as an independent category.[34] Theoretically, if "Don't know" does indicate villagers' apathy toward grassroots democracy, then the mean value of trust in village committees for those who chose "Don't know" should be low and close to the mean value of trust for those who chose private solutions as most effective in regulating and supervising village cadres' behavior. The results are presented in Table 6.3.

As shown in Table 6.3, the mean value of respondents' trust in village committees for the "Don't know" group is 4.45, significantly higher than that for the group of villagers who prefer private solutions, 4.27.[35] Moreover, the mean value of the "Don't know" group, as expected, is significantly less than that of the group that believes in the effectiveness of grassroots democracy in regulating and supervising village cadres' behavior.[36] Thus, it is safe to argue that "Don't know" is not primarily driven by villagers' cynical attitudes toward China's rural grassroots democracy but is instead more likely the consequence of a complicated psychological process that involves various factors.[37] Therefore, in subsequent analysis,

Table 6.3. AVERAGE TRUST IN VILLAGE COMMITTEES FOR VILLAGERS
WITH DIFFERENT CHOICES OF MOST EFFECTIVE MEANS OF REGULATING
AND SUPERVISING VILLAGE CADRES

	Mean (1–6)	Obs.
Indigenous relation-based institutions	4.27 (0.149)	159
Imposed rule-based institutions	4.57 (0.050)	1,983
Private solutions	4.27 (0.083)	492
Don't know	4.45 (0.057)	1,571

Source: 2008 ABSMCS Rural Subpopulation (*N* = 4,205).
Note: Weighted mean.
Standard errors in parentheses, corrected for complex sampling.

"Don't know" is addressed with the conventional technique of dealing with missing values for survey item non-responses.

Theoretically, villagers' evaluations of the effectiveness of grassroots democracy in holding village cadres accountable to the public interest should follow the same logic presented in the previous section on villagers' contextualized institutional choices in resolving conflict, alleviating disasters and crises, and securing modest credit and small loans. As outward migration in a village increases from a low level, which weakens the capacity of indigenous relation-based institutions to regulate and supervise village cadres' behavior, using grassroots democracy to hold village cadres accountable becomes more attractive. Nevertheless, if the level of outward migration increases even further, the atomized and paralyzed social environment cannot support even a required minimal level of coordination among villagers for the effective performance of grassroots democracy, which, in turn, may lead to more frequent use of private solutions among the villagers to deal with village cadres.[38]

Again, probit regressions are used to explore the conditions under which grassroots democracy is more likely to be perceived by average villagers as most effective in holding village cadres accountable to the public interest. Given the political nature of the accountability issue, in addition to all of the individual features and village characteristics used in the previous section on Chinese villagers' contextualized institutional choices, three variables that capture individual socio-psychological features are also included as controls: political interest,[39] internal political efficacy,[40] and satisfaction with the performance of democracy in China.[41]

According to the regression results of probit models, after controlling for various individual-level and village-level features, cityward migration

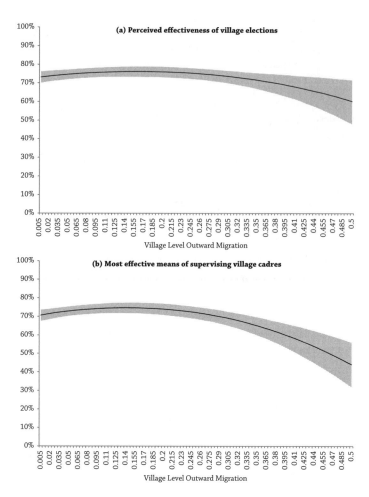

Figure 6.2:
Predicted Probabilities on Villagers' Evaluations of Grassroots Democracy

still plays a significant and persistent role in explaining villagers' assessment of the effectiveness of village elections in selecting quality village cadres who can improve local governance as well as grassroots democracy as the most effective means of supervising and regulating village cadres' behavior.[42] The negative but significant coefficient associated with the quadratic term of outward migration again confirms an inverted-U relationship between cityward migration and villagers' evaluations of grassroots democracy's effectiveness in holding village cadres accountable.

To visualize the impacts of cityward migration on villagers' evaluations of China's rural grassroots democracy, I run simulations to demonstrate the change in an average villager's propensity to believe in the effectiveness of village elections in selecting quality village cadres for better local governance as well as grassroots democracy as the most effective means in regulating and supervising village cadres' behavior, as the village level outward migration increases from 0.5% to 50%.[43] Other variables are set at their respective means and medians. The predicted probabilities and their associated 95% confidence intervals are displayed in Figure 6.2.

As shown in Figure 6.2a, the curvilinear impact of outward migration on villagers' assessment of the effectiveness of village elections is statistically and substantively significant. In a typical village with a low level of outward migration (0.5%), the propensity of an average villager's believing in the effectiveness of village elections in selecting quality village cadres for better local governance is 73.1%. This propensity increases as outward migration grows and reaches its largest value of 76.2%, when the village-level outward migration reaches 15.5%. Further growth in outward migration decreases this propensity, which drops to 60.2% when outward migration increases to 50%. The inverted-U relationship between outward migration and villagers' belief in grassroots democracy as the most effective means for regulating and supervising village cadres is presented in Figure 6.2b: In a close-knit village with a low level of outward migration (0.5%), the propensity that an average villager regards grassroots democracy as the most effective institution in holding village cadres accountable is 70.6%. As an increasing number of villagers leave to work as migrants in other cities or provinces, the average villager becomes more likely to believe in the effectiveness of grassroots democracy for regulating and supervising village cadres' behavior. This propensity achieves its maximum value, 74.6%, when outward migration reaches 16%. Even more villagers' leaving can exert a negative influence on the average villager's belief in the effectiveness of grassroots democracy for holding village cadres accountable: This propensity falls dramatically to 44.1% as outward migration approaches 50%. Essentially, Chinese villagers of a village with a medium level of outward migration, *ceteris paribus*, are more likely to (1) believe in the effectiveness of village elections in selecting quality village cadres for better local governance and (2) regard grassroots democracy as the most effective means for regulating and supervising village cadres' behavior.[44]

To summarize, examining Chinese rural residents' assessment of the effectiveness of grassroots democracy in (1) selecting quality local leaders for better village governance and (2) regulating and supervising village cadres' behavior, compared to possible alternatives, offers direct and systematic evidence on how effective imposed rule-based institutions, primarily embodied via grassroots democracy, are addressing the problem of accountability in Chinese villages. This analysis also identifies the conditions under which such imposed institutions are likely to be well established and perform effectively in sustaining China's rural governance. More specifically, a majority of Chinese villagers believe in the effectiveness of grassroots democracy for selecting quality village cadres for better local governance and holding them accountable to the public interest. Moreover, these subjective evaluations change across Chinese villages, following a curvilinear function of village-level outward migration. It is in villages with a medium level of outward migration that Chinese rural residents are more likely to hold positive perceptions and better evaluations of the effectiveness of imposed grassroots democracy for selecting quality village cadres for better local governance and holding them accountable to the public interest.

6.4 CONCLUSION

Good governance, as resulting in citizens' prosperous and peaceful lives, involves more than just the sufficient provision of local public goods. The effective resolution of possible conflicts to ensure social order, timely delivery of assistance and resources to alleviate disasters and crises, and convenient access to credit and loans for economic activities all are important for quality governance. Using the 2008 ABSMCS and 2008 NVS, this chapter examines (1) Chinese villagers' contextualized choices among different institutions to resolve conflict, alleviate disasters and crises, and raise credit and loans for economic activities as well as (2) their assessment of the effectiveness of different institutions that can hold village cadres accountable to the public interest and for better governance, with particular emphasis on their evaluations of rural China's grassroots democracy.

The coexistence of indigenously developed relation-based institutions, externally imposed rule-based institutions, and private solutions has been widely observed in Chinese villages in regard to conflict resolution, disaster and crisis relief, and modest credit and small loans. In addition to contacting village committees, villager councils, relevant local official agencies, or the RCCs, some Chinese villagers (1) contact clan/lineage organizations or upright and fair fellow villagers with recognized authority to resolve conflict, (2) seek assistance from clan/lineage organizations or neighbors in the event of unexpected disasters or crises, and (3) organize associations such as ROSCAs to raise modest credit and small loans. Meanwhile, some also rely on themselves, families, friends, or other people they know to address their problems in these domains. In today's rural China, imposed rule-based institutions play a major role in resolving local conflict, while private solutions based on personal connections dominate Chinese villagers' institutional choices in alleviating disasters and crises and raising the necessary capital for economic activities.

Moreover, Chinese villagers' institutional choices for local governance issues are indeed contextualized; they are significantly shaped by the communal structural features of Chinese rural communities. Multiple regression results confirm that imposed rule-based institutions are more likely to be the choice for resolving conflict, alleviating disasters and crises, and raising credit and loans for economic activities in villages with a medium level of outward migration. As discussed in detail in Chapter 2 and summarized in Table 2.2, in such loosely coupled rural communities, impaired indigenous relation-based institutions (due to weakened social sanctions) generate sufficient incentives for Chinese villagers to embrace imposed rule-based institutions, and the still-functioning social networks ensure effective coordination among villagers with regard to their institutional choices. In contrast, in close-knit villages with a low level of outward migration, thanks to their convenient access to the still-effective but less costly indigenous institutions, imposed institutions are more expensive to use and, thus, are less attractive to Chinese villagers. Further, in atomized communities with paralyzed social networks, a high level of outward migration drains the "social nutrition" needed for the effective performance of any institutions, and, thus, private solutions based on personal connections or brute force are more likely to be the default choice for Chinese villagers.

To ensure the effectiveness of imposed rule-based institutions in sustaining governance in rural China, the Chinese government introduced grassroots democracy as the key institution to address the accountability issue (i.e., holding village cadres accountable to the public interest and for better village governance). Contrary to some China scholars' conclusions on the impotency of grassroots democracy in holding village cadres accountable, a large percentage of Chinese villagers believe that grassroots democracy is the most effective means of regulating and supervising village cadres' behavior, and more than a simple majority believe that village elections can select quality village cadres for better governance in their respective villages.[45] Further statistical analyses and simulations confirm that villagers' evaluations of the effectiveness of China's rural grassroots democracy in selecting quality village cadres and holding them accountable to the public interest follow the same logic as do contextualized institutional choices. Essentially, in close-knit villages, effective indigenous means of holding village cadres accountable via powerful social sanctions make grassroots democracy relatively less appealing to Chinese villagers. In atomized villages with a high level of migration, grassroots democracy cannot perform effectively due to a hostile social environment that cannot even sustain a minimum level of within-village coordination. Thus, grassroots democracy is most likely to be endorsed by Chinese villagers in rural communities with a medium level of outward migration and evaluated much more positively for its effectiveness in selecting quality village cadres for better local governance and holding them accountable to the public interest.

In summary, Chinese villagers use different institutional alternatives to address local governance issues in their villages. Their choices among available institutions are contextualized and embedded in the social environment of their respective villages. As the communal structures of Chinese villages are unevenly transformed, *inter alia*, by the large-scale cityward migration, the transformed social environment accordingly shapes their residents' institutional choices. In loosely coupled villages characterized by a medium level of outward migration, externally imposed rule-based institutions, *ceteris paribus*, are more likely to attract Chinese villagers' attention and become their preferred choice for addressing local governance issues and holding village cadres accountable. Such findings on Chinese villagers' contextualized institutional choices shed light on the individual-level dynamics and mechanisms of the varying institutional foundations of local governance, as well as institutional change and performance, in transformed Chinese rural communities.

CHAPTER 7
Conclusion

As is widely recognized among scholars and policymakers, institutions are critical for the quality of governance in local communities. Establishing "good institutions" might be even more significant for local communities in a decentralized system, wherein the community members themselves are required to address issues of collective action and accountability. Although similar sets of rule-based institutions have been promoted through China's legislative and bureaucratic efforts to enhance its decentralized rural governance since the late 1980s, the variance in Chinese villages' governance is dramatic, with respect not only to quality but also to underlying institutional foundations.

In some Chinese villages, indigenously developed relation-based institutions, primarily supported by powerful social sanctions, have successfully coordinated and regulated villagers' behaviors and effectively channeled village cadres' efforts toward the public interest. In these villages, the indigenous institutions are so powerful that they even counteract national policies to enforce community-shared norms, such as regular land reallocation to accommodate local demographic changes. In other villages, externally imposed rule-based institutions, primarily embodied in village democratic elections, have been well established and enforced according to standardized national stipulations, sometimes even despite significant intervention from township officials, to provide institutional support for quality village governance. In these communities with competitive and transparent village elections, residents are significantly empowered and self-conscious in supervising village cadres and holding them accountable through democratic procedures. The recognized authority of elected village cadres, based on the integrity of their electoral institutions and procedures, also has equipped these cadres with effective leverage in coordinating villagers' behaviors and organizing collective efforts to further the interest of these communities.

Meanwhile, in some Chinese villages, neither indigenous relation-based nor imposed rule-based institutions perform well. In these communities, not only do village cadres dodge and ignore their obligations and duties without incurring any penalties but also villagers care little about community affairs and focus exclusively on their private lives. Private solutions prevail in these villages, with everyone's counting on himself or herself to address a range of issues through individual efforts or personal connections. Thus, little attention is paid to and few resources are channeled into public projects, and most community affairs are left unattended. In these villages, one can find dilapidated irrigation projects, unpaved muddy roads, frequent conflicts, and a lack of cooperation among villagers or even the dominance of local bullies or gangsters.

This book has tried to understand the origins of such variance in contemporary rural China's decentralized governance. More specifically, it has tried to identify the conditions under which different types of institutions are likely to perform effectively in sustaining Chinese villages' governance as well as the role of community structural features in transforming the underlying institutional foundations of their governance.

In general, I argue that any institution that can efficiently solve the problems of collective action and accountability should be able to uphold quality governance in local communities, regardless of their nature and origins. The respective performance of different types of institutions, however, is contingent upon the characteristics of the social environment in which they are embedded. Such social environment characteristics are, in turn, closely shaped by the structural features of the local communities. More specifically, frequent and continuous social interaction and dense and extended social networks in close-knit communities favor the performance of indigenously developed relation-based institutions, supported primarily by powerful multilateral social sanctions. Externally imposed rule-based institutions, assisted by specialized agents and complementary organizations, have an advantage in loosely coupled communities with thin and loosened, but still functional, social networks. Further, in atomized communities characterized by a dearth of vibrant, within-community interaction and collapsed social networks, neither indigenous relation-based nor imposed rule-based institutions can survive.

I further argue that, among a variety of factors that might have contributed to the structural transformation of rural communities, which has implications for the establishment and performance of different types of institutions in these communities, the most salient is a major phenomenon witnessed in many developing countries experiencing the transition from agrarian to industrial societies: rural–urban migration. More specifically, in local communities with distinct levels of outward migration, community members' contextualized choices between indigenous relation-based and imposed rule-based institutions for local governance issues are likely to unfold in different ways. This generates distinct dynamics of institutional change in these communities with varying communal structures.

In particular, indigenous relation-based institutions are more likely to be preferred over imposed rule-based institutions if a low level of outward migration has done limited damage to the frequent and continuous interactions among community members or to their dense and extended social networks. Thus, institutional disarticulation or grafting, to use Galvan's (2004) terms, is likely to arise, given the dominance of indigenous institutions in these communities' local governance. As a medium level of outward migration transforms close-knit communities into loosely coupled ones, imposed rule-based institutions are more likely to be favored over indigenous relation-based ones and, thus, provide the institutional support for these communities' governance. Hence, institutional syncretism or even modernizing transformation, again to use Galvan's (2004) terms, is likely to be observed, thanks to the dominance of imposed institutions in these communities' local governance. Moreover, in both close-knit and loosely coupled communities, quality governance is more likely to be effectively sustained, despite their distinct institutional foundations. However, a very high level of outward migration can paralyze and atomize local communities and, thus, deprive them of the minimally required social nutrition for the performance of any institutions. In these communities, neither indigenous nor imposed institutions can perform effectively, and private solutions based on violence or individualized connections are likely to prevail, leading to a radical degeneration in these communities' governance.

7.1 EMPIRICAL FINDINGS

Using the 2008 National Village Survey (NVS), the rural subpopulation of the 2008 ABS Mainland China Survey (ABSMCS), and a number of case studies, this book systematically examines (1) the impacts of indigenous relation-based and imposed rule-based institutions on decentralized local public goods provision in Chinese villages as well as how the quality of these institutions is shaped by rural China's unevenly distributed cityward migration; (2) how cityward migration affects the social environments in rural China, including villagers' access to local information, their perceived power of possible social sanctions, foundations of publicly recognized local authority, and community-shared norms; and (3) the effects of cityward migration on villagers' contextualized institutional choices for conflict resolution, disaster and crisis relief, and modest credit and small loans as well as their evaluations of the effectiveness of rural China's grassroots democracy in supervising village cadres and holding them accountable.

Decentralized Local Public Goods Provision

The village-level information collected from the 356 administrative villages in the 2008 NVS, as well as three case studies, shows a hybrid version of decentralized local public goods provision in rural China, based on varying institutional foundations. These villages' varying institutional foundations for local public goods provision are further tied to their respective communal structures, which have been transformed to varying extents due to the unprecedented large-scale and unevenly distributed outflow of rural labor through cityward migration.

As empirically demonstrated, the provision of local public goods in Chinese villages has been significantly decentralized, particularly after the collapse of the commune system in the early 1980s, subsequent tax-for-fee reforms in the early 2000s, and the final abolition of agricultural taxes in 2006. With limited fiscal transfers from upper-level governments, Chinese villages need to mobilize and secure economic resources by themselves to fund local public projects and provide public welfare. To provide local public goods in this decentralized system, Chinese villages need effective institutional solutions to address the problems of collective action and accountability. The 2008 NVS shows consistent and significant evidence of varieties of governance in Chinese villages and the effectiveness of different institutional solutions in improving these villages' decentralized public goods provision.

On the one hand, indigenously developed relation-based institutions, as supported by powerful social sanctions, can regulate and coordinate villagers' behaviors and relieve the problem of collective action. Village cadres also can be held accountable to the public interest, as long as such indigenous institutions can effectively deter their possible opportunistic and rent-seeking activities via powerful social sanctions. On the other hand, externally imposed rule-based institutions also can be of great help in improving local public goods provision. Transparent and competitive elections can not only make elected village cadres accountable to their electorates and channel their efforts toward the public interest but also generate highly recognized public authority that is indispensable for coordinating villagers' behaviors and mobilizing necessary resources for local public goods provision.

Moreover, both quantitative and qualitative evidence confirm that the effectiveness of these institutions is contingent upon some communal structural features that are significantly but unevenly transformed by the large-scale cityward migration in rural China. In Chinese villages with a very low level of outward migration, indigenous relation-based institutions embedded in the well-maintained, close-knit social environment and supported by powerful social sanctions can effectively address the problems of collective action and accountability. When outward migration increases to a medium level, the effectiveness of these indigenous institutions is weakened. Then, in these loosely coupled villages, imposed rule-based institutions are more likely to be well established and perform effectively in addressing the two problems. In both close-knit and loosely coupled villages, local public goods provision is more likely to be effectively sustained, though with distinct institutional support. As outward migration approaches a high or exodus level, the communal structures of Chinese villages are fundamentally transformed, and their social networks are seriously fragmented and paralyzed. In this atomized environment, neither indigenous institutions nor imposed institutions can effectively address the problem of collective action and hold local leaders accountable. Due to this lack of effective institutional support, local public goods provision in these atomized Chinese villages is insufficient or, worse, close to nonexistent.

Social Environments in Transformed Villages

Quantitative analyses that combine village-level information from the 2008 NVS and individual-level information from the 2008 ABSMCS, as well as a qualitative longitudinal case study, show consistent evidence of the erosive effects of cityward migration on the social environments in Chinese villages. Essentially, as the close-knit communal structure of Chinese villages is transformed, *inter alia*, by large-scale cityward migration, the social foundations of China's rural governance are changed as well.

The transformed social environment in many Chinese villages, particularly those that witness a higher level of outward migration, is no longer favorable for the performance of indigenous relation-based institutions supported by powerful social sanctions.

More specifically, with a large number of rural residents' leaving for economic opportunities in cities, villagers' personal stakes in their home villages are significantly reduced, and their social interaction with fellow villagers is disrupted and becomes less frequent. As expected, the local information environment diminishes, with many villagers' knowing little about their fellow villagers. As their attention shifts to the outside world, the significance that villagers attach to their local reputations also decreases. All the aforementioned changes impair the power of social sanctions and weaken the performance of indigenous relation-based institutions. The increasingly diversified foundations of local public authority further complicate the situation, given the dominant leadership role played by traditional authorities in upholding and enforcing these indigenous institutions.

Moreover, cityward migration erodes some crucial social norms in Chinese villages, which are a critical component of the social foundations for China's rural governance based on indigenous institutions. In Chinese villages with a higher level of outward migration, residents, on average, are less likely to internalize the norms that prioritize collective interests, long-term relationships, and harmonious relationships within the villages. In other words, in these transformed rural communities, villagers are more likely to be self-centered in social interactions, such as caring more about their own interests and short-term benefits and insisting on assigning blame to one party or the other once conflicts arise. All these changes further challenge the performance of indigenous relation-based institutions and generate serious needs for alternative institutional solutions that are more effective in sustaining the governance in Chinese villages with transformed communal structures and social environments.

Contextualized Institutional Choices

By combining village-level information from the 2008 NVS and individual-level information from the 2008 ABSMCS, this book presents further evidence of the implications of the transformed social environments in rural China for their residents' institutional choices. In general, Chinese villagers use a variety of institutional alternatives to address local governance issues, and their choices among the available institutions are contextualized and embedded in the social environment of their respective villages. In loosely coupled villages, characterized by a medium level of outward migration, imposed rule-based institutions, *ceteris paribus*, are more likely to attract Chinese villagers' attention and become their choice in addressing local governance issues. In these villages, rule-based institutions also are more likely to be perceived as most effective in supervising village cadres and holding them accountable.

The coexistence of indigenous relation-based institutions, imposed rule-based institutions, and private solutions, which are used by Chinese villagers for conflict resolution, disaster and crisis relief, and modest credit and small loans, is clearly documented in the survey data from rural China. For instance, in addition to contacting village committees, villager councils, relevant local official agencies, or the Rural Credit Cooperatives, some Chinese villagers also (1) contact clan/lineage organizations or upright and fair fellow villagers with recognized authority to resolve conflict, (2) seek assistance from clan/lineage organizations or neighbors in the event of unexpected disasters or crises, and (3) organize associations such as rotating savings and credit associations to raise modest credit and small loans. Meanwhile, some rely on themselves, families, friends, or other people they know personally to address their concerns. Moreover, Chinese villagers' institutional choices for local governance issues are indeed contextualized; that is, they are significantly shaped by the communal structural features of their villages. The imposed rule-based institutions are more likely to be the choice for resolving conflicts, alleviating disasters and crises, and raising modest credit and small loans for economic activities in loosely coupled villages—that is, those with a medium level of outward migration.

To ensure the effectiveness of the imposed rule-based institutions in upholding China's rural governance, the Chinese government has introduced grassroots democracy to address the issue of accountability (i.e., holding village cadres accountable to the public interest). The survey data show that a large percentage of Chinese villagers believe that grassroots democracy is the most effective means of regulating and supervising village cadres' behavior, and more than a simple majority believe that village elections can select quality village cadres for better governance. Further statistical analyses confirm that Chinese villagers' evaluations of the effectiveness of grassroots democracy in selecting quality village cadres and holding them accountable to the public interest follow the same logic as that of their contextualized institutional choices. Grassroots democracy is more likely to be enthusiastically embraced by the residents of loosely coupled rural communities and evaluated much more positively by these villagers for its effectiveness in selecting quality village cadres for better local governance as well as holding them accountable to the public interest.

In summary, the evidence of the impacts of cityward migration on Chinese villages' social environments and their residents' institutional choices for various local governance issues provides critical micro-level mechanisms that bridge the changes in community structures and the existence of varying institutional foundations of local governance in contemporary rural China. Overall, due to unevenly distributed large-scale cityward migration in rural China, the social environments of Chinese villages have been transformed. These transformed social environments remold the social foundations for the performance of different types of institutions, which, in turn, shape and coordinate villagers' institutional choices for local governance issues. The aggregation of these contextualized institutional choices results in several varieties of governance in Chinese rural communities, each with a distinct institutional foundation.

7.2 CONTEXTUALIZED INSTITUTIONAL CHANGE = EPIPHENOMENAL INSTITUTIONS?

In a thought-provoking paper, Przeworski (2004) raises one of the most challenging questions for scholars of institutions: Are institutions merely epiphenomenal? Przeworski's argument is logically persuasive: If similar institutions survive under some conditions but fail under others, do institutions have autonomous roles to play? In other words, are they simply transmitting the causal effects of those conditions? Przeworski's critique "applies perfectly" to my argument of contextualized institutional change, which features the significance of community structural features in shaping the performance of both indigenously developed relation-based institutions and externally imposed rule-based ones in sustaining the decentralized governance in rural China. It seems on the surface that, for my argument, institutions are merely epiphenomenal and what really matter are the structural features of Chinese villages. If this is the case, why should we care about institutions?

What has been bothering scholars of institutions are the various methodological barriers that they have to overcome when differentiating the impact of institutions from that of surrounding conditions.[1] As long as we can identify some factors that not only significantly shape the institutions of interest but also are exogenous to the structural conditions under examination,[2] we should be able to effectively isolate the impact of institutions from that of surrounding conditions and, thus, shed some light on the question of why we should care about institutions. Fortunately, the experiences of China's rural governance provide some analytic leverage on this, particularly with respect to externally imposed institutions. Essentially, various institutions imposed upon Chinese villages for their governance have never been completely endogenous to these rural communities. What types of institutions should be imposed, as well as how such imposed institutions should operate, have been significantly shaped by Chinese political leaders based on concerns beyond rural China's governance. In other words, institutions in rural China are significantly shaped by socioeconomic and political forces that are exogenous to Chinese villages, in addition to the impact of their surrounding conditions.

As shown in Chapter 3, the rulers of the Ming and Qing dynasties took some structural features of Chinese villages into consideration when designing the *lijia*, *baojiao*, and *xiangyue* systems. They also systematically incorporated some indigenous relation-based institutions into their institutional design to ensure order and stability in rural China, given their insufficient fiscal and administrative resources. Nevertheless, when the rulers designed and imposed the institutions, their concerns over how to effectively extract economic and personnel resources from Chinese villages to finance the empire's gigantic bureaucratic machine and military dwarfed the issue of local governance in these rural communities. These concerns are clearly exogenous to the Chinese villages under examination.

For instance, when the rulers of the Ming and Qing dynasties were in urgent need of economic and personnel resources to support their military campaigns against foreign rivals, "entrepreneurial brokers," as the national government's intermediate agents, dominated the operation of the institutions in rural China with brute force, in place of "protective brokers," who relied more on their public authority embedded in the local cultural nexus to run the same institutions during peacetime (Duara 1988). The then-surrounding conditions of the *lijia*, *baojia*, and *xiangyue* systems in rural China did not change much, but the intermediate agents recruited by the national government to run these institutions had distinct incentives in playing their roles as community leaders. This change in the operation of institutions, which pushed for an almost exclusive emphasis on extracting resources rather than serving rural communities, was clearly independent from the institutions' then-surrounding conditions. Nevertheless, this change significantly transformed the dynamics of governance in rural China and resulted in the deterioration of these communities' governance.

Rural China's experiences under the Chinese Communist Party (CCP) regime also confirm the significant influence of institutions on its governance, which cannot be fully attributed to the institutions' simply transmitting the impact of structural conditions. As the statistics presented in Chapter 3 show, the structural conditions of rural China at the beginning of the CCP regime were not essentially different from those of the Republican era. Nevertheless, for ideological and historical reasons, the CCP imposed a set of totalitarian institutions that were essentially different from those chosen by the Kuomintang to deal with similar problems in governing rural China.

The CCP's penetration into Chinese villages, with the help of widely established party organizations and backed by its despotic power, land reform, and ideological indoctrination, ensured the effectiveness of these imposed totalitarian institutions in aligning local interests with those of the national government. With the help of these institutions, the CCP regime was much more effective in extracting resources from Chinese villages to subsidize its industrialization in urban China than were any other previous regimes. Meanwhile, despite its negative and even catastrophic impacts on the lives of most Chinese peasants, particularly during the Three Years of Natural Disasters (1959–1961), the commune system contributed to the improvement of some aspects of Chinese villages' governance (e.g., widely constructed and regularly maintained irrigation projects and an effective public health system). Again, the significant differences between the governance of rural China under the CCP regime, particularly during the early years after the CCP's victory, and that under the Ming and Qing dynasties and the Kuomintang regime cannot simply be attributed to the impacts of rural China's structural conditions, which did not change dramatically in the 1950s. They were, indeed, the result of different institutions imposed onto Chinese rural communities.

More recently, rural China's grassroots democracy, the newly designed and imposed rule-based institutions for self-governance in Chinese villages since the late 1980s, also was significantly shaped by the political dynamics of upper-level governments (Kennedy 2002; Landry et al. 2010; O'Brien 1994; O'Brien and Li 2000; Shi 1999b, 2000c). This provides a great opportunity to conduct a counterfactual analysis of the possible independent impact of imposed village elections on Chinese villages' governance.[3]

Given the widely observed rigged elections in rural China and the significant influence of township governments in this regard, as documented in Chapter 4, it is easy to imagine decentralized governance in Chinese villages under a system that continues the practice of having village cadres appointed by township governments. Were this system sustained in rural China, village cadres' incentives could have been significantly shifted by the rule-based institutions toward following their upper-level government's instructions rather than toward serving their fellow villagers. In this hypothetical scenario and given the possible conflicts between the interests of the upper-level government and the villagers, as increasing cityward migration weakens the capacity of indigenous relation-based institutions to solve the problems of collective action and accountability in Chinese villages, no alternative rule-based institutions, such as the grassroots democracy, would have been available for the villagers to supervise their village cadres and hold them accountable. Therefore, it would not be an exaggeration to argue that the quality of decentralized governance in Chinese villages witnessing a medium level of cityward migration could have been more worrisome if grassroots democracy had not been imposed.

In other words, the imposed grassroots democracy offers a rule-based institutional alternative for sustaining decentralized governance in these villages by effectively alleviating the challenges posed by cityward migration. For these rural communities, the imposed rule-based institutions do much more than simply transmit the causal effects of surrounding conditions; they provide new institutional alternatives that contribute to better local governance.[4] Therefore, despite the documented significant influence of surrounding structural conditions on the performance of these imposed institutions (Chapters 4 and 6), institutions have independent impacts on rural China's governance and are not merely epiphenomenal.

7.3 CONTEXTUALIZED UNDERSTANDING OF INSTITUTIONS AND INSTITUTIONAL CHANGE

After decades of research, scholars of institutions have gradually come to recognize the significance of informal institutions as underlying constraints that drive path-dependency in institutional change (Greif 2006; Greif and Tabellini 2010; Kuran 2010; North 1990; Roland 2004), as critical components that contribute to institutional syncretism (Galvan 2004; Sil and Galvan 2007), as powerful responses against existing formal institutions (Helmke and Levitsky 2004; K. S. Tsai 2006), or as functional substitutes for formal institutions (K. S. Tsai 2002; L. Tsai 2007a, b). Compared with previous generations of research on institutions, which usually isolates the subjects of examination from their surrounding institutional environment, these scholars have contextualized their understanding on institutional change by incorporating the institutional environment. Unfortunately, with a few exceptions,[5] most scholars of institutions have not sufficiently contextualized their theorization and explanations of institutional change.

I argue that to adequately contextualize our understanding of institutional change and its consequences, we need to (1) develop a more comprehensive framework to examine the possible dynamics among different types of institutions by, for instance, enriching the conceptualization of institutional environment to cover various scenarios and (2) move beyond the institutional environment and bring in the pertinent social environment, in which the institutional environment is embedded. These issues were systematically addressed in this book, with a specific focus on the transformed institutional foundations of local governance in contemporary rural China.

Formal and Informal Institutions

In contemporary political science literature on institutions and institutional change, possible dynamics among different types of institutions have been either absent or, at best, partially captured. Some researchers treat different types of institutions as separate and isolated systems that work simultaneously in specific settings (Y.-t. Chang and Wu 2011; L. Tsai 2007a, b), while others theorize about and incorporate the interactions among different types of institutions but mostly in an incomplete way (Helmke and Levitsky 2004; Mahoney and Thelen 2010b; K. S. Tsai 2006).

Helmke and Levitsky's (2004) well-received research agenda on informal institutions, for example, provides a typology that features four types of informal institutions that are differentiated along two dimensions: (1) how effective related formal institutions are and (2) to what extent the outcomes of formal and informal institutions under examination converge or diverge. This typology implicitly assumes that the effectiveness of formal institutions has nothing to do with informal institutions and is purely exogenous. This assumption might be reasonable for their subsequent focus on the origins of and changes in informal institutions that are endogenous to related formal ones. Nevertheless, there are many other equally plausible dynamics between formal and informal institutions that cannot be captured by Helmke and Levitsky's framework, wherein the change in formal institutions might be endogenous to related informal ones. A clear example of how informal institutions shape the change in formal institutions is the literature on path-dependency in institutional change pioneered by scholars like North (1990, 2005). This is why scholars such as Ledeneva (2006) and Grzymala-Busse (2010) criticize Helmke and Levitsky's framework as prioritizing formal institutions in theoretical deductions (without sufficient justification) and ignoring the role of informal institutions in shaping the performance of formal ones.

This issue is highly salient in regard to decentralized local governance, wherein indigenously developed relation-based institutions, most of which are informal, to use Helmke and Levitsky's terms,[6] have a much longer history of providing institutional support for local communities and were in place long before the externally imposed rule-based institutions that are "created, communicated, and enforced through channels widely accepted as official" (Helmke and Levitsky 2004, p. 727). For instance, as discussed in Chapter 3, indigenous relation-based institutions that have helped sustain social order, ensure public security, and cultivate and enforce reciprocal norms in Chinese villages can be traced back to times when bureaucratic influence was negligible in these communities and such informal institutions bore most responsibility for their governance.

Most of the time, not only in rural China but also in many other regions of different countries, rule-based formal institutions are imposed upon local communities with rich traditions of indigenous relation-based informal institutions. As a result, the relation-based informal institutions constitute a critical component of the institutional environment in which rule-based formal institutions are embedded. And the effectiveness of the imposed formal institutions is highly likely to be contingent upon how the indigenous informal institutions perform in these communities. To further our understanding of institutional change and how local governance can be more effectively improved via appropriate institutional building, we need to seriously engage the possibility and scenarios that the establishment, performance, and effectiveness of formal institutions, again using Helmke and Levitsky's (2004) terms, in local communities are endogenous to the informal institutions indigenously developed in these communities.

With quantitative evidence based on national survey data and qualitative case studies, as well as secondhand empirical evidence from related literature, this book systematically demonstrates the dynamics between imposed rule-based institutions and indigenous relation-based ones in providing institutional support for Chinese villages' local public goods provision (Chapter 4), when the former are imposed upon Chinese villages that have a long tradition of decentralized governance that relies on the latter (Chapter 3). The carefully documented dynamics between imposed formal institutions and indigenous informal ones in the villages' local public goods provision correspond to residents' contextualized choices between the two types of institutions to address local governance issues such as resolving conflicts, relieving disasters and crises, raising modest credit and small loans, and holding local political leaders accountable (Chapter 6). The empirical evidence suggests that imposed rule-based institutions are more attractive to Chinese villagers when key mechanisms that ensure the effectiveness of indigenous relation-based institutions (powerful social sanctions and convenient access to local information) are weakened (Chapter 5) and the indigenous institutions become less competent in addressing local governance issues (Chapter 6). Overall, the imposed institutions are more likely to be well established (e.g., grassroots democracy with a transparent and competitive electoral institution) in Chinese villages with weakened indigenous institutions (Chapter 4).

These findings confirm that different types of institutions work simultaneously in specific settings; nevertheless, they do not necessarily perform independently of each other. The dynamics between them are likely to be realized through numerous agents' contextualized institutional choices. These findings also emphasize the equally important (but generally ignored) fact that the establishment, performance, and effectiveness of formal institutions are likely to be shaped to some extent by related informal institutions, particularly when the latter have a much longer history in serving similar purposes. These findings complement those of previous studies in political science on institutional change that assume the one-way endogeneity of informal institutions to formal institutions. Here, endogeneity is no longer some annoying methodological issue that should be either addressed through technical routines in an agnostic way just for appropriate estimations or intentionally avoided for a more parsimonious and straightforward explanation. Instead, endogeneity provides great opportunities for a much richer understanding of the performance of and change in institutions.

Formal and informal institutions can be endogenous to each other, depending on the issues and processes under examination. Hence, a more comprehensive examination of the possible dynamics among different types of institutions contributes to our contextualized understanding of institutional performance and change. This more comprehensive framework not only further clarifies the issue of endogeneity for contemporary research on institutions but also provides new perspectives to advance our conceptualization and theorization of institutions, institutional environment, and institutional change.

Beyond Institutional Environment

In addition to promoting a richer conceptualization of institutional environment, with informal institutions as a critical component, and emphasizing the possible endogeneity of formal institutions to informal ones, this book further suggests that scholars of institutions, in their theorization and examination of institutions and institutional change, should pay more attention to the impact of the surrounding social environment in which the institutional environment is embedded. Bringing the social environment into our research explicitly theorizes and incorporates the well-documented yet under-theorized effects of social environment in existing studies on institutions in sociology, economic history, anthropology, and legal studies. This book presents a more self-conscious and intentional push for an even deeper contextualized understanding of institutional performance and change, particularly in informal institutions.

More specifically, this book identifies some fundamental and commonly observed mechanisms that underlie the performance of various informal institutions and establishes the role of surrounding social environment in shaping these mechanisms. This is of critical value for understanding the change in informal institutions, which is rarely addressed in contemporary literature.[7] For instance, due to the lack of this "deepened contextualization," contemporary research on informal institutions in local governance has been segmented into isolated areas dominated by their respective pet variables—for example, solidarity groups (L. Tsai 2007a, b), local norms (Gibson et al. 2000; Ostrom 1990), community-shared customs (Platteau 2000; Platteau and Peccoud 2011; Platteau and Seki 2001), or implicit rules (Skarbek 2011). Despite this literature's value in enriching our understanding of how informal institutions work, there is a lack of a unified framework that could synthesize all these related empirical findings and thus provide a more coherent understanding of the origins and performance of informal institutions. Because of this deficiency, this literature is relatively impotent in explaining how informal institutions evolve and change.

This book argues that the performance of indigenous relation-based informal institutions relies on two key underlying mechanisms: convenient and low-cost access to pertinent information and powerful social sanctions (Chapter 2). When the two mechanisms are disrupted, these informal institutions have much more difficulty in enforcing their rules, sustaining their performance, and ensuring their effectiveness.[8] Meanwhile, the convenience and cost of accessing pertinent information and the power of social sanctions in regulating and coordinating community members' behaviors are highly contingent upon the features of the surrounding social environment. More specifically, a close-knit social environment, due to its frequent and continuous social interactions as well as dense and extended social networks, ensures convenient access to pertinent information at a low cost and effective social sanctions against deviant and opportunistic behavior in a timely fashion. Thus, this close-knit social environment favors the performance of informal institutions.

When the surrounding social environment undergoes transformation, the local information environment and the power of social sanctions change accordingly, further affecting the effectiveness of informal institutions. Moreover, as discussed in the previous section, this change in informal institutions has implications for the institutional environment of imposed formal institutions as well as their establishment and performance. In many cases, particularly in rural China, the changes in local communities' social environments are effectively driven by, *inter alia*, their transformed communal structures as a consequence of socioeconomic and political forces that are usually foreign and exogenous to the communities under examination. Focusing on the uneven transformation in Chinese villages' communal structures driven by surplus rural labor's cityward migration, as well as its influence on the practice of indigenous relation-based institutions, this book compiles both quantitative and qualitative evidence of how Chinese villages' transformed social environments affect the performance of indigenous informal institutions, shape the institutional environment for imposed formal institutions, and contribute to the transformed institutional foundations of their decentralized governance.

More specifically, the unprecedented large-scale cityward migration in rural China significantly challenges Chinese villages' close-knit communal structures that had been well maintained before the early 1990s (Chapter 3). As expected, a higher level of cityward migration impairs Chinese villages' capacity to mobilize and establish consensus, primarily through social sanctions, in regard to the regular reallocation of land to accommodate local demographic changes (Chapter 4). In Chinese villages that witness a higher level of cityward migration, villagers report less access to information about their fellow villagers and attach less significance to their local reputations. In addition, in these transformed villages, residents are also less morally obliged to prioritize collective interests over individual interests, cultivate long-term relationships at the cost of immediate benefits, and cherish local harmony by avoiding conflict when dealing with their fellow villagers (Chapter 5).

In other words, as cityward migration impoverishes the local information environment, weakens social sanctions, and erodes moral obligations, indigenous relation-based institutions become less competent in regulating and coordinating villagers' behaviors and less effective in addressing local governance issues. As previously discussed, this generates a greater incentive for villagers to embrace imposed rule-based institutions. Thus, grassroots democracy is much better established and practiced in loosely coupled villages with a medium level of cityward migration (Chapter 4). Additionally, in these loosely coupled communities, villagers are more attracted to imposed rule-based institutions for resolving conflict, relieving disasters and crises, raising modest credit and small loans, and holding local political leaders accountable (Chapter 6). Further, a very high or exodus level of cityward migration can paralyze the social networks in Chinese villages. In these atomized rural communities, even imposed rule-based institutions cannot perform effectively due to the lack of the minimally required coordination capacity and social nutrition. Thus, villagers are left with private solutions based on their own efforts or personal connections, which are inadequate for sustaining quality local governance (Chapters 4 and 6).

These findings establish the significance of social environment in affecting the performance of different institutions, shaping the institutional environment under examination, and moderating the dynamics of institutional change. By moving beyond the institutional environment and incorporating the surrounding social environment, this further-deepened contextualization provides a general framework to understand the performance of informal institutions and contributes to existing research on how informal institutions work and change.[9] This contextualization also makes scholars and policymakers more conscious of the possible impacts of social environment on institutional performance and change. In many cases, the transformation in the surrounding social environment is driven by factors that are exogenous and foreign to the settings under examination. This provides a valuable springboard to launch our investigations, given the notorious issue of endogeneity in the literature on institutions and institutional change. Hence, incorporating social environment into our research to establish a further-deepened contextualized understanding of institutions and institutional change not only enriches our theories but also offers additional analytic leverage in addressing some thorny methodological issues in related empirical work.

Implications for Local Governance

In addition to enriching contemporary literature on institutions and institutional change, this contextualized framework, which pays close attention to the possible dynamics among different types of institutions and incorporates the impacts of the surrounding social environment, also contributes to existing research on local governance. Despite the widely recognized value of appropriate institutions in sustaining high-quality governance (Acemoglu and Robinson 2012; North 1990; North et al. 2009), contemporary empirical literature that evaluates which institutions are critical for decentralized local governance contains contradictory findings and arguments (Manion 1996, 2006; L. Tsai 2007a, b; Y. Yao and Gao 2006; Y. Yao and Shen 2006). Recognizing the existence of varieties of governance is the first step toward establishing a coherent theoretical framework to make sense of these findings, synthesize their arguments, and provide more fruitful policy suggestions for local governance in practice.

This book argues that quality governance in local communities can be sustained as long as the problems of collective action and accountability can be effectively solved. However, which institutional solutions are effective in solving these problems is contingent upon communities' local histories, traditions, institutional inheritances, communal structures, and even the national government's institutional engineering and socioeconomic policies. Assisted by the contextualized understanding of institutions and institutional change, this book presents both quantitative and qualitative evidence on the effectiveness of both indigenous relation-based institutions and imposed rule-based institutions in solving the problems of collective action and accountability in Chinese villages and, thus, improving the decentralized provision of local public goods in rural China (Chapter 4). This book further identifies the conditions under which certain types of institutions are more capable of solving the problems and providing the institutional support for quality governance in Chinese villages. Specifically, in close-knit communities, indigenous relation-based institutions play the dominant role in sustaining local governance, while, in loosely coupled communities, imposed rule-based institutions replace the indigenous institutions as the key institutional foundation for local governance (Chapters 4 and 6).

Thus, as long as we bring the issue of local governance back into its surrounding social environment, the lack of a universally applicable institutional solution for effective local governance should no longer be of concern.[10] Varieties of institutional foundations for governance can simply be the norm. Following Yousfi's (2011, p. 36) call for being "more cognizant of the context-specificity of desirable institutional arrangements" as well as Masbridge's (2010, p. 592) emphasis on making institutions "legitimate in the eyes of users," this book also argues that, in practice, institutional engineering and transplant for local governance should be viewed and implemented with local communal structures and institutional inheritances in mind. To some extent, locally tailored institutional design and building—despite being stripped of the standardization that could save some implementation and administration costs—might be a much more productive approach to promoting quality local governance.

Moreover, the impotence of both indigenous relation-based institutions and imposed rule-based ones in upholding the governance of atomized communities sends a critical message to policymakers. In addition to crafting appropriate institutional designs for more effective local governance, more attention should be paid to how to revive local communities and cultivate sufficient social nutrition for the effective performance of these institutions. In other words, community building should be a critical and complementary component to institution building for better local governance.

CHAPTER 8

Epilogue: New Opportunities for Rural China's Governance?

The world economic recession of 2008 has reduced the growth rate of China's economy: The GDP growth rate in the first six months of 2012 was 7.8%. This was the very first time over the past three years that the GDP growth rate was lower than 8%.[1] As a consequence, since late 2008, many Chinese villages have witnessed a wave of returning migrant workers. According to the report from the Ministry of Agriculture released in early 2009, due to the downturn in China's economy, about 20 million migrant workers lost their jobs and had to return to their home villages.[2] It is very likely that, if this decreased economic growth in China continues and its labor-intensive industries in urban areas are forced to upgrade by substituting advanced technology for inexpensive labor, the number of migrant workers who cannot find jobs might increase further. Then the question arises: Will these returned migrant workers offer new opportunities for decentralized governance in rural China? Will they be able to help recover the fragmented and loosened social networks in their communities and restore the collective action and coordination capacity among their fellow villagers?

8.1 QUITE LIKELY, IF THEY STAY

For me, the answer depends on how these returned migrant workers settle in their home communities as well as how local governments make effective use of these returned high-quality human resources, who, compared to their fellow villagers staying at home, have a better education and variety of work skills.

According to a survey conducted in Guizhou Province in Southwest China, by the end of 2008, there were five hundred thousand returned migrant workers, two thirds of whom were unemployed due to the world financial crisis. Moreover, around 48% of interviewed returned migrant workers were not looking for temporary or permanent jobs, and approximately 75% held strong intentions of leaving again once the economic situation in urban areas improved (X. Hu and Wang 2009). These findings, based on local samples, confirms what the National Bureau of Statistics reported in early 2009 in regard to the situation of returned migrant workers in rural China: Approximately 80% of returned migrant workers may leave again for jobs in urban areas when economic opportunities become available.[3]

In addition, detailed qualitative studies of villages in labor-exporting provinces such as Sichuan, Henan, Hunan, and Hubei show that the majority of retuned migrant workers are relatively young, have gotten used to the lifestyle in urban areas, and generally hold negative attitudes toward agricultural production. Although these young migrant workers know that there are fewer choices in urban areas due to the economic downturn, they still regard the life in villages as boring (*mei yisi*) or backward (*luo hou*). Most of them prefer to stay in urban areas, despite lower salaries, provided they can get jobs (X. He et al. 2010; Y. Liu 2009; Tian 2012). Given these findings, it is clear that, due to the lack of a strong attachment to their home villages, returned migrant workers may eventually leave again. For them, rural communities are just temporary shelters during an economic downturn. Thus, they pay little attention to the governance in their home villages.

As discussed in Chapters 2 and 5, villagers' attachment and attention to their home communities are indispensable to the performance of any institution in sustaining rural China's decentralized governance. A key reason that frequent and continuous social interaction can be sustained in Chinese villages and local information can be quickly spread through village social networks is that villagers care about their lives in these rural communities. Given the attachment and high stakes involved, social sanctions are sufficiently powerful in regulating and coordinating villagers' behaviors and deterring deviant and opportunistic activities. The effective performance of grassroots democracy also relies heavily on villagers' participation, which is significantly driven by their attachment to their home communities and their interest in community affairs (J. Lu and Shi 2009; Yusheng Yao 2012). Despite their presence in villages, due to their lack of interest in local governance and related issues, these returned migrant workers might simply be temporary visitors who are not willing to make an effort to help revive their home communities. Therefore, whether this large number of returned migrant workers can be successfully channeled back into their home villages and transformed into critical resources for reviving these communities' governance is critically dependent on how to effectively attract the migrant workers to resettle in Chinese villages and regenerate and strengthen their attachment to their home villages.

One possible solution, as discussed in Chapters 3 and 4, might be that the Chinese government tries various programs to promote and facilitate re-employment of the returned migrant workers in local non-agricultural sectors. Although the township and village enterprises model may not be applicable to all Chinese villages, the possibility of keeping a larger number of villagers' leaving the land without leaving villages (*litu bu lixiang*) via expanding local non-agricultural economies should be seriously explored in the Chinese government's future rural policies. The significance of rebuilding rural communities into meaningful homes for Chinese villagers in terms of improving rural China's decentralized governance cannot be overemphasized. Effective community building, assisted by expanded local non-agricultural economies, is vital for strengthening and consolidating the social foundations for the performance of any institution in sustaining the governance in Chinese villages.

In addition to keeping returned migrants with attractive local employment opportunities, another solution might lie in organizing those who (for whatever reasons) choose to stay in Chinese villages (particularly those atomized by a high level of cityward migration) to help revive their paralyzed communities. As shown in Chapters 2 and 6, the key reason that externally imposed rule-based institutions cannot work in atomized rural communities lies in the infertile social environment that cannot sustain the minimally required cooperation and coordination among the villagers. If such cooperation and coordination cannot be effectively provided by the villagers themselves, external inputs could be indispensable to jump-start the momentum needed for cultivating the required social environment, which can generate the minimally required social nutrition for the effective establishment and performance of the imposed institutions. Some field experiments conducted by the Center of Rural Governance (CRG) at Huazhong University of Science and Technology, with which I worked closely to compile the qualitative case studies and implement the pilot project for the national surveys used in this book, have shown some encouraging results of such external inputs in reviving, through community building, the governance in atomized rural communities.[4]

8.2 FIELD EXPERIMENTS OF ORGANIZING VILLAGERS IN ATOMIZED VILLAGES

The project was originally designed to examine the impact of civil associations in Chinese villages on the quality of life of the seniors who stay in the villages via providing a space for them to get together and to be entertained. In 2004, the CRG selected three villages in Jingmen City, Hubei Province, all with a high level of outward migration, to determine whether the quality of life of the senior villagers left behind could be improved through external inputs, such as the establishment of Senior People Associations (SPAs) and the sponsoring of SPA activities.[5] After securing necessary research grants, the CRG worked with the village committees of the selected villages to establish SPAs. The CRG provided a fund of 40,000 RMB (around 6,350 USD) for each of the villages to establish an SPA, equip a room allocated to the SPA with entertainment facilities such as a television and mahjong sets, and sponsor SPA activities such as the yangko dance, drum dance, and aerobics over the next two years.

In the beginning, the organization and operation of the SPAs were difficult and highly dependent upon assistance from the CRG. Researchers from the CRG needed to stay in these villages for weeks to provide step-by-step instructions on how to run the SPAs and organize SPA activities. They even visited the seniors individually to invite them to join the SPAs and to participate in the SPA activities. Things changed quickly, and, after approximately a half year's operation under the guidance of the CRG, all three SPAs were able to perform independently. They regularly organized activities for the seniors, and the rooms allocated for the SPAs were frequently visited by the senior villagers and gradually became a public space for the villages.

Later, the CRG researchers were surprised to find that, far beyond their original expectation, these "organized" seniors gradually began to exert their influence over the governance of their respective villages. For instance, in 2005, the village committee in one of the selected villages tried to collect extra fees for allocating homestead land.[6] When a senior villager complained about his unpleasant experience of being asked for extra fees when applying for a piece of homestead land for his son at the SPA, the other seniors became furious. Later, around twenty seniors went together to the village committee and asked the chairman to abolish these illegal fees. They even threatened to mobilize other villagers to vote this chairman out of office in the forthcoming election if their demand could not be satisfied. Facing this collective pressure from the seniors, the chairman called the CRG for help and mediation. Soon, the fee-charging policy was abolished, and the extra fees already levied were paid back.[7]

Given my experiences of staying in these villages and other CRG researchers' descriptions, I believe that the SPAs did strengthen the seniors' collective action and coordination capacity and empowered their participation in the governance of their respective communities over time. Specifically, the SPAs served as a hub of local information transmission in the villages. Plenty of information about their fellow villagers was exchanged and was spread among the seniors when they chatted or played cards or mahjong in the SPA center, or danced and exercised together. This facilitated the seniors' and even other villagers' access to local information. It was not surprising that even some village cadres visited the SPAs often and talked to the activists and leaders of the SPAs to acquire information to which they might not otherwise have access, such as violations of family-planning policy and abnormal deaths.[8] Clearly, access to such information could have been much more difficult, if not impossible, had SPAs not been established.

Moreover, over time, with accumulated experience and confidence, the SPAs also gradually expanded their organized collective activities from pure entertainment to some crucial aspects of community governance. The senior villagers' involvement in conflict resolution (particularly the conflicts between mothers-in-law and daughters-in-law) and public sanitary services (collecting garbage and cleaning within-village roads) were well received. For instance, in the posters outside its center, one SPA praised some young villagers who took good care of their parents and in-laws. This same SPA also threatened to reveal, in posters, the bad behaviors of those who disrespected senior villagers and who did not support their parents or in-laws. Another SPA charged the village committee nominal fees (used for its organized activities) and organized its members to collect garbage and clean within-village roads by turns.[9] Gradually, in all three villages, the SPAs' involvement in the governance of their respective villages became widely accepted, regularized, and even recognized with semiofficial status. As witnessed and documented by the CRG researchers (X. He 2007b, 2009), this helped improve not only the quality of life of the senior villagers but also the governance of these villages in general.

These stories may sound familiar to what Putnam and his colleagues (1993) found in Italy. However, in addition to confirming their argument on the positive effects of social capital on institutional performance, these experiments also present a dynamic picture of how social capital might be cultivated through community building assisted and jump-started by external inputs. Similar to the case of South Italy examined by Putnam and colleagues, which was characterized by a lack of social capital, these villages were initially haunted by paralyzed social networks and impoverished social environment that prevented the establishment and performance of any institution to sustain their decentralized governance. However, with external inputs from the CRG and establishment of SPAs, their community lives were jump-started and gradually revived. This further strengthened the collective action and coordination capacity among their villagers, empowered their participation in local governance, and enabled and facilitated the performance of both formal and informal institutions. All these contributed to and improved the governance in these villages.

Of course, SPAs are not the only feasible means of cultivating a favorable social environment for the performance of various institutions in sustaining the decentralized governance in rural China. Nevertheless, the spillover effects of SPAs in the governance of these formerly atomized villages speak to the feasibility of reviving Chinese rural communities that have been paralyzed due to a high level of outward migration. The key is community building through well-placed external inputs. Although villagers who stay in these communities do not have sufficient capability and resources to overcome the barriers to effective cooperation and coordination by themselves, once assisted by sufficient external inputs, they can effectively revive their communities and cultivate the self-propelling momentum needed to support various institutions for better local governance.

In general, to promote its institutional building for decentralized governance in Chinese villages and ensure the effective performance of imposed rule-based institutions, the Chinese government should pay more attention to community building in rural China. Accordingly, how to effectively use the increasing budget for *Sannong* (agriculture, villages, and peasants) from the national government,[10] channel critical resources into rural communities (particularly those significantly eroded by outward migration), and intentionally cultivate the cooperation and coordination capacity among Chinese villagers should be at the top of the policy agenda of Chinese leaders.

2008 Asian Barometer Survey Mainland China Survey (ABSMCS) and 2008 National Village Survey (NVS)

The two surveys were conducted in 2008 in mainland China in cooperation with the Research Centre for Contemporary China (RCCC) at Peking University. The survey sample represents the adult population over 18 years of age residing in family households at the time of the survey, excluding those living in the Tibetan Autonomous Region. The sampling frame was based on the information collected by the Sociological Institute of the Chinese Academy of Social Sciences (CASS) for a 2006 nationwide representative survey.

A stratified multistage area sampling procedure with probabilities proportional to size measures (PPS) was employed to select the sample. The Primary Sampling Units (PSUs) were districts (*qu*) in metropolitan areas and counties (*xian*) in other areas. All PSUs were stratified according to their population and economic features. Altogether, using hierarchical cluster analysis based on the Ward method, thirty-seven strata were identified and 212 PSUs were selected. The Secondary Sampling Units (SSPs) were street councils (*jiedao*) in urban areas and townships (*xiang*) in rural areas, and the third stage of sampling was geared toward resident committees (*juweihui*) in urban areas and administrative villages (*cun*) in rural areas. A total of 424 SSUs and 848 TSUs were selected. Within each selected family household, a Kish table was used to select an eligible respondent.

Local retired high school teachers in selected counties and townships were employed as interviewers for this survey. In October 2008, the RCCC contacted local associations for retired middle school teachers or bureaus of education in selected counties and townships to ask for their help in identifying newly retired teachers. Letters were sent to those aged between fifty-five and sixty-two to inform them about the survey and ask them to apply for jobs as interviewers. All recruited interviewers received formal training implemented by professional staffs from the RCCC, with standardized training materials, before the fieldwork.

Before the interviews began, we sent letters to all sampling spots to check whether there were any changes in addresses. We then removed some invalid addresses from our sampling frame and thereby eliminated a majority of non-contacts. The survey scheduled interviews with 7,293 people. For various reasons (e.g., invalid address, no eligible candidates, and migration), 583 prospective respondents could not be located. Five thousand ninety-eight of the prospective respondents completed the questionnaire, and the response rate was 75.98%. Poststratification techniques were used to adjust sampling errors. Weighting variables were calculated along the three dimensions of gender, age, and educational level to make the data consistent with the entire population. Given the focus of this book (i.e., rural China), only the data from rural areas were used for analysis, which included 4,205 completed interviews in administrative villages.

Information on villagers and their villages was collected through two sets of questionnaires, respectively. With the help of face-to-face interviews, following standardized mass questionnaires, the 2008 ABSMCS collected the following information from each interviewed villager: (1) demographic features; (2) migration experience; (3) socio-psychological features; (4) normative orientations and cultural values; (5) perceptions and evaluations of local information environment, social sanctions, and public authority; and (6) choices among different institutional solutions for a variety of issues.

Through interviewing key village cadres, particularly the clerks (*wenshu*) who are responsible for bookkeeping and preserving archives and records, following standardized village questionnaires, the 2008 NVS collected the following information from each sampled village: (1) village population size; (2) the number of villagers engaged in different economic activities, including working as migrant workers in urban areas; (3) collective income from various resources; (4) geographic and ecological features; (5) activities and structures of solidarity groups (e.g., lineage organizations); (6) the performance of grassroots democracy (i.e., institutional features of most recent village committee elections); (7) the village's experiences with issues like land reallocation; and (8) the provision of local public goods and maintenance of public projects. Moreover, interviewers were required to make records of some ecological features of selected administrative villages, such as the housing pattern and the existence of public space for collective activities. At the end of the survey, 356 village questionnaires were completed and returned.

APPENDIX 2

Multivariate Probit Regression (MPR)

As previously discussed, the provision of specific public goods is likely to be under the same budget and other socioeconomic constraints. Statistically, the error terms are not independent across the regression equations for specific public goods. To accommodate and model these correlated error terms, I follow the literature on public goods provision (L. Tsai 2007a, b) and adopt the more appropriate approach of seemingly unrelated regression (SUR) (Greene 2008; Zellner 1962, Chapter 14). The conventional SUR approach can deal only with continuous dependent variables, whereas all dependent variables here are dichotomous and, thus, cannot be analyzed with conventional SUR. Multivariate probit regression (MPR) is the appropriate and most efficient statistical modeling choice (Cappelari and Jenkins 2003).

As demonstrated by Greene (2008, pp. 817–826) and Pindyck and Rubinfeld (1998), MPR's statistical structure is similar to that of bivariate probit regression (BPR). The only difference is that more than two dichotomous dependent variables are simultaneously estimated. This significantly increases the challenge for estimation and calls for more efficient algorithms and simulation methods. To effectively accommodate such statistical challenges, I follow the strategy of MPR and implement statistical analysis in the framework of structural equation modeling (SEM). More specifically, I specify five simultaneous equations for tap water, within-village paved roads, maintenance of irrigation projects, maintenance of other public facilities, and provision of other public welfare, respectively, and specify the error terms of all five dichotomous dependent variables to be correlated with each other as free parameters for simultaneous estimation.

Table A2.1. SUMMARY STATISTICS OF KEY VILLAGE-LEVEL VARIABLES

Variable Name	Mean	Mode	Std. Dev.	Max	Min
Total population	2215.46		1542.78	10,877	118
Total migrant workers	230.6		296.02	1946	1
Percentage of migrant workers	0.096		0.105	0.578	0.0001
Annual per capita income	3469.65		5048.35	86,000	200
Distance to township seat	6.12		6.27	65	0
Land per capita	1.38		1.2	7.58	0.057
Model village in self-governance		0		1	0
Public space in village		0		1	0
Rice as the key agricultural product		0		1	0

Source: 2008 National Village Survey (*N* = 356).

APPENDIX 3

Table A3.1. PROBIT MODELS ON INFORMATION ENVIRONMENT, LOCAL REPUTATION, AND PUBLIC AUTHORITIES IN RURAL CHINA

Individual features	Extensive Knowledge about Fellow Villagers	Caring about Local Reputation	Recognizing Traditional Local Authorities
Age	0.033 (0.011)***	−0.019 (0.008)**	−0.009 (0.008)
Age squared	−0.0002 (0.0001)*	0.0002 (0.0001)**	0.0001 (0.0001)
Education	0.004 (0.022)	0.001 (0.016)	0.084 (0.018)***
Male	0.105 (0.056)*	−0.061 (0.043)	−0.104 (0.047)**
Media exposure	0.030 (0.022)	−0.010 (0.019)	0.042 (0.018)**
Migration experience	−0.037 (0.088)	−0.085 (0.063)	−0.008 (0.066)
Chinese Communist Party affiliation	−0.043 (0.100)	0.152 (0.078)*	0.051 (0.076)
Economic situation	−0.048 (0.041)	0.071 (0.030)**	−0.023 (0.030)
Community features			
Size of population staying in village	0.031 (0.048)	0.078 (0.033)**	−0.013 (0.035)
Village level migration	−0.466 (0.271)*	−0.409 (0.205)**	−0.963 (0.233)***
Annual income per capita	0.009 (0.041)	−0.067 (0.032)**	−0.208 (0.032)***

(continued)

Individual features	Extensive Knowledge about Fellow Villagers	Caring about Local Reputation	Recognizing Traditional Local Authorities
Village collective income	0.0005 (0.007)	0.010 (0.005)*	0.001 (0.006)
Distance to the township seat	0.152 (0.045)***	−0.046 (0.033)	−0.011 (0.034)
Clustered housing	−0.162 (0.044)***	0.004 (0.033)	0.212 (0.036)***
A dominant clan	−0.043 (0.095)	−0.198 (0.068)***	0.085 (0.074)
Competing clans	0.010 (0.084)	−0.015 (0.060)	−0.070 (0.062)
Intercept	−2.616 (0.507)***	0.444 (0.382)	1.671 (0.375)***

Model information

F-statistic	F (16, 186566.2) = 6.30***	F (16, 3408.6) = 3.50***	F (16, 2208.3) = 10.92***
Number of strata	34		
Number of PSUs	127		

Source: 2008 ABSMCS Rural Subpopulation (*N* = 4,127).
Note: Coefficients are averaged results over the estimation of five imputed datasets.
Averaged standard errors in parentheses, corrected for complex sampling.
*$p < 0.1$ **$p < 0.05$ ***$p < 0.01$.

Table A3.2. MPR MODEL ON SOCIAL NORMS IN RURAL CHINA

Individual features	Collective Interest	Long-term Relationship	Conflict Avoidance	Averaged Joint Chi-square Test
Age	0.0002 (0.002)	−0.003 (0.002)*	−0.004 (0.002)*	
Education	0.101 (0.018)***	0.085 (0.016)***	0.035 (0.016)**	
Male	−0.016 (0.047)	0.029 (0.042)	0.026 (0.044)	
Media exposure	−0.011 (0.017)	−0.038 (0.019)**	−0.122 (0.019)***	
Migration experience	−0.071 (0.067)	0.051 (0.066)	−0.096 (0.069)	
Chinese Communist Party affiliation	−0.048 (0.076)	−0.011 (0.074)	0.033 (0.069)	
Economic situation	0.037 (0.034)	0.015 (0.028)	−0.009 (0.028)	

Community features

Size of population staying in village	−0.085 (0.036)**	0.054 (0.034)	0.053 (0.035)	
Village level migration	−0.430 (0.214)**	−0.485 (0.207)**	−0.893 (0.222)***	F (3, 559.9) = 6.73***
Annual income per capita	0.060 (0.033)*	0.073 (0.030)**	0.073 (0.032)**	
Village collective income	0.017 (0.006)***	0.010 (0.006)*	−0.001 (0.006)	
Distance to the township seat	0.009 (0.038)	0.039 (0.033)	0.126 (0.034)***	
Clustered housing	0.072 (0.038)*	0.088 (0.037)**	−0.020 (0.004)	
A dominant clan	0.135 (0.076)*	−0.066 (0.072)	−0.229 (0.074)***	
Competing clans	−0.0009 (0.071)	0.163 (0.071)**	0.123 (0.062)**	
Intercept	0.107 (0.357)	−1.152 (0.336)***	−0.873 (0.344)**	

Error term correlation

Long-term relationship	0.396 (0.032)***	
Conflict avoidance	0.197 (0.029)***	0.218 (0.026)***

Model information

Number of strata	34
Number of PSUs	127
F-statistic	F (45, 6107.3) = 6.02***

Source: 2008 ABSMCS Rural Subpopulation (N = 4,127).
Note: Coefficients are averaged results over the estimation of five imputed datasets. Averaged standard errors in parentheses, corrected for complex sampling.
*$p < 0.1$ **$p < 0.05$ ***$p < 0.01$.

APPENDIX 4

Table A4.1. PROBIT REGRESSIONS ON CHINESE VILLAGERS'
CONTEXTUALIZED CHOICE OF IMPOSED RULE-BASED
INSTITUTIONS FOR LOCAL GOVERNANCE ISSUES

Individual features	Conflict Resolution	Disaster and Crisis Relief	Modest Credit and Small Loans
Age	0.001 (0.002)	0.009 (0.002)***	0.005 (0.002)***
Education	−0.005 (0.020)	−0.040 (0.018)**	0.040 (0.019)**
Male	0.006 (0.051)	0.164 (0.047)***	0.208 (0.050)***
Media exposure	0.089 (0.020)***	0.021 (0.018)	0.044 (0.018)**
Migration experience	0.020 (0.081)	−0.175 (0.070)**	0.055 (0.070)
Chinese Communist Party affiliation	−0.183 (0.083)**	0.003 (0.079)	0.057 (0.085)
Economic situation	0.095 (0.036)***	−0.003 (0.033)	−0.002 (0.035)
Community features			
Size of population staying in village	−0.109 (0.046)**	−0.128 (0.036)***	−0.167 (0.040)***
Village-level migration	3.921 (0.670)***	2.937 (0.603)***	2.312 (0.659)***
Village-level migration squared	−8.828 (1.837)***	−6.263 (1.620)***	−4.054 (1.763)**
Annual income per capita	0.140 (0.039)***	0.084 (0.033)**	0.086 (0.038)**
Village collective income	−0.011 (0.007)	−0.041 (0.006)***	−0.023 (0.006)***
Distance to the township seat	0.006 (0.039)	0.004 (0.036)	0.152 (0.038)***
Clustered housing	0.158 (0.040)***	0.028 (0.036)	0.145 (0.038)***

(continued)

Table A4.1. (CONTINUED)

Individual features	Conflict Resolution	Disaster and Crisis Relief	Modest Credit and Small Loans
A dominant clan	−0.193 (0.083)**	−0.443 (0.084)***	−0.216 (0.084)***
Competing clans	−0.061 (0.079)	−0.257 (0.067)***	−0.295 (0.084)***
Constant	−0.153 (0.404)	−0.535 (0.356)	−1.408 (0.404)***

Model information

F-statistic	F (16, 5906.6) = 6.33***	F (16, 5132.3) = 12.96***	F (16, 5539.6) = 8.21***
Number of strata	34		
Number of PSUs	127		

Source: 2008 ABSMCS Rural Subpopulation (N = 4,127).
Note: Coefficients are averaged results over the estimation of five imputed datasets.
Averaged robust standard errors in parentheses, corrected for complex sampling.
*$p < 0.1$ **$p < 0.05$ ***$p < 0.01$.

Table A4.2. PROBIT REGRESSIONS ON VILLAGERS' EVALUATIONS OF GRASSROOTS DEMOCRACY

Individual features	Effectiveness of Village Elections	Grassroots Democracy as the Most Effective Means of Supervising Village Cadres
Age	0.002 (0.002)	−0.001 (0.002)
Education	−0.061 (0.017)***	0.029 (0.018)
Male	0.034 (0.049)	0.002 (0.055)
Media exposure	−0.025 (0.021)	0.008 (0.020)
Migration experience	−0.134 (0.087)	−0.199 (0.069)***
Chinese Communist Party affiliation	0.047 (0.076)	0.197 (0.081)**
Economic situation	0.189 (0.032)***	0.017 (0.037)
Political interest	0.024 (0.039)	−0.052 (0.042)
Internal political efficacy	0.086 (0.062)	0.026 (0.056)
Satisfaction with democracy in China	0.303 (0.043)***	0.253 (0.049)***

Community features

Size of population staying in village	−0.045 (0.038)	−0.119 (0.040)***
Village-level migration	1.209 (0.641)*	1.804 (0.691)**
Village-level migration squared	−3.830 (1.774)**	−6.347 (1.885)***

Annual income per capita	0.055 (0.036)	0.038 (0.035)
Village collective income	−0.016 (0.038)	−0.007 (0.008)
Distance to the township seat	0.011 (0.038)	−0.023 (0.040)
Clustered housing	0.002 (0.037)	0.054 (0.045)
A dominant clan	−0.173 (0.074)**	0.051 (0.102)
Competing clans	−0.136 (0.066)**	−0.231 (0.082)***
Constant	0.661 (0.395)*	1.626 (0.386)

Model information

F-statistic	F (19, 1113.0) = 6.76***	F (19, 660.4) = 4.02***
Number of strata	34	
Number of PSUs	127	

Source: 2008 ABSMCS Rural Subpopulation (N = 4,127).
Note: Coefficients are averaged results over the estimation of five imputed datasets.
Averaged robust standard errors in parentheses, corrected for complex sampling.
*$p < 0.1$ **$p < 0.05$ ***$p < 0.01$.

NOTES

CHAPTER 1

1. Decentralization is a multifaceted concept. In this book, I primarily focus on the administrative and fiscal aspects of decentralization in China. More detailed information in this regard is provided in Chapter 3.

2. "Loose coupling" was introduced by Weick (1976) into organizational studies to describe a system whose components are "tied together either weakly or infrequently or slowly with minimal interdependence" (p. 5). For further discussions on "loosely coupled systems," see Orton and Weick (1990). For this book, loosely coupled communities differ from close-knit communities in terms of the lower frequency of social interaction and weaker social connections among their residents.

3. Putnam and his colleagues' work (1993) on the performance of democratic institutions in Italy is a clear example of this.

4. Berkowitz and his colleagues' work (2003b) on the "transplant effect" of institutional change is a clear example of this.

5. Galvan's work (2004) on the performance of government imposed land-tenure institutions in Senegal is a clear example of this.

6. Putnam and his colleagues' work (1993) on the performance of democratic institutions in Italy suggests that one critical social factor (i.e., social capital) determines the performance of imposed democratic institutions in local communities. Nevertheless, Putnam and his colleagues treat social capital as an exogenous variable, shaped primarily by historical traditions and legacies. As Krishna (2007) argues, social capital also grows or diminishes. In his work, Krishna attributes the accumulation of social capital to the existence of community-shared rules and self-initiated organizations. In actuality, the existence of community-shared rules and self-initiated organizations could be the result of certain communal structures. Galvan and his colleagues (2004, 2007) also suggest a framework for understanding the performance of externally imposed institutions in local communities. Unfortunately they focus only on successful cases of institutional syncretism and fail to explain why varying results could persist. All these issues are systematically addressed in this book. The significance of the China case for addressing these issues is discussed in later sections.

7. Definitions of "indigenously developed institutions" and "externally imposed institutions" are provided in the next section.

8. Accordingly, "local governance" is understood as the exercise of power to structure, regulate, and coordinate the relationships among the residents of a locality in the management of local public affairs.

9. Some scholars (e.g., Przeworski 2004) have challenged the conclusion that institutions matter, as there are many problems in isolating the impacts of institutions from those of surrounding conditions. Such challenges are addressed later in this book, after the presentation of pertinent empirical evidence.

10. The literature on legal pluralism has long recognized the lack of a universally applicable institutional template or formula for legal issues (Galanter 1981; Merry 1988; Qiang 2003; L. Su 2000, 2002).

11. Putnam and his colleagues are interested in the performance of nationally imposed formal democratic institutions in different regions, rather than local governance per se. Although there are some connections between the performance of imposed formal institutions and the quality of governance, good performance of imposed formal institutions is not a necessary condition for good governance in local communities. This point is systematically developed in Chapter 2.

12. Although Manion (1996, 2006) as well as Yao and Shen (2006) do not take local governance as the dependent variable in their studies, increased trust between elected officials and electorates and reduced income inequality among villagers are theoretically associated with quality local governance. Their work suggests the positive role of grassroots democracy in local governance.

13. L. Tsai's work focuses on the provision of local public goods in Chinese villages, which is a very important aspect of local governance. Nevertheless, local governance means much more than just the provision of local public goods. In Chapter 6, other critical aspects of local governance, like conflict resolution, disaster and crisis relief, and modest credit and small loans, are examined within a coherent framework.

14. There is no consensus on the definition of institutions, and there are numerous typologies to categorize them. For North (1990, p. 3), institutions are "the rules of the game in a society or, more formally, are the humanly designed constraints that shape human interaction"; and organizations, as players of the game, are not part of institutions. North further differentiates between formal and informal constraints, with the latter largely determined by culture. Knight (1992, p. 2) follows North's definition in suggesting that "an institution is a set of rules that structure social interaction in particular ways," but he adds that "for a set of rules to be an institution, knowledge of these rules must be shared by the members of the relevant community or society." Knight differentiates between externally forced and self-enforcing institutions, with the former resembling North's formal constraints and the latter resembling informal constraints. Greif (2006, p. 30) is more comprehensive in his definition of institutions: "An institution is a system of social factors that conjointly generate a regularity of behavior." For Greif, to have a coherent, comprehensive, and dynamic understanding of institutional change, "rules, beliefs, norms, and organizations" should work together to generate a regularity of social behavior. In this book, I follow Greif and, thus, define an institution as a system of social factors. The differences between formal and informal institutions are the focus of another ongoing debate among the scholars. Helmke and Levitsky (2004) differentiate between formal and informal institutions according to whether the rules of the game are "enforced outside of officially sanctioned channels"

and develop their typology of informal institutions according to the relationships between informal and formal institutions. Boettke and colleagues (2008) suggest another typology for institutions that include three types: indigenously introduced endogenous (IEN) institutions, indigenously introduced exogenous (IEX) institutions, and foreign-introduced exogenous (FEX) institutions. This typology puts more emphasis on the relationship between the initiators of institutions and surrounding communities or societies. Because the key issue of this book is decentralized local governance, Boettke and colleagues' typology is relevant for examining the interaction between indigenously developed institutions and externally imposed institutions. However, the distinction between IEX and FEX institutions is not relevant, given this book's exclusive focus on China's rural governance.

15. Atomized communities are characterized by paralyzed with-community social networks. Detailed discussions on the differences between close-knit, loosely coupled, and atomized communities are provided in Chapter 2.

16. This is the term used by Shue (1988) to describe the community structural features of rural China between the 1950s and 1970s: Village and family were the key units that defined villagers' lives. As Shue (1988, pp. 134–135) argues, "the honeycomb pattern established in the countryside meant that households tended to thicken ties within hamlets and villages while dissolving ties to the outside. . . . Even local gossip networks tended to be circumscribed, and peasant communities became even more self-absorbed than before." In her work, Shue further emphasizes that this honeycomb socioeconomic structure of rural China secured sufficient independence and autonomy for local cadres. And, through the cadres' intermediation and formalities, policies from the top were adapted to local needs. Thus, Shue questions the validity of the totalitarian model to explain Chinese politics during the Maoist period. In this book, I only use the term "honeycomb" to capture rural China's socioeconomic structure and locally circumscribed social interactions.

17. The reasons that close-knit communities favor the operation of indigenous relation-based institutions in local governance are systematically examined in Chapter 2.

18. As previously discussed, I only use "honeycomb" to capture rural China's socioeconomic structure and locally circumscribed social interactions under the Maoist period. Even in his scathing review of Shue's work, Unger (1989, p. 124) actually agrees with Shue regarding the community structural features of rural China during that time: "Peasants no longer took an active interest either in the town or in the other villages of their marketing district. Lateral trade between villages, after all, had been cut off, making the villages dependent instead upon the state both as the purchaser of its products and as the provider of consumer and investment goods. As observed in the anecdote from Shue, quoted above, neighboring villages could no longer even trade peanuts for sugar legally. . . . The attention of the peasantry and of village cadres became refocused, more strongly than even before, upon their own neighborhood and village. . . . They now shared a common harvest and a common fate with their immediate neighbours. At the very same time, the village became tied directly and strongly into national movements and national demands." Of course, Unger disagrees with Shue on whether the CCP effectively controlled rural China during the Maoist period with its centralized administrative system.

19. http://www.stats.gov.cn/tjgb/ndtjgb/qgndtjgb/t20120222_402786440.htm

20. Most migrant workers come from Central and West China and find their jobs in East China. Even within one province, the level of outward migration varies across counties, townships, and even villages. Features of rural–urban migration in China and its evolution are systematically examined in Chapter 3.

21. For more information on the sampling of the 2008 ABSMCS and 2008 NVS, other technical issues, and key survey instruments included, see Appendix 1.

22. During the fieldwork, we lived either in villagers' houses or in empty rooms at the village committee's office. In this way, we maximized the experiences and possibilities of knowing each village as comprehensively as possible. In each village, we usually spent two to three weeks, long enough to build villagers' trust in us, which enabled us to receive honest answers during interviews.

23. This pilot survey included 870 villagers in twenty-five administrative villages. The selection of communities for this pilot survey, for logistic and financial reasons, was based on convenience rather than probability sampling, and the selection of villagers within each village followed strictly a systematic sampling procedure. Using the newly updated household registration information (as a result of the then just-finished second national agriculture census) as the sampling frame, we randomly selected fifty villagers within each village for face-to-face interviews using standardized mass questionnaires. Following our previous teamwork strategy, each group worked independently in a village, and then all groups in adjacent villages met every two days for in-depth discussions. Surveys were usually conducted in the middle of each group's two- or three-week stay in a selected community, after each group got familiar with the community and gained sufficient trust from villagers and village cadres through casual conservations and semistructured interviews. These local surveys offered abundant and systematic information on local governance and the operation of different institutions in these twenty-five villages. This pilot survey significantly facilitated the selection and refining of survey instruments that were later included in the 2008 national survey.

24. For more information on the ABS, visit its official website at http://www.asianbarometer.org.

25. Case studies in this book are based on information from villages that are not part of the 2008 NVS. Thus, these case studies provide out-of-sample tests for whatever conclusions derived from statistical analyses.

CHAPTER 2

1. I use "rule-based institutions" and "parchment institutions" interchangeably.

2. Social control can be broadly defined as "virtually all of the human practices and arrangements that contribute to social order and, in particular, that influence people to conform" (D. Black 1984b, p. 4), or it can be narrowly defined as "how people define and respond to deviant behavior" (D. Black 1984b, p. 5). For more information on social control, see the edited volume by Donald Black (1984b).

3. I am not romanticizing communities like these in Sub-Saharan Africa, East Asia, or other continents, for there is also a dark side of these communities in their culture, norms, and social life. What I argue here is simply that order and governance can be secured and sustained, particularly in local communities, without resorting to parchment institutions. For information on the darker side of these communities, see Edgerton (1992).

4. Reputation-based mechanisms for regulating and coordinating business transactions are not a recent development. The history of these mechanisms dates back to medieval times (Greif 1989, 1993, 2006; Greif et al. 1995). Reputation-based mechanisms also play an important role in today's e-commerce (Cabral and Hortaçsu 2010; Picci 2011; Resnick et al. 2006). Although Bernstein (1992, pp. 120–134) emphasizes the consideration of "secrecy" in favoring the extralegal system over the legal one among diamond businessmen, "secrecy" is neither sufficient nor necessary for choosing the extralegal system over the legal one.

5. Ellickson (1991, pp. 178–181) identifies the "central attributes of close-knittedness" as (1) future power to administer sanctions and (2) access to information about the past and present. But I argue that such attributes are contingent upon the two community structural features: (1) frequent and continuous within-community interaction and (2) extended and dense social networks that connect community members. When such structural features change, the capacity of administering sanctions, as well as access to pertinent information, can change accordingly. Because a key concern of this book is the impact of community structural changes, primarily driven by outward migration, on local governance, I follow a structure-centered approach, rather than the function-anchored view, to define close-knit communities.

6. The structural constraints may also include the professional features of Maghribi traders in medieval times (Greif 1993), contemporary diamond businessmen (L. Bernstein 1992), or street gangs (Skarbek 2011).

7. Stylized game-theory models have been widely adopted by social scientists to examine people's interactions and the associated social consequences. For detailed information and descriptions of these game-theory models, as well as their applications in political science, see McCarty and Meirowitz (2007) and Morrow (1994).

8. A Nash-equilibrium is "a profile of strategies that each player's strategy is an optimal response to the other players' strategies" (Fudenberg and Tirole 1991, p. 11).

9. According to the Folk Theorem, any combination of strategies might show up as a Nash-equilibrium in an infinitely iterated PD game. Therefore, it is not always the case that close-knit communities can find effective ways to solve the problems of collective action and accountability. For an example of close-knit communities that suffer from the problems of collective action and accountability, see Banfield (1967). In Chapter 3, I present a historical narrative on how some macro-dynamics, in addition to close-knittedness, have facilitated the emergence of indigenous institutional solutions to the problems of collective action and accountability in Chinese villages.

10. In her work on trade and credit in local communities in Mexican California, Clay (1997, p. 497) notes, "Continued interaction with other individuals was valuable. These gains and the threat of punishment by multiple individuals for deviation from accepted norms created incentives that allowed individuals to trust one another."

11. Issue linkages also are used by scholars of international relations to explain the role of international institutions in promoting cooperation among nation-states (e.g., Davis 2004; Haas 1980; Keohane 1984).

12. Cross-issue linkages also contribute to achieving socially optimal results with a division of labor among players that would not have been possible if left to isolated individuals. For related information, see Ellickson (1991, pp. 162–164).

13. Information is critical for any reputation-based governance, with or without the support of rule-based institutions (Picci 2011). For the role of information in the reputation systems in e-commerce, see Cabral and Hortaçsu (2010) and Resnick and colleagues (2006).
14. In this sense, Burt's (1992) social network with structural holes is loose rather than dense. If there are structural holes within a community's social networks, some community members can manipulate the flow of information due to their structural privilege in receiving and sending information. This might hamper the performance of indigenous institutions in sustaining governance.
15. There is a large body of literature on gossip in psychology. According to the research, people enjoy gossiping (Barkow 1992; Brison 1992; Merry 1984). Regardless of whether psychological incentives are involved, gossiping serves a functional purpose for my argument (i.e., easing the transmission of information).
16. In his work on the economic activities in Sub-Saharan African villages, Platteau (1994a, p. 549) particularly notes: "In the village community everyone is watching everyone. Gossip about one's misconduct is circulated by word of mouth faster than any modern means of communication. In such an environment, a significant cost could be incurred to a person who would violate a contract with his fellow villager, since not only would he lose benefits from the contract but the resulting bad reputation would deprive him of future opportunities to enter into contracts with other villagers as well."
17. My arguments on governance without parchment institutions in close-knit communities rely on the role of powerful social sanctions in sustaining the operation of indigenous institutions. Thus, multilateral sanctions and the efficient spread of information are the linchpins. My arguments are not specifically associated with the homogeneity or heterogeneity of local communities. In the literature on collective action, there are arguments for both the positive and negative impacts of heterogeneity in solving the problem of collective action, facilitating rebels' collective efforts, and driving unexpected social movements and revolutions (R. Hardin 1982; Kuran 1989, 1991, 1995; Lichbach 1995; Mancur Olson 1971; Sandler 1992). Nevertheless, for my arguments, both homogeneity and heterogeneity can play positive roles. For example, on the one hand, community members' commonly shared norms and cultural values that emphasize reciprocity and collectivism (i.e., one type of homogeneity) can facilitate collective action. On the other hand, community members' different thresholds in denouncing deviant behavior in public (i.e., one type of heterogeneity) also can empower efficacious social sanctions by enabling the sanction cascade. Therefore, it is not necessary for my arguments to be specific in regard to whether community homogeneity or heterogeneity matters most for the performance of indigenous institutions. Some new research on collective action emphasizes the role of hierarchical social relationships like clientelist networks dominated by landlords (Shami 2012). Thanks to the Chinese government's socioeconomic and fiscal reforms since the early 2000s, the influence of clientelist networks on collective action is not an issue for my argument. Related issues are discussed in detail in Chapter 3.
18. Modernization is a multidimensional phenomenon. It has been conceptualized as a process that involves industrialization, urbanization, and other socioeconomic and political changes. Although this concept has been conventionally

associated with social evolutionism and ethnocentrism, I use this concept without such connotations. For this book, modernization's most important dimension is economic development, as promoted and facilitated by technological innovations, and associated impacts on institutional change. For more information on modernization and its role in the twentieth century, see Black (1966, 1967), Eisenstadt (1966), Lerner and Pevsner (1962), Smelser (1966), Weiner (1966), and Wood (1966). For critiques on modernization theory, see Bendix (1967), Nisbet (1969), Rudolph and Rudolph (1967), Shils (1962), and Tipps (1973).

19. The literature on the effectiveness of rule-based institutions in solving the problems of collective action and accountability is extensive (e.g., Fukuyama 2011; G. Hardin 1968; R. Hardin 1995; Olken 2010; Mancur Olson 1971; Przeworski et al. 1999; Sandler 1992; Seabright 1996; Strom et al. 2003). Therefore, I do not review that literature here but focus instead on the distinct processes that have pushed for the development and establishment of rule-based institutions due to social transition.

20. As Lerner and Pevsner (1962, p. 48) note in their seminal research on the social transition in the Middle East: "Physical mobility so experienced naturally entrained social mobility, and gradually there grew institutions appropriate to the process."

21. According to Wong (1997a, p. 138), before the Republican era, the Chinese government actually intentionally limited the introduction of a market economy into its rural areas and constrained mobility in rural China: "While they believed markets to be socially useful, late imperial officials worried about people leaving the land to take to the road in search for profit. Their concerns included worries that people in perpetual or periodic movement were potentially dangerous to social order, which was defined in terms of a sedentary agrarian society in which men worked the fields and women wove cloth and tended the home."

22. For similar arguments on China's state-building and development of rule-based formal institutions for rural governance, see Brandtstädter and Schubert (2005), He (2013), Wong (1997a), and Zhang (2006).

23. To make the argument analytically focused, I intentionally separate the bottom-up momentum from the top-down incentives for institutional change. In reality, they are interrelated. For instance, high mobility makes both citizens and national leaders realize the weakened capacity of indigenous institutions to sustain good governance as well as the need for new institutional solutions. However, even without the issue of high mobility, political leaders of nation-states still face the challenge of using indigenous relation-based institutions for effective governance over substantially expanded territories that include residents with different backgrounds, experiences, and cultural traditions. The problem of scale is most relevant for political leaders, and this is also the focus of my argument on the top-down incentives for institutional change.

24. Some indigenous institutions do have stipulated rules and codes (e.g., village compacts in rural China). But even for such indigenous institutions, the implementation of these rules and codes is still based on social sanctions that hinge upon the significance of locally valued relations. Therefore, relation-based regulation mechanisms are central to indigenous institutions.

25. Again, as Scott (1998) argues, with the help of rule-based institutions, national leaders make their societies more legible.

26. When supply meets demand, it is likely to find improved governance in transformed societies, with rule-based institutions' supporting governance by regulating and coordinating social interaction. However, if supply does not meet demand, disruptions are likely to emerge. In most cases, when the supply of rule-based institutions lags behind the demand for them, institutional change or innovation can occur in one of two ways. In some cases, social elites can either establish new institutions or transform old institutions in an adaptive way to accommodate the demand (Mahoney and Thelen 2010a; Thelen 2002; K. S. Tsai 2006). In other cases, if social elites cannot launch institutional changes as requested, more radical approaches might be adopted on the societal side by rejecting old institutions and establishing a new system from scratch (S. P. Huntington 1968; S. P. Huntington and Nelson 1976).

27. These political leaders may intentionally learn or borrow rule-based institutions that have been practiced and established in developed countries. In addition to widely embraced modern economic institutions such as stock and futures markets and corporate systems, political institutions are also intentionally borrowed by developing countries to transform their old systems—for example, the diffusion of communism and the communist system in the East European region and China as well as various waves of democratization in South Europe, Latin America, East Asia, and Africa. The political leaders may also be pressured to establish rule-based economic and political institutions. For instance, the IMF, World Bank, and some developed countries have promoted the Washington Consensus through their aid packages for liberal economic reforms in developing countries. Democracy also has been "exported" to developing countries through economic sanctions/rewards and even military actions.

28. This is primarily due to political leaders' paying much less attention to or even ignoring the socioeconomic and political environments, as well as the unevenness across localities, of their societies.

29. Historical evolution and development of village elections in rural China will be discussed in detail in Chapter 3.

30. Helmke and Levitsky (2004) propose a framework for examining the origins and changes in informal institutions, which, in many cases, are what I call indigenous institutions. In their framework, informal institutions are conceptualized as a societal response to the performance and efficacy of formal institutions (what I call parchment or rule-based institutions). Helmke and Levitsky implicitly assume the exogeneity, effectiveness, and priority of formal institutions. Some scholars follow this framework in their research on informal institutions and institutional change (Helmke and Levitsky 2006; K. S. Tsai 2006). However, others criticize this line of research for its assumed effectiveness and priority of formal institutions (Grzymala-Busse 2010; Ledeneva 2006). Similarly, in their research on the growth of capitalism and change in economic institutions in contemporary China, Nee and Opper (2012) argue for the causal priority of informal institutions over formal institutions. This is particularly the case when we study local governance, wherein indigenous relation-based institutions supported by social sanctions have a much longer history of serving as the institutional foundation of governance and were in place long before imposed rule-based institutions. Thus, as the following sections demonstrate, the performance and effectiveness of imposed rule-based institutions (formal institutions) are highly contingent upon the effectiveness and performance of

indigenous institutions (informal institutions). Moreover, the effectiveness and performance of indigenous institutions also cannot be assumed but, rather, are endogenous to their surrounding social environments.

31. According to Galvan and Sil (2007, p. 4), contemporary research on institutional change has been "emphasizing transnational processes of change rather than the parallel evolution of independent systems. Yet, they too rest on teleological foundational assumptions in that they assign a priori epistemological and causal primacy to homogenizing forces of social transformation and uniform logics of social action rather than to sources of variation across space and mechanisms of historical continuity with locales." Some important sources of variation across space and mechanisms, such as norms, informal rules, and cultures, also have been addressed by scholars in the mainstream literature on institutional change. For instance, North (1990) emphasizes the role of informal institutions in explaining "path-dependency" in institutional change. Greif (2006, p. 195) argues that "institutions more compatible with the environment spanned by existing ones, those reflecting the coordinating influence of past institutional elements and incorporating institutional elements inherited from the past, are more likely to result." However, for most mainstream studies on institutional change, norms, values, cultures, and informal rules are just a "theoretical and empirical" residual, rather than an integrated part of a coherent theoretical framework for understanding institutional change.

32. These are what I mean by externally imposed institutions (EIIs), as defined in Chapter 1.

33. Other scholars use different concepts to capture the institutional infrastructure identified by Galvan. For instance, "metis" is the term used by Scott (1998) and Boettke and colleagues (2008), while "slow-moving institutions" is the term used by Roland (2004).

34. Galvan's argument is compatible with Roland's (2004) differentiation between fast-moving and slow-moving institutions. Basically, Galvan's "institutional superstructure" corresponds to Roland's "fast-moving institutions," while Galvan's "institutional infrastructure" corresponds to Roland's "slow moving institutions."

35. Using this framework, Galvan (2004) examines the fates of *Taile* pawning, rural councils, and its national domain law in Senegal. This framework is adopted by scholars to explain the development of local-level democracy in rural Senegal (Galvan 2007), the evolution of Chinese armed forces' engagement in economic activities (Bickford 2007), the change in Argentina's party system (Ostiguy 2007), the managerial syncretism in Japan (Sil 2007), and the nature of economic stabilization plans in Latin American countries (Kearney 2007).

36. Given Galvan and his colleagues' emphasis on the legitimacy of imposed or transplanted modern institutions, as well as the difficulty of cultural transformation, it is understandable that institutional syncretism is their preferred way of institutional change in developing countries. Galvan (2004, pp. 221–222) does not have much confidence in the feasibility of modernizing transformation, as he argues that "this had only really worked in societies where the carriers of pre-modern culture and institutional infrastructure have been wiped out through genocide or massive demographic exclusion"; "setting aside genocidal displacement and apartheid, there are two serious obstacles to imposition and modernizing transformation. Genuine transformation of culture and institutional infrastructure to support new superstructure requires

extraordinarily expensive mechanisms of re-education and re-socialization to construct a hegemonic culture wholly alien to subordinates." Galvan rightly identifies the significance of re-education and re-socialization processes in transforming institutional infrastructure; but, unfortunately, he wrongly equates these processes to what had been done through projects such as assimilation in colonial eras. Culture and institutional infrastructure do change as a response to the transformed social environment in which they are embedded (e.g., Bikhchandani et al. 1992; Eckstein 1988; Inglehart 2003; Inglehart and Welzel 2005; A. Patten 2011). This can be the result of some intentional projects, such as the assimilation mentioned by Galvan, but also may be the result of individuals and communities' adaptive responses to socioeconomic changes induced by, *inter alia*, modernization. The second possibility is one focus of this book.

37. Galvan and his colleagues (2007) assume invariance in the performance and effectiveness of indigenous institutions across regions and examine how institutional syncretism works.

38. Eggertsson (2005, p. 31) argues, "Actors respond to rules aimed at creating new institutions by forming (1) perceptions about the transition path from the old to the new regime; (2) perceptions about the properties of the new system when it is in equilibrium—for example, whether it will involve hard or soft constraints; and (3) perceptions about responses by fellow actors to issues (1) and (2) and how best to adjust to these responses." The effectiveness of distinct institutions is the essence of Eggertsson's second point, while his first and third points correspond to the switching and coordination costs in my argument, respectively.

39. Self-help has been identified by scholars of legal studies, sociology, and anthropology as a form of social control, most likely to be witnessed in atomized communities (e.g., D. Black 1983, 1984a).

40. There are numerous potential sources of the breakdown of indigenous relation-based institutions in local communities, including outward migration, cultural and normative changes caused by economic changes, and exposure to pluralistic mass media. Nevertheless, the outflow of community members through rural–urban migration is a significant phenomenon in all developing countries, and it can exacerbate the impacts of other potential sources on the breakdown of indigenous institutions. Therefore, rural–urban migration is identified as the key structural variable in this book. The impacts of other potential sources are incorporated as critical controls in subsequent empirical chapters.

41. Rural–urban migration happens within a country as well as across national borders. Because this book focuses exclusively on the impacts of rural–urban migration on local governance, domestic rural–urban migration is the key concern.

42. http://www.stats.gov.cn/tjgb/ndtjgb/qgndtjgb/t20120222_402786440.htm. A similar phenomenon has been widely documented in the history of developed countries (Hagood and Sharp 1951; Hochstadt 1999; J. Patten 1973) and in contemporary developing societies (Chaudhuri 1993; Jha 1989; Joshi and Verma 2004; Singh 2001).

43. Household registration systems have been used in some countries, including China, Japan, Vietnam, and North Korea, for population regulation and management. In China, it was originally adopted not for population regulation and

management, per se, but as a complementary institution for its industrialization program (K. W. Chan and Zhang 1999; F.-L. Wang 2005; X. Wu and Treiman 2004).

44. This exit strategy is similar to what Hirschman (1970) examines in his seminal work on exit, voice, and loyalty as well as Tiebout's (1956) ground-breaking work on local provision of public goods. According to both Hirschman and Tiebout, the availability of an exit strategy can create pressure for the provision of products with better quality from manufacturers and more public goods from local governments. Their assumption is that both manufacturers and local governments have to rely on keeping their consumers and constituencies with higher physical mobility for consumption and taxes, respectively. Nevertheless, for many rural communities in developing countries, including China, there is little such pressure for cultivating community members' loyalty. Thus, Hirschman and Tiebout's arguments do not apply to the issues examined in this book.

45. The impact of migration on migrants' home communities is not always negative. For example, Magee and Thompson (2010) claim that the success of the British empire between the 1850s and 1910s should be partly attributed to the effectiveness of the networks among British emigrants in the empire's colonies around the world in providing critical information for economic investments. These emigrants were strongly connected through material support, symbolic attractions, and cultural identity even after their leaving the UK. According to Magee and Thomson (2010), the key reason that British emigrants closely identified with the UK and their fellow citizens in different colonies was that they emigrated from what was then the most developed country with a higher level of civilization to much less developed societies with a lower level of civilization. The situation is essentially different from that of contemporary rural–urban migration in developing countries, where people leave relatively poorer and underdeveloped regions for much more developed urban areas. In this situation, migrants' home communities cannot provide the same type of support and attractions that the UK provided for its emigrants in various colonies in the late nineteenth and early twentieth centuries.

46. This corresponds to the documented change from "communities of acquaintances" (Fei 1992) to "communities of quasi-acquaintances" or even "communities of strangers" (X. He 2003a, 2003b; Y. Xu 2000; Y. Xu and Xu 2003) in contemporary literature on social transformation in Chinese villages.

47. The characteristics of rural–urban migration in contemporary China are discussed in detail in Chapter 3.

48. The general consensus in the literature on rural–urban migration, with evidence from all over the world, is that economic disparity between rural and urban areas is the key underlying driving force (Hare 1999; Lall and Selod 2006; Lobo 2004; Oberai et al. 1989; Roberts 1997; Singh 2001; Stark and Taylor 1991; Wightman 1990; Y. Zhao 1999). In mainland China, this rural–urban disparity is caused primarily by the Chinese government's policies since the early 1950s that prioritize its industrialization and economic growth in urban areas. This is discussed in detail in Chapter 3.

49. The national programs of establishing and imposing rule-based institutions in rural China are also discussed in detail in Chapter 3.

CHAPTER 3

1. For the significance of China's agricultural economy in shaping its socioeconomic and political institutions, see Rosenthal and Wong (2011) and Wong (1997a, 1999).

2. According to the National Bureau of Statistics of China (NBSC), those who have been living in urban areas continuously for more than one year are counted as urban residents.

3. According to the most updated statistics from the NBSC, at the end of 2011, 48.7% of the Chinese population lived in rural areas. This is the first time in Chinese history that its urban population outnumbers its rural population. http://www.stats.gov.cn/tjgb/ndtjgb/qgndtjgb/t20120222_402786440.htm

4. The household registration system is discussed in detail later. Generally speaking, it was originally designed to control the movement of population between rural and urban regions, as an institution complementary to the CCP's early industrialization program.

5. Approximately 79% of the total working population in 1933 was engaged in farming, and 73% percent of the total population lived in families who had agriculture as their main occupation (Feuerwerker 1977, p. 9). According to Feuerwerker (1976, p. 97), at least 90% of the Chinese population lived in rural areas in the eighteenth century.

6. Cohen (2005, p. 64) states, "In China, however, Western influence and pre-Communist industrialization and modernization had their greatest impact in the cities, especially the major foreign-dominated treaty ports." Scholars have varying perspectives on the lack of industrial revolution in China. Scholars such as Feuerwerker (1958) and Greif and Tabellini (2010) attribute retarded industrialization in China to various institutional, cultural, and ideological obstacles. Scholars such as Pomeranz (2000) and Wong (1997a) argue that the isolated geographic location of fossil fuels such as coal in China, as well as China's lack of access to resources from other regions such as the New Continent, causes its retarded industrialization.

7. Although there are different estimates of the role of secondary industry in the national economy in the Republican era, taken together, they indicate that it contributed from 10% to 20% of the national economy in the 1930s (Feuerwerker 1977, pp. 10–40).

8. During this period, the Great Leap Forward (1958–1961) contributed to China's industrial production, which, unfortunately, also generated catastrophic consequences for Chinese society. For more information on this, see Bachman (1991), Dhawan (1990), Domenach (1995), MacFarquhar (1983), and Thaxton (2008).

9. Wong (1997a, p. 29) also agrees that "[t]he view of agrarian China as a massive society in which population and resources broadly stayed in a balance over many centuries remains persuasive."

10. Wong (1997a, p. 131) argues, "Reliance on agricultural revenues became basic to Chinese state administration after the fourteenth century, when the Ming dynasty's founder, Ming Taizu, promoted an agrarian social order with little place for commerce."

11. Skinner (1971, 2001) establishes a model of rural Chinese markets that features an economic hierarchy that focuses on higher-level economic activities in a few centers, wherein successively lower-level services become increasingly dispersed in a triangular-lattice spatial structure. Skinner argues against viewing a family or a village as an entirely self-reliant and closed system and,

instead, stresses the role of standard market towns in China's rural economy. Nevertheless, Skinner's empirical evidence comes primarily from the west part of Sichuan, where the market economy has a long tradition due to abundant resources and rich natural endowments. I am arguing not that rural villages in Chinese history were entirely self-reliant and closed, but rather that socioeconomic activities within respective residential communities played a dominant role in their residents' lives. This also should be the case for the Chinese people who live in relatively developed areas such as those in Skinner's cases.

12. For more information on the civil service examination system in China and its evolution, see Elman (2000), Miyazaki (1981), and Woodside (2006).

13. The ecological status of clan/lineage organizations varies across regions in rural China: more prosperous and powerful in South China but much less so in North China. Nevertheless, even in North China, where scholars have suggested a lack of strong or active clan/lineage organizations, lineage in some villages brings the "ability to display considerable congregational solidarity" (Cohen 2005, p. 12).

14. The "honeycomb" (Shue 1988) structure of rural China was well maintained before the initiation of economic reforms in the late 1970s. I return to this point in later sections.

15. Decentralization is a multifaceted phenomenon. Literally, decentralization means redistributing or dispersing functions, powers, people, or things away from a central location or authority. Nevertheless, as a UNDP report summarizes (1999, p. 1), "In fact, a quick review of the literature shows that there is no common definition or understanding of decentralization, although much work has gone into exploring its differing applications." In contemporary literature on decentralization in China, researchers differentiate between political, economic, fiscal, and administrative decentralization (Y. Huang 1996; Y. Huang and Sheng 2009; Ko and Zhi 2012; Landry 2008; C. Shen et al. 2012; S. Wang and Hu 2001). For this book, fiscal and administrative decentralization are the two key aspects of rural China's decentralized governance. The most widely accepted measure of fiscal decentralization is the subnational share of total government expenses. Basically, fiscal decentralization captures the extent to which local governments are autonomous in determining the allocation of their expenditures and responsible for providing varying kinds of services to their residents. Administrative decentralization features the transfer of responsibility for the planning, financing, and management of certain public functions from the central government and its agencies to subnational governments at different levels.

16. As shown in Section 3.1, before the 1950s, agricultural production dominated the national economy in China. Agriculture's low production rate, as well as the Ming and Qing governments' relatively low agricultural tax (R. Huang 1998; Myers and Wang 2002; R.B. Wong 1997a, b, 1999), constrained the resources that could be extracted by the national governments.

17. Wong (1997b, p. 311) argues, "The Confucian agenda for local order in eighteenth-century China did not pit state and elites against each other in a European manner. Nor did it privilege either of them as the guardians of local order. It admitted both in spatially variable ways to sustain social stability." For more information on direct and indirect controls in Late Imperial China, see Wong and colleagues (1997) and Xiao (1960).

18. The salience of decentralization and intentional incorporation of local resources and indigenous institutions in Late Imperial China's rural governance has also been emphasized by scholars who examined China's water control in this period of time (Elvin 1996; Perdue 1987; Scheineson 2008).

19. For more information on the *lijia*, *baojia*, and *xiangyue* systems in Late Imperial China, see Niou (2005), Qu (1962), and Watt (1972).

20. As Elvin (1996, p. 130) describes similar institutional settings in the Qing dynasty's local water control projects, "The new system, which relied on a network of personal obligations, effectively limited corruption and created an organic system for water control by playing community members in charge whose reputations would be tarnished by any foul play."

21. Xiao (1960, p. 273) also observed, "They [the intermediate agents] were recognized rather than elected."

22. For the roles of gentries and clan/lineage organizations in providing disaster relief, education, and other public welfare in Chinese villages in Late Imperial China, see Leung (1994), Schneewind (2006), Shiue (2004), Will and Wong (1991), Wong (1997b), and Xiao (1960).

23. The performance of such institutions also varied within the Ming and Qing dynasties as the dynastic cycle unfolded. A key issue in the dynastic cycle is the pressure of taxation on Chinese peasants (C. Y. C. Chu and Lee 1994; Usher 1989; Q. Yang 2006). The influence of evolving taxation on the performance of such institutions will be discussed in the context of the late Qing dynasty.

24. Many of these entrepreneurial brokers lived outside villages in towns and even cities. They usually made their living as tax farmers, usurers, and businessmen (Duara 1988). In other words, their alternative ways of making a living outside villages, *inter alia*, enabled them to ignore potential social sanctions from their fellow villagers. Thus, as discussed in Chapter 2, indigenous relation-based institutions could not effectively hold the entrepreneurial brokers accountable.

25. According to some estimates, 50% to 99% of these traditional landed gentries became absentee landlords in the Republican era (Thornton 2007, p. 103).

26. This does not necessary mean that local governance was completely unattended in the Republican era. In some regions, to more effectively extract resources for military purposes and to consolidate their political power, some warlords, such as Xishan Yan in Shanxi Province, did pay attention to institutional engineering for the governance of rural communities (J. Dong 2002). Nevertheless, most measures were based on either the previously discussed *lijia*, *baojia*, and *xiangyue* systems or some mixture of these old systems with pseudo-democratic components. Although the close-knit communal structures of Chinese villages were not substantially challenged in the Republican era, the constant military conflicts and swift power fluctuations seriously disrupted people's expectations of each other's behavior and deterred long-term investment in social relations and economic activities. Thus, indigenous relation-based institutions could not work effectively in this chaotic situation. For a similar interpretation of this chaotic situation, see Olson (1993).

27. In some communities, against the entrepreneurial brokers' predatory activities, local militias launched acts of tax resistance (Perry 1980, 2006). And the ecological features of local communities played a significant role in shaping how these communities responded to such predatory activities (Perry 1980).

28. Different categories were used for classifying villagers in rural China (e.g., poor, middle, and rich peasant, landlord). The key indicator of this social class designation was the economic status of villagers, particularly their properties in land and farm tools. For more information on class categories and their influence, see Friedman and colleagues (1991), Kraus (1981), and Zhang (2013).

29. Collectivism has been intentionally promoted by the CCP ever since the Yan'an period, through its mass media, education system, and family and workplace socialization. Role models promoted in the media, such as Norman Bethune, Zhang Side, and Lei Feng, add to the numerous editorials and comments in newspapers such as the *People's Daily* that speak to how national interests should be voluntarily served even at the cost of individual interests. As Yan (2010, p. 492) argues, "The ultimate goal was to create a new type of socialist subjects, known in Chinese as 'Chairman Mao's good soldiers,' who prioritize their loyalty to the party-state over their filial duties to their parents and family and devote themselves to the grand revolutionary goals instead of individual interests."

30. For detailed information on the operation of the commune system in rural China, see Li (2009).

31. The commune system made some astonishing achievements in improving rural residents' access to medical resources, decreasing the rate of illiteracy among villagers, and promoting equality, particularly economic equality within rural communities. The commune system also contributed significantly to the construction of irrigation projects in rural China. For more information on the socioeconomic impacts of the People's Commune on rural China, see Bennett and colleagues (1978), Dutt (1967), Nargolkar (1982), Parish (1985), Powell (1992), Printz and Steinle (1977), and Wang (2011).

32. I am not arguing that all rural cadres of production teams, brigades, and communes worked fully for the interests of the CCP. As Li (2009), Oi (1989), and Shue (1988) suggest, even under the commune system, there was still some collusion between rural cadres and their villagers to protect their communal interests. This occurred because of the embeddedness generated by the "honeycomb" communal structure, in which rural cadres cared about their reputations among villagers, and their lives were affected by social sanctions. In these cases, rural cadres, at least to some extent, resembled "protective brokers" in the Ming and Qing dynasties. Nevertheless, Chinese communists' effective ideological indoctrination in rural communities and their firm political control of rural cadres dramatically reduced potential collusion between the cadres and villagers (Unger 1989), at the cost of the government, although that possibility of collusion was not completely eliminated.

33. On the issues of coercion, terror, and violence under the commune system, see Dikotter (2011), Thaxton (2008), and Yang (1996).

34. For information on the industrialization programs launched by the CCP in the 1950s and 1960s, as well as their consequences, see Lardy (1987a, b).

35. Before the 1980s, for Chinese rural residents, joining the army, marrying urban residents, and pursuing higher education were the only likely ways of changing their household registration type.

36. As previously discussed, despite his disagreement with Shue on the effectiveness of the CCP's totalitarian system in controlling rural China, Unger (1989) agrees with Shue on the close-knit communal structures of rural China.

37. Brandtstädter and Schubert (2005, p. 813) also observe that "With the end of the planned economy, and the erosion of the socialist collective, the village community emerged from under the state."

38. In addition to distorted incentive mechanisms under the commune system, the Chinese government's intentional extraction of agricultural resources and strict control over rural residents' free migration and choice of occupation are also emphasized as critical factors that restrained China's rural economic growth before the late 1970s. For detailed discussions on these points, see Huang and colleagues (2008), Li (2009), Meng (2012), and Walder and Zhao (2006).

39. This trial version only recommended the implementation of this grassroots democracy rather than making it compulsory.

40. For more information on the continuing debates on the OLVC and village committee elections, see O'Brien and Han (2009), O'Brien and Li (2000), and Shi (1999b, 2000c).

41. Most local officials, particularly township officials, have good reasons to oppose village committee elections, especially before the abolishment of agricultural taxes in 2006. Given the size of rural China, township officials cannot get government policies effectively implemented or resources efficiently extracted without the help of their local agents, who are familiar with village situations and, most of the time, even live in villages. In addition to these practical concerns for implementing policies and extracting resources, the CCP's cadre evaluation system, particularly after the economic reforms beginning in the late 1970s, pays more attention to cadres' performance in boosting local economies and in implementing unfavorable policies such as population control and tax collection (Bo 2002; Landry 2003, 2008). This institutionalized evaluation system makes the local agents who live in villages even more indispensable to township officials. Under the old political appointment system, township officials could directly select villagers who could be relied on. Because township officials, under the old political appointment system, also were in charge of the salaries, material rewards, and sometimes kickbacks that village cadres received, their local agents were usually diligent in implementing policies and levying taxes and fees. Once village cadres are elected, which makes them accountable to villagers rather than to upper-level governments, township officials are in a much less favorable situation and have much less leverage in securing help from village cadres, especially when government policies are not favored by villagers. That is exactly why many township officials opposed village committee elections by claiming that they would become "crabs without legs" once villagers were granted the autonomy for self-governance. Moreover, "the overwhelming roles and powers of local governments often provide township leaders with enormous opportunities to control and manipulate elections" (B. He 2007, p. 148). Thus, township officials are often deeply involved in organizing the leadership groups for village elections. They also can influence villagers' voting choices through personal authority and local connections. As expected, manipulating and circumventing the OLVC are widely reported in various regions of China (B. He 2007; Kelliher 1997; Kennedy 2002; J. Lu 2012; O'Brien 1994; O'Brien and Li 2000; L. Tsai 2010). This issue is systematically addressed in Chapter 4.

42. Before the TFR, Chinese villagers usually were confronted with four types of formal and informal taxes and fees. First tax stands for the real taxes levied,

namely the agricultural tax, the tax on agricultural special products, the slaughter tax, and the animal husbandry tax. Second tax stands for the village retention (*cun tiliu*) and the township comprehensive fee (*xiang tongchou*). These important quasi-taxes were, in their combination (*santi wutong*), not allowed to exceed 5% of peasant revenue. The third tax denotes irregular but legal extractions such as the road construction fee, the education fund, and so forth. The fourth tax stands for illegal fee taking (Göbel 2010, pp. 29–30). The main reforms of TFR include (1) abolition of the various fees, funds, and allotments, including the township comprehensive fee and the village education fund; (2) abolition of the slaughter tax; (3) gradual abolition of compulsory labor; (4) increasing the agricultural tax to a maximum of 7%; (5) standardization of the special product tax; (6) inclusion of the village retention into the agricultural and special product taxes as a surcharge of a maximum of 20% of the root tax rates; and (7) democratic approval of village-level projects directly financed by the peasants (Göbel 2010, p. 88). After the TFR, remuneration of village cadres and expenses for administration and social relief were financed by the return of agricultural tax surcharges from township governments.

43. These were proposed as reforms complementary to the TFR, including (1) reduction of territorial entities by merging villages and townships and bypassing prefecture- and township-level governments; (2) reduction of the number of offices and employees in counties, townships, and villages; (3) strict regulation for the process of hiring, evaluating, remunerating, and promoting local government employees; (4) outsourcing of government services; (5) strict limitation of local-level fiscal capacities; (6) separation of government and business; and (7) creation of a supervisory system (Göbel 2010, p. 89).

44. To overcome their fiscal shortfalls, an increasing number of township governments and village committees rely on selling land for resources (Hsing 2006, 2010; Takeuchi 2013). Therefore, land-related disputes have become a key issue for China's rural governance since the late 2000s (Whiting 2011).

45. The "one task, one meeting" system was introduced to rural China during the TFR in the early 2000s. After the abolition of the agricultural tax, this "one task, one meeting" system provides the only legitimate channel to raise funds from villagers. Basically, any public project should be discussed and democratically voted on at either the villager meeting or villager representative meeting. Once approved, villagers should equally share the expenditure.

46. There were large-scale migrations in Chinese history, but they were driven primarily by natural disasters, military mobilization, and other administrative projects. This type of migration, however, is essentially different from the rural–urban migration discussed here. For related information on population change and migration in modern China since the Ming dynasty, as well as the then Chinese government's control on rural mobility, see He (1959) and Wong (1997a, 1999).

47. This information has not been reported in the China Agricultural Development Report after 2007.

48. There have been numerous studies on the political economy of the origins and evolution of TVEs as well as their implications for Chinese local economies and politics. Most research focuses on the institutional features of the credit and loan system, embedded partial economic reforms, and the corporatism between local cadres and economic entrepreneurs. For more information on the political economy of TVEs in China, see Huang (2008), Oi (1999), and Oi and Walder

(1999). Scholars also have different definitions of TVEs, many focusing on the ownership features. Nevertheless, as Huang argues (2008, p. 77), "TVEs, as used by the Chinese, are a locational concept — enterprises located in the townships and villages." For this book, TVEs are relevant only in terms of their capacity to absorb rural surplus labor released from agriculture.

49. Large-scale layoffs due to the SOE reforms began in 1992, when the Chinese government began reporting related statistics.

50. This compulsory nine-year education program, officially sanctioned by the CCP, requires that all school-aged children complete an elementary (six years) and junior high school (three years) education. However, many rural families cannot afford the expense of the nine-year education program. Since 2006, the central government has been promoting a free nine-year education program in rural China; that is, rural families no longer need to pay tuition and registration fees. With fiscal transfers from the government, the CCP tries to make it possible for all rural school-aged children to complete the nine-year education program.

51. In addition to their prominent role in labor-intensive manufacturing industries, rural migrants also are widely found in urban areas, working as janitors, safety guards, wait staff in restaurants, and maids. For related information on migrant workers' lives in cities, see Becker (2012), Fong and Murphy (2006), and Solinger (1999).

52. In receiving regions, such as Guangdong, Fujian, and Zhejiang, migrant workers are a key component of local economies. In sending regions, such as Jiangxi, Sichuan, Chongqing, and Anhui, remittances from migrant workers play an important role in boosting local income, reducing poverty, and sustaining expenditures (C. Luo and Yue 2012). Some provinces, such as Sichuan and Anhui, are actively engaged in the organized export of rural labor to coastal areas and urban areas for employment (Mobrand 2009).

53. Ever since the early 2000s, the central government has issued a series of rules and regulations to facilitate rural–urban migration and to improve the living of migrant workers in urban areas, such as eliminating various fees charged against them and abolishing restrictions on the recruitment of migrant workers (Hussain and Wang 2010).

54. Generally speaking, a majority of rural migrant workers (more than 60%) stay in urban areas far away from their home communities (i.e., other counties in their home provinces or other provinces). This is compatible with Hussain and Wang's (2010) findings based on survey data: The percentage of rural migrants who stay nine months or more in urban areas is around 58.4%.

55. The impacts of cityward migration on the lives of rural residents who remain as villagers are widely examined by policymakers and scholars (e.g., Du et al. 2004; Jacka 2012; Murphy 2002; Xun 2007). However, this book focuses on the impacts of cityward migration on the communal structures, social environments, institutional change, and the quality of governance in rural China.

56. The national surveys that I use in subsequent chapters were completed in 2008. Thus, I choose the information in 2008 for illustrative purposes. According to China's official definition, "East China" includes Beijing, Tianjin, Hebei, Shanghai, Jiangsu, Zhejiang, Fujian, Shandong, Guangdong, and Hainan; "Central China" includes Shanxi, Anhui, Jiangxi, Hunan, Hubei, and Henan; "West China" includes Inner Mongolia, Guangxi, Chongqing, Sichuan, Yunnan,

Guizhou, Tibet, Shaanxi, Gansu, Ningxia, Qinghai, and Xinjiang; and "Northeast China" includes Liaoning, Jilin, and Heilongjiang.

57. These are the most recent statistics on temporary residents who work in industries in each provincial-level administrative unit that I can find.

58. This regional difference in cityward migration is observed not just at the provincial level but also at the village level (X. Zhou 2011). I will come back to this point in Chapter 4.

59. There are a few exceptions, such as Li and Xu (2000), Murphy (2002), Xu (2000), Xu and Xu (2003), and Yang (2008). Nevertheless, except for some empirical narratives and case studies, no author theorizes the impact of rural–urban migration on rural governance and institutional change or identifies the underlying causal mechanisms. Further, none generalizes or tests his or her findings in a systematic and rigorous way.

CHAPTER 4

1. Numerous indicators have been developed for the quality of governance, and the Kaufmann-Kraay-Mastruzzi worldwide governance indicators might be the most widely used in comparative studies. There are, however, some serious problems with these indicators (Arndt and Oman 2006).

2. In addition to the challenge of operationalization, there are also methodological concerns, particularly the issue of measurement validity. Some public goods can be precisely and objectively measured for rigorous analysis, thus minimizing the influence of measurement errors in statistical inference (Achen 1983).

3. Sufficient provision of public goods also improves the state–society relationship in contemporary China as well as rural residents' views of the Chinese government (Michelson 2011). Thus, local public goods provision is a critical issue for China's rural governance.

4. As discussed in Chapter 3, this book focuses on the fiscal and administrative decentralization in China's contemporary rural governance.

5. China tightened its administrative and fiscal regulation in the mid-1990s. Since then, the central state has taken power over economic resources that were once under the control of village and township cadres (Edin 2003; Oi et al. 2012). Nevertheless, the shift toward tightened fiscal and administration regulation in rural China does not necessarily lead to the recentralization of China's village governance. On the contrary, as some China scholars demonstrate (X. He 2011; Kennedy 2007a; J. Wang 2012), the tightened fiscal and administrative regulation actually has undermined Chinese township governments' incentives to intervene in village affairs and increased their indifference to and detachment from village governance. In other words, Chinese villagers have to rely more on themselves for their community governance.

6. This well-established infrastructural foundation later contributed to the economic growth in rural China after the economic reforms.

7. Village retention was collected by administrative villages and was intended to be used for (1) maintaining irrigation projects, planting trees, and investing in collective enterprises; (2) subsidizing the poor and childless, public health, and other public welfare; and (3) paying village administration expenses and salaries of village cadres. The township comprehensive fee was collected by administrative villages but transferred to townships. It was intended to be used for subsidizing village public goods provision, education, family-planning programs, militia training, and other public welfare. In addition to these fiscal

resources, village cadres also could call for contribution of in-kind labor (*yiwu-gong*) from villagers for local public goods provision.

8. This result is very similar to the information reported by the Ministry of Water Resources in 2011 (54.7%), taking into account sampling errors and sample size, which at least partially confirms the validity of the 2008 NVS data.

9. Since the early 2000s, the Ministry of Education in China, to improve the quality of China's rural education and raise the human capital of students in poor rural areas, has been promoting an ambitious program of elementary school mergers by shutting down small village schools and opening up larger centralized schools in township and county seats. At the end of 2010, the number of elementary schools in rural China was 260,000, down from 550,000 in 2000. Therefore, education facilities and resources are not included in this analysis as part of local public goods in Chinese villages. For detailed information on the merger program and its consequences, see Luo and colleagues (2009, 2012) and Mo and colleagues (2012).

10. Administrative villages in China do not have the right to levy taxes, which makes taxation, a conventional means of collecting resources for local public goods provision, no longer a feasible funding strategy for Chinese villages.

11. In 2002, the Chinese central government, with the promulgation of new legislation known as the Rural Land Contract Law, stipulated a fixed land tenure of thirty years. For detailed information on China's land-tenure system in China and its evolution, see Brandt and colleagues (2002), Dong (1996), Kung and Liu (1997), Li and colleagues (1998), Liu and Chen (2007), and Zhu and Jiang (1993).

12. Wang and colleagues (2011, p. 810) also find: "For the four related questions respectively, 62.79%, 61.98%, 59.95% and 61.10% of interviewees did not endorse the central government's attempt to stabilize farmland tenure. On the opposite end, around 30% of our interviewees agreed that the central government's policy was reasonable (32.01%, 28.98%, 30.38% and 29.59% for the four questions, respectively)."

13. In his examination of land reallocations in some Chinese villages of Anhui Province, Unger (2012) recognizes that the decision to undertake land reallocations usually requires a three-quarters approval vote, but often by unanimous consensus. The clear identification of winners and losers in land reallocation makes it very different from the provision of local public goods, from which everyone can benefit. Of course, people can argue that, over generations, land reallocation can be beneficial for everyone. Nevertheless, the time horizon involved for such evaluation is much longer than that involved in local public goods provision. Thus, I argue that, given the distinct dynamics involved, land reallocation is essentially different from local public goods provision.

14. This is based on my fieldwork in Shandong Province in summer 2006.

15. Due to the underestimation in my measure of the strength of social sanctions, villages with powerful social sanctions and functional indigenous institutions could have been labeled as lacking these features, but these villages actually may have sufficient provision of local public goods because of the powerful social sanctions and functional indigenous institutions that were not captured by the measure. Therefore, in subsequent analyses, these villages are negative cases against my arguments.

16. Veto players are conventionally defined as collective or individual actors or organizations whose agreement is necessary to change the status quo. For detailed discussions on veto players, see Tsebelis (2002).

17. Such findings are further confirmed by Xia's recent work on the basis of a 2005 national survey of rural China (which covered 410 villages from 24 provinces on municipalities): "out of 410 surveyed villages, 114 villages were identified as having a clan organization. Of these 114 villages, 35 have a clan temple, which means that these 35 villages can be said to have a well-organized clan" (Xia 2011, p. 150). In addition to their insufficient coverage of rural China before 1949 and in 2008, as shown in Table 4.4, clan/lineage organizations' strong inertia and historical inheritance prevent these organizations from being created easily in rural China, which demands effective institutions to improve their local public goods provision.

18. Party branches in Chinese villages also play significant roles in local governance. The OLVC stipulates that:

> Article 3: The primary organization of the Communist Party of China in the countryside shall carry out its work in accordance with the Constitution of the Communist Party of China, playing its role as a leading nucleus; and, in accordance with the Constitution and laws, support villagers and ensure that they carry out self-government activities and exercise their democratic right directly.

This article blurs the role of party branches in village governance. Some scholars also see the problem of "dual centers" in Chinese villages (J. Dong 2005; Z. Guo and Bernstein 2004; Jing 2004; Oi and Rozelle 2000; Sun et al. 2013). However, in practice, some villages have adopted the two-ballot system (*liangpiaozhi*) that has candidates of the secretary of the party branch elected by villagers and then CCP members of the village's selecting one of the candidates to be the secretary through an anonymous election. This system makes secretaries of party branches also accountable to villagers (Bai and Zhao 2001; Jing 2003; L. Li 1999). In 2002, the CCP central committee and the State Council jointly endorsed the practice of selecting a single individual to head both the village committee and the village party branch, also known as "concurrent office holding" (*yijiantiao*). The practice has been promoted for streamlining China's rural governance and reducing tensions between the secretary of village party branch and the chair of village committee. This official policy further increases the pressure of villagers' voices, via grassroots elections, on the party branches in Chinese villages (J. Dong 2007; Sun et al. 2013). According to some estimates, as many as 60% to 70% of Chinese villages are currently characterized by this practice of concurrent office holding (S. Zhao 2011).

19. For comprehensive reviews of the literature on village elections in rural China, see Lu (2012), Manion (2009), and O'Brien and Han (2009).

20. All these village elections were organized between 2006 and 2008. China's agricultural taxes were officially abolished on January 1, 2006.

21. For detailed information on the 2002 and 2005 national village surveys, see Lu (2012). The 2005 survey was sponsored by the Ministry of Civil Affairs, which is in charge of China's grassroots democracy in both urban and rural areas. Due to its official sponsorship, the 2005 survey might have overestimated the quality of village elections.

22. There were nineteen villages with missing information land allocation. It is worth noting that, as shown in Table 4.8, powerful social sanctions and high-quality village elections did not often come together in the sampled villages,

and they seem to be found in different communal environments. The variation in the institutional environments is systematically addressed in the next section.

23. Summary statistics of the key variables are provided in Appendix 2 as Table A2.1.

24. This is a reported average within a village, which includes various incomes from agricultural production, sidelines, and remittances from migrant workers. Due to its distributional skewness, a logarithmic transformation is used.

25. This consists of different incomes of a village, including rents collected for collectively owned land, profits from collective economies, and donations from various sources. Due to its distributional skewness, a logarithmic transformation is used.

26. The size of the population who stays in villages could have different impacts on the provision of public goods. As a proxy for the impact of group size, a larger population is expected to exacerbate the problem of collective action. However, as a proxy for possible varying demand for public goods, a larger population might generate more pressure for the provision of public goods. Hence, the regression result might reflect the combination of the two contrasting effects. Due to its distributional skewness, a logarithmic transformation is used.

27. The reported clan structural features from village cadres and the number of ancestor halls with spirit tablets are used as alternative measures; they yield almost identical results.

28. The pattern of housing is an ordinal variable with three categories: (1) scattered housing with significant distance in between, (2) scattered housing with some distance in between, and (3) clustered housing.

29. Compared with other crops, rice needs much more water, which makes irrigation facilities much more important. This is a dummy variable that indicates whether rice is the dominant crop in local agricultural production. For a similar argument on how the structure of agricultural production may shape villagers' collective action, see Zhou (2011).

30. Due to its distributional skewness, a logarithmic transformation is used.

31. This is a binary variable, with 1 indicating the existence of such political contracts.

32. This is a binary variable, with 1 indicating the status of a model village. It is possible that those villages with better local public goods provision are more likely to be selected and rewarded as model villages of self-governance. Then the relationship between local public goods provision and the status of being a model village is endogenous. Nevertheless, it also is common in rural China that some village cadres try everything (e.g., personal connections) to get this status for more fiscal transfers from upper-level governments. For my statistical analysis, this is simply a control for possible extra fiscal transfers from upper-level governments. The causal relationship between the status of being a model village and local public goods provision is not the focus of this analysis.

33. Detailed information on the MPR model is provided in Appendix 2.

34. The overall goodness-of-fit of this MPR model can be assessed by four indexes: Chi-square for the whole model as well as the other three comparative model fit indexes (e.g., Comparative Fit Index [CFI], Tucker-Lewis Index [TLI], and Root Mean Square Error of Approximation [RMSEA]). First, the averaged Chi-square statistic is not statistically significant at the conventional level (i.e., the

highlighted cell in the lower right corner of Table 4.10 that contains the insignificant F-statistic). In other words, the specified MPR model can satisfactorily recover the variance-covariance matrix of the raw data and, thus, in a statistical sense, perform very well. Second, the large values of CFI and TLI and the small value of RMSEA further confirm the satisfying performance of the MPR model in fitting the data. If the values of CFI and TLI are larger than 0.9 and the value of RMSEA is less than 0.08, then the specified model has effectively recovered the variance-covariance matrix of the raw data (Bentler 1990; Browne and Cudeck 1993; Hoyle 1995; Kline 2005).

35. When each specific public facility or project is examined, except for the insignificant negative coefficient of a transparent and competitive village election in regard to local maintenance of irrigation projects, all the other coefficients are positive, as expected. Further, some of these coefficients are statistically significant by themselves: access to tap water (indigenous relation-based institutions), access to within-village paved roads (imposed rule-based institutions), and provision of other public welfare (both indigenous and imposed institutions).

36. Kung and colleagues' (2009) work examines 345 randomly sampled villages in Guangdong Province. Their measure of informal institutions (i.e., a sizeable group sharing the same surname in a village) is closely tied to clan/lineage organizations, which makes sense for regions like Guangdong with a rich tradition of clan/lineage activities. As previously discussed, the validity of this type of measure is suspicious in any comparative study that covers many regions with different institutional traditions, where informal institutions may have distinct facades.

37. The criteria for qualified migrant workers are specific and clearly defined in the questionnaire: (1) working as migrants for more than a month in 2007 (to ensure time endurance) and (2) working in other cities of home provinces or other provinces (to ensure geographic distance from home villages).

38. For instance, the first group includes the sampled villages with a percentage of migrant workers that range from the lowest value (0.01%) to the tenth quantile (0.37%) of the distribution. The tenth group includes villages with a percentage of migrant workers that range from the ninetieth quantile (26.3%) to the largest value (57.8%).

39. Due to its distributional skewness, a logarithmic transformation is used.

40. These variables follow the same operationalization used for the MPR analysis presented in Table 4.10.

41. To rigorously examine whether cityward migration has only indirect effects on local public goods provision, I also specify and estimate another SEM, with extra direct paths from cityward migration to all specific public goods. With the help of nested Chi-square tests, I confirm that, once all indirect effects are specified, the direct impact is not statistically significant. For simplicity of presentation, I drop the direct paths.

42. This is based on the clan structure information reported by village cadres.

43. This is based on village cadres' answers to the following question: "Which of the following statements describes the relationship between the village committee (VC) and the township government (TG)?" Answer categories are: "1: VC tries its best to fulfill all tasks assigned by the TG"; "2: VC does whatever can be done and puts aside what cannot be done"; "3: VC completes the assigned tasks that are compatible with villagers' interests and puts aside the rest"; and "4: VC

completes the assigned tasks that are compatible with villagers' interests, re-sists the rest, and reports the tasks that are incompatible with villagers' inter-ests to higher-level governments." The answers are reverse-coded, with a larger value's indicating a more dominant role of township governments when deal-ing with village committees.

44. I also try different model specifications to examine the dynamics between in-digenous and imposed institutions: (1) a direct path from indigenous institu-tions to imposed institutions and (2) a bidirectional path between indigenous and imposed institutions. Neither model gives significant coefficients for the path(s) between indigenous and imposed institutions after controlling for out-ward migration and other factors.

45. Again, all missing values are filled in through model-based imputations. All results are averaged across five imputed complete datasets, following Rubin's rule. Notably, the overall goodness-of-fit of the integrated SEM is satisfying. The average Chi-square statistic is statistically insignificant, as indicated by the F-test result in the lower right corner of Table 4.11. All three comparative fit indexes (i.e., CFI, TLI, and RMSEA) suggest the statistically satisfying perfor-mance of the SEM.

46. Fieldwork in Qingzhou, Shandong Province, summer 2006.

47. Fieldwork in Qingzhou, Shandong Province, summer 2006.

48. In Qianhouzhai, the village party branch and the village committee are headed by the same person.

49. Fieldwork in Qingzhou, Shandong Province, summer 2006.

50. Fieldwork in Qingzhou, Shandong Province, summer 2006.

51. This was actually against the then national policy on collecting money from villagers for local public projects, which set the upper limit at 15 RMB per person.

52. Fieldwork in Songzhuang, Henan Province, summer 2007.

53. Fieldwork in Songzhuang, Henan Province, summer 2007.

54. Songzhuang follows the practice of concurrent office holding.

55. Fieldwork in Songzhuang, Henan Province, summer 2007.

56. Fieldwork in Songzhuang, Henan Province, summer 2007.

57. In Su Village, it is difficult for a man to get married if he or his parents cannot build a decent house for him.

58. Fieldwork in Su Village, Henan Province, summer 2007.

59. Fieldwork in Su Village, Henan Province, summer 2007.

CHAPTER 5

1. A very famous example of the salience of social sanctions in Chinese villages is presented in a film, *Defendant: Mr. Shangangye (Beigao Shangangye),* in which a woman committed suicide after a village cadre, Mr. Shangangye, revealed her maltreatment of her in-laws to the public and punished her, following local cus-toms. For more information on this, see Su (2000, 2002).

2. It is critical to point out that economic resources or physical power alone have rarely ensured publicly recognized authority in rural China throughout his-tory. When resources or power were combined with moral character, including such qualities as uprightness, fairness, or generosity, the combination was more likely to ensure publicly recognized authority. Otherwise, the rich or powerful villagers could simply be considered "local bullies and bad gentries" (*tuhao lieshen*). Even in today's rural China, "power" (*quanli*) and "authority"

(*quanwei/weiwang*) are two essentially distinct concepts for most villagers, and, in many cases, they do not go hand in hand. For related information and discussion, see Xiao (2010).

3. Response categories are "Almost nothing," "Something superficial," "Something," and "Almost everything."
4. Response categories are "Not at all," "Care," and "Care a lot."
5. This is a close-ended question with preselected response categories. It is reasonable to assume that, if an open-ended question had been used, there would have been potential for confusion in the villagers' answers, as someone might earn publicly recognized local authority for multiple reasons and villagers may randomly report any factors as their answers. This would make it difficult to differentiate among distinct foundations of local public authority. For example, a villager might enjoy this public authority because he is a village cadre and has senior status in the clan/lineage hierarchy. It is important for me to know which of the two attributes is perceived as *more* important among his fellow villagers in generating the public authority. That is why I used a close-ended question, with preselected response categories. When forced to choose among preselected response categories, hopefully, villagers can identify the attributes that are mostly respected in their villages. I do acknowledge the deficiency in this survey instrument, but it is the most effective approach that I could think of.
6. Only the rural subpopulation of the 2008 ABSMCS is used here and in subsequent sections. STATA 11's SVY commands for subpopulation analysis in complex surveys are used.
7. Fieldwork in Henan Province, summer 2007.
8. It is worth noting that (as discussed previously) I used a close-ended question, with preselected response categories. When forced to choose among preselected response categories, villagers were expected to identify the attributes that are mostly respected in their villages. Despite its deficiencies, with this instrument, I can maximize the analytic leverage of differentiating among distinct foundations of local public authority.
9. Instead of using hierarchical models, I pool individual features and village-level information for analysis. The methodological concerns are twofold: (1) the within-village sample size, on average eleven respondents per village, is not large enough for accurate estimation of separate relationships for each village and (2) the sample size varies significantly across villages, ranging from two to thirty, which can lead to unreliable estimates at the village level. After matching individual-level information with village-level information, only 4,127 cases within 350 villages are available for analysis.
10. Age is measured with a continuous variable recording the real age of respondents.
11. Educational attainment is measured with an ordinal variable that ranges from 0 (illiterate or incomplete elementary education) to 8 (postgraduate).
12. A dichotomous variable indicates whether the respondent is a male.
13. Media exposure is measured with an ordinal variable that gauges how frequently a respondent listens to, reads, or watches news. It ranges from 1 (less than once a week) to 5 (several times a day).
14. A dichotomous variable indicates whether a respondent has the experience of working as a migrant in other cities or provinces.
15. A dichotomous variable indicates whether a respondent is affiliated with the CCP.

16. Economic situation is measured with an ordinal variable that gauges the extent to which the family incomes of a respondent can cover all expenditures. It has three values: 1 (family incomes cannot cover expenditures), 2 (family incomes can just cover expenditures without difficulty), and 3 (family incomes can sufficiently cover expenditures, with some extra money for saving).
17. Detailed regression results are in Appendix 3 as Table A3.1.
18. Given her fieldwork in Fujian, a province with rich traditions of clan/lineage activities, Hansen (2008) also argues that outward migration weakens senior authority in rural communities.
19. For the simulation, all other continuous variables are assigned to their respective means, and all ordinal and binary variables are assigned to their respective medians. Simulations are run using the statistical package of CLARIFY. For more information on this package, see King and colleagues (2000) and King's website at http://gking.harvard.edu/stats.shtml.
20. As shown in Table 5.1, only 9.3% of Chinese villagers report extensive familiarity with their fellow villagers. Relatively speaking, this drop of 3.7% is substantial.
21. The reason that I categorize "possible sanctions" as a norm-related intervening variable is that social sanctions per se are discouraged by the curse of collective action (e.g., the second-order collective action problem). With the help of internalized norms, social sanctions can be much more effective in deterring deviant and opportunistic behavior. This point will be discussed in detail later. For information on the second-order collective action problem as well as the significance and functions of internalized norms in social sanctions, see Coleman (1990, pp. 272–289).
22. Such norms could be the result of spontaneous responses from local communities, based on their experiences of social interaction. They also could be the result of intentional cultivation and indoctrination by governing regimes to reduce the cost of local governance—for instance, the *xiangyue* or *jiangyue* system adopted by the Ming and Qing dynasties in China, as discussed in Chapter 3. Empirically, it is difficult to tell which process dominates. The emergence of such norms is more likely to be the result of the interaction between the bottom-up and top-down processes. Regardless of the origins of such norms, they are more likely to emerge, and be diffused and internalized, in close-knit communities.
23. This explanation has been borrowed by students of institutions to explain the origins, evolution, and change of institutions (Mantzavinos 2001; North 2005).
24. In some cases, the impacts of the policies of national governments on the social norms in local communities could be paramount (MacLean 2010). However, given this book's focus on contemporary rural China, the CCP government's policies can be treated as a variable that affects all Chinese villages to a similar extent, particularly in regard to promoting socialist core values such as collectivism.
25. For students of political culture, these norms are not just particular to rural China; they are key features of the Chinese and the more general East Asian culture. For more information on this point, see Antlov and Nog (2000), de Bary (2004), Fingarette (1972), Mote (1989), Pye (1968), Pye and Pye (1985), Shi (2000a, b, 2001), Shin (2011). The cross-national survey project Asian Barometer Survey (ABS) has been focusing on the evolution and transformation in the political culture of East Asian societies since the early 1990s. For the

most recent results of this project, see Chue and colleagues (2008), Shi (forth-coming), and Shin (2011).

26. Although courts and police systems are widely established in developing countries, the available resources are simply not sufficient to meet the demand. This is particularly the case in the rural areas of developing countries, where access to such resources is even more limited and difficult. For information on how limited legal resources are in rural China, see Chen (2008a, b, 2011a, b) and Su (2000, 2002).

27. This also makes it easier to compare the results with previously run probit models.

28. One methodological concern is that because all three dependent variables tap Chinese villagers' normative orientations, due to some commonly shared but unobservable normative or psychological attributes they might be correlated with each other. Thus, the error terms of the three statistical equations are no longer independent from each other but are correlated (Cappelari and Jenkins 2003; Greene 2008; Pindyck and Rubinfeld 1998). Because of this, compared to probit models, MPR is methodologically more appropriate and statistically more efficient. Moreover, these three variables do not tap the same dimension but tap different dimensions of a latent construct. Therefore, a scale score based on factor analysis is theoretically not appropriate and empirically not reliable.

29. Detailed regression results are in Appendix 3 as Table A3.2. The significant joint Chi-square test suggests that the coefficients of the level of outward migration in Chinese villages cannot be fixed to be zero simultaneously for all three social norms without compromising the performance of the MPR model.

30. These findings are compatible with Yan's documentation on the individualization process in contemporary China. Yan (2010, pp. 497–498) argues that "mobility serves as an important agent of transformation as it enables disembedment, making it possible for the individual to break out of the shadow of the various sorts of collectives. This is precisely the direct social impact of the rural-urban labour migration."

31. Such findings are further confirmed by what Tao and his colleagues have found in their most recent study on social trust in rural China, using a different national rural survey in 2008: "those communities that have a higher proportion of people having left home as migrant workers tend to face more challenges; they have lower social trust scores, especially on the childcare question and on helping those in need" (Tao et al., 2014, p. 249).

32. One *mu* is roughly equal to 667 square meters.

33. Fieldwork in Three-Spring Village, Hubei Province, summer 2006.

34. Fieldwork in Three-Spring Village, Hubei Province, summer 2006.

35. Fieldwork in Three-Spring Village, Hubei Province, summer 2006.

36. Before the abolition of agricultural taxes, in a year with great weather and abundant water, the annual production for one-*mu* farmland was around 1,000 kilograms of rice and wheat, which generated a net profit of around 750 RMB (about 112 USD). The per capita farmland in Three-Spring is less than one *mu*. As a migrant worker, it is not difficult to earn a monthly salary of 400 RMB (about 60 USD) or even more, which is an annual income of 4,800 RMB (about 720 USD).

37. Lee and Meng's (2010) survey data show that among their 6,677 surveyed Chinese rural–urban migrants aged 16 to 65, 5,571 reported no interruption

of three months or more. And the average duration of migration was 7.3 years (8 years among men and 6.2 years among women).

38. Fieldwork in Three-Spring Village, Hubei Province, summer 2006.
39. Fieldwork in Three-Spring Village, Hubei Province, summer 2006.
40. Fieldwork in Three-Spring Village, Hubei Province, summer 2006.
41. Fieldwork in Three-Spring Village, Hubei Province, summer 2006.
42. To have a baby in China, a couple has to apply for a certificate issued by local governments. In urban areas, residents' committees are responsible for this, while in rural communities, village committees are responsible. Premarital pregnancy is a very serious issue for most villager cadres, as pregnancy without the required certificate is regarded as violation of the one-child policy, which can result in penalties on village cadres and even ruin their annual evaluations.
43. Fieldwork in Three-Spring Village, Hubei Province, summer 2006.
44. Fieldwork in Three-Spring Village, Hubei Province, summer 2006.

CHAPTER 6

1. Researchers can count the number of cases of conflict between villagers that are resolved through village committees, but it is very difficult to count similar cases resolved in other ways, such as the intermediation of senior villagers. Scholars also can determine the amount of money that village committees distribute to respond to disasters and crises each year but find it difficult to determine the amount of resources voluntarily contributed by other villagers to help those who are affected. The records of credit and loans from collectively owned Rural Credit Cooperatives (RCCs) can be compiled, but little information on informal borrowing and lending among villagers for such purposes is available. Essentially, at the village level, the role of externally imposed rule-based institutions in these aspects of local governance can relatively easily be gauged and examined, but those of indigenously developed relation-based institutions can be difficult to establish. Thus, to comprehensively evaluate the performance of different institutions in China's rural governance, villagers' self-reported choices among alternative institutions for a variety of issues are a more appropriate measure.

2. There is some research on conflict resolution (e.g., L. Dong 2006a, b; L. Dong 2008; Michelson 2007, 2008; Read and Michelson 2008; X. Zhao 2003), credit and loan raising (e.g., Bislev 2012; W. He et al. 2005; B. Hu 2007; G. Li 2005; Ong 2012; K. S. Tsai 2002; J. Zhang 2003; L. Zhou and Takeuchi 2010), and disaster and crisis relief (e.g., Croll 1999; Hebel 2003; G. Wang 2004; Lirong Zhang and Li 2000) in rural China, but most of this research either is primarily descriptive or focuses on the performance of one specific institution in a specific issue domain. Few have examined all of these issues using a coherent local governance framework, and even fewer have searched for the common underlying mechanisms that drive such phenomena.

3. Harmony presumes the elimination of interest conflict and the existence of commonly shared goals. According to Keohane (1984, pp. 51–54), "Cooperation must be distinguished from harmony. Harmony refers to a situation in which actors' policies (pursued in their own self-interest without regard for others) automatically facilitate the attainment of others' goals. . . . When harmony reigns, cooperation is unnecessary. . . . Cooperation requires that the actions of separate individuals or organizations—which are not in pre-existent

harmony—be brought into conformity with one another through a process of negotiation."

4. In some rural communities, some senior villagers commit suicide after quarreling with daughters-in-law, and some women commit suicide after serious arguments with their husbands (B. Chen 2008a, 2011a; L. Dong 2006a, b, 2008).

5. The division of family assets in rural China usually has nothing to do with the daughters of a family; they are expected to be married into other families and, therefore, are not entitled to any family assets, except for their dowry.

6. Fieldwork in Jiangxi Province, summer 2004.

7. For more information on the CCP's efforts in formalizing China's legal institutions and promoting legal education, see Liebman (2012).

8. For more information on the evolution of the mediation system in China, as well as its performance and effectiveness, see Lubman (1967), Read and Michelson (2008), and Wall and Blum (1991).

9. The Chinese government has been trying to rebuild the social security system in rural China, including medical insurance, pension insurance, and the program for guaranteeing the minimum standard of living. Unfortunately, the empirical evidence on the effect of medical insurance is mixed (Wagstaff et al. 2007; Hong Wang et al. 2005), and pension insurance and the program for guaranteeing a minimum standard of living provide limited coverage. A critical consideration in rural China is that, in response to the abolition of agricultural taxes and the initiation of official subsidies for agricultural production, the insurance function of land for Chinese villagers has expanded. Thus, in rural China, to some extent, land can serve as a substitute for the social security system.

10. The granary system comprised three related sets of granaries: (1) ever-normal granaries (*changpingcang*), (2) charity granaries (*yicang*), and (3) community granaries (*shecang*). The first one was sponsored and managed by local governments, and the other two were sponsored through voluntary contributions from and managed by villagers. For detailed information on the performance and evolution of the granary system, see Xiao (1960, Chapter 5).

11. Fieldwork in Shandong Province, summer 2006.

12. The elderly, the disabled, or veterans with no ability to work, no income, and no family support are eligible for the "five guarantees" of food, clothing, shelter, medical care, and burial expenses, as well as subsidies for social services and aid for establishing income-generating activities. The money is guaranteed and comes directly from fiscal transfers from upper-level governments.

13. To decide who should receive social relief, in terms of money and resources, from upper-level governments, local agencies of civil affairs must rely on village cadres, who have more information about each case. Thus, village committees are directly and heavily involved in the delivery of social relief from local governments, and, on most occasions, village committees have veto power in terms of the eligibility of potential beneficiaries in their villages.

14. Hebel's (2003) examination of the "welfare pluralism" in rural China shows four different types of institutions: (1) state and related agencies (e.g., local agencies of civil affairs and village committees), (2) intermediate organizations (e.g., neighborhood and communal mutual help), (3) kinship, and (4) market. For social relief in Chinese villages, market-based institutions rarely work, except for a few unique cases in which rich villagers can afford commercial insurance.

15. A key difference between Hebel (2003) and me lies in our categorization of clan/lineage organizations. For Hebel, clan/lineage organizations and relatives/families are similar in terms of providing assistance during disasters and crises. For me, they are essentially different. The performance of clan/lineage organizations relies on powerful within-community social sanctions, while assistance from relatives/families is based more on consanguineous obligations. Thus, communal structures matter significantly for the former but much less for the latter. In this chapter, I treat clan/lineage organizations like other solidarity groups, as a specific type of indigenous relation-based institution for social relief, and assistance from relatives/families/friends as a private solution for alleviating disasters and crises.

16. This is part of the reason why the "one-child policy" has been quite difficult to implement and enforce in rural China, given the traditional important role of family-based private solutions in providing social welfare. This is less salient for social relief but more critical to providing "pensions" for the elderly. In Chinese villages, intergenerational transfer plays a dominant role in providing support for the elderly. For more information on this, see Croll (1999), Hebel (2003), Lin (1995), and Wong (1998).

17. There are different forms of ROSCAs. According to Hu (2007, pp. 103–104), "Financing-oriented ROSCAs take different forms. They include rotating savings and credit associations in terms of whose money is used by its members on a rotating basis ('rotating associations'); 'dice-shaking associations' that shake dice to decide the order of granting loans; 'bidding associations' that decide the order of granting loans through bidding for the interest; and 'escalating associations' which are a mixture of large and small associations."

18. For reviews on the problems of RCCs in extending credit and loans to Chinese villagers, see Ong (2006, 2009).

19. As previously discussed, a similar strategy and procedure is used by local agencies of civil affairs to deliver social relief in Chinese villages. Village committees and village cadres play indispensable roles in the performance of these rule-based institutions in rural China.

20. Zhou and Takeuchi (2010) argue that China's rural finance faces four key problems: asymmetric information, a lack of collateral, the unique structure of costs and risks, and the nonproductive use of loans. They further suggest that informal lenders have an advantage in solving these problems. Clearly, RCCs intentionally use village cadres' evaluations and village committees' endorsement to address these problems when extending modest credit and small loans to Chinese villagers.

21. Village cadres' significant influence over who can get social relief resources and their official endorsement (in many cases, required) on villagers' applications for modest credit and small loans from RCCs offer them opportunities to take bribes and even embezzle social relief resources. For example, during my visit to a village in Hubei Province in the summer of 2006, I was told by several villagers that if anyone wanted to get a loan from the RCC located at the township seat, he or she had to send gifts or money to village cadres for their official endorsement. I also heard stories of village cadres' favoring their families, relatives, and friends' receipt of social relief resources during my fieldwork in this village.

22. There are some empirical studies on Chinese rural residents' behavior in conflict resolution, particularly their propensity to go up the institutional

hierarchy, with increasing transaction costs for issues with different levels of stakes involved (X. Guo and Wang 2004; Michelson 2007, 2008; Read and Michelson 2008). There is a key problem with this literature: Almost all studies assume that various institutions for conflict resolution are available in most, if not all, Chinese villages, ranging from mediation through senior villagers or other local authoritative figures, to village committees, to local judicial agencies at township seats or even higher-level judicial agencies. However, in many villages, neither local authoritative figures, including senior villagers, nor village committees have the capacity for effective conflict resolution (B. Chen 2011a, b; L. Dong 2006a, 2008). For me, the concern is to identify the primary institutional choice of Chinese villagers and examine whether some institutions with low transaction costs for conflict resolution work in rural China. If such institutions do work, they are more likely to be villagers' first choice, particularly for resolving the conflict with their fellow villagers. Whether Chinese villagers go up the institutional hierarchy to address issues with different stakes involved is not the concern here.

23. In the 2008 ABSMCS, these questions were asked only of rural respondents. Therefore, analyses are based on the rural subpopulation of the national sample.

24. That only a few respondents chose to contact clan/lineage councils first for conflict resolution and disaster/crisis relief is compatible with the finding presented in Chapter 4, that only a small percentage of Chinese villages have active clan/lineage organizations. This is a national sample that covers both urban and rural China. Given the probability sampling, it is understandable that only a few villagers with access to active clan/lineage organizations were interviewed.

25. When their respective transaction costs are taken into consideration, the differences in Chinese villagers' choices of imposed rule-based institutions in various issue domains are understandable. For either disaster/crisis relief or modest credit and small loans, working with imposed rule-based institutions demands extra time, skills, and even other activities such as preparing documents and proofs. Thus, villagers' access to imposed rule-based institutions for conflict resolution is much easier and carries significantly lower transaction costs.

26. A second observable implication of my arguments is that there is a positive linear relationship between the propensity of villagers' preferring imposed institutions to indigenous ones and the level of cityward migration. A key difference between this hypothesis and the one tested in the chapter lies in the baseline for comparison. This hypothesis takes indigenous institutions as the benchmark for comparison, while the one tested in the chapter lumps indigenous institutions and private solutions together as the benchmark for comparison. To test this hypothesis, I use multinomial probit models, setting indigenous relation-based institutions as the base category. The results of the multinomial probit models confirm the validity of this conjecture. Additionally, I create a series of binary variables for Chinese villagers' choices of indigenous relation-based institutions in these issue domains and run similar regression analysis. A significant and negative linear relationship is found between the level of outward migration and villagers' choice of indigenous institutions. In other words, as outward migration increases, Chinese villagers are less inclined to choose indigenous institutions for local governance issues.

27. For conflict resolution, "clan/lineage council" and "other upright and fair villagers with recognized authority" are coded as indigenous relation-based institutions. For disaster and crisis relief, "clan/lineage council" and "neighbors" are coded as indigenous institutions. For modest credit and small loans, "organizations such as ROSCAs" and "neighbors" are coded as indigenous institutions. "Villager council," "village committee," "judicial agencies at the township seat," "agencies of civil affairs at the township seat," and "RCCs" are coded as imposed rule-based institutions for respective issue domains. The remaining choices are coded as private solutions. Due to the same concerns explained in Chapter 5, I do not use hierarchical models for regression analysis here. After matching individual-level and village-level information, I have 4,127 respondents from 350 villages for statistical analysis.
28. Detailed regression results are provided in Appendix 4 as Table A4.1.
29. In addition to cityward migration, the size of population who stay in villages and the existence of a dominant clan also have persistent and significant impacts on Chinese villagers' contextualized institutional choices to address their problems. A larger population generates more obstacles for the adoption of imposed institutions, which is compatible with the conventional wisdom on the negative impacts of group size on coordination (e.g., Mancur Olson 1971; Platteau 2000). The existence of a dominant clan discourages villagers' adoption of imposed institutions. This finding seems compatible with the findings of previous studies on the role of encompassing and embedding clan/lineage organizations in China's rural governance as a specific type of informal institution (e.g., L. Tsai 2007a, b). Nevertheless, as shown in Chapter 4 and 5, the existence of a dominant clan neither significantly facilitates local public goods provision nor effectively contributes to the social environment that favors the performance of indigenous relation-based institutions. Therefore, what this measure really captures merits further examination.
30. Following the same strategies of simulation used in Chapter 5, simulations are generated through CLARIFY with five imputed datasets.
31. The term, "a medium level of outward migration," might sound too ambiguous to provide accurate information for identifying loosely coupled communities in rural China. Nevertheless, it is worth noting that any empirical exercise based on snapshot surveys can only suggest a very rough range for the level of outward migration that might transform a Chinese village into a loosely coupled community. This "ambiguity" is further exacerbated by the distinctiveness of the local governance issues selected for empirical examination. In other words, using different surveys to analyze distinct local governance issues, researchers may get different estimations for the substantive meaning of "a medium level of outward migration." This chapter's empirical exercise (as summarized in Figs. 6.1 and 6.2) suggests that various imposed rule-based institutions, *ceteris paribus*, are most likely to be embraced in Chinese villages with 15.5% to 28.5% of their villagers working as migrants in cities far away from their homes, depending on the specific issues under examination. Thus, I would argue that it is reasonable to identify Chinese villages with 10% to 30% of their villagers working as migrants in cities far away from their homes as "loosely coupled communities." In the 2008 NVS, around 28.09% of the sampled villages met this criterion.
32. Previous studies on Chinese villagers' participation in village elections fail to take into account the various means used by village committees, various

candidates, and even upper-level governments to mobilize and increase villagers' participation, such as paying each villager an allowance for attending a
meeting or using roving ballot boxes to collect votes from those who do not
want to make the effort to cast their ballot in a prespecified location. Therefore,
villagers' participation in local elections may not be an appropriate indicator of
their evaluations of the election-based accountability mechanism.

33. I do not categorize "petitioning to county or higher-level governments" as an
imposed rule-based institution for holding village cadres accountable for two
reasons: (1) Asking for help from local leaders' supervisors has long been used
by Chinese villagers to address their grievances and correct the wrongs that
have been done to them by local leaders and (2) The existing petitioning system
in China does not provide enough transparency or well-articulated rules on
how petitions should be addressed. In many cases, petitioners must take radical
measures to get their cases heard and addressed. Many petition cases are addressed on an ad hoc basis. And petition is also intentionally used by Chinese
political leaders for other purposes. Therefore, I categorize "petitioning to
county or higher-level governments" as a private solution that Chinese villagers
can use all by themselves or together with fellow villagers. For more information on China's petitioning system and villagers' appealing to upper-level governments, see Li and colleagues (2012), Li and O'Brien (2008), Michelson
(2007), and O'Brien and Li (2005, 2006).

34. Rural respondents were asked to indicate their trust in their respective village
committee on a 6-point scale, with 1 = "no trust at all" and 6 = "a great deal of
trust." The coding scheme for the respondents' choices of the most effective
means of regulating and supervising village cadres is as follows: "clan/lineage
council" and "gossip and public opinion" are coded as indigenous relation-based
institutions; "villager council" and "village election" are coded as imposed rule-
based institutions; and "appealing to county or higher-level governments,"
fighting," and "other people with connections" are coded as private solutions.

35. The difference between the two group means is statistically significant
($t = 1.98, p = 0.05$).

36. The difference between the two group means is statistically significant ($t = 2.16,$
$p = 0.034$).

37. This conclusion is compatible with that of contemporary research on the origins
of "Don't know" in political surveys conducted in mainland China. For related
information, see Shi (1996), Ren (2009), Yan (2008), and Yan and Ren (2010).

38. Yao (2012, p. 328) also argues that when ample opportunities to make a decent
living are available outside of rural communities, "villagers no longer felt a high
stake at the result of elections." I argue that this significantly reduced stake
attached to village elections is most salient when the outflow of rural labor
through cityward migration reaches a high level.

39. Respondents were asked, "How often do you talk about politics and national
affairs with your families or friends?" Response categories are "Often," "Occasionally," and "Never." This is an ordinal variable, with a larger value's indicating more interest in politics.

40. Respondents were asked to say whether they "Completely agree," "Agree," "Disagree," or "Completely disagree" with following statement: "I think I understand well the major political problems our country faces." This is an ordinal
variable, with a larger value's indicating a higher level of internal political
efficacy.

41. Respondents were asked, "How satisfied are you with the performance of democracy in our country?" Response categories are "Very satisfied," "Satisfied,"
"Dissatisfied," and "Very dissatisfied." This is an ordinal variable, with a larger
value's indicating a higher level of satisfaction with the performance of democracy in China.
42. Detailed regression results are provided in Appendix 4 as Table A4.2.
43. Again, the CLARIFY package is used for simulation, with five imputed datasets.
44. As discussed in Chapter 4, thanks to the officially promoted practice of the
two-ballot system (*liangpiaozhi*) and concurrent office-holding (*yijiantiao*),
there is increasing pressure of villagers' voices, via grassroots elections, on
village party branches in rural China. Moreover, in the accountability instruments of the 2008 ABSMCS, "village cadres" (*cunganbu*), rather than "village
committee cadres" (*cunweihui ganbu*), was used. It is reasonable to argue that
when villagers were approached with these survey instruments, they were
likely to include the cadres of both village committees and village party
branches for assessment.
45. As previously discussed, in existing research, there is no consensus on whether
grassroots democracy effectively generates accountability in rural China; this is
particularly the case for those studies that exclusively focus on village-level
data (e.g., L. Tsai 2007b, 2011; S. Wang and Yao 2010; Y. Yao and Gao 2006).
Using individual-level survey data on political attitudes and behavior from
rural China, most researchers agree on the effectiveness of grassroots democracy (despite its deficiencies and problems) in boosting perceived accountability
among Chinese villagers, particularly after several rounds of its practice (e.g.,
Landry et al. 2010; J. Lu and Shi 2009; Manion 1996, 2006; Sun 2014). In this
chapter, I use Chinese villagers' self-reported measures, and my findings are in
line with those of the second group of scholars. In addition to the difference
regarding the unit of analysis, timing and background information might also
contribute to the different conclusions. The 2008 ABSMCS was implemented
after the Chinese government's tax-for-fee reform and eventual abolition of its
agricultural taxes. As discussed in Chapter 3, such fiscal and related administrative reforms have significant implications for China's rural governance and,
thus, may also affect the dynamics of grassroots democracy in Chinese villages.
Nevertheless, without access to appropriate longitudinal data, it is difficult to
assess the influence of such timing and background information. This is beyond
the scope of this book but definitely merits further research.

CONCLUSION

1. In his paper, Przeworski identifies five biases that could affect the inferences
on the impact of institutions: (1) baseline difference, (2) effect of the treatment on the treated, (3) post-treatment effect, (4) distance effect, and (5) aggregate effect. For detailed discussions on these biases, see Przeworski (2004,
pp. 537–540).
2. Methodologically, this addresses the issue of identifiability.
3. For various pitfalls associated with counterfactual analysis in social sciences,
see Fearon (1991), Hawthorn (1991), King and Zeng (2006), and Przeworski
(2004).
4. Although this book focuses on the role of communal structures in shaping the
institutional environment and the performance of various institutions in Chinese villages and treats bureaucrats at upper-level governments as actors in the

background, this does not necessarily mean that the performance of various institutions in Chinese villages is independent from the socioeconomic and political forces foreign to these rural communities. For instance, some scholars have speculated about and tentatively shown the possible impacts of tax-for-fee reform and the abolition of agriculture taxes on the performance of grassroots democracy in Chinese villages (X. He 2007a; Kennedy 2007a). As previously discussed, such national policies affect most Chinese villages simultaneously. Therefore, for this book, these national-level macro-structural and institutional changes are in the background, as fixed parameters for all Chinese villages. They cannot explain the variance in Chinese villages' institutional environments and governance, in which this book is interested. Again, to systematically examine these impacts, scholars need more than one wave of cross-sectional data, or even panel data, which is beyond the scope of this book.

5. Studies that systematically examine the contextualized interaction between formal and informal institutions are found primarily in legal studies, institutional economics, and economic history (Ellickson 1991; Galvan 2004; Greif 2006; Greif and Tabellini 2010; Kuran 2010; North 1990, 2005).

6. For Helmke and Levitsky (2004, p. 727), informal institutions are "socially shared rules, usually unwritten, that are created, communicated, and enforced outside officially sanctioned channels."

7. MacLean (2010) examines how informal institutions in rural African communities are transformed due to distinct state-building processes. As I demonstrate in Chapter 3, national governments' institutional engineering and policies also have serious implications for the performance of informal institutions in Chinese rural communities. However, for this book, as previously discussed, the Chinese national government's policies and institutional engineering affect all Chinese villages to a similar extent and thus are unlikely to be the key factor in driving the varying institutional foundations of local governance in contemporary rural China.

8. MacLean (2010, p. 19) also argues for the dominant role of social sanctions in enforcing informal institutions: "The breach of informal rules was not necessarily enforced by the central state but was often self-enforcing by the group through joking, gossip, social stigmatization, or even violence." Internal sanctions also play a role in the performance of these informal institutions—for instance, moral obligations identified by Tsai (2007a, b). Without the help of social sanctions, however, internal sanctions have limited capacity to sustain the performance of these informal institutions. On the limited role of internalized values and norms in sustaining social order, see Shlapentokh (2006).

9. This further-deepened contextualized understanding of informal institutions has serious implications for two other lines of research in political science. For the literature on social capital (Krishna 2002, 2007; Putnam 2000; Putnam et al. 1993), bringing in the social environment helps explain the change and continuity in social capital. For the literature on institutional syncretism (Berkowitz et al. 2003a, b; Boettke et al. 2008; Galvan 2004, 2007; Sil and Galvan 2007), bringing in the social environment helps researchers identify the conditions under which different results of institutional engineering or transplant may emerge.

10. Although addressing state-building rather than local governance, Fukuyama (2004, p. 43) also forcefully argues that "there is no optimal form of organization, both in the private sector and for public sector agencies. . . . Most good

solutions to public administration problems, while having certain common features of institutional design, will not be clear-cut 'best practices' because they will have to incorporate a great deal of context-specific information."

EPILOGUE

1. http://www.oushinet.com/172-4427-184,787.aspx
2. http://news.sina.com.cn/c/2009-02-02/103817133291.shtml
3. http://www.gov.cn/wszb/zhibo301/content_1,212,373.htm.
4. I was involved in these experiments in 2005 and visited these villages several times in 2005 and 2006, during which I interviewed villagers and local cadres. For more detailed information on the experiments, see He (2007b). For other field experiments on local governance in Chinese villages, see Ma and Xu (2012).
5. In some regions of South China such as Fujian, SPAs are initiated by villagers themselves and play an important role in village governance (Hansen 2008). For discussions on the role played by SPAs in China's rural politics, see Deng and O'Brien (2014).
6. Chinese villagers are entitled to homestead land allocated by their village committees for building their houses. This has been interpreted as a kind of social welfare for Chinese villagers; it is usually free, except for some nominal fees for related paperwork.
7. Interviews of the CRG researchers in Wuhan, summer 2006.
8. Fieldwork in Hubei Province, summer 2006.
9. Fieldwork in Hubei Province, summer 2006.
10. The national budget for *Sannong* in 2012 is 1228.7 billion RBM (around 192.6 billion USD), with an increase of 17.9% from that in 2011. For related information, see http://www.gov.cn/gzdt/2012-04/27/content_2,124,858.htm.

REFERENCE LIST

Abel, Richard L. 1974. "A Comparative Theory of Dispute Institutions in Society." *Law & Society Review* 8(2):217–347.

Acemoglu, D., and J. Robinson. 2012. *Why Nations Fail: The Origins of Power, Prosperity, and Poverty*. New York, NY: Crown Business.

Achen, C. 1983. "Toward Theories of Data: The State of Political Methodology." In *Political Science: The State of the Discipline*, ed. A. W. Finifter. Washington, DC: American Political Science Association.

Anderson, Siwan, and Patrick Francois. 2008. "Formalizing Informal Institutions: Theory and Evidence from a Kenyan Slum." In *Institutions and Economic Performance*, ed. E. Helpman. Cambridge, MA: Harvard University Press.

Anderson, Terry L., and Peter J. Hill. 2004. *The Not So Wild, Wild West*. Stanford, CA: Stanford University Press.

Antlov, Hans, and Tak-Wing Ngo. 2000. *The Cultural Construction of Politics in Asia*. New York, NY: St. Martin's Press.

Aoki, Masahiko. 2001a. "Community Norms and Embeddedness: A Game-Theoretical Approach." In *Communities and Markets in Economic Development*, ed. M. Aoki and Y. Hayami. New York, NY: Oxford University Press.

———. 2001b. *Toward a Comparative Institutional Analysis*. Cambridge, MA: MIT Press.

Aoki, Masahiko, and Y. Hayami, eds. 2001. *Communities and Markets in Economic Development*. New York, NY: Oxford University Press.

Arendt, Hannah. 1958. "What Was Authority?" In *Authority*, ed. C. J. Friedrich. Cambridge, MA: Harvard University Press.

Arndt, Christiane, and Charles Oman. 2006. *Uses and Abuses of Governance Indicators*. Paris: Development Centre of the Organisation for Economic Co-operation and Development.

Axelrod, Robert M. 1984. *The Evolution of Cooperation*. New York, NY: Basic Books.

———. 1997. *The Complexity of Cooperation: Agent-Based Models of Competition and Collaboration*. Princeton, NJ: Princeton University Press.

Bachman, David M. 1991. *Bureaucracy, Economy, and Leadership in China: The Institutional Origins of the Great Leap Forward*. New York, NY: Cambridge University Press.

Bai, Gang, and Shouxing Zhao. 2001. *Xuanju yu Zhili: Zhongguo Cunmin Zizhi Yanjiu (Election and Governance: Studies on Self-governance in China)*. Beijing: Zhongguo Shehui Kexue Chuban She.

Bakken, Borge. 1998. *Migration in China*. Copenhagen: NIAS.

Banerjee, Abhijit, and Lakshmi Iyer. 2005. "History, Institutions, and Economic Performance: The Legacy of Colonial Land Tenure Systems in India." *American Economic Review* 94(4):1190–1213.

Banerjee, Abhijit, Rohini Somanathan, and Lakshmi Iyer. 2005. "History, Social Divisions, and Public Goods in Rural India." *Journal of the European Economic Association* April-May (3):639–647.

Banfield, Edward C. 1967. *The Moral Basis of a Backward Society.* New York, NY: Free Press.

Barkow, Jerome H. 1992. "Beneath New Culture Is Old Psychology: Gossip and Social Stratification." In *The Adapted Mind: Evolutionary Psychology and the Generation of Culture,* ed. J. H. Barkow, L. Cosmides, and J. Tooby. New York, NY: Oxford University Press.

Becker, Jeffrey. 2012. "The Knowledge to Act: Chinese Migrant Labor Protests in Comparative Perspective." *Comparative Political Studies* 45(11):11.

Bendix, Richard. 1967. "Tradition and Modernity Reconsidered." *Comparative Studies in Society and History* 9(3):292–346.

Bennett, Gordon A., Ken Kieke, and Ken Yoffy. 1978. *Huadong: The Story of a Chinese People's Commune.* Boulder, CO: Westview Press.

Bentler, P. M. 1990. "Comparative Fit Indexes in Structural Models." *Psychological Bulletin* 107:238–246.

Berkowitz, Daniel, Katharina Pistor, and Jean-Francois Richard. 2003a. "Economic Development, Legality, and the Transplant Effect." *European Economic Review* 47:165–195.

———. 2003b. "The Transplant Effect." *American Journal of Comparative Law* 51(1):163–203.

Bernstein, Lisa. 1992. "Opting Out of the Legal System: Extralegal Contractual Regulations in the Diamond Industry." *Journal of Legal Studies* 21(1):115–157.

Bernstein, Thomas, and Xiaobo Lu. 2008. *Taxation without Representation in Contemporary Rural China.* New York, NY: Cambridge University Press.

Besley, Timothy, Stephen Coate, and Glenn Loury. 1993. "The Economics of Rotating Savings and Credit Associations." *American Economic Review* 83:792–810.

———. 1994. "Rotating Savings and Credit Associations, Credit Markets and Efficiency." *Review of Economic Studies* 61:701–719.

Besley, Timothy, and Alec R. Levenson. 1996. "The Role of Informal Finance in Household Capital Accumulation: Evidence from Taiwan." *Economic Journal* 106:39–59.

Bhuyan, Ayubur Rahman, Harun-ar-Rashid Khan, and Sultan Uddin Ahmad. 2001. *Rural-Urban Migration and Poverty: The Case for Reverse Migration in Bangladesh.* Dhaka: Centre on Integrated Rural Development for Asia and the Pacific.

Bickford, Thomas J. 2007. "Institutional Syncretism and the Chinese Armed Forces." In *Reconfiguring Institutions across Time and Space,* ed. D. C. Galvan and R. Sil. New York, NY: Palgrave Macmillan.

Bikhchandani, Sushil, David Hirshleifer, and Ivo Welch. 1992. "A Theory of Fads, Fashion, Custom, and Cultural Change as Informational Cascades." *Journal of Political Economy* 100(5):992–1026.

Bislev, Ane. 2012. "Embedded Microcredit—Creating Village Cohesion on the Basis of Existing Social Networks." In *Organizing Rural China, Rural China Organizing,* ed. A. Bislev and S. Thøgersen. Lanham, MD: Lexington Books.

Bislev, Ane, and Stig Thøgersen, eds. 2012. *Organizing Rural China, Rural China Organizing.* Lanham, MD: Lexington Books.

Black, Cyril Edwin. 1966. "Change as a Condition of Modern Life." In *Modernization: The Dynamics of Growth*, ed. M. Weiner. New York, NY: Basic Books.

————. 1967. *The Dynamics of Modernization: A Study in Comparative History*. New York, NY: Harper & Row.

Black, Donald. 1983. "Crime as Social Control." *American Sociological Review* 48(1):34–45.

————. 1984a. "Social Control as A Dependent Variable." In *Toward A General Theory of Social Control*, ed. D. Black. New York, NY: Academic Press.

————, ed. 1984b. *Toward a General Theory of Social Control*. 2 vols. New York, NY: Academic Press.

Bo, Zhiyue. 2002. *Chinese Provincial Leaders: Economic Performance and Political Mobility Since 1949*. Armonk, NY: M.E. Sharpe.

Boehm, Christopher. 1984. *Blood Revenge: The Anthropology of Feuding in Montenegro and Other Tribal Societies*. Lawrence, KS: University Press of Kansas.

Boettke, Peter, Christopher J. Coyne, and Peter T. Leeson. 2008. "Institutional Stickiness and the New Development Economics." *American Journal of Economics and Sociology* 67(2):331–358.

Boix, C. 1999. "Setting the Rules of the Game: The Choice of Electoral Systems in Advanced Democracies." *American Political Science Review* 93(3):609–624.

Brady, H. E., and D. Collier. 2004. *Rethinking Social Inquiry: Diverse Tools, Shared Standards*. Lanham, MD: Rowman & Littlefield.

Brandt, Loren, Jikun Huang, Guo Li, and Scott Rozelle. 2002. "Land Rights in Rural China: Facts, Fictions and Issues." *China Journal* (47):67–97.

Brandtstädter, Susanne, and Gunter Schubert. 2005. "Democratic Thought and Practice in Rural China." *Democratization* 12(5):801–819.

Brison, Karen J. 1992. *Just Talk: Gossip, Meetings, and Power in a Papua New Guinea Village*. Berkeley, CA: University of California Press.

Browne, M. W., and R. Cudeck. 1993. "Alternative Ways of Assessing Model Fit." In *Testing Structural Equation Models*, ed. K. A. Bollen and J. S. Long. Newbury Park, CA: Sage Publication.

Burt, Ronald S. 1992. *Structural Holes: The Social Structure of Competition*. Cambridge, MA: Harvard University Press.

Cabral, Luis, and A. L. I. Hortaçsu. 2010. "The Dynamics of Seller Reputation: Evidence from eBay." *Journal of Industrial Economics* 58(1):54–78.

Cai, Fang, and Nansheng Bai. 2006. *Labor Migration in Transition China*. Beijing: Social Sciences Academic Press.

Camerer, Colin. 2003. *Behavioral Game Theory*. Princeton, NJ: Princeton University Press.

Cappelari, Lorenzo, and Stephen P. Jenkins. 2003. "Multivariate Probit Regression Using Simulated Maximum Likelihood." *Stata Journal* 3(3):278–294.

Chan, Anita, Richard Madsen, and Jonathan Unger. 1984. *Chen Village: The Recent History of a Peasant Community in Mao's China*. Berkeley, CA: University of California Press.

————. 1992. *Chen Village under Mao and Deng*. Berkeley, CA: University of California Press.

Chan, Kam Wing, and Li Zhang. 1999. "The Hukou System and Rural-Urban Migration in China: Processes and Changes." *China Quarterly* 160:818–855.

Chang, Chung-li. 1955. *The Chinese Gentry: Studies on Their Role in Nineteenth-Century Chinese Society*. Seattle, WA: University of Washington Press.

Chang, Yu-tzung, and Chen-chia Wu. 2011. "Grassroots Democracy in China and the Development of Rural Welfare Provision." *Taiwan Political Science Review* 15(2):177–232.

Chaudhuri, Jayasri Ray. 1993. *Migration and Remittances: Inter-Urban and Rural-Urban Linkages*. Newbury Park, CA: Sage Publications.

Chen, Baifeng. 2008a. "Jiazhiguan Bianqian Beijingxia de Nongmin Zishan Wenti: Wanbei Liyucun Diaocha (Suicide in Rural China and Value Change: Liyu Village in North Anhui.)" *Zhongguo Xiangcun Yanjiu* 6.

———. 2008b. "Zhongxibu Nongcun Jiceng Falv Fuwuye de Kunjing (The Difficult Situation of Grassroots Legal Service in West and Central Rural China.)" *Zhanjiang Shifanxueyuan Xuebao (Journal of Zhanjiang Normal College)* (2).

———. 2011a. *Baoli yu Zhiyu (Violence and Order)*. Beijing: China Social Sciences Press.

———. 2011b. *Xiangcun Jianghu: Lianghu Pingyun Hunhun Yanjiu (Jianghu in Rural China: Studies on Rural Hooligans in Hubei and Hunan)*. Beijing: China University of Political Science and Law Press.

Chen, J., and Y. Zhong. 2002. "To Vote or Not To Vote: An Analysis of Peasants' Participation in Chinese Village Elections." *Comparative Political Studies* 35(6):686–712.

Chen, Jie, and Narisong Huhe. 2013. "Informal Accountability, Socially Embedded Officials, and Public Goods Provision in Rural China: The Role of Lineage Groups." *Journal of Chinese Political Science* 18(2):101–116.

Cheng, Linshun. 2003. *Banking in Modern China*. New York, NY: Cambridge University Press.

Cheng, Tiejun, and Mark Selden. 1994. "The Origins and Social Consequences of China's Hukou System." *China Quarterly* (139):644–668.

Chimhowu, Admos, and Phil Woodhouse. 2006. "Customary vs. Private Property Rights? Dynamics and Trajectories of Vernacular Land Markets in Sub-Saharan Africa." *Journal of Agrarian Change* 6(3):346–371.

Chu, C. Y. Cyrus, and Ronald D. Lee. 1994. "Famine, Revolt, and the Dynastic Cycle." *Journal of Population Economics* 7(4):351–378.

Chu, Yun-han, Larry Diamond, A. Nathan, and Doh Chull Shin, eds. 2008. *How East Asians View Democracy*. New York, NY: Columbian University Press.

Clay, Karen. 1997. "Trade, Institutions, and Credit." *Explorations in Economic History* 34:495–521.

Cohen, Myron L. 2005. *Kinship, Contract, Community, and State: Anthropological Perspectives on China*. Stanford, CA: Stanford University Press.

Coleman, J. S. 1986. "Social Structure and the Emergence of Norms among Rational Actors." In *Paradoxical Effects of Social Behavior*, ed. A. Diekman and P. Mitter. Heidelberg: Physica-Verlag.

———. 1990. *Foundations of Social Theory*. Cambridge, MA: Harvard University Press.

Collier, D. 2011. "Understanding Process Tracing." *PS: Political Science & Politics* 44(4):745–748.

Cook, Karen S., and R. Hardin. 2001. "Norms of Cooperativeness and Networks of Trust." In *Social Norms*, ed. M. Hechter and K.-D. Opp. New York, NY: Russell Sage Foundation.

Croll, Elisabeth J. 1999. "Social Welfare Reform: Trends and Tensions." *China Quarterly* 159:684–699.

Cronin, Bruce. 1999. *Community Under Anarchy: Transnational Identity and the Evolution of Cooperation*. New York, NY: Columbia University Press.

Cuscak, T. R., T. Iversen, and D. W. Soskice. 2007. "Economic Interests and the Origins of Electoral System." *American Political Science Review* 101(3):373–391.

Daley, Elizabeth. 2005a. "Land and Social Change in a Tanzanian Village 1: Kinyanambo, 1920s-1990s." *Journal of Agrarian Change* 5(3):363–404.

———. 2005b. "Land and Social Change in a Tanzanian Village 2: Kinyanambo in the 1990s." *Journal of Agrarian Change* 5(4):526–572.

Davis, Christina L. 2004. "International Institutions and Issue Linkage: Building Support for Agricultural Trade Liberalization." *American Political Science Review* 98(1):153–169.

Day, Lincoln H., and Xia Ma. 1994. *Migration and Urbanization in China*. Armonk, NY: M.E. Sharpe.

de Bary, William Theodore. 2004. *Nobility & Civility: Asian Ideals of Leadership and the Common Good*. Cambridge, MA: Harvard University Press.

de Hooge, Ilona E., Marcel Zeelenberg, and Seger M. Breugelmans. 2007. "Moral Sentiments and Cooperation: Differential Influences of Shame and Guilt." *Cognition & Emotion* 21(5):1025–1042.

Deng, Yanhua, and K. J. O'Brien. 2014. "Societies of Senior Citizens and Popular Protest in Rural Zhejiang Research Report." *China Journal* 71:172–188.

Dhawan, Neerja. 1990. *Great Leap Forward: An Appraisal*. New Delhi: R.K. Gupta & Co.

Dikotter, Frank. 2011. *Mao's Great Famine: The History of China's Most Devastating Catastrophe, 1958–1962*. New York, NY: Walker & Company.

DiMaggio, P. J. 1997. "Culture and Cognition." *Annual Review of Sociology* 23: 263–287.

Dixit, Avinash K. 2004. *Lawlessness and Economics: Alternative Modes of Governance*. Princeton, NJ: Princeton University Press.

Domenach, Jean-Luc. 1995. *The Origins of the Great Leap Forward: The Case of One Chinese Province*. Boulder, CO: Westview Press.

Dong, Jiangai. 2002. *Shanxi Cunzhi yu Junfa Zhengzhi, 1917–1927 (Village Governance in Shanxi Province and Warlord Politics, 1917–1927)*. Beijing: Zhongguo Shehui Chubanshe.

———. 2005. "Cunji Xuanju zhong Xingcheng de Liangwei Guanxi Duili ji Chulu (Confrontation between Party Branches and Villagers Committees in Village Elections.)" *Huazhong Shifan Daxue Xuebao* 44(1):54–59.

———. 2007. "Liangpiaozhi, Liangtui Yixuan yu Yijiantiao de Chuanxinxing (Creative Institutions for Rural Governances: Two-Ballot System, Two-Recommendations-One-Ballot, and Two-Leaderships-One-Person)." *Shehui Zhuyi Yanjiu* 6:73–76.

Dong, Leiming. 2006a. "Cunzhuang Jiufen Tiaojie Jizhi de Yanjiu Lujing (How to Examine the Mechanisms of Conflict Resolution in Villages)" *Xuexi yu Tansuo* (1):107–110.

———. 2006b. "Nongcun Tiaojie Jizhi de Yujinghua Lijie yu Quyu Bijiao Yanjiu (A Contextualized Understanding and Comparative Study of the Mechanisms of Conflict Resolution in Villages)." *Shehui Kexue Jikan* (1):56–61.

———. 2008. *Songcun de Tiaojie: Jubian Shidai de Quanwei yu Chixu (Conflict Resolution in Song Village: Authority and Order in a Time of Radical Change)*. Beijing: Falu Chubanshe.

Dong, Xiao-yuan. 1996. "Two-Tier Land Tenure System and Sustained Economic Growth in Post-1978 Rural China." *World Development* 24(5):915–928.

Du, Peng, Zhihong Ding, Quanmian Li, and Jiangfeng Gui. 2004. "Nongcun Zinv Waichu Wugong Dui Liushou Laoren de Yingxiang (Impacts of Out-flowing Labors on the Life of Their Parents in Villages)." *Renkou Yanjiu* (6):44–52.

Duan, Wenyou. 2007. *Huanghe Zhongxiayou Jiazu Cunluo Minsu yu Shehui Xiandaihua (Clans, Villages, Folk-customs and Social Modernization in the Middle and Lower Reaches of the Yellow River)*. Beijing: Zhonghua Shuju.

Duara, Prasenjit. 1988. *Culture, Power, and the State: Rural North China, 1900–1942*. Stanford, CA: Stanford University Press.

Dutt, Gargi. 1967. *Rural Communes in China: Organizational Problems*. Bombay: Asia Pub. House.

Easton, David. 1955. *A Theoretical Approach to Authority*. Stanford, CA: Stanford University Press.

———. 1958. "The Perception of Authority and Political Change." In *Authority*, ed. C. J. Friedrich. Cambridge, MA: Harvard University Press.

Eckstein, Harry. 1988. "A Culturalist Theory of Political Change." *American Political Science Review* 82(3):789–804.

Edgerton, Robert B. 1992. *Sick Societies: Challenging the Myth of Primitive Harmony*. New York, NY: Free Press.

Edin, Maria. 2003. "State Capacity and Local Agent Control in China: CCP Cadre Management from a Township Perspective." *China Quarterly* 173:35–52.

Eggertsson, T. 2005. *Imperfect Institutions: Possibilities and Limits of Reform*. Ann Arbor, MI: University of Michigan Press.

Eisenstadt, S. N. 1966. *Modernization: Protest and Change*. Englewood Cliffs, NJ: Prentice-Hall.

Ellickson, Robert C. 1991. *Order without Law: How Neighbors Settle Disputes*. Cambridge, MA: Harvard University Press.

———. 2001. "The Evolution of Social Norms: A Perspective from the Legal Academy." In *Social Norms*, ed. M. Hechter and K.-D. Opp. New York, NY: Russell Sage Foundation.

———. 2008. *The Household: Informal Order around the Hearth*. Princeton, NJ: Princeton University Press.

Elman, Benjamin A. 2000. *A Cultural History of Civil Examination in Late Imperial China*. Berkeley, CA: University of California Press.

Elvin, Mark. 1996. *Another History: Essays on China from a European Perspective*. Honolulu, HI: University of Hawaii Press.

Evans, Peter B. 1995. *Embedded Autonomy: States and Industrial Transformation*. Princeton, NJ: Princeton University Press.

Fafchamps, Marcel. 2011. "Markets and the Diffusion of Institutional Innovations." In *Culture, Institutions, and Development*, ed. J. P. Platteau and R. Peccoud. New York, NY: Routledge.

Fearon, J. D. 1991. "Counterfactuals and Hypothesis Testing in Political Science." *World Politics* 43(2):169–195.

Fei, X. 1939. *Peasant Life in China*. New York, NY: E. P. Dutton & Company.

———. 1992. *From the Soil: The Foundations of Chinese Society*. Translated by G. G. Hamilton and Z. Wang. Berkeley, CA: University of California Press.

Felstiner, William L. F. 1974. "Influences of Social Organization on Dispute Processing." *Law & Society Review* 9(1):63–94.

Feuerwerker, Albert. 1958. *China's Early Industrialization: Sheng Hsuan-huai (1844–1916) and Mandarin Enterprise*. Cambridge, MA: Harvard University Press.

———. 1976. *State and Society in Eighteenth-Century China: The Ch'ing Empire in Its Glory*. Ann Arbor, MI: University of Michigan Press.

———. 1977. *Economic Trends in the Republic of China, 1912–1949*. Ann Arbor, MI: University of Michigan Press.

Fingarette, Herbert. 1972. *Confucius: The Secular as Sacred*. 1st ed. New York, NY: Harper & Row.

Fong, Vanessa L., and Rachel Murphy. 2006. *Chinese Citizenship: Views from the Margins*. New York, NY: Routledge.

Freedman, Maurice. 1958. *Lineage Organization in Southeastern China*. London: Athlone Press.

———. 1966. *Chinese Lineage and Society: Fukien and Kwangtung*. New York, NY: Humanities Press.

Friedman, Edward, Paul Pickowicz, and Mark Selden. 1991. *Chinese Village, Socialist State*. New Haven, CT: Yale University Press.

Friedrich, Carl J. 1958. "Authority, Reason, and Discretion." In *Authority*, ed. C. J. Friedrich. Cambridge, MA: Harvard University Press.

———. 1972. *Tradition and Authority*. New York, NY: Praeger.

Fudenberg, Drew, and Jean Tirole. 1991. *Game Theory*. Cambridge, MA: MIT Press.

Fukuyama, Francis. 2004. *State-Building: Governance and World Order in the 21st Century*. Ithaca, NY: Cornell University Press.

———. 2011. *The Origins of Political Order: From Prehuman Times to the French Revolution*. New York, NY: Farrar, Straus and Grioux.

Galanter, Marc. 1981. "Justice in Many Rooms: Courts, Private Ordering, and Indigenous Law." *Legal Pluralism* 19(1):1–47.

Galvan, Dennis Charles. 2004. *The State Must Be Our Master of Fire: How Peasants Craft Sustainable Development in Senegal*. Berkeley, CA: University of California Press.

———. 2007. "Syncretism and Local-Level Democracy in Senegal." In *Reconfiguring Institutions across Time and Space*, ed. D. C. Galvan and R. Sil. New York, NY: Palgrave Macmillan.

Galvan, Dennis Charles, and Rudra Sil. 2007. "The Dilemma of Institutional Adaptation and the Role of Syncretism." In *Reconfiguring Institutions across Time and Sapce*, ed. D. C. Galvan and R. Sil. New York, NY: Palgrave Macmillan.

Geertz, Clifford. 1973. *The Interpretation of Cultures*. New York, NY: Basic Books.

———. 1980. *Negara: The Theatre State in Nineteenth Century Bali*. Princeton, NJ: Princeton University Press.

Gibson, Clark C., Margaret A. McKean, and Elinor Ostrom. 2000. *People and Forests: Communities, Institutions, and Governance*. Cambridge, MA: MIT Press.

Gilbert, Paul. 2003. "Evolution, Social Roles, and the Differences in Shame and Guilt." *Social Research: An International Quarterly* 70(4):1205–1230.

Ginat, J. 1997. *Blood Revenge: Family Honor, Mediation and Outcasting*. Portland, OR: Sussex Academic Press.

Gintis, Herbert. 2005. *Moral Sentiments and Material Interests: The Foundations of Cooperation in Economic Life*. Cambridge, MA: MIT Press.

Göbel, Christian. 2010. *The Politics of Rural Reform in China*. New York, NY: Routledge.

Greene, William H. 2008. *Econometric Analysis*. 6th ed. Upper Saddle River, NJ: Prentice Hall.

Greif, A. 1989. "Reputation and Coalitions in Medieval Trade: Evidence on the Maghribi Traders." *Journal of Economic History* 49(4):857–882.

———. 1993. "Contract Enforceability and Economic Institutions in Early Trade: The Maghribi Traders' Coalition." *American Economic Review* 83(3):525–548.

———. 2006. *Institutions and the Path to the Modern Economy: Lessons from Medieval Trade*. New York, NY: Cambridge University Press.

Greif, A., and Eugene Kandel. 1995. "Contract Enforcement Institutions: Historical Perspective and Current Status in Russia." In *Economic Transition in Eastern Europe and Russia*, ed. E. P. Lazear. Stanford, CA: Hoover Institution Press.

Greif, A., and D. Laitin. 2004. "A Theory of Endogenous Institutional Change." *American Political Science Review* 98(4):633–652.

Greif, A., Paul Milgrom, and B. Weingast. 1995. "Coordination, Commitment, and Enforcement: The Case of the Merchant Guild." In *Explaining Social Institutions*, ed. J. Knight and I. Sened. Ann Arbor, MI: University of Michigan Press.

Greif, A., and G. Tabellini. 2010. "Cultural and Institutional Bifurcation: China and Europe Compared." *American Economic Review* 100(2):135–140.

Greif, A., and Steven Tadelis. 2010. "A Theory of Moral Persistence: Crypto-Morality and Political Legitimacy." *Journal of Comparative Economics* 38(3):229–244.

Grould, Roger V. 1993. "Collective Action and Network Structure." *American Sociological Review* 58(2):182–196.

Grzymala-Busse, Anna. 2010. "The Best Laid Plans: The Impact of Informal Rules on Formal Institutions in Transitional Regimes." *Studies in Comparative International Development* 45(3):311–333.

Guang, Lei, and Lu Zheng. 2005. "Migration as the Second-Best Option: Local Power and Off-farm Employment." *China Quarterly* 181:22–45.

Guo, Liang. 2010. Land Politics. Dissertation, Department of Sociology, Huazhong University of Science and Technology, Wuhan.

Guo, Peigui. 2006. "Mingdai Keju Geji Kaoshi de Guimo ji Luqulv (The Scale of Different Levels of Imperial Examinations in the Ming Dynasty and its Enrollment Rate.)" *Journal of Historical Science* (12).

Guo, Xinghua, and Ping Wang. 2004. "Zhongguo Nongcun de Jiufen yu Jiejue Tujing (Disputes and Means of Resolution in Rural China)." *Sociological Studies* (2):71–77.

Guo, Xinghua, and Chaoguo Xing. 2010. "Cong Songfa Xialiang dao Lixing Xuanze: Xiangtu Shehui de Falv Shijian (From Sending Law of Rural China to Rational Choice: Legal Practice in Chinese Villages)." *Heilongjiang Shehui Kexue* 1:129–133.

Guo, Zhenglin, and Thomas Bernstein. 2004. "The Impact of Elections on the Village Structure of Power: The Relations between Village Committees and Village Party Branches." *Journal of Contemporary China* 13(39):257–275.

Haas, Ernst B. 1980. "Why Collaborate? Issue-Linkage and International Regimes." *World Politics* 32(3):357–405.

Habyarimana, James, Macartan Humphreys, Daniel N. Posner, and Jeremy M. Weinstein. 2007. "Why Does Ethnic Diversity Undermine Public Goods Provision?" *American Political Science Review* 101(4):709–725.

Hagood, Margaret Jarman, and Emmit F. Sharp. 1951. *Rural-Urban Migration in Wisconsin, 1940–1950*. Madison, WI: University of Wisconsin Press.

Hansen, Mette Halskov. 2008. "Organising the Old: Senior Authority and the Political Significance of a Rural Chinese 'Non-Governmental Organisation.'" *Modern Asian Studies* 42(5):1057–1078.

Hardin, Garrett. 1968. "The Tragedy of the Commons." *Science* 162(3859):1243–1248.

Hardin, R. 1982. *Collective Action*. Baltimore, MD: Johns Hopkins University Press.

———. 1995. *One for All: The Logic of Group Conflict*. Princeton, NJ: Princeton University Press.

Hare, Denise. 1999. "Push versus Pull Factors in Migration Outflows and Returns: Determinants of Migration Status and Spell During Among China's Rural Population." *Journal of Developmental Studies* 35(3):45–72.

Harris, J., and M. Todaro. 1970. "Migration, Unemployment and Development: A Two Sector Analysis." *American Economic Review* 40(1):126–142.

Hawthorn, Geoffrey. 1991. *Plausible Worlds: Possibility and Understanding in History and the Social Sciences*. New York, NY: Cambridge University Press.

Hayami, Yujiro, and Toshihiko Kawagoe. 2001. "Middlemen in a Peasant Community: Vegetable Marketing in Indonesia." In *Communities and Markets in Economic Development*, ed. M. Aoki and Y. Hayami. New York, NY: Oxford University Press.

He, Annai, and Biliang Hu, eds. 2000. *Nongcun Jinrong yu Fazhan (Finance and Development in Rural China)*. Beijing: Jingji Kexue Shubanshe.

He, Baogang. 2003. "Kinship, Village Elections and Structural Conditions in Zhejiang." In *Damage Control: The Chinese Communist Party in the Jiang Zemin Era*, ed. G. Wang and Y. Zheng. Singapore: Times Media Private Limited.

———. 2007. *Rural Democracy in China: The Role of Village Elections*. New York, NY: Palgrave Macmillan.

He, Bingdi. 1959. *Studies on the Population of China, 1368–1953*. Cambridge, MA: Harvard University Press.

He, Wenguang, Xingyuan Feng, Pei Guo, Lili Li, Jing Yang, Hong Wang, and Xiaojia Li. 2005. *Zhongguo nongcun Jinrong Fazhan yu Zhidu Bianqian (Development and Institutional Change in Chinese Rural Finance)*. Beijing: Zhongguo Caizheng Jingji Chubanshe.

He, Wenkai. 2013. *Paths Toward the Modern Fiscal State: England, Japan, and China* Cambridge, MA: Harvard University Press.

He, Xuefeng. 2000. "On Some Issues to Be Clarified in the Study of Village Self-government." *China Rural Survey* 2:66.

———. 2003a. *Xiangcun Zhili de Shehui Jichu (Social Foundation of Rural Governance)*. Beijing: China Social Sciences Press.

———. 2003b. *Xin Xiangtu Zhongguo (New Rural China)*. Guilin: Guangxi Normal University Press.

———. 2007a. "Shilun Zhongguo Ershi Shijie Xiangcun Zhili de Luoji (On the Logic of Rural Governance in China in the Twentieth Century)." *Rural China* 5:157–173.

———. 2007b. *Xiangcun de Qiantu (The Future of Villages in China)*. Jinan: Shandong People's Press.

———. 2009. *Cunzhi de Luoji (The Logic of Village Governance)*. Beijing: Zhongguo Shehui Kexue Press.

———. 2011. "Lun Xiangcun Zhili Neijuanhua: Yi Henan Sheng K Zhen Diaocha Weili (On the Involution of Rural Governance: A Case Study of Township K in Henan Province)." *Kaifang Shidai* (2):86–101.

———. 2013. *Xiaonong Lichang (Peasants' Perspectives)*. Beijing: China University of Political Science and Law Press.

He, Xuefeng, Song Yuan, and Lina Song. 2010. *Nongmingong Fanxiang Yanjiu (Studies on Returned Rural Migrant Workers)*. Shandong: Shandong Renmin Press.

Hebel, Jutta. 2003. "Social Welfare in Rural China." *Journal of Peasant Studies* 30(3):224–251.

Hechter, M. 1987. *Principles of Group Solidarity*. Berkeley, CA: University of California Press.

Hechter, M., and Karl-Dieter Opp. 2001. *Social Norms*. New York, NY: Russell Sage Foundation.

Helmke, Gretchen, and S. Levitsky, eds. 2006. *Informal Institutions and Democracy: Lessons from Latin Americ*a. Baltimore, MD: Johns Hopkins University Press.

Helmke, Gretchen, and Steven Levitsky. 2004. "Informal Institutions and Comparative Politics: A Research Agenda." *Perspectives on Politics* 2(4):725–740.

Hirschman, A. O. 1970. *Exit, Voice, and Loyalty: Responses to Decline in Firms, Organizations, and States*. Cambridge, MA: Harvard University Press.

Hobbes, Thomas. 1982 [1651]. *Leviathan*. Harmondsworth: Penguin.

Hochstadt, Steve. 1999. *Mobility and Modernity: Migration in Germany, 1820–1989*. Ann Arbor, MI: University of Michigan Press.

Horne, Christine. 2001. "Sociological Perspectives on the Emergence of Social Norms." In *Social Norms*, ed. M. Hechter and K.-D. Opp. New York, NY: Russell Sage Foundation.

Hoyle, Rick H. 1995. *Structural Equation Modeling: Concepts, Issues, and Applications*. Thousand Oaks, CA: Sage Publications.

Hsing, You-tien. 2006. "Land and Territorial Politics in Urban China." *China Quarterly* 187:575–591.

———. 2010. *The Great Urban Transformation: Politics of Land and Property in China*. New York, NY: Oxford University Press.

Hu, Biliang. 2004. "Active Informal Financing in Rural China: A Case Study of Rotating Savings and Credit Associations in a Chinese Village." In *Rural Finance and Credit Infrastructure in China*, ed. OECD. Paris: OECD.

———. 2007. *Informal Institutions and Rural Development in China*. New York, NY: Routledge.

Hu, Rong. 2005. "Economic Development and the Implementation of Village Elections in Rural China." *Journal of Contemporary China* 14(44):427–444.

Hu, Xiaodeng, and Guannan Wang. 2009. "Jinrong Weiji Yingxiang xia Guizhou Nongmingong Fanxiang de Yingxiang yu Duice Yanjiu (The Impacts of Returned Migrant Workers due to Financial Crisis in Guizhou and Policy Suggestions.)" *Lilun yu Dangdai* (1): 14–17.

Huang, Bihong, and Kang Chen. 2012. "Are Intergovernmental Transfers in China Equalizing?" *China Economic Review* 23(3):534–551.

Huang, Jikun, Keijiro Otsuka, and Scott Rozelle. 2008. "Agriculture in China's Development: Past Disappointments, Recent Successes, and Future Challenges." In *China's Great Economic Transformation*, ed. L. Brandt and T. G. Rawski. New York, NY: Cambridge University Press.

Huang, Philip C. 1985. *The Peasant Economy and Social Change in North China*. Stanford, CA: Stanford University Press.

———. 1990. *The Peasant Family and Rural Development in the Yangzi Delta, 1350–1988*. Stanford, CA: Stanford University Press.

———. 1996. *Civil Justice in China: Representation and Practice in the Qing*. Stanford, CA: Stanford University Press.

———. 2001. *Code, Custom, and Legal Practice in China: The Qing and the Republic Compared*. Stanford, CA: Stanford University Press.

Huang, Ray. 1998. "The Ming Fiscal Administration." In *The Ming Dynasty, 1398–1644, Part 2*, ed. D. Twitchett and J. K. Fairbank. New York, NY: Cambridge University Press.

Huang, Yasheng. 1996. *Inflation and Investment Controls in China: The Political Economy of Central-Local Relations During the Reform Era*. New York, NY: Cambridge University Press.

———. 2008. *Capitalism with Chinese Characteristics: Entrepreneurship and the State*. New York: NY: Cambridge University Press.

Huang, Yasheng, and Yumin Sheng. 2009. "Political Decentralization and Inflation: Sub-National Evidence from China." *British Journal of Political Science* 39:389–412.

Huntington, S. P. 1968. *Political Order in Changing Societies*. New Haven, CT: Yale University Press.

Huntington, S. P., and J. M. Nelson. 1976. *No Easy Choice: Political Participation in Developing Countries*. Cambridge, MA: Harvard University Press.

Huntington, Samuel P. 1991. *The Third Wave: Democratization in the Late Twentieth Century*. Norman, OK: University of Oklahoma Press.

Hussain, Athar, and Youjuan Wang. 2010. "Rural-Urban Migration in China: Scale, Composition, Pattern and Deprivation." In *Marginalization in Urban China: Comparative Perspectives*, ed. F. Wu and C. Webster. Hampshire, NY: Palgrave Macmillan.

Inglehart, R. 2003. *Human Values and Social Change: Findings from the Values Surveys*. Boston, MA: Brill Academic Publishing.

Inglehart, R., and C. Welzel. 2005. *Modernization, Cultural Change, and Democracy: The Human Development Sequence*. New York, NY: Cambridge University Press.

Jacka, Tamara. 2005. *Rural Women in Urban China: Gender, Migration, and Social Change*. Armonk, NY: M.E. Sharpe.

———. 2012. "Migration, Householding and the Well-Being of Left-Behind Women in Rural Ningxia." *China Journal* 67:1–22.

Jackson, Samuel. 2011. "A Tale of Two State-Builders: Kuomintang and Communist Compared." *Columbia East Asia Review* 4:76–88.

Jha, S. D. 1989. *Policy Implication of Rural-Urban Migration in India*. New Delhi: Vani Prakashan.

Jing, Yuejin. 2003. "Liangpiaozhi Zuzhi Jishu yu Xuanju Moshi (The Model and Organizating Strategies of Two-Ballot System)." *Renmin Daxue Xuebao* 3 (124–130).

———. 2004. *Dangdai Zhongguo Nongcun Linagwei Guanxi de Weiguan Jieshi yu Hongguan Toushi (Micro- and Macro-Analysis on the Relationship between Party Branches and Villagers Committees in Contemporary Rural China)*. Beijing: Zhongyang Wenxian.

Joshi, Y. G., and Verma, D. K. 2004. *In Search of Livelihood: Labour Migration from Chattisgarh*. New Delhi: Dr. Babasaheb Ambedkar National Institute of Social Sciences.

Kearney, Christine A. 2007. "Brazil's 1964–1967 Economic Stabilization Plan as Institutional Syncretism." In *Reconfiguring Institutions across Time and Space*, ed. D. C. Galvan and R. Sil. New York, NY: Palgrave MacMillan.

Kelliher, Daniel Roy. 1992. *Peasant Power in China: The Era of Rural Reform, 1979–1989*. New Haven, CT: Yale University Press.

———. 1997. "The Chinese Debate Over Village Self-Government." *China Journal* 37:63–86.

Kennedy, John James. 2002. "The Face of 'Grassroots Democracy' in Rural China: Real versus Cosmetic Elections." *Asian Survey* 42(3):456–482.

———. 2007a. "From the Tax-for-Fee Reform to the Abolition of Agricultural Taxes: The Impact on Township Governments in North-West China." *China Quarterly* 189 (43–59).

———. 2007b. "The Implementation of Village Elections and Tax-for-Fee Reform in Rural Northwest China." In *Grassroots Political Reform in Contemporary China*, ed. E. J. Perry and M. Goldman. Cambridge, MA: Harvard University Press.

———. 2009. "State Capacity and Support for Village Institutions in Rural Shaanxi." *China Information* 23(3):383–410.

Kennedy, John James, Scott Rozelle, and Yaojiang Shi. 2004. "Elected Leaders and Collective Land: Farmers' Evaluation of Village Leaders' Performance in Rural China." *Journal of Chinese Political Science* 9(1):1–22.

Keohane, Robert O. 1984. *After Hegemony: Cooperation and Discord in the World Political Economy.* Princeton, NJ: Princeton University Press.

King, G., James Honaker, Anne Joseph, and Kenneth Scheve. 2001. "Analyzing Incomplete Political Science Data: An Alternative Algorithm for Multiple Imputation." *American Political Science Review* 95(1):49–69.

King, G., R. Keohane, and S. Verba. 1994. *Designing Social Inquiry.* Princeton, NJ: Princeton University Press.

King, G., Michael Tomz, and Jason Wittenberg. 2000. "Making the Most of Statistical Analyses: Improving Interpretation and Presentation." *American Journal of Political Science* 44(2):347–361.

King, G., and L. Zeng. 2006. "The Dangers of Extreme Counterfactuals." *Political Analysis* 14:131–159.

Kline, Rex B. 2005. *Principles and Practice of Structural Equation Modeling.* 2nd ed. New York, NY: Guilford Press.

Knight, Jack. 1992. *Institutions and Social Conflict.* New York, NY: Cambridge University Press.

Ko, Kilkon, and Hui Zhi. 2012. "Fiscal Decentralization: Guilty of Aggravating Corruption in China?" *Journal of Contemporary China* 22(79):35–55.

Kraus, Richard Curt. 1981. *Class Conflict in Chinese Socialism.* New York, NY: Columbia University Press.

Krishna, A. 2002. *Active Social Capital: Tracing the Roots of Development and Democracy.* New York, NY: Columbia University Press.

———. 2007. "How Does Social Capital Grow? A Seven-Year Study of Villages in India." *Journal of Politics* 49(4):941–956.

Kuhn, Philip A. 1975. "Local Self-government Under the Republic: Problems of Control, Autonomy, and Mobilization." In *Conflict and Control in Late Imperial China*, ed. F. E. Wakeman and C. Grant. Berkeley, CA: University of California Press.

Kung, James Kai-sing. 2000. "Common Property Rights and Land Reallocations in Rural China: Evidence from a Village Survey." *World Development* 28(4):701–719.

Kung, James Kai-Sing, Yongshun Cai, and Xiulin Sun. 2009. "Rural Cadres and Governance in China: Incentive, Institutions and Accountability." *China Journal* 62:61–77.

Kung, James Kai-Sing, and Shouying Liu. 1997. "Farmers' Preferences Regarding Ownership and Land Tenure in Post-Mao China: Unexpected Evidence from Eight Counties." *China Journal* (38):33–63.

Kuran, T. 1989. "Sparks and Prairie Fires: A Theory of Unanticipated Political Revolution." *Public Choice* 61:41–74.

———. 1991. "Now Out of Never: The Element of Surprise in the East European Revolution of 1989." *World Politics* 44(1):7–48.

———. 1995. *Private Truths, Public Lies: The Social Consequences of Preference Falsification.* Cambridge, MA: Harvard University Press.

———. 1998. "Ethnic Norms and Their Transformation through Reputational Cascades." *Journal of Legal Studies* 27(2):623–659.

———. 2010. *The Long Divergence: How Islamic Law Held Back the Middle East.* Princeton, NJ: Princeton University Press.

Kutsche, Paul. 1994. *Voices of Migrants: Rural-Urban Migration in Costa Rica*. Gainesville, FL: University Press of Florida.

La Ferrara, Eliana. 2011. "Family and Kinship Ties in Development: An Economist's Perspective." In *Culture, Institutions, and Development*, ed. J. P. Platteau and R. Peccoud. New York, NY: Routledge.

Lacy, Dean, and Emerson Niou. 2004. "A Theory of Economic Sanctions and Issue Linkage: The Roles of Preferences, Information, and Threats." *Journal of Politics* 66(1):25–42.

Lall, Somik V., and Harris Selod. 2006. *Rural-Urban Migration in Developing Countries: A Survey of Theoretical Predictions and Empirical Findings*. Washington, DC: World Bank.

Landry, Pierre F. 2003. "The Political Management of Mayors in Post-Deng China." *Copenhagen Journal of Asian Studies* 17:31–58.

———. 2008. *Decentralized Authoritarianism in China: The Communist Party's Control of Local Elites in the Post-Mao China*. New York, NY: Cambridge University Press.

Landry, Pierre F., Deborah Davis, and Shiru Wang. 2010. "Elections in Rural China: Competition Without Parties." *Comparative Political Studies* 43(6):763–790.

Lardy, Nicholas R. 1987a. "The Chinese Economy under Stress, 1958–1965." In *The People's Republic, Part 1: The Emergence of Revolutionary China 1949–1965*, ed. R. MacFarcuhar and J. K. Fairbank. New York, NY: Cambridge University Press.

———. 1987b. "Economy Recovery and the 1st Five-Year Plan." In *The People's Republic, Part 1: The Emergence of Revolutionary China 1949–1965*, ed. R. MacFarcuhar and J. K. Fairbank. New York, NY: Cambridge University Press.

Ledeneva, Alena V. 2006. *How Russia Really Works: The Informal Practices That Shaped Post-Soviet Politics and Business*. Ithaca, NY: Cornell University Press.

Lee, Leng, and Xin Meng. 2010. "Why Don't More Chinese Migrate from the Countryside? Institutional Constraints and the Migration Decision." In *The Great Migration: Rural-Urban Migration in China and Indonesia*, ed. X. Meng, C. Manning, L. Shi, and T. Noer Effendi. Northampton, MA: Edward Elgar Publishing, Inc.

Lerner, Daniel, and Lucille W. Pevsner. 1962. *The Passing of Traditional Society: Modernizing the Middle East*. Glencoe, IL: Free Press.

Lesorogol, Carolyn K. 2008. *Contesting the Commons: Privatizing Pastoral Lands in Kenya*. Ann Arbor, MI: University of Michigan Press.

Leung, Angela K. C. 1994. "Elementary Education in the Lower Yangtze Region in the 17th and 18th Centuries." In *Education and Society in Late Imperial China*, ed. B. A. Elman and A Woodside. Berkeley, CA: University of California Press.

Lewis, W. A. 1954. "Economic Development with Unlimited Supplies of Labor." *The Manchester School* 22:139–191.

Li, Guang. 2005. *Zhongguo Nongcun Tourongzi Tizhi Gaige Yanjiu (Reform in the Institutions of Raising Capital and Credits in Rural China)*. Beijing: Zhongguo Caizheng Jingji Chubanshe.

Li, Guo, Scott Rozelle, and Loren Brandt. 1998. "Tenure, Land Rights, and Farmer Investment Incentives in China." *Agricultural Economics* 19(1):63–71.

Li, Huaiyin. 2005. *Village Governance in North China, 1875–1936*. Stanford, CA: Stanford University Press.

———. 2009. *Village China under Socialism and Reform: A Micro-History, 1948–2008*. Stanford, CA: Stanford University Press.

Li, John Shuhe. 2003. "Relation-based versus Rule-based Governance: An Explanation of the East Asian Miracle and Asian Crisis." *Review of International Economics* 11(4):651–673.

Li, Lianjiang. 1999. "The Two-Ballot System in Shanxi Province: Subjecting Village Party Secretaries to a Popular Vote." *China Journal* 42:103–118.

Li, Lianjiang, Mingxing Liu, and K. J. O'Brien. 2012. "Petitioning Beijing: The High Tide of 2003–2006." *China Quarterly* 210:313–334.

Li, Lianjiang, and K. J. O'Brien. 2008. "Protest Leadership in Rural China." *China Quarterly* 193:1–23.

Li, Lianjiang, and Jingming Xiong. 1998. "Cong Zhengfu Zhudao de Cunmin Zizhi Maixiang Minzhu Xuanju (From Government-Guided Village Governance to Democratic Elections)." *Twenty-First Century* 50:151–156.

Li, Linda Chelan. 2006. "Differentiated Actors: Central-Local Politics in China's Rural Tax Reforms." *Modern Asian Studies* 40(1):151–174.

Liang, Jingzhi. 2004. *Qingdai Minjin Zongjiao yu Xiangtu Shehui (Folk Religions and Rural Society in the Qing Dynasty)*. Beijing: Shehui Kexu Chubanshe.

Liang, Linxia. 2008. *Delivering Justice in Qing China: Civil Trials in the Magistrate's Court*. New York, NY: Oxford University Press.

Liang, Zhiping. 1996. *Qingdai Xiguanfa: Shehui yu Guojia (Habitual Law in Qing Dynasty: Society and State)*. Beijing: Zhongguo Zhengfa University Press.

————. 2002. *Xunqiu Ziran Chixu Zhongde Hexie (Seeking for Harmony in Natural Order)*. Beijing: Zhongguo Zhengfa University Press.

Lichbach, Mark Irving. 1995. *The Rebel's Dilemma*. Ann Arbor, MI: University of Michigan Press.

Liebman, Benjamin L. 2012. "Professionals and Populists: The Paradoxes of China's Legal Reforms." In *China in and beyond the Headlines*, ed. T. B. Weston and L. M. Jensen. Lanham, MD: Rowman & Littlefield Publishers, Inc.

Lin, Jiang. 1995. "Changing Kinship Structure and its Implications for Old Age Support in Urban and Rural China." *Population Studies* 49:127–145.

Lin, Justin Yifu, and Mingxing Liu. 2007. "Rural Informal Taxation in China: Historical Evolution and an Analytic Framework." *China & World Economy* 15(3):1–18.

Lin, Wanlong. 2003. *Zhongguo Nongcun Shequ Gonggong Wupin Gongji Zhidu Bianqian Yanjiu (Institutional Evolution in the Provision of Public Goods in Chinese Rural Communities)*. Beijing: Chinese Finance Press.

Liu, Guangdong, and Jiumiao Chen. 2007. "1949 Yilai Zhongguo Nongcun Tudi Zhidu Bianqian de Lilun he Shijian (Theory and Practice: Evolution of the Land-Tenure System in Rural China Since 1949)." *Zhongguo Nongcun Guancha* 2:70–80.

Liu, Liangqun, and Rachel Murphy. 2006. "Lineage Networks, Land Conflicts and Rural Migration in Late Socialist China." *Journal of Peasant Studies* 33(4):612–645.

Liu, Yanwu. 2009. "Fanxiang Nongmingong de Jiben Leixing (Basic Types of Returned Migrant Workers)." *Shehui Kexue Bao*, April 02.

Lobo, Norbert. 2004. *Migration and Migrants*. New Delhi: Mohit Publications.

Locke, John. 1980 [1689]. *Second Treaties of Government*. Indianapolis, IN: Hackett Publishing Company, Inc.

Lu, J. 2012. "Varieties of Electoral Institutions in China's Grassroots Democracy: Cross-Sectional and Longitudinal Evidence from Rural China." *China Quarterly* 210:482–493.

Lu, J., and T. Shi. 2009. "Political Experience: A Missing Variable in the Study of Political Transformation." *Comparative Politics* 42(1):103–120.

Lu, Xiaobo. 1997. "The Politics of Peasant Burden in Reform China." *Journal of Peasant Studies* 25(1):116–134.

Lubman, Stanley. 1967. "Mao and Mediation: Politics and Dispute Resolution in Communist China." *California Law Review* 55(5):1284–1359.

Luo, Chuliang, and Ximing Yue. 2012. "Rural-Urban Migration and Poverty in China." In *The Great Migration: Rural-Urban Migration in China and Indonesia*, ed. X. Meng, C. Manning, L. Shi, and T. Noer Effendi. Northampton, MA: Edward Elgar.

Luo, Renfu, Yaojiang Shi, Linxiu Zhang, Chengfang Liu, Scott Rozelle, and Brian Sharbono. 2009. "Malnutrition in China's Rural Boarding Schools: The Case of Primary Schools in Shaanxi Province." *Asia Pacific Journal of Education* 29(4):481–501.

Luo, Renfu, Yaojiang Shi, Linxiu Zhang, Chengfang Liu, Scott Rozelle, Brian Sharbono, Ai Yue, Qiran Zhao, and Reynaldo Martorell. 2012. "Nutrition and Educational Performance in Rural China's Elementary Schools: Results of a Randomized Control Trial in Shaanxi Province." *Economic Development and Cultural Change* 60(4):735–772.

Luo, Renfu, Linxiu Zhang, Jikun Huang, and Scott Rozelle. 2007. "Elections, Fiscal Reform and Public Goods Provision in Rural China." *Journal of Comparative Economics* 35(3):583–611.

Luskin, Robert C., and John G. Bullock. 2011. "'Don't Know' Means 'Don't Know': DK Responses and the Public's Level of Political Knowledge." *Journal of Politics* 73(2):547–557.

Ma, Hua, and Yong Xu. 2012. "Reorganizing Rural China from the Bottom: A Discussion of Recent Experiments with Rural Reconstruction." In *Organizing Rural China, Rural China Organizing*, ed. A. Bislev and S. Thøgersen. Lanham, MD: Lexington Books.

MacFarquhar, Roderick. 1983. *The Great Leap Forward, 1958–1960*. New York, NY: Columbia University Press.

MacLean, Lauren M. 2010. *Informal Institutions and Citizenship in Rural Africa*. New York, NY: Cambridge University Press.

Madsen, Richard. 1984. *Morality and Power in a Chinese Village*. Berkeley, CA: University of California Press.

Magee, Gary B., and Andrew S. Thompson. 2010. *Empire and Globalisation: Networks of People, Goods and Capital in the British World, 1850–1914*. New York, NY: Cambridge University Press.

Mahoney, J. 2010. "After KKV: The New Methodology of Qualitative Research." *World Politics* 62(1):120–147.

Mahoney, J., and K. Thelen. 2010a. "A Theory of Gradual Institutional Change." In *Explaining Institutional Change: Ambiguity, Agency, and Power*, ed. J. Mahoney and K. Thelen. New York, NY: Cambridge University Press.

———, eds. 2010b. *Explaining Institutional Change: Ambiguity, Agency, and Power*. New York, NY: Cambridge University Press.

Manion, M. 1996. "The Electoral Connection in the Chinese Countryside." *American Political Science Review* 90(4):736–748.

———. 2006. "Democracy, Community, Trust: The Impact of Elections in Rural China." *Comparative Political Studies* 39(3):301–324.

_____. 2009. "How to Assess Village Elections in China." *Journal of Contemporary China* 18(60):379–383.

Mansbridge, Jane. 2010. "Beyond the Tragedy of the Commons: A Discussion of Governing the Commons: The Evolution of Institutions for Collective Action." *Perspectives on Politics* 8(02):590–593.

Mantzavinos, Chrysostomos. 2001. *Individuals, Institutions, and Markets.* New York, NY: Cambridge University Press.

Martin, Lisa L. 1993. "Credibility, Costs, and Institutions: Cooperation on Economic Sanctions." *World Politics* 45(03):406–432.

McCarty, Nolan, and A. Meirowitz. 2007. *Political Game Theory: An Introduction.* New York, NY: Cambridge University Press.

Meng, X., and Li Zhang. 2011. "Democratic Participation, Fiscal Reform and Local Governance: Empirical Evidence on Chinese Villages." *China Economic Review* 22(1):88–97.

Meng, Xin. 2000. *Labour Market Reform in China.* Melbourne: Cambridge University Press.

_____. 2012. "Labor Market Outcomes and Reforms in China." *Journal of Economic Perspectives* 26(4):75–102.

Merry, Sally Engle. 1984. "Rethinking Gossip and Scandal." In *Toward A General Theory of Social Control*, ed. D. Black. New York: Academic Press.

_____. 1988. "Legal Pluralism." *Law & Society Review* 22(5):869–896.

Michelson, Ethan. 2007. "Climbing the Dispute Pagoda: Grievances and Appeals to the Official Justice System in Rural China." *American Sociological Review* 72(2):459–485.

_____. 2008. "Justice from Above or Below? Popular Strategies for Resolving Grievances in Rural China." *China Quarterly* 193:43–64.

_____. 2011. "Public Goods and State-Society Relations: An Impact Study of China's Rural Stimulus." In *Research Center for Chinese Politics and Business Working Paper #4*: Indiana University.

Michelson, Ethan, and Benjamin L. Read. 2011. "Public Attitudes toward Official Justice in Beijing and Rural China." In *Chinese Justice: Civil Dispute Resolution in Contemporary China*, ed. M. Y. K. Woo and M. Gallagher. New York, NY: Cambridge University Press.

Miguel, Edward, and Mary Key Gugerty. 2005. "Ethnic Diversity, Social Sanctions, and Public Goods in Kenya." *Journal of Public Economics* 89:2325–2368.

Miller, Harry. 2009. *State versus Gentry in Late Ming Dynasty China, 1572–1644.* New York, NY: Palgrave Macmillan.

Ministry of Agriculture, China, ed. 2007. *2007 China Agricultural Development Report.* Beijing: China Agriculture Press.

Ministry of Water Resources, China, ed. 2011. *2010 Statistic Bulletin on China Water Activities.* Beijing: Zhongguo Shuili Shuidian Chubanshe.

Miyazaki, Ichisada. 1981. *China's Examination Hell: The Civil Service Examinations of Imperial China.* Translated by C. Schirokauer. New Haven, CT: Yale University Press.

Mo, Di, Hongmei Yi, Linxiu Zhang, Yaojiang Shi, Scott Rozelle, and Alexis Medina. 2012. "Transfer Paths and Academic Performance: The Primary School Merger Program in China." *International Journal of Educational Development* 32(3):423–431.

Mobrand, Erik. 2009. "Endorsing the Exodus: How Local Leaders Backed Peasant Migration in 1980s Sichuan." *Journal of Contemporary China* 18(58):137–156.

Moe, Terry. 1984. "The New Economics of Organization." *American Journal of Political Science* 28(4):739–777.

Mokyr, Joel. 2002. *The Gifts of Athena: Historical Origins of the Knowledge Economy.* Princeton, NJ: Princeton University Press.

———. 2008. "The Institutional Origins of the Industrial Revolution." In *Institutions and Economic Performance*, ed. E. Helpman. Cambridge, MA: Harvard University Press.

Morrow, James D. 1994. *Game Theory for Political Scientists.* Princeton, NJ: Princeton University Press.

Mortuza, Syed Ali. 1992. *Rural-Urban Migration in Bangladesh: Causes and Effects.* Berlin: D. Reimer.

Mote, Frederick W. 1989. *Intellectual Foundations of China.* 2nd ed. New York, NY: Knopf.

Murphy, Rachel. 2002. *How Migrant Labor Is Changing Rural China.* New York, NY: Cambridge University Press.

Myers, Ramon H. 1980. "North China Villages During the Republican Period: Socioeconomic Relationships." *Modern China* 6(3):243–266.

Myers, Ramon H., and Yeh-Chien Wang. 2002. "Economic Development, 1644–1800." In *The Ch'ing Empire to 1800*, ed. W. Peterson. New York, NY: Cambridge University Press.

Nachbar, John H. 1989. *The Evolution of Cooperation in the Finitely Repeated Prisoner's Dilemma.* Santa Monica, CA: Rand.

Nakane, Chie. 1967. *Kinship and Economic Organization in Rural Japan.* London: Athlone Press.

Nargolkar, Vasant. 1982. *Rural Development Through Communes in China.* New Delhi: S. Chand.

Nee, Victor, and Sonja Opper. 2012. *Capitalism from Below: Markets and Institutional Change in China.* Cambridge, MA: Harvard University Press.

Niou, Emerson. 2005. *Zhongguo Lidai Xiangyue (Village Compacts in Chinese History).* Beijing: Zhongguo Shehui Chubanshe.

Nisbet, Robert A. 1969. *Social Change and History: Aspects of the Western Theory of Development.* New York, NY: Oxford University Press.

Noland, Soraya. 1981. "Dispute Settlement and Social Organization in Two Iranian Rural Communities." *Anthropological Quarterly* 54(4):190–202.

North, D. C. 1990. *Institutions, Institutional Change, and Economic Performance.* New York, NY: Cambridge University Press.

———. 2005. *Understanding the Process of Economic Change.* Princeton, NJ: Princeton University Press.

North, D. C., John Joseph Wallis, and B. Weingast. 2009. *Violence and Social Orders: A Conceptual Framework for Interpreting Recorded Human History.* New York, NY: Cambridge University Press.

Nye, John. 2008. "Institutions and Institutional Environment." In *New Institutional Economics: A Guidebook*, ed. E. Brousseau and J.-M. Glachant. New York, NY: Cambridge University Press.

O'Brien, K. J. 1994. "Implementing Political Reform in China's Villages." *Australian Journal of Chinese Affairs* 32:33–59.

O'Brien, K. J., and Rongbin Han. 2009. "Path to Democracy? Assessing Village Elections in China." *Journal of Contemporary China* 18(60):359–378.

O'Brien, K. J., and Lianjiang Li. 2000. "Accommodating 'Democracy' in a One-Party State: Introducing Village Elections in China." *China Quarterly* 162:465–489.

———. 2005. "Popular Contention and Its Impact in Rural China." *Comparative Political Studies* 38(3):235–259.

———. 2006. *Rightful Resistance in Rural China*. New York, NY: Cambridge University Press.

Oberai, A. S., Pradhan H. Prasad, and M. G. Sardana. 1989. *Determinants and Consequences of Internal Migration in India: Studies in Bihar, Kerala, and Uttar Pradesh*. New York, NY: Oxford University Press.

Oi, Jean. 1985. "Communism and Clientelism: Rural Politics in China." *World Politics* 37(2):238–266.

———. 1989. *State and Peasant in Contemporary China: The Political Economy of Village Government*. Berkeley, CA: University of California Press.

———. 1996. "Economic Development, Stability, and Democratic Village Self-Governance." In *China Review 1996*, ed. M. Brosseau, S. Pepper, and S.-k. Tsang. Hong Kong: Chinese University of Hong Kong.

———. 1999. *Rural China Takes Off: Institutional Foundations of Economic Reform*. Berkeley, CA: University of California Press.

Oi, Jean, Kim Singer Babiarz, Linxiu Zhang, Renfu Luo, and Scott Rozelle. 2012. "Shifting Fiscal Control to Limit Cadre Power in China's Townships and Villages." *China Quarterly* 211:649–675.

Oi, Jean, and Scott Rozelle. 2000. "Elections and Power: The Locus of Decision-making in Chinese Villages." *China Quarterly* 162:513–539.

Oi, Jean, and Andrew G. Walder, eds. 1999. *Property Rights and Economic Reform in China*. Stanford, CA: Stanford University Press.

Oi, Jean, and Shukai Zhao. 2007. "Fiscal Crisis in China's Townships: Causes and Consequences." In *Grassroots Political Reform in Contemporary China*, ed. E. J. Perry and M. Goldman. Cambridge, MA: Harvard University Press.

Olken, Benjamin A. 2010. "Direct Democracy and Local Public Goods: Evidence from a Field Experiment in Indonesia." *American Political Science Review* 104(2):243–267.

Olson, M. 1982. *The Rise and Decline of Nations: Economic Growth, Stagflation, and Social Rigidities*. New Haven, CT: Yale University Press.

———. 1993. "Dictatorship, Democracy, and Development." *American Political Science Review* 87(3):567–576.

Olson, Mancur. 1971. *The Logic of Collective Action: Public Goods and the Theory of Groups*. Cambridge, MA: Harvard University Press.

Ong, Lynette. 2006. "Multiple Principals and Collective Action: China's Rural Credit Cooperatives and Poor Households' Access to Credit." *Journal of East Asian Studies* 6(2):177–204.

———. 2009. "Communist Party and Financial Institutions: Institutional Design of China's Post-Reform Rural Credit Cooperatives." *Pacific Affairs* 82(2): 251–278.

———. 2012. *Prosper or Perish: Credit and Fiscal Systems in Rural China*. Ithaca, NY: Cornell University Press.

Onoma, Ato Kwamena. 2010. "The Contradictory Potential of Institutions: The Rise and Decline of Land Documentation in Kenya." In *Explaining Institutional Change: Ambiguity, Agency and Power*, ed. J. Mahoney and K. Thelen. New York, NY: Cambridge University Press.

Opp, Karl-Dieter. 1986. "The Evolution of A Prisoner's Dilemma in the Market." In *Paradoxical Effect of Social Behavior*, ed. A. Diekmann and P. Mitter. Heidelberg: Physica-Verlag.

Orton, J. Douglas, and Karl E. Weick. 1990. "Loosely Coupled Systems: A Reconceptualization." *Academy of Management Review* 15(2):203–223.

Ostiguy, Pierre. 2007. "Syncretism in Argentina's Party System and Peronist Political Culture." In *Reconfiguring Institutions across Time and Space*, ed. D. C. Galvan and R. Sil. New York, NY: Palgrave MacMillan.

Ostrom, Elinor. 1990. *Governing the Commons*. New York, NY: Cambridge University Press.

Parish, William L. 1985. *Chinese Rural Development: The Great Transformation*. Armonk, NY: M.E. Sharpe.

Parish, William L., and Martin King Whyte. 1978. *Village and Family in Contemporary China*. Chicago, IL: University of Chicago Press.

Parthasarathi, Prasannan. 2011. *Why Europe Grew Rich and Asia Did Not: Global Economic Divergence, 1600–1850*. New York, NY: Cambridge University Press.

Patten, Alan. 2011. "Rethinking Culture: The Social Lineage Account." *American Political Science Review* 105(4):735–749.

Patten, John. 1973. *Rural-Urban Migration in Pre-Industrial England*. Oxford: University of Oxford.

Peerenboom, R. P. 2007. *China Modernizes: Threat to the West or Model for the Rest?* New York, NY: Oxford University Press.

Perdue, Peter. 1987. *Exhausting the Earth: State and Peasant in Hunan, 1500–1850*. Cambridge, MA: Harvard University Press.

Perry, Elizabeth J. 1980. *Rebels and Revolutionaries in North China, 1845–1945*. Stanford, CA: Stanford University Press.

———. 2006. *Patrolling the Revolution: Worker Militias, Citizenship and the Modern Chinese State*. Lanham, MD: Rowman & Littlefield Publishers, Inc.

Pesqué-Cela, Vanesa, Ran Tao, Yongdong Liu, and Laixiang Sun. 2009. "Challenging, Complementing or Assuming 'the Mandate of Heaven'? Political Distrust and the Rise of Self-Governing Social Organizations in Rural China." *Journal of Comparative Economics* 37(1):151–168.

Picci, Lucio. 2011. *Reputation-Based Governance*. Stanford, CA: Stanford University Press.

Pindyck, R. S., and D. L. Rubinfeld. 1998. *Econometric Models and Economic Forecasts*. New York, NY: McGraw-Hill.

Platteau, J. P. 1994a. "Behind the Market Stage Where Real Societies Exist—Part I: The Role of Public and Private Order Institutions." *Journal of Development Studies* 30(3):533–577.

———. 1994b. "Behind the Market Stage Where Real Societies Exist—Part II: The Role of Moral Norms." *Journal of Development Studies* 30(3):753–817.

———. 1995. *Reforming Land Rights in Sub-Saharan Africa: Issues of Efficiency and Equity*. Geneva: United Nations Research Institute for Social Development.

———. 2000. *Institutions, Social Norms, and Economic Development*. Amsterdam: Harwood Academic.

———. 2008. "The Causes of Institutional Inefficiency: A Development Perspective." In *New Institutional Economics: A Guidebook*, ed. E. Brousseau and J.-M. Glachant. New York: Cambridge University Press.

Platteau, J. P., and Robert Peccoud, eds. 2011. *Culture, Institutions, and Development*. New York, NY: Routledge.

Platteau, J. P., and Erika Seki. 2001. "Community Arrangements to Overcome Market Failures: Pooling Groups in Japanese Fisheries." In *Communities and*

Markets in Economic Development, ed. M. Aoki and Y. Hayami. New York, NY: Oxford University Press.

Pomeranz, Kenneth. 1993. *The Making of a Hinterland: State, Society, and Economy in Inland North China, 1853–1937*. Berkeley, CA: University of California Press.

————. 2000. *The Great Divergence: China, Europe and the Making of the Modern World Economy*. Princeton, NJ: Princeton University Press.

Potter, Jack M. 1970. "Land and Lineage in Traditional China." In *Family and Kinship in Chinese Society*, ed. M. Freedman. Stanford, CA: Stanford University Press.

Powell, Simon. 1992. *Agricultural Reform in China: From Communes to Commodity Economy, 1978–1990*. Manchester: Manchester University Press.

Printz, Peggy, and Paul Steinle. 1977. *Commune: Life in Rural China*. New York, NY: Dodd, Mead.

Przeworski, A. 2004. "Institutions Matter?" *Government and Opposition* 39(4):527–540.

Przeworski, A., S. Stokes, and B. Manin. 1999. *Democracy, Accountability, and Representation*. New York, NY: Cambridge University Press.

Przeworski, A., and Henry Teune. 1970. *The Logic of Comparative Social Inquiry*. New York, NY: Wiley-Interscience.

Putnam, R. D. 2000. *Bowling Alone: The Collapse and Revival of American Community*. New York, NY: Simon & Schuster.

Putnam, R. D., R. Leonardi, and R. Nanetti. 1993. *Making Democracy Work: Civic Traditions in Modern Italy*. Princeton, NJ: Princeton University Press.

Pye, Lucian W. 1968. *The Spirit of Chinese Politics: A Psychocultural Study of the Authority Crisis in Political Development*. Cambridge, MA: MIT Press.

Pye, Lucian W., and Mary W. Pye. 1985. *Asian Power and Politics: The Cultural Dimensions of Authority*. Cambridge, MA: Belknap Press.

Qian, Hang. 1994. *Zhongguo Zongzu Zhidu Xintan (Studies on Clan/Lineage Institutions in China)*. Hong Kong: Chung Hwa Book Corporation.

Qiang, Shigong. 2003. *Fazhi yu Zhili: Guojia Zhuanxin Zhongde Falv (Rule of Law and Governance: Law in State Transition)*. Beijing: Zhongguo Zhengfa University Press.

Qu, Tongzu. 1962. *Local Government in China under the Ch'ing*. Cambridge, MA: Harvard University Press.

Ragin, C. 1989. *The Comparative Method*. Berkeley, CA: University of California Press.

Read, Benjamin L., and Ethan Michelson. 2008. "Mediating the Mediation Debate: Conflict Resolution and the Local State in China." *Journal of Conflict Resolution* 52(5):737–764.

Reed, Christopher A. 2004. *Gutenberg in Shanghai: Chinese Print Capitalism, 1876–1937*. Vancouver: UBC Press.

Ren, Liying. 2009. Surveying Public Opinion in Transitional China: An Examination of Survey Response. Dissertation, Political Science, University of Pittsburgh, Pittsburgh, PA.

Resnick, Paul, Richard Zeckhauser, John Swanson, and Kate Lockwood. 2006. "The Value of Reputation on eBay: A Controlled Experiment." *Experimental Economics* 9(2):79–101.

Roberts, Kenneth D. 1997. "China's 'Third Wave' of Migrant Labor: What Can We Learn from Mexican Undocumented Migration to the United States." *International Migration Review* 31(2):249–293.

Rodrik, Dani. 2007. *One Economics, Many Recipes: Globalization, Institutions, and Economic Growth.* Princeton, NJ: Princeton University Press.

Roland, Gerard. 2004. "Understanding Institutional Change: Fast-Moving and Slow-Moving Institutions." *Studies in Comparative International Development* 38(4):109–131.

Rosenthal, Jean-Laurent, and R. Bin Wong. 2011. *Before and Beyond Divergence: The Politics of Economic Change in China and Europe.* Cambridge, MA: Harvard University Press.

Rousseau, Jean-Jacques. 1968 [1762]. *The Social Contract.* Translated by M. W. Cranston. Baltimore, MD: Penguin.

Rubin, Donald B. 1987. *Multiple Imputation for Nonresponse in Surveys.* New York, NY: Wiley.

Rudolph, Lloyd I., and Susanne Hoeber Rudolph. 1967. *The Modernity of Tradition: Political Development in India.* Chicago, IL: University of Chicago Press.

Ruf, Gregory A. 1998. *Cadres and Kin: Making a Socialist Village in West China, 1921–1991.* Stanford, CA: Stanford University Press.

Sandler, Todd. 1992. *Collective Action: Theory and Applications.* Ann Arbor, MI: University of Michigan Press.

Sato, H. 2008. "Public Goods Provision and Rural Governance in China." *China: An International Journal* 6(2):281–298.

Sato, H., Shi Li, and Ximing Yue. 2007. "The Redistributive Impact of Taxation in Rural China, 1995–2002: An Empirical Study using the 1995––2002 CASS CHIP Surveys." In *Inequality and Public Policy in China*, ed. B. A. Gustafsson, S. Li, and T. Sicular. New York, NY: Cambridge University Press.

Scheff, Thomas J. 1988. "Shame and Conformity: The Deference-Emotion System." *American Sociological Review* 53(3):395–406.

Scheineson, Andrew. 2008. "From Laws to Levees: Methods of Water Control in the Qing Dynasty." *Columbia East Asia Review* 1:56–70.

Schneewind, Sarah. 2006. *Community Schools and the State in Ming China.* Stanford, CA: Stanford University Press.

Scott, J. C. 1998. *Seeing Like A State: How Certain Schemes to Improve the Human Condition Have Failed.* New Haven, CT: Yale University Press.

Seabright, Paul. 1996. "Accountability and Decentralization in Government: An Incomplete Contracts Model." *European Economic Review* 40:61–89.

Shami, Mahvish. 2012. "Collective Action, Clientelism, and Connectivity." *American Political Science Review* 106(03):588–606.

Shen, Chunli, Jing Jin, and Heng-fu Zou. 2012. "Fiscal Decentralization in China: History, Impact, Challenges and Next Steps." *Annals of Economics and Finance* 13(1):1–51.

Shen, Duanfeng. 2006. "Ershi Shiji Zhongguo Xiangcun Zhili de Luoji (The Logic of Rural Governance in the 20th Century)." *Journal of Huazhong Normal University (Humanities and Social Sciences)* (4).

Shi, T. 1996. "Survey Research in China." In *Rethinking Rationality, Research in Micropolitics, Vol. 5*, ed. M. Delli-Carpini, L. Huddy and I. Shapiro. Greenwich, CT: JAI Press.

———. 1999a. "Economic Development and Election in Rural China." *Journal of Contemporary China* 8(22):425–442.

———. 1999b. "Village Committee Elections in China: Institutionalist Tactics for Democracy." *World Politics* 51(3):385–412.

_____. 1999c. "Voting and Non-voting in China." *Journal of Politics* 61(4):1115–1139.

_____. 2000a. "Cultural Values and Democracy in Mainland China." *China Quarterly* 162:540–559.

_____. 2000b. "Political Culture: A Prerequisite for Democracy." *American Asian Review* 18(2):53–83.

_____. 2000c. *Rural Democracy in China*. Singapore: Singapore University Press.

_____. 2001. "Cultural Values and Political Trust: A Comparison of the People's Republic of China and Taiwan." *Comparative Politics* 33(4):401–419.

_____. forthcoming. *The Logic of Politics in Mainland China and Taiwan: A Cultural Basis of Attitudes and Behavior*. New York, NY: Cambridge University Press.

Shils, Edward. 1962. *Political Development In the New States*. The Hague: Mouton.

Shin, Doh Chull. 2011. *Confucianism and Democratization in East Asia*. New York, NY: Cambridge University Press.

Shiue, Carol H. 2004. "Local Granaries and Central Government Disaster Relief: Moral Hazard and Intergovernmental Finance in Eighteenth- and Nineteenth-Century China." *Journal of Economic History* 64(1):100–124.

Shlapentokh, Vladimir. 2006. *Fear in Contemporary Society: Its Negative and Positive Effects*. New York, NY: Palgrave Macmillan.

Shue, Vivienne. 1988. *The Reach of the State: Sketches of the Chinese Body Politic*. Stanford, CA: Stanford University Press.

_____. 2012. "Modern/Rural China: State Institutions and Village Values." In *Organizing Rural China, Rural China Organizing*, ed. A. Bislev and S. Thøgersen. Lanham, MD: Lexington Books.

Sil, Rudra. 2007. "The Dynamics of Institutional Adaptation and the Fruitful Emergence of Managerial Syncretism in Japan." In *Reconfiguring Institutions across Time and Space*, ed. D. C. Galvan and R. Sil. New York, NY: Palgrave Macmillan.

Sil, Rudra, and Dennis Charles Galvan. 2007. *Reconfiguring Institutions across Time and Space: Syncretic Responses to Challenges of Political and Economic Transformations*. New York, NY: Palgrave.

Singh, Archana. 2001. *Rural Outmigration*. Lucknow, India: New Royal Book Company.

Skarbek, David. 2011. "Governance and Prison Gangs." *American Political Science Review* 105(4):702–716.

Skinner, William G. 1971. "Chinese Peasants and the Closed Community: An Open and Shut Case." *Comparative Studies in Society and History* 13(3):270–281.

_____. 2001. *Marketing and Social Structure in Rural China*. Ann Arbor, MI: Association for Asian Studies.

Smelser, Neil J. 1966. "The Modernization of Social Relations." In *Modernization: The Dynamics of Growth*, ed. M. Weiner. New York, NY: Basic Books.

Smith, Arthur Henderson. 1899. *Village Life in China: A Study in Sociology*. Chicago, IL: F. H. Revell Company.

Smith, Robert J. 1967. "The Japanese Rural Community: Norms, Sanctions, and Ostracism." In *Peasant Society: A Reader*, ed. J. M. Potter, M. N. Diaz, and G. M. Foster. Boston, MA: Little, Brown and Company.

Solinger, Dorothy J. 1999. *Contesting Citizenship in Urban China: Peasant Migrants, the State, and the Logic of the Market*. Berkeley, CA: University of California Press.

Stark, Oded, and J. Edward Taylor. 1991. "Migration Incentives, Migration Types: The Role of Relative Deprivation." *Economic Journal* 101(408):1163–1178.

Strom, K., W. C. Muller, and T. Bergman. 2003. *Delegation and Accountability in Parliamentary Democracies*. New York, NY: Oxford University Press.

Su, Fubing, Ran Tao, Xin Sun, and Mingxing Liu. 2011. "Clans, Electoral Procedures and Voter Turnout: Evidence from Villagers' Committee Elections in Transitional China." *Political Studies* 59(2):432–457.

Su, Li. 2000. *Songfa Xiaxiang: Zhongguo Jiceng Sifa Zhidu Yanjiu (Sending Law to Rural Communities: Studies on Grassroots Legal Institutions in China)*. Beijing: China University of Political Science and Law Press.

———. 2002. *Fazhi Jiqi Bentu Ziyuan (Rule of Law and Its Indigenous Resources)*. Beijing: China University of Political Science and Law Press.

Sun, Xin. 2014. "Autocrats' Dilemma: The Dual Impacts of Village Elections on Public Opinion in China." *China Journal* 71:109–131.

Sun, Xin, Travis J. Warner, Dali L. Yang, and Mingxing Liu. 2013. "Patterns of Authority and Governance in Rural China: Who's in Charge? Why?" *Journal of Contemporary China* 22(83):733–754.

Svensson, Marina. 2012. "Lineages and the State: Re-inventing Lineages and Ancestor Ceremonies as Cultural Heritage." In *Organizing Rural China, Rural China Organizing*, ed. A. Bislev and S. Thøgersen. Lanham, MD: Lexington Books.

Tabellini, G. 2008. "Institutions and Culture." *Journal of European Economic Association* 6(2/3):255–294.

Takeuchi, Hiroki. 2013. "Survival Strategies of Township Governments in Rural China: from predatory taxation to land trade." *Journal of Contemporary China* 22(83):755–772.

Tan, Qingshan. 2004. "Building Institutional Rules and Procedures: Village Election in China." *Policy Science* 37(1):1–22.

Tang, Jun. 2001. *Zhefu yu Mianyan: Dangdai Huabei Cunluo Jiazu de Shengzhang Licheng (Continuity and Change: History of Village Clans in Contemporary North China)*. Beijing: China Social Sciences Press.

Tang, Wenfang, and Qing Yang. 2008. "The Chinese Urban Caste System in Transition." *China Quarterly* 196:759–779.

Tao, Ran, and Ping Qin. 2007. "How Has Rural Tax Reform Affected Farmers and Local Governance in China?" *China & World Economy* 15(3):19–32.

Tao, Ran, Dali Yang, Ming Li, and Xi Lu. 2014. "How Does Political Trust Affect Social Trust? An Analysis of Survey Data from Rural China Using An Instrumental Approach." *International Political Science Review* 35 (2): 237–253.

Thaxton, Ralph. 2008. *Catastrophe and Contention in Rural China: Mao's Great Leap Forward Famine and the Origins of Righteous Resistance in Da Fo Village*. New York, NY: Cambridge University Press.

Thelen, K. 2002. "The Political Economy of Business and Labor in the Developed Democracies." In *Political Science: The State of the Discipline*, ed. I. Katznelson and H. V. Milner. New York, NY: W. W. Norton & Company.

———. 2003. "How Institutions Evolve: Insights From Comparative Historical Analysis." In *Comparative Historical Analysis in the Social Sciences*, ed. J. Mahoney and D. Rueschemeyer. New York, NY: Cambridge University Press.

———. 2004. *How Institutions Evolve: The Political Economy of Skills in Germany, Britain, the United States, and Japan*. New York, NY: Cambridge University Press.

Thireau, Isabelle, and Hua Linshan. 2007. "New Institutions in Practice: Migrant Workers and Their Mobilization of the Labor Law." In *Social Change in Contemporary China: C. K. Yang and the Concept of Institutional Diffusion*, ed. W. Tang and B. Holzener. Pittsburgh, PA: University of Pittsburgh Press.

Thornton, Patricia M. 2007. *Disciplining the State: Virtue, Violence, and State-Making in Modern China*. Cambridge, MA: Harvard University Press.

Tian, Xianhong. 2012. "Zaidi Shiminhua: Nongmingong Fanxiang de Cunzhuang Shehui Houguo (Citizens in Chinese Villages: The Social Effects of Returned Migrant Workers in Rural China.") *Journal of South China Agricultural University (Social Science Edition)* 11(2):109–117.

Tiebout, Charles M. 1956. "A Pure Theory of Local Expenditures." *Journal of Political Economy* 64(5):416–424.

Tipps, Dean C. 1973. "Modernization Theory and the Comparative Study of Societies: A Critical Perspective." *Comparative Studies in Society and History* 15(2):199–226.

Tourangeau, Roger, Lance J. Rips, and Kenneth A. Rasinski. 2000. *The Psychology of Survey Response.* New York, NY: Cambridge University Press.

Tsai, K. S. 2002. *Back-Alley Banking: Private Entrepreneurs in China.* Ithaca, NY: Cornell University Press.

———. 2005. "Capitalists without a Class: Political Diversity among Private Entrepreneurs in China." *Comparative Political Studies* 38(9):1130–1158.

———. 2006. "Adaptive Informal Institutions and Endogenous Institutional Change in China." *World Politics* 59(1):116–141.

Tsai, L. 2002. "Cadres, Temple, and Lineage Institutions, and Governance in Rural China." *China Journal* 48:1–27.

———. 2007a. *Accountability without Democracy: How Solidary Groups Provide Public Goods in Rural China.* New York, NY: Cambridge University Press.

———. 2007b. "Solidary Groups, Informal Accountability, and Local Public Goods Provision in Rural China." *American Political Science Review* 101(2):355–372.

———. 2008. "Understanding the Falsification of Village Income Statistics." *China Quarterly* 196:805–826.

———. 2010. "Governing One Million Rural Communities after Two Decades: Are China's Village Elections Improving?" In *Growing Pains: Tensions and Opportunity in China's Transformation*, ed. J. Oi, S. Rozelle, and X. Zhou. Stanford, CA: Asia-Pacific Research Center.

———. 2011. "Friends or Foes? Nonstate Public Goods Providers and Local State Authorities in Nondemocratic and Transitional System." *Studies in Comparative International Development* 46(1):46–69.

Tsebelis, G. 2002. *Veto Players: How Political Institutions Work.* Princeton, NJ: Princeton University Press.

Ullmann-Margalit, Edna. 1977. *The Emergence of Norms.* Oxford: Clarendon Press.

Unger, Jonathan. 1989. "State and Peasant in Post-Revolution China." *Journal of Peasant Studies* 17(1):114–136.

———. 2002. *The Transformation of Rural China.* Armonk, NY: M.E. Sharpe, Inc.

———. 2005. "Family Customs and Farmland Reallocations in Contemporary Chinese Villages." In *Social Transformations in Chinese Societies*, ed. Y. Bian, K.-b. Chan, and T.-s. Cheung. Leiden: Brill.

———. 2012. "Continuity and Change in Rural China's Organization." In *Organizing Rural China, Rural China Organizing*, ed. A. Bislev and S. Thøgersen. Lanham, MD: Lexington Books.

United Nations, Dept. of International Economic and Social Affairs, Dept. for Economic and Social Information and Policy Analysis United Nations, and Dept. of Economic and Social Affairs United Nations. 2005. *World Urbanization Prospects: The 2005 Revision.* New York, NY: United Nations.

United Nations Development Program. 1999. *Decentralization: A Sampling of Definitions.* United Nations Development Programme.

Usher, Dan. 1989. "The Dynastic Cycle and the Stationary State." *American Economic Review* 79(5):1031–1044.

Wagstaff, Adam, Magnus Lindelow, Jun Gao, Ling Xu, and Juncheng Qian. 2007. *The Impact of Health Insurance in Rural China: Evidence from the New Cooperative Medical Scheme*. iHEA 2007 6th World Congress: Explorations in Health Economics Paper.

Wakeman, Frederic E., and Carolyn Grant. 1975. *Conflict and Control in Late Imperial China*. Berkeley, CA: University of California Press.

Walder, Andrew G., and Litao Zhao. 2006. "Political Office and Household Wealth: Rural China in the Deng Era." *China Quarterly* 186:357–376.

Wall, James A., and Michael Blum. 1991. "Community Mediation in the People's Republic of China." *Journal of Conflict Resolution* 35(1):3–20.

Wang, Fei-ling. 2004. "Reformed Migration Control and New Targeted People: China's Hukou System in the 2000s." *China Quarterly* 177:115–132.

———. 2005. *Organizing through Division and Exclusion: China's Hukou System*. Stanford, CA: Stanford University Press.

Wang, Guojun. 2004. "Zhongguo Nongcun Shehui Baozhang Zhidu de Bianqian (Institutional Change in Social Welfare in Rural China)." *Zhejiang Shehui Kexue* 1:141–149.

Wang, Hong, Winnie Yip, Licheng Zhang, Lusheng Wang, and William Hsiao. 2005. "Community-Based Health Insurance in Poor Rural China: The Distribution of Net Benefits." *Health Policy and Planning* 20(6):366–374.

Wang, Hui, Juer Tong, Fubing Su, Guoxue Wei, and Ran Tao. 2011. "To Reallocate or Not: Reconsidering the Dilemma in China's Agricultural Land Tenure Policy." *Land Use Policy* 28(4):805–814.

Wang, Juan. 2012. "Shifting Boundaries between the State and Society: Village Cadres as New Activists in Collective Petition." *China Quarterly* 211:697–717.

Wang, S., and Y. Yao. 2007. "Grassroots Democracy and Local Governance: Evidence from Rural China." *Journal of Peking University (Philosophy and Social Sciences)* (2):121–130.

———. 2010. "Grassroots Democracy and Local Governance: Evidence from Rural China." *Procedia—Social and Behavioral Sciences* 2(5):7164–7180.

Wang, Shaoguang. 2011. "Learning through Practice and Experimentation: The Financing of Rural Health Care." In *Mao's Invisible Hand: The Political Foundations of Adaptive Governance in China*, ed. S. Heilmann and E. J. Perry. Cambridge, MA: Harvard University Press.

Wang, Shaoguang, and Angang Hu. 2001. *The Chinese Economy in Crisis: State Capacity and Tax Reform*. Armonk, NY: M.E. Sharpe.

Wang, Zongpei. 1935. *Zhongguo zhi Hehui (Rotating Savings and Credit Associations in China)*. Beijing: Zhongguo Hezuo Xueshe.

Watt, John R. 1972. *The District Magistrate in Late Imperial China*. New York, NY: Columbia University Press.

Watts, Duncan J., and Peter S. Dodds. 2007. "Influentials, Networks, and Public Opinion Formation." *Journal of Consumer Research* 34:441–458.

Weick, Karl E. 1976. "Educational Organizations as Loosely Coupled Systems." *Administrative Science Quarterly* 21(1):1–19.

Weiner, Myron, ed. 1966. *Modernization: The Dynamics of Growth*. New York, NY: Basic Books.

Weston, Timothy B. 2012. "China's Historic Urbanization: Explosive and Challenging." In *China In and Beyond the Headlines*, ed. T. B. Weston and L. M. Jensen. Lanham, MD: Rowman & Littlefield Publishers, Inc.

Whiting, Susan. 2011. "Values in Land: Fiscal Pressures, Land Disputes and Justice Claims in Rural and Peri-urban China." *Urban Studies* 48(3):569–587.

Wightman, Ann M. 1990. *Indigenous Migration and Social Change: The Forasteros of Cuzco, 1570–1720*. Durham, NC: Duke University Press.

Will, P. E., and R. Bin Wong. 1991. *Nourish the People: The State Civilian Granary System in China, 1650–1850*. Ann Arbor, MI: University of Michigan Press.

Wong, Linda. 1998. *Marginalization and Social Welfare in China*. New York, NY: Routledge.

Wong, R. Bin. 1997a. *China Transformed: Historical Change and the Limits of European Experience*. Ithaca, NY: Cornell University Press.

———. 1997b. "Confucian Agendas for Material and Ideological Control in Modern China." In *Culture and State in Chinese History*, ed. T. Huters, R. B. Wong, and P. Yu. Stanford, CA: Stanford University Press.

———. 1999. "The Political Economy of Agrarian Empire and Its Modern Legacy." In *China and Historical Capitalism*, ed. T. Brook and G. Blue. London: Cambridge University Press.

Wong, R. Bin, Theodore Huters, and Pauline Yu. 1997. "Shifting Paradigms of Political and Social Order." In *Culture and State in Chinese History*, ed. R. B. Wong, T. Huters, and P. Yu. Stanford, CA: Stanford University Press.

Wood, Robert C. 1966. "The Future of Modernization." In *Modernization: The Dynamics of Growth*, ed. M. Weiner. New York, NY: Basic Books.

Woodside, Alexander. 2006. *Lost Modernities: China, Vietnam, Korea, and the Hazards of World History*. Cambridge, MA: Harvard University Press.

Wu, Shijian. 2002. "Shilun Nongcun Gonggong Chanpin Gongji Zhidu de Gaige yu Wanshan (Reform and Improvement on the Institutions for the Provision of Public Goods in Villages)." *Nongye Jingji Wenti* 7:48–52.

Wu, Xiangang, and Donald J. Treiman. 2004. "The Household Registration System and Social Stratification in China: 1955–1996." *Demography* 41(2):363–384.

Xia, Min. 2011. "Social Capital and Rural Grassroots Governance in China." *Journal of Current Chinese Affairs* 40(2):135–163.

Xiao, Gongquan. 1960. *Rural China: Imperial Control in the Nineteenth Century*. Seattle, WA: University of Washington Press.

Xiao, Tangbiao. 2002. *Zongzu, Xiangcun Quanli yu Xuanju: Dui Jiangxisheng Shier ge Cunweihui Xuanju de Guancha Yanjiu (Kinships, Rural Power, and Elections: A Study of 12 Village Elections in Jiangxi Province)*. Xi'an: Xibei University Press.

———. 2010. *Zongzu Zhengzhi: Cunzhi Quanli Wangluo de Fenxi (Politics of Clans and Lineages: An Analysis of the Nexus of Power in Village Governance)*. Beijing: Shangwu Yinshu Guan Press.

Xu, Xin. 2005. *Lun Sili Jiuji (On Private Remedy)*. Beijing: Zhongguo Zhengfa University Press.

Xu, Yong. 2000. "Zhengtuo Tudi Sufu Zhihou de Xiangcun Kunjing Jiqi Yingdui (Dilemma of the Floating Population and the Shock of Rural Ruling Order)." *Journal of Huazhong Normal University (Humanities and Social Sciences)* (2).

Xu, Yong, and Zengyang Xu. 2003. *Liudong Zhong de Xiangcun Zhili (Rural Governance and Floating Population)*. Beijing: Chinese Social Sciences Press.

Xun, Jianli. 2007. "Cunmin Waichu Dagong Dui Liushou Jiaren de Yingxiang (Influences of Migrant Workers on the Life of Their Families Left Behind)." *Youth Studies* (6).

Yadava, K. N. S. 1989. *Rural-Urban Migration in India: Determinants, Patterns and Consequences*. New Delhi, India: Independent Pub. Co.

Yan, Jie. 2008. "Distribution of Non-response in Chinese Political Survey Research." *Wuhan University Journal (Philosophy & Social Sciences)* 61(2):225–231.

Yan, Jie, and Liying Ren. 2010. "The Application of Multiple Imputation in Answering Sensitive Political Issues." *Journal of Huazhong Normal University (Humanities and Social Sciences)* 49(2):29–34.

Yan, Yongfu. 2004. *Zhongguo Nongcun Jinrongye: Xianxiang Poxi yu Zouxiang Tansuo (Financial Industry in Rural China: Analysis and Suggestions)*. Beijing: Zhongguo Jinrong Chubanshe.

Yan, Yunxiang. 2010. "The Chinese Path to Individualization." *British Journal of Sociology* 61(3):489–512.

Yang, Da. 2008. *Ganan 90 Cun: Laodongli Zhuanyi Beijing Xiade Cunji Shequ Kaocha (90 Villages in Gannan Area: An Investigation on Village Communities with Rural-Urban Migration)*. Beijing: Social Sciences Academic Press.

Yang, Dali. 1996. *Calamity and Reform in China: State, Rural Society, and Institutional Change Since the Great Leap Famine*. Stanford, CA: Stanford University Press.

Yang, Liansheng. 1961. *Studies in Chinese Institutional History*. Cambridge, MA: Harvard University Press.

Yang, Qingping. 2006. *Evolution of Taxation Systems and the Dynastic Cycle in China (Huangliang Guoshui: Shuizhi Liubian yu Wangchao Xingshuai)*. Hunan: Hunan People's Press.

Yang, Xiushi. 1993. "Household Registration, Economic Reform and Migration." *International Migration Review* 27(4):796–818.

———. 1996. "Patterns of Economic Development and Patterns of Rural-Urban Migration in China." *European Journal of Population* 12:195–218.

Yao, Y., and Mengtao Gao. 2006. "Grassroots Democracy Benefits the Poor in China." In *Chinese Social Policy*, ed. X. Gu. Beijing: Beijing Normal University Press.

Yao, Y., and Yan Shen. 2006. "Village Election and Income Distribution." *Economic Research Journal* 41(4):97–105.

Yao, Yusheng. 2012. "Village Elections and the Rise of Capitalist Entrepreneurs." *Journal of Contemporary China* 21(74):317–332.

Ye, Qingxing. 1997. "Lun Nongcun Gonggong Chanpin Gongji Zhidu de Gaige (Reform on the Institutions for the Provision of Public Goods in Villages)." *Jingji Yanjiu* 6:57–62.

Yep, Ray. 2003. *Manager Empowerment in China: Political Implications of Rural Industrialization in the Reform Era*. New York, NY: RoutledgeCurzon.

———. 2004. "Can 'Tax-for-Fee' Reform Reduce Rural Tension in China? The Process, Progress and Limitations." *China Quarterly* 177:42–70.

Yousfi, Hela. 2011. "Culture and Development: The Continuing Tension Between Modern Standards and Local Contexts." In *Culture, Institutions, and Development*, ed. J. P. Platteau and R. Peccoud. New York, NY: Routledge.

Zellner, Arnold. 1962. "An Efficient Method of Estimating Seemingly Unrelated Regression Equations and Tests for Aggregation Bias." *Journal of the American Statistical Association* 57:348–368.

Zhang, Bin, and Yongsheng Chu. 2006. "Nongcun Gonggong Wupin Gongzhi Zhidu Tanxi (Institutions for the Provision of Public Goods in Villages)." *Jianghai Xuekan* 5:95–100.

Zhang, Jie. 2003. *Zhongguo Nongcun Jinrong Zhidu: Jiegou, Bianquan yu Zhengce (Financial Institutions of Rural China: Structure, Change, and Policy)*. Beijing: Renmin University Press.

Zhang, Jing. 2006. *Modern Public Rules and Rural Society (Xiandai Gonggong Guize yu Xiangcun Shehui)*. Shanghai: Shanghai Bookstore Publishing House.

Zhang, Linxiu, Songqing Jin, Scott Rozelle, Klaus Deininger, and Jikun Huang. 2010. "Rights and Rental: Are Rural Cultivated Land Policy and Management Constraining or Facilitating China's Modernization?" In *Growing Pains: Tensions and Opportunity in China's Transformation*, ed. J. Oi, S. Rozelle, and X. Zhou. Stanford, CA: Asia-Pacific Research Center.

Zhang, Lirong, and Haihua Li. 2000. "Zhongguo Nongcun Shehui Baozhang: Xianzhuang Fenxi yu Duice Gouxiang (Social Welfare in Rural China: Current Situation and Policy Suggestions)." *Huazhong Shifan Daxue Xuebao* 39(6):47–56.

Zhang, Mei. 2003. *China's Poor Regions' Rural-Urban Migration, Poverty, Economic Reform, and Urbanisation*. New York, NY: Routledge Curzon.

Zhang, Weiguo. 2013. "Class Categories and Marriage Patterns in Rural China in the Mao Era." *Modern China* 39(4):438–471.

Zhang, Xiaobo, Shenggen Fan, Linxiu Zhang, and Jikun Huang. 2004. "Local Governance and Public Goods Provision in Rural China." *Journal of Public Economics* 88(12):2857–2871.

Zhao, Changbao. 2004. "Zhongguo Xianjieduan de Nongcun Laodongli Liudong yu Mingong Duanque Xianxiang (Rural Labor Migration and the Shortage of Migrant Workers in Contemporary China)." In *Zhongguo Nongcun Yanjiu Baogao (Research Report on Rural China)*, ed. N. N. J. Y. Zhongxin. Beijing: Zhongguo Caizheng Jingji Chubanshe.

Zhao, Dingxin. 1998. "Ecologies of Social Movements: Student Mobilization during the 1989 Prodemocracy Movement in Beijing." *American Journal of Sociology* 103(6):1493–1529.

Zhao, Litao. 1999. "Family Lineage and Village Politics 1950–1970." *Twenty-First Century* 55:45–52.

Zhao, Shukai. 2011. *Nongmin de Zhengzhi (Peasant Politics)*. Beijing: The Commercial Press.

Zhao, Xudong. 2003. *Quanli yu Gongzheng: Xiangtu Shehui de Jiufen Jiejue yu Quanwei Duoyuan (Authority and Fairness: Conflict Resolution and Multi-dimensional Authority in Rural China)*. Tianjin: Tianjin Guji Press.

Zhao, Yaohui. 1999. "Labor Migration and Earnings Differences: The Case of Rural China." *Economic Development and Cultural Change* 47(4):767–782.

———. 2002. "Causes and Consequences of Return Migration: Recent Evidence from China." *Journal of Comparative Economics* 30:376–394.

Zhou, Kate Xiao. 1996. *How the Farmers Changed China: Power of the People*. Boulder, CO: Westview Press.

Zhou, Li, and Hiroki Takeuchi. 2010. "Informal Lenders and Rural Finance in China: A Report from the Field." *Modern China* 36(3):302–328.

Zhou, Xueguang. 2011. "The Autumn Harvest: Peasants and Markets in Post-Collective Rural China." *China Quarterly* 208:913–931.

Zhu, Ling, and Zhongyi Jiang. 1993. "From Brigade to Village Community: The Land Tenure System and Rural Development in China." *Journal of Economics* 17(4):441–461.

Zweig, David. 2010. "To the Courts or To the Barricades? Can New Political Institutions Manage Rural Conflict?" In *Chinese Society: Change, Conflict and Resistance*, ed. E. J. Perry and M. Selden. New York, NY: Routledge.

INDEX

Figures and tables are indicated by f and t following the page number.

Camerer, Colin, 23
Cappelari, Lorenzo, 105
CCP. *See* Chinese Communist Party
Center of Rural Governance (CRG) at
    Huazhong University of Science
    and Technology, 202–205
Central China, migrant workers in
    urban areas in, 77
Centralized governance, with imposed
    totalitarian institutions, 61–65
Ceremonies, leaders for, 151–152
Chan, Anita, 64, 65
Chan, Kam Wing, 64
Chang, Chung-li, 59
Chang, Yu-tzung, 3, 36, 98, 192
Changsha Liao, 148–149
Chen, Baifeng, 8, 41, 67, 90, 160
Chen, Jie, 3, 8, 69, 172
Chen, Xiaolin, 151
Cheng, Linshun, 28
Cheng, Tiejun, 64
Chimhowu, Admos, 6–7
China. *See also* Chinese Communist
    Party (CCP); Rural China; *specific
    dynasty*
    economic growth rate, 200
    economic structure, 51–52
Chinese Communist Party (CCP)
    administration, centralization of, 10
    cadre evaluation system, 234*n*41
    conflict resolution by, 159
    formalized judicial institutions,
        establishment of, 33–34
    industrialization launched by,
        51–52
    role in government, 239*n*18
    rural China under, 190
    rural governance under, 61–65,
        68–69, 82
Chu, Yongsheng, 86
Chuanmen (dropping in), 150, 151
Cityward migration. *See* Rural-urban
    migration
Clan/lineage organizations, 62, 64,
    94–96, 105, 160
Class loyalty, 62
Clay, Karen, 25, 133, 223*n*10
Close-knit communities. *See also*
    Atomized communities; Loosely
    coupled communities

under CCP, 63–65, 69
communal structures of, 133–134,
    153–154
effects of rural-urban migration on,
    43, 83
governance without parchment
    institutions in, 20–26
grassroots democracy in, 179–180
imposed institutions in, 40, 46,
    179
indigenous institutions in, 9, 38, 40,
    45, 110, 130, 164–165, 182,
    185, 198
in Japan, 20
Qianhouzhai Village as, 121, 123
rural communities as, 55
social norms in, 141–142
in Sub-Saharan Africa, 20
Coalitions, 140
Coercive power, 63
Cohen, Myron L., 51, 54, 90, 134, 160,
    230*n*6
Coleman, J. S., 11–12, 23, 25, 42, 141
Collective action problem, solutions
    for, 26, 89–90, 184–185
Collective interest, 142–144, 145–146
Collective responsibility of *baojia*
    system, 58
Collier D., 148
Commercial guilds, 28
Communal structures. *See also*
    Rural-urban migration
    under CCP, 63–64
    in close-knit communities, 133–134
    influence on institutions, 42, 109,
        113
    influence on social environments, 9,
        182
Commune system, 10, 63–65, 69, 150,
    161, 190
Communities (societies) of
    acquaintances, 22, 54, 121, 150
Community building, 204
Community granaries, 160
Community-level relationships, 11, 21,
    38
Community mediation system, 159
Compulsory education, 236*n*50
Conflict avoidance, 142–144, 145–146
Conflict resolution

effectiveness of, 190–191

in loosely coupled communities, 109, 119, 197

self-governance based on, 65, 66–68, 69, 82

uneven development of, 7–8

village committees as, 2

villagers' participation in, importance of, 201

Great Leap Forward, 230n8

Greif, A., 4, 5, 6, 7, 25, 28, 31, 32, 34, 43, 133, 141, 191, 220n14

Grould, Roger V., 89

Grzymala-Busse, Anna, 193

Guang, Lei, 70

Gugerty, Mary Key, 85

Guilt, 23

Guo, Liang, 92

Guo, Peigui, 54

Guo, Xinghua, 34, 36, 159

Habitual responses, 141

Habyarimana, James, 84

Hagood, Margaret Jarman, 73

Hansen, Mette Halskov, 69, 244n18

Hardin, Garrett, 19, 23, 141

Hare, Denise, 73

Harris, J., 73

Hayami, Yujiro, 5, 7, 33, 162

He, Annai, 36, 163

He, Beogang, 115

He, Wenkai, 34, 162, 163, 164

He, Xuefeng, 24, 25, 36, 66, 90, 94, 134, 201, 204

Hebel, Jutta, 160, 247n14, 248n15

Hechter, M., 23, 141

Helmke, Gretchen, 5, 191, 192–193, 220n14, 226n30, 253n6

Hill, Peter J., 33

Hirschman, A. O., 229n44

Hobbes, Thomas, 6

Hochstadt, Steve, 73

Home communities, villagers' attachment to, 42, 147, 154, 201

Honeycomb structure (of rural China), 10–11, 64, 82

Horne, Christine, 23, 141

House construction in Qianhouzhai Village, 121

Household income, 77, 79, 124, 126

Household populations, working in TVEs vs. as migrant workers, 72–73

Household registration (hukou) system, 10, 50–51, 64, 69, 73–74

Household responsibility system (jiating lianchan chengbao zerenzhi), 65, 82, 161

Housing patterns, 105, 107, 121, 124, 126

Hu, Biliang, 3, 8, 36, 162, 163, 248n17

Hu, Rong, 33, 99

Hu, Xiaodeng, 201

Huang, Bihong, 67

Huang, Philip C., 21, 28, 51, 70, 158

Huang, Yasheng, 236n48

Huhe, Narisong, 3, 8

Hukou (household registration) system, 10, 50–51, 64, 69, 73–74

Huntington, Samuel P., 6

Hussain, Athar, 73

Hybrid version of local public goods provision, rural-urban migration and, 109–120

IDIs (indigenously developed institutions), 8–9. See also Indigenous institutions

Immediate benefits, long-term relationships vs., 142–144, 145–146

Imperial examinations (keju kaoshi), 54

Imposed grassroots democracy. See Grassroots democracy

Imposed institutions (rule-based institutions). See also Grassroots democracy

accountability mechanism for, 171–178

in close-knit communities, 40, 179

close-knit communities without, 20–26

for conflict resolution, 159, 166, 167t

for disaster and crisis relief, 166–167

effectiveness of, 38–40, 46, 177–178

exogenous factors shaping, 189

imposed, and modernization, 26–32

Imposed institutions (*Continued*)
    influence of rural-urban migration
        on choice of, 168–171
    land allocation and, 92
    local public goods provision and, 185
    in loosely coupled communities, 9,
        40, 46, 113, 119, 130,
        164–165, 171, 179, 180, 182,
        186, 197, 199
    for solving problem of collective
        action, 130
    totalitarian, centralized governance
        with, 61–65
    transaction costs of, 30–31, 38–39
Incentives, top-down, 28–32
Incorporated indigenous institutions,
        decentralized governance with,
        55–61
Indian villages, conflict resolution in, 7
Indigenous and imposed institutions,
        in decentralized provision of
        local public goods, 102–109
Indigenous institutions (relation-based
        institutions). *See also* Rural
        governance and rural-urban
        migration; Social sanctions
    accountability of village cadres and,
        172–173
    under CCP, 64, 68
    in close-knit communities, 9, 40, 45,
        110, 130, 164–165, 182, 185,
        198
    collective action problem and, 130
    for conflict resolution, 158–159,
        166–167
    decentralized governance with
        incorporated, 55–61
    under Deng Xiaoping, 69
    for disaster and crisis relief, 167
    effectiveness of, 38–40, 45–46
    effects of modernization on, 27–32
    effects of rural-urban migration on,
        43
    fixed vs. marginal costs of, 38
    incorporated, decentralized
        governance with, 55–61
    land allocation and, 92
    local public goods provision and,
        184–185
    in Qianhouzhai Village, 128

raising capital, role in, 162–163
in rural communities, 55
social relief by, 160–161
in Songzhuang, 129
in Su Village, 127
Indigenously developed institutions
        (IDIs), 8–9. *See also* Indigenous
        institutions
Indigenous social sanctions, in
        decentralized provision of local
        public goods, 90–97
Individual interest, collective interest
        vs., 142–144, 145–146
Individual-level relationships, 11
Indonesia, informal institutions in, 7
Industrialization programs, 51
Informal institutions, 191–196. *See
        also* Indigenous institutions
Information
    influence on indigenous institutions,
        196
    influence on social sanctions and
        public authority, 133–140
    transmission of, 25, 27–28, 30, 43,
        56, 57, 204
Institutional choices. *See also*
        Rural-urban migration,
        contextualized institutional
        choices and
    for accountability, 171–178
    for conflict resolution, 166, 167*t*,
        178–179
    for disaster and crisis relief,
        166–167, 178–179
    factors determining, 39, 141, 164
    findings on, 186–187
    institutional syncretism and, 32–41
    for local governance issues, 179–180
    for modest credit and small loans,
        167–168, 178–179
    research methodology on, 168
    rural-urban migration and
        governance quality and, 44*t*
Institutional costs, 29–30
Institutional disarticulation, 35, 183
Institutional effectiveness, 4–5, 9,
        31–32, 114
Institutional environments, 103, 104*t*
Institutional infrastructure and
        superstructure, 35

Su Village case study, 126–128, 129*t*
Local public goods provision, decentralized, 89–109
  imposed grassroots democracy and, 97–102
  indigenous and imposed institutions, 102–109
  indigenous social sanctions and, 90–97
  overview, 89–90
Locke, John, 6
Long-term relationships, immediate benefits vs., 142–144, 145–146
Loosely coupled communities. *See also* Atomized communities; Close-knit communities
  grassroots democracy in, 119, 187–188, 197
  imposed institutions in, 9, 40, 46, 113, 119, 130, 164–165, 171, 179, 180, 182, 186, 197, 199
  indigenous institutions in, 110
  institutional choice in, 187
Lu, Jie, 3, 7, 13–15, 33, 66, 69, 99, 115, 172, 201
Lu, Xiaobo, 66
Luo, Chuliang, 73
Luo, Renfu, 3, 36, 67, 68, 84, 85, 87, 98, 172
Luskin, Robert C., 174

Ma, Xia, 73
MacLean, Lauren M., 5, 253*nn*7–8
Madsen, Richard, 62, 64
Magee, Gary B., 229*n*45
Magistrates, 56
Mahoney, J., 4, 34, 148, 192
Manion, M., 5, 8, 69, 98, 172, 198, 220*n*12
Mansbridge, Jane, 199
Mantzavinos, Chrysostomos, 23
Marginal costs, institutional, 29–30
Market-oriented economic reforms, 11
Marriage ceremonies, 151–152
Martin, Lisa L., 25
Maxims, of *jiangyue* system, 58
Meng, Xin, 68, 70, 245*n*37
Michelson, Ethan, 8, 34, 39, 158
Migrant workers, 74–77, 78*t*. *See also* Rural-urban migration

Migration. *See* Rural-urban migration
Miguel, Edward, 85
Miller, Harry, 59
Ming dynasty
  administrative units, 56
  imperial examination enrollment rates, 54
  indigenous institutions in governance, 58, 189
  intermediate agents, 81
  rural population, 51
  xiangyue system, 57–58
Ming Taizu, Emperor, 56
Ministry of Agriculture, 200
Ministry of Civil Affairs, 239*n*21
Ministry of Education, 238*n*9
Ministry of Water Resources, 86
Mobility, 27–28, 64. *See also* Rural-urban migration
Model village of self-governance, 105, 106, 107
Modernization, imposed parchment institutions and, 26–32
Modernizing transformation, 35–36
Modern states, nature of, 29
Modest credit and small loans, 88, 89, 162–164, 167*t*, 168–171, 178–179, 187
Moe, Terry, 90
Mokyr, Joel, 31
Mortuza, Syed Ali, 73
Multilevel system of propositions, 11, 12*f*
Multivariate probit regression (MPR), 105–109, 114
Murphy, Rachel, 11, 24, 54, 76
Mutual help, 161
Myers, Ramon H., 60

Nachbar, John H., 23, 89
Nakane, Chie, 20, 25
National Bureau of Statistics of China (NBSC), 201, 230*nn*2–3
National leaders, challenges of rural government, 49, 52–53
National markets, influence on guilds, 28
National regulations, on migrant workers, 74
National Village Survey (NVS), 13–14, 86–87, 88

Nation-states, 26–27, 28–29, 38–39
Nature, state of, 40, 157
NBSC (National Bureau of Statistics of China), 230*nn*2–3
Nee, Victor, 8, 38, 70, 72, 226*n*30
Neighborhood administrative system (*lijia*), 56–57, 58, 81, 189
Niou, Emerson, 21, 25, 161
Noland, Soraya, 158
Non-agricultural sectors, 70–72
Norms. *See* Egalitarian norms; Local norms; Social norms; Social sanctions
North, D. C., 4, 6, 23, 33, 34, 191, 193, 198, 220*n*14, 227*n*31
Northeast China, migrant workers in urban areas in, 77
Nye, John, 39

Oberai, A. S., 73
O'Brien, K. J., 2, 7, 33, 66, 97, 190
Official bureaucracies, in rural communities, 55
Oi, Jean, 33, 63, 67, 99
Olson, Mancur, 6, 23, 89, 105, 119
One-child policy, 162, 248*n*16
One task, one meeting (*yishi yiyi*) system, 68, 236*n*45
Ong, Lynette, 3, 8, 36, 163, 164
Onoma, Ato Kwamena, 38
Opp, Karl-Dieter, 8, 23, 43, 140, 141
Opper, Sonja, 38, 70, 72, 226*n*30
Organic Law of the Urban Residents Committees (1989), 159
Organic Law of Village Committees (OLVC, 1987, 1998, 2010), 2–3, 33, 66–67, 97–99, 159, 239*n*18
Ostracism, 25. *See also* Social sanctions
Ostrom, Elinor, 19, 89, 195
Outward migration. *See* Rural-urban migration

Parchment institutions. *See* Imposed institutions
Parish, William L., 10, 63, 65, 142
Parthasarathi, Prasannan, 4
Path diagram for SEM on local public goods provision, 114
Patten, John, 73
Paved roads, 87, 104

PD (Prisoners' Dilemma) game, 22–23, 27, 140
Peasants, under KMT, 60
Peccoud, Robert, 5, 141, 195
Peerenboom, R. P., 33
People's Commune (*renmin gongshe*), 63. *See also* Commune system
Per capita disposable income, rural vs. urban, 73–74
Personal reputations. *See* Reputation; Social sanctions
Pesqué-Cela, Vanesa, 11, 68
Pevsner, Lucille W., 225*n*20
Place of origin, as ascribed status, 54
Platteau, J. P., 5, 7, 20, 33, 43, 133, 141, 160, 195, 224*n*16
Police, conflict resolution and, 159
Political contracts for public goods provision, 105, 107
Political features in analysis of local public goods provision, 105–109
Pomeranz, Kenneth, 4, 28, 51, 94, 134
Population size in analysis of local public goods provision, 105, 107
Potter, Jack M., 54, 134, 160
Premarital pregnancy, 152–153
Prisoners' Dilemma (PD) game, 22–23, 27, 140
Private capital raising, 164
Private solutions, 40–41, 47, 48, 166–167
Production teams (*shengchan xiaodui*), 63
Propositions, multilevel system of, 11
Protective brokers, 60, 61, 68, 81, 189
Przeworski, A., 14, 90, 188, 252*n*1
Pseudo-syncretic grafting, 35
Public authority, social sanctions, and information environment in transformed communities, 133–140
Public authority vacuum, in villages, 66
Public facilities, 88–89, 104. *See also* Local public goods provision
Public goods provision. *See* Local public goods provision
Public sanitary services, SPA participation in, 204
Public security, *baojia* (watch-group) system, 56, 57, 58, 81, 189

Public welfare activities, 104
Putnam, R. D., 6, 204–205, 219*nn*3–4, 220*n*11

Qian, Hang, 24, 54, 134, 160
Qiang, Shigong, 34, 36, 159
Qianhouzhai Village case study, 1–2, 120–123
Qin, Ping, 67, 68
Qing dynasty
    administrative units, 56
    granary systems, 160
    incorporation of indigenous institutions in governance, 58, 189
    intermediate agents, 81
    military expenses, 60
    rural population, 51
    xiangyue system, 58
Qu, Tongzu, 56, 59, 137, 142

Ragin, C., 14
RCCs (Rural Credit Cooperatives), 162, 163, 167–168, 170, 187, 246*n*1
Read, Benjamin, 8, 39
Reed, Christopher A., 28
Relation-based institutions. *See* Indigenous institutions
Religious solidarity groups, 8
Renmin gongshe (People's Commune), 63. *See also* Commune system
Republican era, 51, 60, 81–82, 232*n*26
Republic of China, rural governance under, 60
Reputation, 58, 134, 136, 137–140, 186. *See also* Social sanctions
Reputation-based multilateral social sanctions, 182
Resources, extraction of, rural institutions and, 59, 61
Returned migrant workers, 18, 200–203
Rice, dominance in agricultural production, 105, 107
Roads, quality of, 1–2
Roberts, Kenneth D., 11
Robinson, J., 6, 198
Rodrik, Dani, 6
Roland, Gerard, 33, 191
ROSCAs (rotating savings and credit associations), 162–163, 165, 168, 187
Rosenthal, Jean-Laurent, 4
Rotating savings and credit associations (ROSCAs), 162–163, 165, 168, 187
Rousseau, Jean-Jacques, 142
Rubin, Donald B., 106, 174
Ruf, Gregory A., 64
Rule-based institutions. *See* Imposed institutions
Rules, indigenously developed, 20–21
Rural China. *See also* Rural-urban migration; *additional entries beginning "rural"*
    evolution from indigenous to imposed institutions, 10–11
    overview of history of, 50–55
    population of, 51*f*
Rural communities. *See also* Atomized communities; Close-knit communities; Loosely coupled communities
    limited resources of, 86
    self-governance of, 55
    as societies of acquaintances, 54
Rural Credit Cooperatives (RCCs), 162, 163, 167–168, 170, 187, 246*n*1
Rural district pledge system (*xiangyue*), 56, 57–58, 81, 189
Rural economy, after Cultural Revolution, 65
Rural governance and rural-urban migration, 49–83
    under CCP, 61–65, 68–69
    conclusions, 81–83
    in contemporary China, 70–81
    under Deng Xiaoping, 65–68
    history of, 50–55
    under Late Imperial China, 55–61, 68
    overview, 16, 49–50
Rural household net income, 79*t*
Rural institutional environments, 103
Rural labor
    employed as migrant workers, 74, 75*t*
    employed in non-agricultural production, 70–72
Rural Land Contract Law (2002), 238*n*11

loan payments, collecting, 163
in loosely coupled communities, 165
in Qianhouzhai Village, 122–123, 128
in Qianhouzhai Village vs. Su Village, 1, 2
Senior People Associations and, 204
in Songzhuang Village, 125–126
in Su Village, 127, 129
villagers' rejection of, 65–66, 82
Village Committee Elections (VCEs), 1, 3, 7–8, 66
Village committees. *See also* Organic Law of Village Committees
establishment of, 2
roles of, 97–98, 163, 165
social relief by, 161–162
in Songzhuang, 129
trust in, 175*t*
Village compacts, 21
Village elections
imposed, counterfactual analysis of, 190–191
influence of rural-urban migration on, 119
in loosely coupled communities, 165
OLVC on, 98, 99
opposition to, 234*n*41
in Qianhouzhai Village, 122
quality of, 99–102
rigged, 1, 102
in Songzhuang Village, 125–126, 128–129
in Su Village, 128
transparent and competitive, 98–99, 112–113, 130
uneven implementation of, 33, 99–100
villagers' evaluations of effectiveness of, 172–173
Village lecture (*jiangyue*) system, 58, 81
Village-owned collective income, 87–89
Village retention (*tiliu*), 86, 237*n*7
Villages, rural-urban migration and institutional change in
case studies, 120–131
conclusions on, 181–199
contextualized institutional choices and, 156–180

local governance in transformed communities, 19–48
local public goods provision, 84–109
local public goods provision and rural-urban migration, 109–120
overview, 1–18
rural governance and, 49–83, 200–206
social environments and, 132–155

Wakeman, Frederic E., 10, 56, 59, 90
Wang, Fei-ling, 64
Wang, Guannan, 201
Wang, Guojun, 160
Wang, Hui, 91–92, 238*n*12
Wang, Ping, 159
Wang, S., 3, 8, 68, 172
Wang, Shaoguang, 86, 160
Wang, Youjuan, 73, 163
Washington Consensus, 226*n*27
Watch-group system (*baojia*), 56, 57, 58, 81, 189
Water, access to, 86–87, 104
Watt, John R., 10, 56
Watts, Duncan J., 154
Weick, Karl E., 219*n*2
Welfare pluralism, 247*n*14
Welfare system, 160
West China, migrant workers in urban areas in, 77
Weston, Timothy B., 74
Whyte, Martin King, 63
Wong, R. Bin, 4, 52–53, 57, 225*n*21, 230*nn*9–10, 231*n*17
Woodhouse, Phil, 7
Wu, Chen-chia, 3, 36, 98, 192
Wu, Shijian, 86
Wu, Xiangang, 64

Xia, Min, 3, 8, 239*n*17
Xiangyue (rural district pledge system), 56, 57–58, 81, 189
Xiao, Gongquan, 10, 21, 56, 59, 90, 134, 137, 142, 158, 160, 161, 232*n*21
Xiao, Tangbiao, 33, 69, 94, 105
Xing, Chaoguo, 34, 36
Xinhai Revolution (1911), 60
Xiong, Jingming, 66
Xu, Xin, 41

Xu, Yong, 11
Xu, Zengyang, 11

Yadava, K. N. S., 73
Yan, Jie, 233n29
Yan, Xishan, 232n26
Yan, Yongfu, 163
Yan, Yunxiang, 245n30
Yang, Da, 76
Yang, Liangsheng, 10, 163
Yang, Xiushi, 64, 73
Yansong (anti-litigation culture), 34,
    158
Yao, Mr., 161–162
Yao, Y., 3, 5, 8, 68, 69, 172, 198,
    220n12
Yao, Yusheng, 201, 251n38
Yep, Ray, 10, 67–68, 86
Yongzheng emperor, 58
Yousfi, Hela, 199
Yue, Ximing, 73

Zhang, Bin, 86
Zhang, Jie, 163
Zhang, Li, 64, 68
Zhang, Linxiu, 73
Zhang, Lirong, 160
Zhang, Mei, 73
Zhang, Ming, 121
Zhang, Xiaobo, 3, 8, 36, 85, 87, 98, 172
Zhao, Changbao, 76
Zhao, Dingxin, 105
Zhao, Litao, 24, 54, 65, 134
Zhao, Shukai, 67
Zhao, Xudong, 34, 90, 94, 137, 158
Zhao, Yaohui, 70, 73
Zheng, Lu, 70
Zhike (emcees), for ceremonies,
    151–152
Zhong, Y., 69, 172
Zhou, Kate Xiao, 65, 142
Zhou, Li, 248n20
Zweig, David, 159